Kawasaki
Bayou 220/300 &
Prairie 300 ATV
Owners
Workshop
Manual

by Alan Ahlstrand
and John H Haynes
Member of the Guild of Motoring Writers

Models covered:
Kawasaki KLF220 Bayou, 1988 thru 2001
Kawasaki KLF300 Bayou, 1986 thru 2001
Kawasaki KLF300 Bayou 4X4, 1989 thru 2001
Kawasaki KVF300 Prairie, 1999 thru 2001
Kawasaki KVF300 Prairie 4X4, 1999 thru 2001

ABCDE
FGHIJ
KLMNO
PQRST

Haynes Publishing
Sparkford Nr Yeovil
Somerset BA22 7JJ England

Haynes North America, Inc
861 Lawrence Drive
Newbury Park
California 91320 USA

Acknowledgments

Our thanks to Grand Prix Sports, Santa Clara, California, for providing the facilities used for these photographs; to Anthony Morter, service manager, for arranging the facilities and fitting the mechanical work into his shop's busy schedule; and to Craig Wardner, service technician, for doing the mechanical work and providing valuable technical information.

A book in the Haynes Owners Workshop Manual Series

Printed in the U.S.A.

ISBN 1 56392 437 4

Library of Congress Control Number 2001095540

British Library Cataloguing in Publication Data
A catalogue record for this book is available from the British Library

We take great pride in the accuracy of information given in this manual, but vehicle manufacturers make alterations and design changes during the production run of a particular vehicle of which they do not inform us. No liability can be accepted by the authors or publishers for loss, damage or injury caused by any errors in, or omissions from, the information given.

Contents

Introductory pages

Introduction to the Kawasaki Bayou and Prairie	0-4
About this manual	0-5
Buying parts	0-5
Identification numbers	0-6
General specifications	0-8
Maintenance techniques, tools and working facilities	0-10
Safety first!	0-14
ATV chemicals and lubricants	0-15
Troubleshooting	0-16

Chapter 1   Tune-up and routine maintenance   **1**

Part A	Bayou models	1A-1
Part B	Prairie models	1B-1

Chapter 2   Engine, clutch and transmission   **2**

Part A	Bayou models	2A-1
Part B	Prairie models	2B-1

Chapter 3   Fuel and exhaust systems   **3**

Part A	Bayou models	3A-1
Part B	Prairie models	3B-1

Chapter 4   Ignition and electrical systems   **4**

Part A	Bayou models	4A-1
Part B	Prairie models	4B-1

Chapter 5   Steering, suspension and final drive   **5**

Part A	Bayou models	5A-1
Part B	Prairie models	5B-1

Chapter 6   Brakes, wheels and tires   **6**

Part A	Bayou models	6A-1
Part B	Prairie models	6B-1

Chapter 7   Frame and bodywork   **7**

Part A	Bayou models	7A-1
Part B	Prairie models	7B-1

Chapter 8   **8**

Wiring diagrams	8-1

Conversion factors

Fraction/decimal/millimeter equivalents

Index   **IND**

2001 Kawasaki 300 Bayou 4X4

Introduction to the Kawasaki Bayou and Prairie

The Kawasaki Bayou and Prairie are highly successful and popular all-terrain vehicles.

Five basic models are covered in this manual:

KLF220 Bayou
KLF300 Bayou
KLF300 Bayou 4X4
KVF300 Prairie
KVF300 Prairie 4X4

The engine on all models is an air-cooled single with an overhead camshaft. Bayou models use a gear transmission, similar to a conventional motorcycle-type transmission, mounted inside the crankcase. Prairie models use a variable ratio belt drive transmission.

Fuel is delivered to the cylinder by a single Mikuni carburetor.

The front suspension on 220 Bayou models uses a single control arm with kingpin and a coil spring/shock absorber on each side of the vehicle.

The front suspension on 300 Bayou models uses upper and lower control arms and a coil spring/shock absorber on each side of the vehicle.

The rear suspension on Bayou models consists of two trailing links, supported by two coil spring/shock absorber units. Lateral location of the suspension is provided by two lateral links. The right-hand link is a one-piece rod. The left-hand link is made up of two rods, which curve to straddle the rear differential.

The Prairie front suspension consists of a lower control arm and coil spring/shock absorber strut on each side of the vehicle. The rear suspension is a swingarm, supported by a single coil spring/shock absorber unit.

Bayou 220 models use a mechanical (cable-operated) drum brake at each front wheel. 1986 and 1987 Bayou 300 models use a hydraulic drum brake at each front wheel. 1988 and later Bayou models and all Prairie models use a hydraulic disc brake at each front wheel. Bayou 2WD models use a mechanical drum brake at each rear wheel. Bayou 220, 300 4WD and all Prairie models use a single mechanically actuated drum brake at the rear.

Shaft final drive is used at the rear of all models covered in this manual. On 4WD models, power is transmitted to the front wheels by a sub-transmission (Bayou) or output bevel gear case (Prairie) bolted to the left side of the engine. The Bayou sub-transmission includes gearing for the high and low ranges. This unit operates the front driveshaft, which in turn powers the front differential, driveaxles and wheel hubs.

About this manual

Its purpose

The purpose of this manual is to help you get the best value from your vehicle. It can do so in several ways. It can help you decide what work must be done, even if you choose to have it done by a dealer service department or a repair shop; it provides information and procedures for routine maintenance and servicing; and it offers diagnostic and repair procedures to follow when trouble occurs.

We hope you use the manual to tackle the work yourself. For many simpler jobs, doing it yourself may be quicker than arranging an appointment to get the vehicle into a shop and making the trips to leave it and pick it up. More importantly, a lot of money can be saved by avoiding the expense the shop must pass on to you to cover its labor and overhead costs. An added benefit is the sense of satisfaction and accomplishment that you feel after doing the job yourself.

Using the manual

The manual is divided into Chapters. Each Chapter is divided into numbered Sections, which are headed in bold type between horizontal lines. Each Section consists of consecutively numbered paragraphs.

At the beginning of each numbered Section you will be referred to any illustrations which apply to the procedures in that Section. The reference numbers used in illustration captions pinpoint the pertinent Section and the Step within that Section. That is, illustration 3.2 means the illustration refers to Section 3 and Step (or paragraph) 2 within that Section.

Procedures, once described in the text, are not normally repeated. When it's necessary to refer to another Chapter, the reference will be given as Chapter and Section number. Cross references given without use of the word "Chapter" apply to Sections and/or paragraphs in the same Chapter. For example, "see Section 8" means in the same Chapter.

References to the left or right side of the vehicle assume you are sitting on the seat, facing forward.

All-terrain vehicle manufacturers continually make changes to specifications and recommendations, and these, when notified, are incorporated into our manuals at the earliest opportunity.

Even though we have prepared this manual with extreme care, neither the publisher nor the author can accept responsibility for any errors in, or omissions from, the information given.

NOTE

A **Note** provides information necessary to properly complete a procedure or information which will make the procedure easier to understand.

CAUTION

A **Caution** provides a special procedure or special steps which must be taken while completing the procedure where the Caution is found. Not heeding a Caution can result in damage to the assembly being worked on.

WARNING

A **Warning** provides a special procedure or special steps which must be taken while completing the procedure where the Warning is found. Not heeding a Warning can result in personal injury.

Buying parts

Once you have found all the identification numbers, record them for reference when buying parts. Since the manufacturers change specifications, parts and vendors (companies that manufacture various components on the machine), providing the ID numbers is the only way to be reasonably sure that you are buying the correct parts.

Whenever possible, take the worn part to the dealer so direct comparison with the new component can be made. Along the trail from the manufacturer to the parts shelf, there are numerous places that the part can end up with the wrong number or be listed incorrectly.

The two places to purchase new parts for your vehicle - the accessory store and the franchised dealer - differ in the type of parts

they carry. While dealers can obtain virtually every part for your vehicle, the accessory dealer is usually limited to normal high wear items such as shock absorbers, tune-up parts, various engine gaskets, cables, chains, brake parts, etc. Rarely will an accessory outlet have major suspension components, cylinders, transmission gears, or cases.

Used parts can be obtained for roughly half the price of new ones, but you can't always be sure of what you're getting. Once again, take your worn part to the wrecking yard (breaker) for direct comparison.

Whether buying new, used or rebuilt parts, the best course is to deal directly with someone who specializes in parts for your particular make.

Identification numbers

The frame serial number is stamped into the left side of the frame. The engine number is stamped into the right side of the crankcase. Both of these numbers should be recorded and kept in a safe place so they can be furnished to law enforcement officials in the event of a theft.

The frame serial number, engine serial number and carburetor identification number should also be kept in a handy place (such as with your driver's license) so they are always available when purchasing or ordering parts for your machine.

The models covered by this manual are as follows:
KLF220 Bayou, 1988 through 2001
KLF300 Bayou, 1986 through 2001
KLF300 Bayou 4X4, 1989 through 2001
KVF300 Prairie, 1999 through 2001
KVF300 Prairie 4X4, 1999 through 2001

Identifying model years

The procedures in this manual identify the machines by model year. The model year is included in a decal on the frame, but in case the decal is missing or obscured, the following table identifies the initial frame number of each model year.

The vehicle identification number is stamped on the frame

The engine number is stamped into the crankcase (Prairie shown)

Year and model	Initial frame number
1986	
KLF300-A1	GA000001, GB500001 or LF300A-000001
1987	
KLF300-A2	HA009501, HB517101 or LF300A-009501
1988	
KLF220-A1 Bayou	JB500001 or LF220A-600001
KLF300-B1 Bayou	JA000001, JB500001 or LF300B-600001
1989	
KLF220-A2 Bayou	KB510601 or LF220A-600301
KLF300-B2 Bayou	KB507851, LF300B-600750
KLF300-C1 Bayou 4X4	KB500001, LF300C-600001
1990	
KLF220-A3 Bayou	LB518601 or LF220A-601101
KLF220-A3A Bayou (late production)	LF220A-101332
KLF300-B3 Bayou	LB511401, LF300B-602001
KLF300-B3A Bayou	LF300B-602396
KLF300-C2 Bayou 4X4	LB507501, LF300C-600951
1991	
KLF220-A4 Bayou	MB52890 or LF220A-601701
KLF300-B4 Bayou	MB5616401, LF300B-603401
KLF300-C3 Bayou 4X4	MB515401, LF300C-602101
1992	
KLF220-A5 Bayou	NB539001 or LF220A-602501
KLF300-B5 Bayou	NB519501, LF300B-604301
KLF300-C4 Bayou 4X4	NB521201, LF300C-603201
1993	
KLF220-A6 Bayou	PB549351 or LF220A-603001
KLF300-B6 Bayou	PB522901, LF300B-604301
KLF300-C5 Bayou 4X4	PB527201, LF300C-603651
1994	
KLF220-A7 Bayou	RB560438
KLF300-B7 Bayou	RB526601
KLF300-C6 Bayou 4X4	RB532701
1995	
KLF220-A8/A8A Bayou	SB577001 or LF220A-604101
KLF300-B8/B8A Bayou	SB533701, LF300B-607201
KLF300-C7/C7A Bayou 4X4	SB540601, LF300C-604701
1996	
KLF220-A9 Bayou	TB700001 or LF220A-604701
KLF300-B9 Bayou	TB541451, LF300B-607901
KLF300-C8 Bayou 4X4	TB548951, LF300C-606801
1997	
KLF220-A10 Bayou	VB716001 or LF220A-604901
KLF300-B10 Bayou	VB548301, LF300B-608301
KLF300-C9 Bayou 4X4	VB557001, LF300C-606501
1998	
KLF220-A11 Bayou	WB727201
KLF300-B11 Bayou	WB554101
KLF300-C10 Bayou 4X4	WB563201, LF300C-607501
1999	
KLF220-A12 Bayou	XB743501
KLF300-B12 Bayou	XB559101
KLF300-C11 Bayou 4X4	XB570901
KVF300-A1 Prairie 4X4	XB500051
KVF300-B1 Prairie	XB500051
2000	
KLF220-A13 Bayou	YB760901
KLF300-B13 Bayou	YB561901
KLF300-C12 Bayou 4X4	YB576901
KVF300-A2 Prairie 4X4	YB513101
KVF300-B2 Prairie	YB507001
2001	
KLF220-A14 Bayou	1B788301
KLF300-B14 Bayou	1B566401
KLF300-C13 Bayou 4X4	1B582101
KVF300-A3 Prairie 4X4	1B524801
KVF300-B3 Prairie	1B515501

General specifications

Wheelbase
    Bayou 220 .... 1115 mm (43.89 inches)
    Bayou 300
        1986 and 1987 .... 1200 mm (47.24 inches)
        1988 on .... 1210 mm (47.64 inches
    Bayou 300 4X4 .... 1200 mm (47.24 inches)
    Prairie 300, Prairie 300 4X4 .... 1250 mm (49.21 inches)
Overall length
    Bayou 220 .... 1745 mm (68.70 inches)
    Bayou 300
        1986 and 1987 .... 1850 mm (72.83 inches)
        1988 on .... 1910 mm (75.20 inches)
    Bayou 300 4X4 .... 1860 mm (73.23 inches)
    Prairie 300, Prairie 300 4X4 .... 2065 mm (81.30 inches)
Overall height
    Bayou 220 .... 1015 mm (39.96 inches)
    Bayou 300
        1986 and 1987 .... 1045 mm (41.14 inches)
        1988 on .... 1035 mm (40.74 inches)
    Bayou 300 4X4 .... 1105 mm (43.50 inches)
    Prairie 300, Prairie 300 4X4 .... 1145 mm (45.08 inches)
Seat height
    Bayou 220 .... 730 mm (28.74 inches)
    Bayou 300 .... 750 mm (29.53 inches)
    Bayou 300 4X4 .... 805 mm (31.69 inches)
    Prairie 300 .... 860 mm (33.86 inches)
    Prairie 300 4X4 .... 852 mm (33.54 inches)
Ground clearance
    Bayou 220 .... 155 mm (6.10 inches)
    Bayou 300 .... 195 mm (7.68 inches)
    Bayou 300 4X4 .... 225 mm (8.86 inches)
    Prairie 300, Prairie 300 4X4 .... 163 mm (6.42 inches)

Dry weight
  Bayou 220
    1988 and 1989
      Except UK and Canada.. 183 kg (402.6 lbs)
      UK and Canada.. 181 kg (398.2 lbs)
    1990
      Except Australia A3A (late production)............................ 183 kg (402.6 lbs)
      Australia A3A (late production)....................................... 184 kg (404.8 lbs)
    1991 (all)... 183 kg (402.6 lbs)
    1992
      Except Australia, Canada, Europe................................... 183 kg (402.6 lbs)
      Australia, Canada, Europe.. 183.5 kg (403.7 lbs)
    1993 through early 1995
      Except Australia, Canada, Europe................................... 183 kg (402.6 lbs)
      Australia, Canada, Europe.. 185 kg (407 lbs)
    Late 1995 on
      US.. 183 kg (402.6 lbs)
      Australia, Europe, UK... 185 kg (407 lbs)
      Canada... 183.5 kg (403.7 lbs)
  Bayou 300
    1986 and 1987
      US and Canada.. 223 kg (490.6 lbs)
      All others... 226 kg (97.2 lbs)
    1988 and 1989
      US.. 223 kg (490.6 lbs)
      Australia, UK.. 226 kg (497.2 lbs)
    1990
      All except late 1990 Australia.. 226 kg (497.2 lbs)
      Late 1990 Australia... 228 kg (501.6 lbs)
    1991
      All except Australia... 226 kg (497.2 lbs)
      Australia... 228 kg (501.6 lbs)
    1992
      US.. 226 kg (497.2 lbs)
      Australia... 228 kg (501.6 lbs)
      UK, Canada, Europe... 227 kg 499.4 lbs
    1993 on
      US.. 226 kg (497.2 lbs)
      Australia, UK, Europe... 229 kg (503.8 lbs)
      Canada... 227 kg 499.4 lbs
  Bayou 300 4X4
    1989 through 1994
      US.. 257 kg (565.4 lbs)
      Canada, UK.. 260 kg (572 lbs)
    1995 on
      US.. 260 kg (572 lbs)
      Canada... 261 kg (574.2 lbs)
      UK, Europe, Australia... 263 kg 578.6 lbs
  Prairie 300
      US.. 256 kg (563.2 lbs)
      Australia, Canada... 257 kg (565.4 lbs)
  Prairie 300 4X4
      US.. 274 kg (602.8 lbs)
      Australia, Canada... 275 kg (605 lbs)

General tightening torques*

5 mm thread diameter .... 3.4 to 4.9 Nm (30 to 43 inch-lbs)
6 mm thread diameter .... 5.9 to 7.8 Nm (52 to 69 inch-lbs)
8 mm thread diameter .... 14 to 19 Nm (120 to 162 inch-lbs)
10 mm thread diameter .... 25 to 34 Nm (10 to 25 ft-lbs)
12 mm thread diameter .... 44 to 61 Nm (33 to 45 ft-lbs)
14 mm thread diameter .... 73 to 98 Nm (55 to 72 ft-lbs)

Use these when a torque is not specified for a particular fastener. Threads are dry and cleaned with solvent in all cases.

Maintenance techniques, tools and working facilities

Basic maintenance techniques

There are a number of techniques involved in maintenance and repair that will be referred to throughout this manual. Application of these techniques will enable the amateur mechanic to be more efficient, better organized and capable of performing the various tasks properly, which will ensure that the repair job is thorough and complete.

Fastening systems

Fasteners, basically, are nuts, bolts and screws used to hold two or more parts together. There are a few things to keep in mind when working with fasteners. Almost all of them use a locking device of some type (either a lock washer, locknut, locking tab or thread adhesive). All threaded fasteners should be clean, straight, have undamaged threads and undamaged corners on the hex head where the wrench fits. Develop the habit of replacing all damaged nuts and bolts with new ones.

Rusted nuts and bolts should be treated with a penetrating oil to ease removal and prevent breakage. Some mechanics use turpentine in a spout type oil can, which works quite well. After applying the rust penetrant, let it "work" for a few minutes before trying to loosen the nut or bolt. Badly rusted fasteners may have to be chiseled off or removed with a special nut breaker, available at tool stores.

If a bolt or stud breaks off in an assembly, it can be drilled out and removed with a special tool called an E-Z out (or screw extractor). Most dealer service departments and vehicle repair shops can perform this task, as well as others (such as the repair of threaded holes that have been stripped out).

Flat washers and lock washers, when removed from an assembly, should always be replaced exactly as removed. Replace any damaged washers with new ones. Always use a flat washer between a lock washer and any soft metal surface (such as aluminum), thin sheet metal or plastic. Special locknuts can only be used once or twice before they lose their locking ability and must be replaced.

Tightening sequences and procedures

When threaded fasteners are tightened, they are often tightened to a specific torque value (torque is basically a twisting force). Over-tightening the fastener can weaken it and cause it to break, while under-tightening can cause it to eventually come loose. Each bolt, depending on the material it's made of, the diameter of its shank and the material it is threaded into, has a specific torque value, which is noted in the Specifications. Be sure to follow the torque recommendations closely.

Fasteners laid out in a pattern (i.e. cylinder head bolts, engine case bolts, etc.) must be loosened or tightened in a sequence to avoid warping the component. Initially, the bolts/nuts should go on finger tight only. Next, they should be tightened one full turn each, in a criss-cross or diagonal pattern. After each one has been tightened one full turn, return to the first one tightened and tighten them all one half turn, following the same pattern. Finally, tighten each of them one quarter turn at a time until each fastener has been tightened to the proper torque. To loosen and remove the fasteners the procedure would be reversed.

Disassembly sequence

Component disassembly should be done with care and purpose to help ensure that the parts go back together properly during reassembly. Always keep track of the sequence in which parts are removed. Take note of special characteristics or marks on parts that can be installed more than one way (such as a grooved thrust washer on a shaft). It's a good idea to lay the disassembled parts out on a clean surface in the order that they were removed. It may also be helpful to make sketches

or take instant photos of components before removal.

When removing fasteners from a component, keep track of their locations. Sometimes threading a bolt back in a part, or putting the washers and nut back on a stud, can prevent mixups later. If nuts and bolts can't be returned to their original locations, they should be kept in a compartmented box or a series of small boxes. A cupcake or muffin tin is ideal for this purpose, since each cavity can hold the bolts and nuts from a particular area (i.e. engine case bolts, valve cover bolts, engine mount bolts, etc.). A pan of this type is especially helpful when working on assemblies with very small parts (such as the carburetors and the valve train). The cavities can be marked with paint or tape to identify the contents.

Whenever wiring looms, harnesses or connectors are separated, it's a good idea to identify the two halves with numbered pieces of masking tape so they can be easily reconnected.

Gasket sealing surfaces

Throughout any vehicle, gaskets are used to seal the mating surfaces between components and keep lubricants, fluids, vacuum or pressure contained in an assembly.

Many times these gaskets are coated with a liquid or paste type gasket sealing compound before assembly. Age, heat and pressure can sometimes cause the two parts to stick together so tightly that they are very difficult to separate. In most cases, the part can be loosened by striking it with a soft-faced hammer near the mating surfaces. A regular hammer can be used if a block of wood is placed between the hammer and the part. Do not hammer on cast parts or parts that could be easily damaged. With any particularly stubborn part, always recheck to make sure that every fastener has been removed.

Avoid using a screwdriver or bar to pry apart components, as they can easily mar the gasket sealing surfaces of the parts (which must remain smooth). If prying is absolutely necessary, use a piece of wood, but keep in mind that extra clean-up will be necessary if the wood splinters.

After the parts are separated, the old gasket must be carefully scraped off and the gasket surfaces cleaned. Stubborn gasket material can be soaked with a gasket remover (available in aerosol cans) to soften it so it can be easily scraped off. A scraper can be fashioned from a piece of copper tubing by flattening and sharpening one end. Copper is recommended because it is usually softer than the surfaces to be scraped, which reduces the chance of gouging the part. Some gaskets can be removed with a wire brush, but regardless of the method used, the mating surfaces must be left clean and smooth. If for some reason the gasket surface is gouged, then a gasket sealer thick enough to fill scratches will have to be used during reassembly of the components. For most applications, a non-drying (or semi-drying) gasket sealer is best.

Hose removal tips

Hose removal precautions closely parallel gasket removal precautions. Avoid scratching or gouging the surface that the hose mates against or the connection may leak. Because of various chemical reactions, the rubber in hoses can bond itself to the metal spigot that the hose fits over. To remove a hose, first loosen the hose clamps that secure it to the spigot. Then, with slip joint pliers, grab the hose at the clamp and rotate it around the spigot. Work it back and forth until it is completely free, then pull it off (silicone or other lubricants will ease removal if they can be applied between the hose and the outside of the spigot). Apply the same lubricant to the inside of the hose and the outside of the spigot to simplify installation.

If a hose clamp is broken or damaged, do not reuse it. Also, do not reuse hoses that are cracked, split or torn.

Spark plug gap adjusting tool

Feeler gauge set

Control cable pressure luber

Hand impact screwdriver and bits

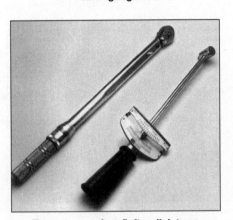

Torque wrenches (left - click type; right, beam type)

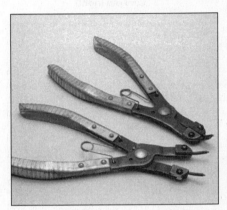

Snap-ring pliers (top - external; bottom - internal)

Tools

A selection of good tools is a basic requirement for anyone who plans to maintain and repair a vehicle. For the owner who has few tools, if any, the initial investment might seem high, but when compared to the spiraling costs of routine maintenance and repair, it is a wise one.

To help the owner decide which tools are needed to perform the tasks detailed in this manual, the following tool lists are offered: Maintenance and minor repair, Repair and overhaul and Special. The newcomer to practical mechanics should start off with the Maintenance and minor repair tool kit, which is adequate for the simpler jobs. Then, as confidence and experience grow, the owner can tackle more difficult tasks, buying additional tools as they are needed. Eventually the basic kit will be built into the Repair and overhaul tool set. Over a period of time, the experienced do-it-yourselfer will assemble a tool set complete enough for most repair and overhaul procedures and will add tools from the Special category when it is felt that the expense is justified by the frequency of use.

Maintenance and minor repair tool kit

The tools in this list should be considered the minimum required for performance of routine maintenance, servicing and minor repair work. We recommend the purchase of combination wrenches (box end and open end combined in one wrench); while more expensive than open-ended ones, they offer the advantages of both types of wrench.

Combination wrench set (6 mm to 22 mm)
Adjustable wrench - 8 in
Spark plug socket (with rubber insert)
Spark plug gap adjusting tool
Feeler gauge set
Standard screwdriver (5/16 in x 6 in)
Phillips screwdriver (No. 2 x 6 in)

Allen (hex) wrench set (4 mm to 12 mm)
Combination (slip-joint) pliers - 6 in
Hacksaw and assortment of blades
Tire pressure gauge
Control cable pressure luber
Grease gun
Oil can
Fine emery cloth
Wire brush
Hand impact screwdriver and bits
Funnel (medium size)
Safety goggles
Drain pan
Work light with extension cord

Repair and overhaul tool set

These tools are essential for anyone who plans to perform major repairs and are intended to supplement those in the Maintenance and minor repair tool kit. Included is a comprehensive set of sockets which, though expensive, are invaluable because of their versatility (especially when various extensions and drives are available). We recommend the 3/8 inch drive over the 1/2 inch drive for general vehicle maintenance and repair (ideally, the mechanic would have a 3/8 inch drive set and a 1/2 inch drive set).

Alternator rotor puller tool
Socket set(s)
Reversible ratchet
Extension - 6 in
Universal joint
Torque wrench (same size drive as sockets)
Ball peen hammer - 8 oz
Soft-faced hammer (plastic/rubber)
Standard screwdriver (1/4 in x 6 in)

Allen wrenches (left), and Allen head sockets (right)

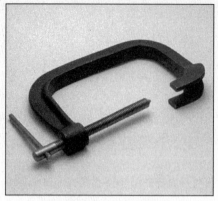
Valve spring compressor

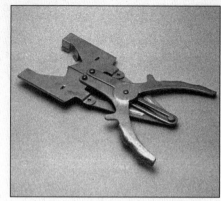
Piston ring removal/installation tool

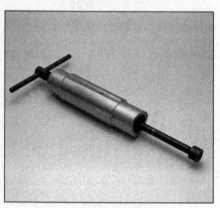
Piston pin puller

Telescoping gauges

0-to-1 inch micrometer

Standard screwdriver (stubby - 5/16 in)
Phillips screwdriver (No. 3 x 8 in)
Phillips screwdriver (stubby - No. 2)
Pliers - locking
Pliers - lineman's
Pliers - needle nose
Pliers - snap-ring (internal and external)
Cold chisel - 1/2 in
Scriber
Scraper (made from flattened copper tubing)
Center punch
Pin punches (1/16, 1/8, 3/16 in)
Steel rule/straightedge - 12 in
Pin-type spanner wrench
A selection of files
Wire brush (large)

Note: *Another tool which is often useful is an electric drill with a chuck capacity of 3/8 inch (and a set of good quality drill bits).*

Special tools

The tools in this list include those which are not used regularly, are expensive to buy, or which need to be used in accordance with their manufacturer's instructions. Unless these tools will be used frequently, it is not very economical to purchase many of them. A consideration would be to split the cost and use between yourself and a friend or friends (i.e. members of a vehicle club).

This list primarily contains tools and instruments widely available to the public, as well as some special tools produced by the vehicle manufacturer for distribution to dealer service departments. As a result, references to the manufacturer's special tools are occasionally included in the text of this manual. Generally, an alternative method of doing the job without the special tool is offered. However, sometimes there is no alternative to their use. Where this is the case, and the tool can't be purchased or borrowed, the work should be turned over to the dealer service department or a vehicle repair shop.

Valve spring compressor
Piston ring removal and installation tool
Piston pin puller
Telescoping gauges
Micrometer(s) and/or dial/Vernier calipers
Cylinder surfacing hone
Cylinder compression gauge
Dial indicator set
Multimeter
Adjustable spanner
Manometer or vacuum gauge set
Small air compressor with blow gun and tire chuck

Buying tools

For the do-it-yourselfer who is just starting to get involved in vehicle maintenance and repair, there are a number of options available when purchasing tools. If maintenance and minor repair is the extent of the work to be done, the purchase of individual tools is satisfactory. If, on the other hand, extensive work is planned, it would be a good idea to purchase a modest tool set from one of the large retail chain stores. A set can usually be bought at a substantial savings over the individual tool prices (and they often come with a tool box). As additional tools are needed, add-on sets, individual tools and a larger tool box can be purchased to expand the tool selection. Building a tool set gradually allows the cost of the tools to be spread over a longer period of time and gives the mechanic the freedom to choose only those tools that will actually be used.

Tool stores and vehicle dealers will often be the only source of some of the special tools that are needed, but regardless of where

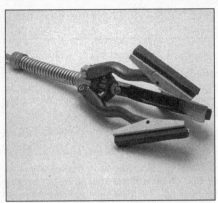

Cylinder surfacing hone

Cylinder compression gauge

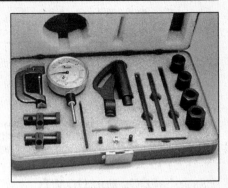

Dial indicator set

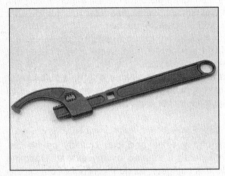

Adjustable spanner

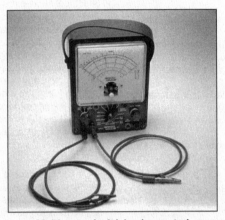

Multimeter (volt/ohm/ammeter)

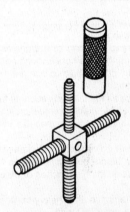

Alternator rotor puller

tools are bought, try to avoid cheap ones (especially when buying screwdrivers and sockets) because they won't last very long. There are plenty of tools around at reasonable prices, but always aim to purchase items which meet the relevant national safety standards. The expense involved in replacing cheap tools will eventually be greater than the initial cost of quality tools.

It is obviously not possible to cover the subject of tools fully here. For those who wish to learn more about tools and their use, there is a book entitled *Motorcycle Workshop Practice Manual* (Book no. 3470) available from the publishers of this manual. It also provides an introduction to basic workshop practice which will be of interest to a home mechanic working on any type of vehicle.

Care and maintenance of tools

Good tools are expensive, so it makes sense to treat them with respect. Keep them clean and in usable condition and store them properly when not in use. Always wipe off any dirt, grease or metal chips before putting them away. Never leave tools lying around in the work area.

Some tools, such as screwdrivers, pliers, wrenches and sockets, can be hung on a panel mounted on the garage or workshop wall, while others should be kept in a tool box or tray. Measuring instruments, gauges, meters, etc. must be carefully stored where they can't be damaged by weather or impact from other tools.

When tools are used with care and stored properly, they will last a very long time. Even with the best of care, tools will wear out if used frequently. When a tool is damaged or worn out, replace it; subsequent jobs will be safer and more enjoyable if you do.

Working facilities

Not to be overlooked when discussing tools is the workshop. If anything more than routine maintenance is to be carried out, some sort of suitable work area is essential.

It is understood, and appreciated, that many home mechanics do not have a good workshop or garage available and end up removing an engine or doing major repairs outside (it is recommended, however, that the overhaul or repair be completed under the cover of a roof).

A clean, flat workbench or table of comfortable working height is an absolute necessity. The workbench should be equipped with a vise that has a jaw opening of at least four inches.

As mentioned previously, some clean, dry storage space is also required for tools, as well as the lubricants, fluids, cleaning solvents, etc. which soon become necessary.

Sometimes waste oil and fluids, drained from the engine or cooling system during normal maintenance or repairs, present a disposal problem. To avoid pouring them on the ground or into a sewage system, simply pour the used fluids into large containers, seal them with caps and take them to an authorized disposal site or service station. Plastic jugs are ideal for this purpose.

Always keep a supply of old newspapers and clean rags available. Old towels are excellent for mopping up spills. Many mechanics use rolls of paper towels for most work because they are readily available and disposable. To help keep the area under the vehicle clean, a large cardboard box can be cut open and flattened to protect the garage or shop floor.

Whenever working over a painted surface (such as the fuel tank) cover it with an old blanket or bedspread to protect the finish.

Safety first

Professional mechanics are trained in safe working procedures. However enthusiastic you may be about getting on with the job at hand, take the time to ensure that your safety is not put at risk. A moment's lack of attention can result in an accident, as can failure to observe simple precautions.

There will always be new ways of having accidents, and the following is not a comprehensive list of all dangers; it is intended rather to make you aware of the risks and to encourage a safe approach to all work you carry out on your bike.

Essential DOs and DON'Ts

DON'T start the engine without first ascertaining that the transmission is in neutral.

DON'T attempt to drain oil until you are sure it has cooled sufficiently to avoid scalding you.

DON'T grasp any part of the engine or exhaust system without first ascertaining that it is cool enough not to burn you.

DON'T allow brake fluid to contact the machine's paint work or plastic components.

DON'T siphon toxic liquids such as fuel, hydraulic fluid or antifreeze by mouth, or allow them to remain on your skin.

DON'T inhale dust - it may be injurious to health (see *Asbestos* heading).

DON'T allow any spilled oil or grease to remain on the floor - wipe it up right away, before someone slips on it.

DON'T use ill fitting wrenches or other tools which may slip and cause injury.

DON'T attempt to lift a heavy component which may be beyond your capability - get assistance.

DON'T rush to finish a job or take unverified short cuts.

DON'T allow children or animals in or around an unattended vehicle.

DON'T inflate a tire to a pressure above the recommended maximum. Apart from over stressing the carcase and wheel rim, in extreme cases the tire may blow off forcibly. ATV tires, which are designed to operate at very low air pressures, may rupture if overinflated.

DO ensure that the machine is supported securely at all times. This is especially important when the machine is blocked up to aid wheel or suspension removal.

DO take care when attempting to loosen a stubborn nut or bolt. It is generally better to pull on a wrench, rather than push, so that if you slip, you fall away from the machine rather than onto it.

DO wear eye protection when using power tools such as drill, sander, bench grinder etc.

DO use a barrier cream on your hands prior to undertaking dirty jobs - it will protect your skin from infection as well as making the dirt easier to remove afterwards; but make sure your hands aren't left slippery. Note that long-term contact with used engine oil can be a health hazard.

DO keep loose clothing (cuffs, ties etc. and long hair) well out of the way of moving mechanical parts.

DO remove rings, wristwatch etc., before working on the vehicle - especially the electrical system.

DO keep your work area tidy - it is only too easy to fall over articles left lying around.

DO exercise caution when compressing springs for removal or installation. Ensure that the tension is applied and released in a controlled manner, using suitable tools which preclude the possibility of the spring escaping violently.

DO ensure that any lifting tackle used has a safe working load rating adequate for the job.

DO get someone to check periodically that all is well, when working alone on the vehicle.

DO carry out work in a logical sequence and check that everything is correctly assembled and tightened afterwards.

DO remember that your vehicle's safety affects that of yourself and others. If in doubt on any point, get professional advice.

IF, in spite of following these precautions, you are unfortunate enough to injure yourself, seek medical attention as soon as possible.

Asbestos

Certain friction, insulating, sealing and other products - such as brake pads, clutch linings, gaskets, etc. - may contain asbestos. *Extreme care must be taken to avoid inhalation of dust from such products since it is hazardous to health*. If in doubt, assume that they *do* contain asbestos.

Fire

Remember at all times that gasoline (petrol) is highly flammable. Never smoke or have any kind of naked flame around, when working on the vehicle. But the risk does not end there - a spark caused by an electrical short-circuit, by two metal surfaces contacting each other, by careless use of tools, or even by static electricity built up in your body under certain conditions, can ignite gasoline (petrol) vapor, which in a confined space is highly explosive. Never use gasoline (petrol) as a cleaning solvent. Use an approved safety solvent.

Always disconnect the battery ground (earth) terminal before working on any part of the fuel or electrical system, and never risk spilling fuel on to a hot engine or exhaust.

It is recommended that a fire extinguisher of a type suitable for fuel and electrical fires is kept handy in the garage or workplace at all times. Never try to extinguish a fuel or electrical fire with water.

Fumes

Certain fumes are highly toxic and can quickly cause unconsciousness and even death if inhaled to any extent. Gasoline (petrol) vapor comes into this category, as do the vapors from certain solvents such as trichloroethylene. Any draining or pouring of such volatile fluids should be done in a well ventilated area.

When using cleaning fluids and solvents, read the instructions carefully. Never use materials from unmarked containers - they may give off poisonous vapors.

Never run the engine of a motor vehicle in an enclosed space such as a garage. Exhaust fumes contain carbon monoxide which is extremely poisonous; if you need to run the engine, always do so in the open air or at least have the rear of the vehicle outside the workplace.

The battery

Never cause a spark, or allow a bare light bulb near the vehicle's battery. It will normally be giving off a certain amount of hydrogen gas, which is highly explosive.

Always disconnect the battery ground (earth) terminal before working on the fuel or electrical systems (except where noted).

Do not charge the battery at an excessive rate or the battery may burst.

Take care when cleaning or carrying the battery. The acid electrolyte, even when diluted, is very corrosive and should not be allowed to contact the eyes or skin. Always wear rubber gloves and goggles or a face shield. If you ever need to prepare electrolyte yourself, always add the acid slowly to the water; never add the water to the acid.

Electricity

When using an electric power tool, inspection light etc., always ensure that the appliance is correctly connected to its plug and that, where necessary, it is properly grounded (earthed). Do not use such appliances in damp conditions and, again, beware of creating a spark or applying excessive heat in the vicinity of fuel or fuel vapor. Also ensure that the appliances meet national safety standards.

A severe electric shock can result from touching certain parts of the electrical system, such as the spark plug wires (HT leads), when the engine is running or being cranked, particularly if components are damp or the insulation is defective. Where an electronic ignition system is used, the secondary (HT) voltage is much higher and could prove fatal.

ATV chemicals and lubricants

A number of chemicals and lubricants are available for use in vehicle maintenance and repair. They include a wide variety of products ranging from cleaning solvents and degreasers to lubricants and protective sprays for rubber, plastic and vinyl.

Contact point/spark plug cleaner is a solvent used to clean oily film and dirt from points, grime from electrical connectors and oil deposits from spark plugs. It is oil free and leaves no residue. It can also be used to remove gum and varnish from carburetor jets and other orifices.

Carburetor cleaner is similar to contact point/spark plug cleaner but it usually has a stronger solvent and may leave a slight oily residue. It is not recommended for cleaning electrical components or connections.

Brake system cleaner is used to remove grease or brake fluid from brake system components (where clean surfaces are absolutely necessary and petroleum-based solvents cannot be used); it also leaves no residue.

Silicone-based lubricants are used to protect rubber parts such as hoses and grommets, and are used as lubricants for hinges and locks.

Multi-purpose grease is an all purpose lubricant used wherever grease is more practical than a liquid lubricant such as oil. Some multi-purpose grease is colored white and specially formulated to be more resistant to water than ordinary grease.

Gear oil (sometimes called gear lube) is a specially designed oil used in transmissions and final drive units, as well as other areas where high friction, high temperature lubrication is required. It is available in a number of viscosities (weights) for various applications.

Motor oil, of course, is the lubricant specially formulated for use in the engine. It normally contains a wide variety of additives to prevent corrosion and reduce foaming and wear. Motor oil comes in various weights (viscosity ratings) of from 5 to 80. The recommended weight of the oil depends on the seasonal temperature and the demands on the engine. Light oil is used in cold climates and under light load conditions; heavy oil is used in hot climates and where high loads are encountered. Multi-viscosity oils are designed to have characteristics of both light and heavy oils and are available in a number of weights from 5W-20 to 20W-50.

Gas (petrol) additives perform several functions, depending on their chemical makeup. They usually contain solvents that help dissolve gum and varnish that build up on carburetor and intake parts. They also serve to break down carbon deposits that form on the inside surfaces of the combustion chambers. Some additives contain upper cylinder lubricants for valves and piston rings.

Brake fluid is a specially formulated hydraulic fluid that can withstand the heat and pressure encountered in brake systems. Care must be taken that this fluid does not come in contact with painted surfaces or plastics. An opened container should always be resealed to prevent contamination by water or dirt.

Chain lubricants are formulated especially for use on the final drive chains of vehicles so equipped (all models covered in this manual are equipped with shaft drive). A good chain lube should adhere well and have good penetrating qualities to be effective as a lubricant inside the chain and on the side plates, pins and rollers. Most chain lubes are either the foaming type or quick drying type and are usually marketed as sprays.

Degreasers are heavy duty solvents used to remove grease and grime that may accumulate on engine and frame components. They can be sprayed or brushed on and, depending on the type, are rinsed with either water or solvent.

Solvents are used alone or in combination with degreasers to clean parts and assemblies during repair and overhaul. The home mechanic should use only solvents that are non-flammable and that do not produce irritating fumes.

Gasket sealing compounds may be used in conjunction with gaskets, to improve their sealing capabilities, or alone, to seal metal-to-metal joints. Many gasket sealers can withstand extreme heat, some are impervious to gasoline and lubricants, while others are capable of filling and sealing large cavities. Depending on the intended use, gasket sealers either dry hard or stay relatively soft and pliable. They are usually applied by hand, with a brush, or are sprayed on the gasket sealing surfaces.

Thread cement is an adhesive locking compound that prevents threaded fasteners from loosening because of vibration. It is available in a variety of types for different applications.

Moisture dispersants are usually sprays that can be used to dry out electrical components such as the fuse block and wiring connectors. Some types can also be used as treatment for rubber and as a lubricant for hinges, cables and locks.

Waxes and polishes are used to help protect painted and plated surfaces from the weather. Different types of paint may require the use of different types of wax polish. Some polishes utilize a chemical or abrasive cleaner to help remove the top layer of oxidized (dull) paint on older vehicles. In recent years, many non-wax polishes (that contain a wide variety of chemicals such as polymers and silicones) have been introduced. These non-wax polishes are usually easier to apply and last longer than conventional waxes and polishes.

Troubleshooting

Contents

Symptom	Section

Engine doesn't start or is difficult to start

Starter motor doesn't rotate ... 1
Starter motor rotates but engine does not turn over ... 2
Starter works but engine won't turn over (seized) ... 3
No fuel flow ... 4
Engine flooded ... 5
No spark or weak spark ... 6
Compression low ... 7
Stalls after starting ... 8
Rough idle ... 9

Poor running at low speed

Spark weak ... 10
Fuel/air mixture incorrect ... 11
Compression low ... 12
Poor acceleration ... 13

Poor running or no power at high speed

Firing incorrect ... 14
Fuel/air mixture incorrect ... 15
Compression low ... 16
Knocking or pinging ... 17
Miscellaneous causes ... 18

Overheating

Engine overheats ... 19
Firing incorrect ... 20
Fuel/air mixture incorrect ... 21
Compression too high ... 22
Engine load excessive ... 23
Lubrication inadequate ... 24
Miscellaneous causes ... 25

Clutch problems (Bayou)

Clutch slipping ... 26
Clutch not disengaging completely ... 27

Automatic transmission problems (Prairie)

Drive belt slipping ... 28
Drive belt upside down in pulleys ... 29
Burn marks or thin spots on drive belt ... 30
Harsh engagement ... 31
Grabby or erratic engagement ... 32
Noisy operation ... 33
Melted belt cover ... 34
Engine rpm too low when vehicle is driven ... 35

Engine rpm too high when vehicle is driven ... 36
Engine rpm erratic when vehicle is driven ... 37

Gear shifting problems

Doesn't go into gear, or lever doesn't return ... 38
Jumps out of gear ... 39
Overshifts ... 40

Abnormal engine noise

Knocking or pinging ... 41
Piston slap or rattling ... 42
Valve noise ... 43
Other noise ... 44

Abnormal driveline noise

Clutch noise ... 45
Transmission noise ... 46
Bevel drive unit (sub-transmission) noise ... 47
Final drive noise ... 48

Abnormal frame and suspension noise

Suspension noise ... 49
Driveaxle noise (4WD models) ... 50
Brake noise ... 51

Neutral or reverse light comes on

Engine lubrication system ... 52
Electrical system ... 53

Excessive exhaust smoke

White smoke ... 54
Black smoke ... 55
Brown smoke ... 56

Poor handling or stability

Handlebar hard to turn ... 57
Handlebar shakes or vibrates excessively ... 58
Handlebar pulls to one side ... 59
Poor shock absorbing qualities ... 60

Braking problems

Front brakes are spongy, don't hold ... 61
Brake lever or pedal pulsates ... 62
Brakes drag ... 63

Electrical problems

Battery dead or weak ... 64
Battery overcharged ... 65

Engine doesn't start or is difficult to start

1 Starter motor does not rotate

1 Engine kill switch Off.
2 Fuse blown. Check fuse (Chapter 4).
3 Battery voltage low. Check and recharge battery (Chapter 4).
4 Starter motor defective. Make sure the wiring to the starter is secure. Test starter relay (Chapter 4). If the relay is good, then the fault is in the wiring or motor.
5 Starter relay faulty. Check it according to the procedure in Chapter 4.
6 Starter switch (button) not contacting. The contacts could be wet, corroded or dirty. Disassemble and clean the switch (Chapter 4).
7 Wiring open or shorted. Check all wiring connections and harnesses to make sure that they are dry, tight and not corroded. Also check for broken or frayed wires that can cause a short to ground (see *Wiring Diagrams*, Chapter 8).
8 Ignition (key) switch defective. Check the switch according to the procedure in Chapter 4. Replace the switch with a new one if it is defective.
9 Engine kill switch defective. Check for wet, dirty or corroded contacts. Clean or replace the switch as necessary (Chapter 4).
10 Neutral switch defective. Check the switches according to the procedure in Chapter 4. Replace the switch with a new one if it is defective.

2 Starter motor rotates but engine does not turn over

1 Starter motor clutch defective. Inspect and repair or replace (Chapter 4).
2 Damaged starter sprockets, chain or torque limiter. Inspect and replace the damaged parts (Chapter 4).

3 Starter works but engine won't turn over (seized)

Seized engine caused by one or more internally damaged components. Failure due to wear, abuse or lack of lubrication. Damage can include seized valves, valve lifters, camshaft, piston, crankshaft, connecting rod bearings, or transmission gears or bearings. Refer to Chapter 2 for engine disassembly.

4 No fuel flow

1 No fuel in tank.
2 Tank cap air vent obstructed. Usually caused by dirt or water. Remove it and clean the cap vent hole.
3 Clogged strainer in fuel tap. Remove and clean the strainer (Chapter 1).
4 Fuel line clogged. Pull the fuel line loose and carefully blow through it.
5 Inlet needle valve clogged. A very bad batch of fuel with an unusual additive may have been used, or some other foreign material has entered the tank. Many times after a machine has been stored for many months without running, the fuel turns to a varnish-like liquid and forms deposits on the inlet needle valve and jets. The carburetor should be removed and overhauled if draining the float chamber doesn't solve the problem.

5 Engine flooded

1 Float level too high. Check as described in Chapter 3 and replace the float if necessary.

2 Inlet needle valve worn or stuck open. A piece of dirt, rust or other debris can cause the inlet needle to seat improperly, causing excess fuel to be admitted to the float bowl. In this case, the float chamber should be cleaned and the needle and seat inspected. If the needle and seat are worn, then the leaking will persist and the parts should be replaced with new ones (Chapter 3).
3 Starting technique incorrect. Under normal circumstances (i.e., if all the carburetor functions are sound) the machine should start with little or no throttle. When the engine is cold, the choke should be operated and the engine started without opening the throttle. When the engine is at operating temperature, only a very slight amount of throttle should be necessary. If the engine is flooded, turn the fuel tap off and hold the throttle open while cranking the engine. This will allow additional air to reach the cylinder. Remember to turn the fuel tap back on after the engine starts.

6 No spark or weak spark

1 Ignition switch Off.
2 Engine kill switch turned to the Off position.
3 Battery voltage low. Check and recharge battery as necessary (Chapter 8).
4 Spark plug dirty, defective or worn out. Locate reason for fouled plug using spark plug condition chart and follow the plug maintenance procedures in Chapter 1.
5 Spark plug cap or secondary (HT) wiring faulty. Check condition. Replace either or both components if cracks or deterioration are evident (Chapter 4).
6 Spark plug cap not making good contact. Make sure that the plug cap fits snugly over the plug end.
7 CDI magneto defective. Check the unit, referring to Chapter 4 for details.
8 CDI unit defective. Check the unit, referring to Chapter 4 for details.
9 Ignition coil defective. Check the coil, referring to Chapter 4.
10 Ignition or kill switch shorted. This is usually caused by water, corrosion, damage or excessive wear. The kill switch can be disassembled and cleaned with electrical contact cleaner. If cleaning does not help, replace the switches (Chapter 8).
11 Wiring shorted or broken between:

a) *Ignition switch and engine kill switch (or blown fuse)*
b) *CDI unit and engine kill switch*
c) *CDI unit and ignition coil*
d) *Ignition coil and spark plug*
e) *CDI unit and pick-up coil*

Make sure that all wiring connections are clean, dry and tight. Look for chafed and broken wires (Chapter 4).

7 Compression low

1 Spark plug loose. Remove the plug and inspect the threads. Reinstall and tighten to the specified torque (Chapter 1).
2 Cylinder head not sufficiently tightened down. If the cylinder head is suspected of being loose, then there's a chance that the gasket or head is damaged if the problem has persisted for any length of time. The head nuts and bolts should be tightened to the proper torque in the correct sequence (Chapter 2).
3 Improper valve clearance. This means that the valve is not closing completely and compression pressure is leaking past the valve. Check and adjust the valve clearances (Chapter 1).
4 Cylinder and/or piston worn. Excessive wear will cause compression pressure to leak past the rings. This is usually accompanied by worn rings as well. A top end overhaul is necessary (Chapter 2).
5 Piston rings worn, weak, broken, or sticking. Broken or sticking piston rings usually indicate a lubrication or carburetion problem that causes excess carbon deposits or seizures to form on the pistons and

rings. Top end overhaul is necessary (Chapter 2).

6   Piston ring-to-groove clearance excessive. This is caused by excessive wear of the piston ring lands. Piston replacement is necessary (Chapter 2).

7   Cylinder head gasket damaged. If the head is allowed to become loose, or if excessive carbon build-up on a piston crown and combustion chamber causes extremely high compression, the head gasket may leak. Retorquing the head is not always sufficient to restore the seal, so gasket replacement is necessary (Chapter 2).

8   Cylinder head warped. This is caused by overheating or improperly tightened head nuts and bolts. Machine shop resurfacing or head replacement is necessary (Chapter 2).

9   Valve spring broken or weak. Caused by component failure or wear; the spring(s) must be replaced (Chapter 2).

10   Valve not seating properly. This is caused by a bent valve (from over-revving or improper valve adjustment), burned valve or seat (improper carburetion) or an accumulation of carbon deposits on the seat (from carburetion or lubrication problems). The valves must be cleaned and/or replaced and the seats serviced if possible (Chapter 2).

11   Compression release stuck in the On position (see Chapter 2).

8   Stalls after starting

1   Improper choke action. Make sure the choke knob or lever is getting a full stroke and staying in the out position.

2   Ignition malfunction. See Chapter 4.

3   Carburetor malfunction. See Chapter 3.

4   Fuel contaminated. The fuel can be contaminated with either dirt or water, or can change chemically if the machine is allowed to sit for several months or more. Drain the tank and float bowl and refill with fresh fuel (Chapter 3).

5   Intake air leak. Check for loose carburetor-to-intake joint connections or loose carburetor top (Chapter 3).

6   Engine idle speed incorrect. Turn throttle stop screw until the engine idles at the specified rpm (Chapter 1).

9   Rough idle

1   Ignition malfunction. See Chapter 4.

2   Idle speed incorrect. See Chapter 1.

3   Carburetor malfunction. See Chapter 3.

4   Idle fuel/air mixture incorrect. See Chapter 3.

5   Fuel contaminated. The fuel can be contaminated with either dirt or water, or can change chemically if the machine is allowed to sit for several months or more. Drain the tank and float bowl (Chapter 3).

6   Intake air leak. Check for loose carburetor-to-intake joint connections, loose or missing vacuum gauge access port cap or hose, or loose carburetor top (Chapter 3).

7   Air cleaner clogged. Service or replace air cleaner element (Chapter 1).

Poor running at low speed

10   Spark weak

1   Battery voltage low. Check and recharge battery (Chapter 4).

2   Spark plug fouled, defective or worn out. Refer to Chapter 1 for spark plug maintenance.

3   Spark plug cap or secondary (HT) wiring defective. Refer to Chapters 1 and 4 for details on the ignition system.

4   Spark plug cap not making contact.

5   Incorrect spark plug. Wrong type, heat range or cap configuration. Check and install correct plug listed in Chapter 1. A cold plug or one with a recessed firing electrode will not operate at low speeds

without fouling.

6   CDI unit defective. See Chapter 4.

7   Pick-up coil or alternator defective. See Chapter 4.

8   Ignition coil defective. See Chapter 4.

11   Fuel/air mixture incorrect

1   Pilot screw out of adjustment (Chapter 3).

2   Pilot jet or air passage clogged. Remove and overhaul the carburetor (Chapter 3).

3   Air bleed holes clogged. Remove carburetor and blow out all passages (Chapter 3).

4   Air cleaner clogged, poorly sealed or missing.

5   Air cleaner-to-carburetor boot poorly sealed. Look for cracks, holes or loose clamps and replace or repair defective parts.

6   Float level too high or too low. Check and replace the float if necessary (Chapter 3).

7   Fuel tank air vent obstructed. Make sure that the air vent passage in the filler cap is open.

8   Carburetor intake joint loose. Check for cracks, breaks, tears or loose clamps or bolts. Repair or replace the rubber boot and its O-ring.

12   Compression low

1   Spark plug loose. Remove the plug and inspect the threads. Reinstall and tighten to the specified torque (Chapter 1).

2   Cylinder head not sufficiently tightened down. If the cylinder head is suspected of being loose, then there's a chance that the gasket and head are damaged if the problem has persisted for any length of time. The head nuts and bolts should be tightened to the proper torque in the correct sequence (Chapter 2).

3   Improper valve clearance. This means that the valve is not closing completely and compression pressure is leaking past the valve. Check and adjust the valve clearances (Chapter 1).

4   Cylinder and/or piston worn. Excessive wear will cause compression pressure to leak past the rings. This is usually accompanied by worn rings as well. A top end overhaul is necessary (Chapter 2).

5   Piston rings worn, weak, broken, or sticking. Broken or sticking piston rings usually indicate a lubrication or carburetion problem that causes excess carbon deposits or seizures to form on the pistons and rings. Top end overhaul is necessary (Chapter 2).

6   Piston ring-to-groove clearance excessive. This is caused by excessive wear of the piston ring lands. Piston replacement is necessary (Chapter 2).

7   Cylinder head gasket damaged. If the head is allowed to become loose, or if excessive carbon build-up on the piston crown and combustion chamber causes extremely high compression, the head gasket may leak. Retorquing the head is not always sufficient to restore the seal, so gasket replacement is necessary (Chapter 2).

8   Cylinder head warped. This is caused by overheating or improperly tightened head nuts and bolts. Machine shop resurfacing or head replacement is necessary (Chapter 2).

9   Valve spring broken or weak. Caused by component failure or wear; the spring(s) must be replaced (Chapter 2).

10   Valve not seating properly. This is caused by a bent valve (from over-revving or improper valve adjustment), burned valve or seat (improper carburetion) or an accumulation of carbon deposits on the seat (from carburetion, lubrication problems). The valves must be cleaned and/or replaced and the seats serviced if possible (Chapter 2).

11   Compression release stuck in the On position (see Chapter 2).

13   Poor acceleration

1   Carburetor leaking or dirty. Overhaul the carburetor (Chapter 3).

2   Timing not advancing. The pick-up coil or the CDI unit may be defective. If so, they must be replaced with new ones, as they can't be

repaired.

3 Engine oil viscosity too high. Using a heavier oil than that recommended in Chapter 1 can damage the oil pump or lubrication system and cause drag on the engine.

4 Brakes dragging. Usually caused by debris which has entered the brake piston sealing boots (disc brakes), corroded wheel cylinders (hydraulic drum brakes), sticking brake cam (mechanical drum brakes), or from a warped drum, warped disc or bent axle. Repair as necessary (Chapter 6).

5 Transmission belt loose (Prairie models). This can cause a flat spot (bogging) when accelerating from idle.

Poor running or no power at high speed

14 Firing incorrect

1 Air cleaner restricted. Clean or replace element (Chapter 1).
2 Spark plug fouled, defective or worn out. See Chapter 1 for spark plug maintenance.
3 Spark plug cap or secondary (HT) wiring defective. See Chapters 1 and 4 for details of the ignition system.
4 Spark plug cap not in good contact. See Chapter 4.
5 Incorrect spark plug. Wrong type, heat range or cap configuration. Check and install correct plugs listed in Chapter 1. A cold plug or one with a recessed firing electrode will not operate at low speeds without fouling.
6 CDI unit or pick-up coil defective. See Chapter 4.
7 Ignition coil defective. See Chapter 4.

15 Fuel/air mixture incorrect

1 Pilot screw out of adjustment. See Chapter 3 for adjustment procedures.
2 Main jet clogged. Dirt, water or other contaminants can clog the main jets. Clean the fuel tap strainer and in-tank strainer, the float bowl area, and the jets and carburetor orifices (Chapter 3).
3 Main jet wrong size. The standard jetting is for sea level atmospheric pressure and oxygen content. See Chapter 3 for high altitude adjustments.
4 Throttle shaft-to-carburetor body clearance excessive. Refer to Chapter 3 for inspection and part replacement procedures.
5 Air bleed holes clogged. Remove and overhaul carburetor (Chapter 3).
6 Air cleaner clogged, poorly sealed, or missing.
7 Air cleaner-to-carburetor boot poorly sealed. Look for cracks, holes or loose clamps, and replace or repair defective parts.
8 Float level too high or too low. Check float level and replace the float if necessary (Chapter 3).
9 Fuel tank air vent obstructed. Make sure the air vent passage in the filler cap is open.
10 Carburetor intake joint loose. Check for cracks, breaks, tears or loose clamps or bolts. Repair or replace the rubber boots (Chapter 3).
11 Fuel tap clogged. Remove the tap and clean it (Chapter 1).
12 Fuel line clogged. Pull the fuel line loose and carefully blow through it.

16 Compression low

1 Spark plug loose. Remove the plug and inspect the threads. Reinstall and tighten to the specified torque (Chapter 1).
2 Cylinder head not sufficiently tightened down. If the cylinder head is suspected of being loose, then there's a chance that the gasket and head are damaged if the problem has persisted for any length of time. The head nuts and bolts should be tightened to the proper torque in the correct sequence (Chapter 2).

3 Improper valve clearance. This means that the valve is not closing completely and compression pressure is leaking past the valve. Check and adjust the valve clearances (Chapter 1).
4 Cylinder and/or piston worn. Excessive wear will cause compression pressure to leak past the rings. This is usually accompanied by worn rings as well. A top end overhaul is necessary (Chapter 2).
5 Piston rings worn, weak, broken, or sticking. Broken or sticking piston rings usually indicate a lubrication or carburetion problem that causes excess carbon deposits or seizures to form on the pistons and rings. Top end overhaul is necessary (Chapter 2).
6 Piston ring-to-groove clearance excessive. This is caused by excessive wear of the piston ring lands. Piston replacement is necessary (Chapter 2).
7 Cylinder head gasket damaged. If a head is allowed to become loose, or if excessive carbon build-up on the piston crown and combustion chamber causes extremely high compression, the head gasket may leak. Retorquing the head is not always sufficient to restore the seal, so gasket replacement is necessary (Chapter 2).
8 Cylinder head warped. This is caused by overheating or improperly tightened head nuts and bolts. Machine shop resurfacing or head replacement is necessary (Chapter 2).
9 Valve spring broken or weak. Caused by component failure or wear; the spring(s) must be replaced (Chapter 2).
10 Valve not seating properly. This is caused by a bent valve (from over-revving or improper valve adjustment), burned valve or seat (improper carburetion) or an accumulation of carbon deposits on the seat (from carburetion or lubrication problems). The valves must be cleaned and/or replaced and the seats serviced if possible (Chapter 2).

17 Knocking or pinging

1 Carbon build-up in combustion chamber. Use of a fuel additive that will dissolve the adhesive bonding the carbon particles to the crown and chamber is the easiest way to remove the build-up. Otherwise, the cylinder head will have to be removed and decarbonized (Chapter 2).
2 Incorrect or poor quality fuel. Old or improper grades of fuel can cause detonation. This causes the piston to rattle, thus the knocking or pinging sound. Drain old fuel and always use the recommended fuel grade.
3 Spark plug heat range incorrect. Uncontrolled detonation indicates the plug heat range is too hot. The plug in effect becomes a glow plug, raising cylinder temperatures. Install the proper heat range plug (Chapter 1).
4 Improper air/fuel mixture. This will cause the cylinder to run hot, which leads to detonation. Clogged jets or an air leak can cause this imbalance. See Chapter 3.

18 Miscellaneous causes

1 Throttle valve doesn't open fully. Adjust the cable slack (Chapter 1).
2 Clutch slipping (Bayou models). May be caused by improper adjustment or loose or worn clutch components. Refer to Chapter 1 for adjustment or Chapter 2 for clutch overhaul procedures.
3 Loose transmission belt (Prairie models). This can cause a flat spot (bogging) just before the vehicle reaches its maximum speed, especially when climbing a hill or carrying a heavy load. Check belt deflection (Chapter 1) and adjust if necessary.
4 Timing not advancing.
5 Engine oil viscosity too high. Using a heavier oil than the one recommended in Chapter 1 can damage the oil pump or lubrication system and cause drag on the engine.
6 Brakes dragging. Usually caused by debris which has entered the brake piston sealing boot, or from a warped drum, warped disc or bent axle. Repair as necessary.

Overheating

19   Engine overheats

1   Engine oil level low. Check and add oil (Chapter 1).
2   Wrong type of oil. If you're not sure what type of oil is in the engine, drain it and fill with the correct type (Chapter 1).
3   Air leak at carburetor intake joint. Check and tighten or replace as necessary (Chapter 3).
4   Fuel level low. Check and adjust if necessary (Chapter 3).
5   Worn oil pump or clogged oil passages. Replace pump or clean passages as necessary.
6   Clogged external oil line. Remove and check for foreign material (see Chapter 2).
7   Carbon build-up in combustion chambers. Use of a fuel additive that will dissolve the adhesive bonding the carbon particles to the piston crown and chambers is the easiest way to remove the build-up. Otherwise, the cylinder head will have to be removed and decarbonized (Chapter 2).
8   Operation in high ambient temperatures.

20   Firing incorrect

1   Spark plug fouled, defective or worn out. See Chapter 1 for spark plug maintenance.
2   Incorrect spark plug (see Chapter 1).
3   Faulty ignition coil (Chapter 4).

21   Fuel/air mixture incorrect

1   Pilot screw out of adjustment (Chapter 3).
2   Main jet clogged. Dirt, water and other contaminants can clog the main jet. Clean the fuel tap strainer, the float bowl area and the jets and carburetor orifices (Chapter 3).
3   Main jet wrong size. The standard jetting is for sea level atmospheric pressure and oxygen content.
4   Air cleaner poorly sealed or missing.
5   Air cleaner-to-carburetor boot poorly sealed. Look for cracks, holes or loose clamps and replace or repair.
6   Fuel level too low. Check fuel level and float level and adjust or replace the float if necessary (Chapter 3).
7   Fuel tank air vent obstructed. Make sure that the air vent passage in the filler cap is open.
8   Carburetor intake manifold loose. Check for cracks or loose clamps or bolts. Check the carburetor-to-manifold gasket and the manifold-to-cylinder head O-ring Chapter 3).

22   Compression too high

1   Carbon build-up in combustion chamber. Use of a fuel additive that will dissolve the adhesive bonding the carbon particles to the piston crown and chamber is the easiest way to remove the build-up. Otherwise, the cylinder head will have to be removed and decarbonized (Chapter 2).
2   Improperly machined head surface or installation of incorrect gasket during engine assembly.

23   Engine load excessive

1   Clutch (Bayou) or automatic transmission belt (Prairie) slipping. Can be caused by damaged, loose or worn clutch components. Refer to Chapter 2 for overhaul procedures.
2   Engine oil level too high. The addition of too much oil will cause pressurization of the crankcase and inefficient engine operation. Check Specifications and drain to proper level (Chapter 1).
3   Engine oil viscosity too high. Using a heavier oil than the one recommended in Chapter 1 can damage the oil pump or lubrication system as well as cause drag on the engine.
4   Brakes dragging. Usually caused by debris which has entered the brake piston sealing boots (disc brakes), corroded wheel cylinders (hydraulic drum brakes), sticking brake cam (mechanical drum brakes) or from a warped drum, warped disc or bent axle. Repair as necessary (Chapter 6).

24   Lubrication inadequate

1   Engine oil level too low. Friction caused by intermittent lack of lubrication or from oil that is overworked can cause overheating. The oil provides a definite cooling function in the engine. Check the oil level (Chapter 1).
2   Poor quality engine oil or incorrect viscosity or type. Oil is rated not only according to viscosity but also according to type. Some oils are not rated high enough for use in this engine. Check the Specifications section and change to the correct oil (Chapter 1).
3   Camshaft or journals worn. Excessive wear causing drop in oil pressure. Replace cam or cylinder head. Abnormal wear could be caused by oil starvation at high rpm from low oil level or improper viscosity or type of oil (Chapter 1).
4   Crankshaft and/or bearings worn. Same problems as paragraph 3. Check and replace crankshaft assembly if necessary (Chapter 2).

25   Miscellaneous causes

Modification to exhaust system. Most aftermarket exhaust systems cause the engine to run leaner, which makes it run hotter. When installing an aftermarket exhaust system, always rejet the carburetor.

Clutch problems (Bayou models)

26   Clutch slipping

1   Secondary clutch friction plates worn or warped. Overhaul the secondary clutch (Chapter 2).
2   Secondary clutch metal plates worn or warped (Chapter 2).
3   Secondary clutch spring(s) broken or weak. Old or heat-damaged spring(s) (from slipping clutch) should be replaced with new ones (Chapter 2).
4   Secondary clutch release mechanism defective. Replace any defective parts (Chapter 2).
5   Secondary clutch boss or housing unevenly worn. This causes improper engagement of the plates. Replace the damaged or worn parts (Chapter 2).
6   Primary (centrifugal) clutch weight linings or drum worn (Chapter 2).

27   Clutch not disengaging completely

1   Secondary clutch improperly adjusted (see Chapter 1).
2   Secondary clutch plates warped or damaged. This will cause clutch drag, which in turn will cause the machine to creep. Overhaul the clutch assembly (Chapter 2).
3   Sagged or broken secondary clutch spring(s). Check and replace the spring(s) (Chapter 2).
4   Engine oil deteriorated. Old, thin, worn out oil will not provide proper lubrication for the discs, causing the secondary clutch to drag.

Replace the oil and filter (Chapter 1).

5   Engine oil viscosity too high. Using a thicker oil than recommended in Chapter 1 can cause the secondary clutch plates to stick together, putting a drag on the engine. Change to the correct viscosity oil (Chapter 1).

6   Secondary clutch housing seized on shaft. Lack of lubrication, severe wear or damage can cause the housing to seize on the shaft. Overhaul of the clutch, and perhaps transmission, may be necessary to repair the damage (Chapter 2).

7   Secondary clutch release mechanism defective. Worn or damaged release mechanism parts can stick and fail to apply force to the pressure plate. Overhaul the release mechanism (Chapter 2).

8   Loose secondary clutch center nut. Causes housing and center misalignment putting a drag on the engine. Engagement adjustment continually varies. Overhaul the clutch assembly (Chapter 2).

9   Weak or broken primary clutch springs (Chapter 2).

Automatic transmission problems (Prairie models)

28   Drive belt slipping

1   Too much belt deflection. Adjust the belt (see Chapter 1).
2   Worn belt. Replace the belt (see Chapter 2).
3   Oil or grease on belt. Clean belt and check for leaking seals (see Chapter 2).
4   Water (not engine coolant) on belt. Check PVT cover for proper sealing.

27   Drive belt upside down in pulleys

1   Wrong drive belt for this model ATV. Check part number on belt and replace with the correct belt if necessary.
2   Clutch out of alignment. Check the alignment and correct if necessary (see Chapter 2).
3   Loose or broken engine mount. Check and tighten or replace as necessary (see Chapter 2).

28   Burn marks or thin spots on drive belt

1   Excessive load on vehicle (weight on racks, heavy trailer, oversized accessory). Remove excessive lead.
2   Brakes dragging. Usually caused by debris which has entered the brake caliper or wheel cylinder sealing boots (hydraulic brakes), corroded calipers or wheel cylinders (hydraulic brakes), sticking brake cams (mechanical brakes), or from a warped disc, warped drum or bent axle. Repair as necessary (see Chapter 6).
3   Applying throttle and continuously raising engine speed when the machine is not moving.

29   Harsh engagement

1   Worn drive belt. Replace the belt (see Chapter 2).
2   Excessive clearance between belt and sheave with new belt. Adjust the clearance by changing the number of shims (see Chapter 2).

30   Grabby or erratic engagement

1   Thin spots or overall wear on drive belt. Inspect the belt and replace if necessary (see Chapter 2). If there are thin spots, check possible causes described in Section 28 above.
2   Drive clutch bushings sticking. Inspect the bushings and replace if necessary (see Chapter 2).

31   Noisy operation

1   Loose belt. Inspect the belt tension and adjust if necessary (see Chapter 1).
2   Worn belt or separated belt plies. Inspect the belt and replace it if necessary (see Chapter 2).
3   Thin spots on belt. Replace the belt and check for causes of thin spots listed in Section 28 above.

32   Melted PVT cover

1   Air intake or outlet clogged. Check the inlet and outlet for obstructions and clean as necessary.
2   Belt slipping due to contamination and rubbing on cover. Clean away contamination. Check the cover for proper sealing against outside water. Check the engine for sources of any oil or grease leaks.
3   Rotating mechanical components hitting cover. Check for damage and repair as necessary.

33   Engine rpm too low when vehicle is driven

1   Engine out of tune. Tune up engine (see Chapter 1).
2   Belt slipping. Inspect belt and adjust or replace as necessary. Clean any excess grease from pulleys.
3   Driven clutch spring broken or installed incorrectly. Inspect the spring and reinstall or replace it.
4   Incorrect drive clutch shift weight for this model ATV. Verify part number and install correct shift weight if necessary.

34   Engine rpm too high when vehicle is driven

1   Incorrect drive clutch shift weight for this model ATV. Verify part number and install correct shift weight if necessary.
2   Incorrect drive clutch spring for this model ATV. Verify part number and install correct spring if necessary.
3   Binding drive clutch. Disassemble the clutch, clean away any dirt and inspect the buttons and shift weights. Reassemble the clutch without the spring and operate it through its full range by hand to check operation.
4   Binding driven clutch. Disassemble the clutch, noting whether the location of the helix spring is correct. Clean away any dirt and inspect the sheave bushing and ramp buttons.

35   Engine rpm erratic when vehicle is driven

1   Thin or burned spots on the drive belt. Replace the belt and check for causes of thin spots listed in Section 28 above.
2   Binding drive clutch. Disassemble the clutch, clean away any dirt and inspect the shift weights. Clean and polish the hub of the stationary shaft, then reassemble the clutch without the spring and operate it through its full range by hand to check operation.
3   Binding driven clutch. Disassemble the clutch, noting whether the location of the helix spring is correct. Clean away any dirt and inspect the sheave bushing and ramp buttons.
4   Wear groove in a sheave face. Replace the affected clutch.

Gear shifting problems

38   Doesn't go into gear or lever doesn't return

1   Clutch not disengaging (Bayou models). See Section 27.

2   Shift fork(s) bent or seized. May be caused by lack of lubrication. Overhaul the transmission (Chapter 2).
3   Gear(s) stuck on shaft. Most often caused by a lack of lubrication or excessive wear in transmission bearings and bushings. Overhaul the transmission (Chapter 2).
4   Shift drum binding. Caused by lubrication failure or excessive wear. Replace the drum and bearing (Chapter 2).
5   Shift lever return spring weak or broken (Chapter 2).
6   Shift lever broken. Splines stripped out of lever or shaft, caused by allowing the lever to get loose. Replace necessary parts (Chapter 2).
7   Shift mechanism pawl broken or worn. Full engagement and rotary movement of shift drum results. Replace shaft assembly (Chapter 2).
8   Pawl spring broken. Allows pawl to float, causing sporadic shift operation. Replace spring (Chapter 2).

39   Jumps out of gear

1   Shift fork(s) worn. Overhaul the transmission (Chapter 2).
2   Gear groove(s) worn. Overhaul the transmission (Chapter 2).
3   Gear dogs or dog slots worn or damaged. The gears should be inspected and replaced. No attempt should be made to service the worn parts.

40   Overshifts

1   Pawl spring weak or broken (Chapter 2).
2   Shift cam stopper lever not functioning (Chapter 2).

Abnormal engine noise

41   Knocking or pinging

1   Carbon build-up in combustion chamber. Use of a fuel additive that will dissolve the adhesive bonding the carbon particles to the piston crown and chamber is the easiest way to remove the build-up. Otherwise, the cylinder head will have to be removed and decarbonized (Chapter 2).
2   Incorrect or poor quality fuel. Old or improper fuel can cause detonation. This causes the pistons to rattle, thus the knocking or pinging sound. Drain the old fuel (Chapter 3) and always use the recommended grade fuel (Chapter 1).
3   Spark plug heat range incorrect. Uncontrolled detonation indicates that the plug heat range is too hot. The plug in effect becomes a glow plug, raising cylinder temperatures. Install the proper heat range plug (Chapter 1).
4   Improper air/fuel mixture. This will cause the cylinder to run hot and lead to detonation. Clogged jets or an air leak can cause this imbalance. See Chapter 3.

42   Piston slap or rattling

1   Cylinder-to-piston clearance excessive. Caused by improper assembly. Inspect and overhaul top end parts (Chapter 2).
2   Connecting rod bent. Caused by over-revving, trying to start a badly flooded engine or from ingesting a foreign object into the combustion chamber. Replace the damaged parts (Chapter 2).
3   Piston pin or piston pin bore worn or seized from wear or lack of lubrication. Replace damaged parts (Chapter 2).
4   Piston ring(s) worn, broken or sticking. Overhaul the top end (Chapter 2).
5   Piston seizure damage. Usually from lack of lubrication or overheating. Replace the pistons and bore the cylinder, as necessary (Chapter 2).
6   Connecting rod upper or lower end clearance excessive. Caused by excessive wear or lack of lubrication. Replace worn parts.

43   Valve noise

1   Incorrect valve clearances. Adjust the clearances by referring to Chapter 1.
2   Valve spring broken or weak. Check and replace weak valve springs (Chapter 2).
3   Camshaft or cylinder head worn or damaged. Lack of lubrication at high rpm is usually the cause of damage. Insufficient oil or failure to change the oil at the recommended intervals are the chief causes.

44   Other noise

1   Cylinder head gasket leaking.
2   Exhaust pipe leaking at cylinder head connection. Caused by improper fit of pipe, damaged gasket or loose exhaust flange. All exhaust fasteners should be tightened evenly and carefully. Failure to do this will lead to a leak.
3   Crankshaft runout excessive. Caused by a bent crankshaft (from over-revving) or damage from an upper cylinder component failure.
4   Engine mounting bolts or nuts loose. Tighten all engine mounting bolts and nuts to the specified torque (Chapter 2).
5   Crankshaft bearings worn (Chapter 2).
6   Camshaft chain tensioner defective. Replace according to the procedure in Chapter 2.
7   Camshaft chain, sprockets or guides worn (Chapter 2).

Abnormal driveline noise

45   Clutch noise (Bayou models)

1   Secondary clutch housing/friction plate clearance excessive (Chapter 2).
2   Loose or damaged secondary clutch pressure plate and/or bolts (Chapter 2).
3   Broken primary clutch springs (Chapter 2).

46   Transmission noise

1   Bearings worn. Also includes the possibility that the shafts are worn. Overhaul the transmission (Chapter 2).
2   Gears worn or chipped (Chapter 2).
3   Metal chips jammed in gear teeth. Probably pieces from a broken gear or shift mechanism that were picked up by the gears. This will cause early bearing failure (Chapter 2).
4   Engine oil level too low. Causes a howl from transmission. Also affects engine power and clutch operation (Chapter 1).

47   Bevel drive unit (sub-transmission) noise

1   Bearings worn. Also includes the possibility that the shafts are worn. Have the unit overhauled (Chapter 6).
2   Gears worn or chipped (Chapter 6).
3   Metal chips jammed in gear teeth. This will cause early bearing failure (Chapter 6).
4   Engine oil level too low. Causes a howl from transmission. Also affects engine power and clutch operation (Chapter 1).

48 Final drive noise

1 Final drive oil level low (Chapter 1).
2 Final drive gear lash out of adjustment. Checking and adjustment require special tools and skills and should be done by a Kawasaki dealer.
3 Final drive gears damaged or worn. Overhaul requires special tools and skills and should be done by a Kawasaki dealer.

Abnormal chassis noise

49 Suspension noise

1 Spring weak or broken. Makes a clicking or scraping sound.
2 Steering shaft bearings worn or damaged. Clicks when braking. Check and replace as necessary (Chapter 5).
3 Shock absorber fluid level incorrect. Indicates a leak caused by defective seal. Shock will be covered with oil. Replace shock (Chapter 5).
4 Defective shock absorber with internal damage. This is in the body of the shock and can't be remedied. The shock must be replaced with a new one (Chapter 5).
5 Bent or damaged shock body. Replace the shock with a new one (Chapter 5).

50 Driveaxle noise (4WD models)

1 Worn or damaged outer joint. Makes clicking noise in turns. Check for cut or damaged seals and repair as necessary (see Chapter 5).
2 Worn or damaged inner joint. Makes knock or clunk when accelerating after coasting. Check for cut or damaged seals and repair as necessary (see Chapter 5).

51 Brake noise

1 Brake linings worn or contaminated. Can cause scraping or squealing. Replace the shoes (drum brakes) or pads (disc brakes) (Chapter 6).
2 Brake linings warped or worn unevenly. Can cause chattering. Replace the linings (Chapter 6).
3 Brake drum out of round or disc warped. Can cause chattering. Replace brake drum or disc (Chapter 6).
4 Loose or worn steering knuckle or rear axle bearings. Check and replace as needed (Chapter 5).

Neutral or reverse light comes on

52 Electrical system

1 Switch defective. Check the switch according to the procedure in Chapter 4. Replace it if it's defective.
2 Neutral or reverse light circuit defective. Check for pinched, shorted, disconnected or damaged wiring (Chapter 4).

53 Engine mechanical system

1 The switches are operated by a pin on the shift drum.
2 Disassemble the crankcase, remove the shift drum and inspect the pin (see Chapter 2). If it doesn't extend by itself when pushed in, disassemble the shift drum stopper and replace the pin or spring.

Excessive exhaust smoke

54 White smoke

1 Piston oil ring worn. The ring may be broken or damaged, causing oil from the crankcase to be pulled past the piston into the combustion chamber. Replace the rings with new ones (Chapter 2).
2 Cylinders worn, cracked, or scored. Caused by overheating or oil starvation. If worn or scored, the cylinders will have to be rebored and new pistons installed. If cracked, the cylinder block will have to be replaced (see Chapter 2).
3 Valve oil seal damaged or worn. Replace oil seals with new ones (Chapter 2).
4 Valve guide worn. Perform a complete valve job (Chapter 2).
5 Engine oil level too high, which causes the oil to be forced past the rings. Drain oil to the proper level (Chapter 1).
6 Head gasket broken between oil return and cylinder. Causes oil to be pulled into the combustion chamber. Replace the head gasket and check the head for warpage (Chapter 2).
7 Abnormal crankcase pressurization, which forces oil past the rings. Clogged breather or hoses usually the cause (Chapter 2).

55 Black smoke

1 Air cleaner clogged. Clean or replace the element (Chapter 1).
2 Main jet too large or loose. Compare the jet size to the Specifications (Chapter 3).
3 Choke stuck, causing fuel to be pulled through choke circuit (Chapter 3).
4 Fuel level too high. Check the fuel level and float level and adjust if necessary (Chapter 3).
5 Inlet needle held off needle seat. Clean the float chamber and fuel line and replace the needle and seat if necessary (Chapter 3).

56 Brown smoke

1 Main jet too small or clogged. Lean condition caused by wrong size main jet or by a restricted orifice. Clean float chamber and jets and compare jet size to Specifications (Chapter 3).
2 Fuel flow insufficient. Fuel inlet needle valve stuck closed due to chemical reaction with old fuel. Float level incorrect; check and replace float if necessary. Restricted fuel line. Clean line and float chamber.
3 Carburetor intake tube loose (Chapter 3).
4 Air cleaner poorly sealed or not installed (Chapter 1).

Poor handling or stability

57 Handlebar hard to turn

1 Steering shaft nut too tight (Chapter 5).
2 Lower bearing or upper bushing damaged. Roughness can be felt as the bars are turned from side-to-side. Replace bearing and bushing (Chapter 5).
3 Steering shaft bearing lubrication inadequate. Causes are grease getting hard from age or being washed out by high pressure car washes. Remove steering shaft and replace bearing (Chapter 5).
4 Steering shaft bent. Caused by a collision, hitting a pothole or by rolling the machine. Replace damaged part. Don't try to straighten the steering shaft (Chapter 5).
5 Front tire air pressure too low (Chapter 1).

58 Handlebar shakes or vibrates excessively

1 Tires worn or out of balance (Chapter 1 or 6).

2   Swingarm bearings worn (Bayou models). Replace worn bearings by referring to Chapter 6.
3   Wheel rim(s) warped or damaged. Inspect wheels (Chapter 6).
4   Wheel bearings worn. Worn front or rear wheel bearings can cause poor tracking. Worn front bearings will cause wobble (Chapter 6).
5   Wheel hubs installed incorrectly (Chapter 5 or Chapter 6).
6   Handlebar clamp bolts or bracket nuts loose (Chapter 5).
7   Steering shaft nut or bolts loose. Tighten them to the specified torque (Chapter 5).
8   Motor mount bolts loose. Will cause excessive vibration with increased engine rpm (Chapter 2).

59   Handlebar pulls to one side

1   Uneven tire pressures (Chapter 1).
2   Frame bent. Definitely suspect this if the machine has been rolled. May or may not be accompanied by cracking near the bend. Replace the frame (Chapter 5).
3   Wheel out of alignment. Caused by incorrect toe-in adjustment (Chapter 1) or bent tie-rod (Chapter 5).
4   Swingarm (Prairie) or trailing link (Bayou) bent or twisted. Caused by age (metal fatigue) or impact damage. Replace the swingarm or trailing link (Chapter 5).
5   Steering shaft bent. Caused by impact damage or by rolling the vehicle. Replace the steering stem (Chapter 5).

60   Poor shock absorbing qualities

1   Too hard:
a)   *Shock internal damage.*
b)   *Tire pressure too high (Chapters 1 and 6).*
2   Too soft:
a)   *Shock oil insufficient and/or leaking (Chapter 5).*
d)   *Springs weak or broken (Chapter 5).*

Braking problems

61   Front brakes are spongy, don't hold

1   Air in brake line (hydraulic brakes). Caused by inattention to master cylinder fluid level or by leakage. Locate problem and bleed brakes (Chapter 6).
2   Linings worn (Chapters 1 and 6).
3   Brake fluid leak (hydraulic brakes). See paragraph 1.
4   Contaminated linings. Caused by contamination with oil, grease, brake fluid, etc. Clean or replace linings. Clean disc or drum thoroughly with brake cleaner (Chapter 6).
5   Brake fluid deteriorated (hydraulic brakes). Fluid is old or contaminated. Drain system, replenish with new fluid and bleed the system (Chapter 6).
6   Master cylinder internal parts worn or damaged causing fluid to bypass (hydraulic brakes) (Chapter 6).
7   Master cylinder bore scratched by foreign material or broken

spring (hydraulic brakes). Repair or replace master cylinder (Chapter 6).
8   Drum warped (drum brakes). Replace drum (Chapter 6).

62   Brake lever or pedal pulsates

1   Axle bent. Replace axle (Chapter 5).
2   Wheel warped or otherwise damaged (Chapter 6).
3   Hub or axle bearings damaged or worn (Chapter 6).
4   Brake drum out of round or disc warped. Replace brake drum or disc (Chapter 6).

63   Brakes drag

1   Master cylinder piston seized (hydraulic brakes). Caused by wear or damage to piston or cylinder bore (Chapter 6).
2   Lever or pedal balky or stuck. Check pivot and lubricate (Chapter 6).
3   Wheel cylinder or caliper piston seized in bore (hydraulic brakes). Caused by wear or ingestion of dirt past deteriorated seal (Chapter 6).
4   Front brake shoes or rear brake pads damaged. Lining material separated from shoes or pads. Usually caused by faulty manufacturing process or from contact with chemicals. Replace shoes or pads (Chapter 6).
5   Shoes or pads improperly installed (Chapter 6).
6   Brake pedal or lever free play insufficient (Chapter 1).
7   Brake springs weak (mechanical drum brakes). Replace brake springs (Chapter 6).

Electrical problems

64   Battery dead or weak

1   Battery faulty. Caused by sulfated plates which are shorted through sedimentation or low electrolyte level. Also, broken battery terminal making only occasional contact (Chapter 4).
2   Battery cables making poor contact (Chapter 4).
3   Load excessive. Caused by addition of high wattage lights or other electrical accessories.
4   Ignition switch defective. Switch either grounds internally or fails to shut off system. Replace the switch (Chapter 4).
5   Regulator/rectifier defective (Chapter 4).
6   Stator coil open or shorted (Chapter 4).
7   Wiring faulty. Wiring grounded or connections loose in ignition, charging or lighting circuits (Chapter 4).

65   Battery overcharged

1   Regulator/rectifier defective. Overcharging is noticed when battery gets excessively warm or boils over (Chapter 4).
2   Battery defective. Replace battery with a new one (Chapter 4).
3   Battery amperage too low, wrong type or size. Install manufacturer's specified amp-hour battery to handle charging load (Chapter 4).

Chapter 1 Part A
Tune-up and routine maintenance (Bayou models)

Contents

	Section
Air cleaner - filter element and drain tube cleaning	7
Battery electrolyte level/specific gravity - check	14
Brake lever and pedal freeplay - check and adjustment	5
Brake system - general check	4
Choke - operation check	10
Clutch - check and freeplay adjustment	8
Cylinder compression - check	22
Differential oil – change	25
Driveaxle and driveshaft boots – inspection	13
Engine oil and filter - change	19
Exhaust system - inspection	16
Fasteners - check	12
Fluid levels - check	3

	Section
Fuel system - check and filter cleaning	20
Idle speed - check and adjustment	17
Introduction to tune-up and routine maintenance	2
Lubrication - general	15
Reverse cable – check and adjustment	11
Spark arrester – cleaning	26
Spark plug - replacement	21
Steering system - inspection and toe-in adjustment	24
Suspension - check	18
Throttle freeplay and speed limiter - check and adjustment	9
Tires/wheels - general check	6
Valve clearances - check and adjustment	23

Specifications

Engine

Compression pressure (at sea level)
  220 models
    Using electric starter .... 1030 to 1570 kPa (149 to 228 psi)
    Using recoil starter .... 1010 to 1540 kPa (146 to 223 psi)
  300 models
    Using electric starter .... 795 to 1240 kPa (115 to 179 psi)
    Using recoil starter .... 825 to 1280 kPa (119 to 185 psi)
Spark plug type
  220 models
    1988 through 1990
      US and Australia .... NGK D8EA
      Except US and Australia .... NGK DR8ES
    1991
      Except Australia .... NGK DR8ES
      Australia .... NGK D8EA
    1992 on ....
      Except Canada, Europe and UK .... NGK D8EA
      Canada, Europe, UK .... NGK DR8ES

Engine (continued)

Spark plug type
    300 2WD models
        Except UK and Canada .... NGK B8ES
        UK and Canada .... NGK BR8ES
    300 4WD models
        1989 and 1990
            US.. NGK D8EA
            Australia, Canada, UK .... NGK DR8ES-L
        1991 on through 1994
            US.. NGK DR7EA
            Australia, Canada .... NGK DR8ES-L
            UK .... NGK DR8EA
        1995 through 1999
            US.. NGK D8EA
            Australia, Canada .... NGK DR8ES-L
            UK, Europe DR7EA
    Gap.. 0.7 to 0.8 mm (0.028 to 0.031 inch)
Engine idle speed .... Lowest stable speed
Valve clearance (COLD engine)
    220 models
        Intake .... 0.15 to 0.20 mm (0.004 to 0.008 inch)
        Exhaust .... 0.18 to 0.23 mm (0.007 to 0.009 inch)
    300 models
        Intake .... 0.10 to 0.15 mm (0.004 to 0.006 inch)
        Exhaust .... 0.15 to 0.20 mm (0.006 to 0.008 inch)
Battery specific gravity .... 1.280 at 20-degrees C (68-degrees F)

Miscellaneous

Front brake shoe lining thickness (drum brakes)
    New .... 4 mm (5/32 inch)
    Limit... 2 mm (5/64 inch)
Front brake pad lining thickness (disc brakes)
    New .... 4.5 mm (3/16 inch)
    Limit... 1 mm (3/64 inch)
Rear brake shoe lining thickness
    2WD models
        New.. 4 mm (5/32 inch)
        Limit .... 2 mm (5/64 inch)
    4WD models
        New.. 5 mm (13/64 inch)
        Limit .... 2.5 mm (7/64 inch)
Front brake lever freeplay
    220 models .... 1 to 2 mm (3/64 to 1/8 inch)
    300 models
        Drum brakes (at lever tip)... 25 to 30 mm (1 to 1-3/16 inch)
        Disc brakes .... Not specified
Rear brake pedal freeplay
    220 models... 25 to 35 mm (1 to 1-3/8 inch)
    300 models
        2WD .... 20 to 30 mm (51/64 to 1-13/64 inch)
        4WD .... 15 to 25 mm (39/64 to 1 inch)
Rear brake pedal height
    220 models... Even with top of footpeg
    300 models
        2WD .... Rider preference
        4WD .... 0 to 5 mm (0 to 13/64 inch) above top of footpeg
Parking brake lever freeplay (at lever gap)
    220 models... 2 to 3 mm (3/64 to 1/8 inch)
    300 4WD models.. 1 to 2 mm (1/32 to 3/64 inch)
Throttle lever freeplay
    220 models... 2 to 3 mm (3/64 to 1/8 inch)
    300 models... 3 to 5 mm (1/8 to 13/64 inch)
Choke freeplay.. Not adjustable
Minimum tire tread depth .... Not specified
Tire pressures (cold)
    2WD models... 3 psi front and rear
    4WD models
        Front.. 5 psi
        Rear... 4 psi

Front wheel toe-in
  220 models .... 30 mm (1-3/16 inch)
  300 models
    2WD .... 27 mm (1-5/64 inch)
    4WD .... 20 mm (25/32 inch)

Torque specifications

Oil drain plug .... 29 Nm (22 ft-lbs)
Oil filter cover bolts .... Not specified
Clutch adjusting screw locknut .... Not specified
Valve adjuster cover bolts .... Not specified
Valve adjusting screw locknuts .... 12 Nm (104 in-lbs)
Spark plug
  220 models .... 20 Nm (174 inch-lbs)
  300 models .... 14 Nm (10 ft-lbs)
Differential filler plug
  220 models .... 15 Nm (132 inch-lbs)
  300 models (front and rear) .... 29 Nm (22 ft-lbs)
Differential drain plug (all models, front and rear).................... 20 Nm (174 in-lbs)
Tie-rod locknuts
  1986 and 1987 .... 29 Nm (22 ft-lbs)
  1988 on .... 27 Nm (20 ft-lbs)

Recommended lubricants and fluids

Engine/transmission oil
  Type .... API grade SE or SF
  Viscosity .... 10W-30, 10W-40, 10W-50, 20W-40 or 20W-50
  Capacity
    220 models .... 2.0 liters 2.1 US qt)
    300 models
      2WD .... 1.7 liters (1.8 US qt)
      4WD .... 2.2 liters (2.4 US qt)
Rear differential oil
  Type .... Hypoid gear oil, API GL-5
  Viscosity
    Below 5-degrees C/41-degrees F .... SAE 80
    Above 5-degrees C/41-degrees F .... SAE 90
  Capacity
    220 models .... 200 cc liters (7 US fl oz)
    300 models
      2WD .... 300 cc (10 US fl oz)
      4WD .... 200 cc liters (7 US fl oz)
Front differential oil (4WD models)
  Type .... Hypoid gear oil for limited slip differentials, API GL-5
  Viscosity .... SAE 140 or 85W-140
  Capacity .... 250 cc (8.5 US fl oz)
Brake fluid .... DOT 3 or DOT 4

Miscellaneous

Wheel bearings .... Medium weight, lithium-based multi-purpose grease (NLGI no. 3)
Swingarm pivot .... Medium weight, lithium-based multi-purpose grease (NLGI no. 3)
Cables and lever pivots .... Chain and cable lubricant or 10W-30 motor oil
Brake pedal/shift pedal/throttle lever pivots............................ Chain and cable lubricant or 10W-30 motor oil

1A

Kawasaki Bayou
Routine maintenance intervals

Note: *The pre-ride inspection outlined in the owner's manual covers checks and maintenance that should be carried out on a daily basis. It's condensed and included here to remind you of its importance. Always perform the pre-ride inspection at every maintenance interval (in addition to the procedures listed). The intervals listed below are the shortest intervals recommended by the manufacturer for each particular operation during the model years covered in this manual. Your owner's manual may have different intervals for your model.*

Daily or before riding

Check the engine oil level
Check the fuel level and inspect for leaks
Check the operation of both brakes - check the front brake fluid level and look for leakage (hydraulic brakes); check the front brake lever (drum brakes), rear brake pedal and lever (all models) for correct freeplay
Check the tires for damage, the presence of foreign objects and correct air pressure
Check the rear final drive (and front differential on 4WD models) for visible oil leaks
Check the throttle for smooth operation and correct freeplay
Make sure the steering operates smoothly
Check for proper operation of the headlight, tail light, brake light (if equipped) and indicator lights
Make sure the engine kill switch works properly
Check the driveaxle boots (4WD models) and driveshaft boots for damage or deterioration
Check the air cleaner drain tube and clean it if necessary
Check all fasteners, including wheel nuts and axle nuts, for tightness; make sure axle nut cotter pins are in place
Check the underbody for mud or debris that could start a fire or interfere with vehicle operation
Make sure any cargo is properly loaded and securely fastened

Every 10 operating days

Perform all of the daily checks plus:
Clean the air filter element (1)
Clean the air cleaner housing drain tube (1)
Check clutch adjustment
Check throttle cable adjustment
Check reverse cable adjustment
Check the rear brake lining wear
Inspect the driveaxle boots (4WD models)

Every 30 operating days

Perform all of the daily checks plus:
Check/adjust the idle speed
Check/adjust the throttle lever freeplay
Check choke operation
Check battery condition and specific gravity
Inspect the suspension
Check the skid plates for looseness or damage
Check the exhaust system for leaks and check fastener tightness
Inspect the wheels and tires
Check disc brake pad wear
Check brake fluid level
Check the wheel bearings for looseness or damage
Lubricate cables and pivot points

Every 90 operating days

Check the cleanliness of the fuel system and the condition of the fuel line
Clean the fuel tap strainer screen
Clean and gap the spark plug
Check and adjust the valve clearances
Change the engine oil and oil filter
Change the final drive oil and front differential oil
Replace the brake fluid
Inspect the steering system and steering shaft bearing

Every year

Change the differential oil
Clean the spark arrester

Every two years

Overhaul the brake master cylinder (hydraulic brakes)
Overhaul the wheel cylinders (hydraulic drum brakes) or calipers (disc brakes)
Replace the brake fluid hoses (2)

(1)   More often in dusty or wet conditions.
(2)   Or whenever cracks or damage are visible.

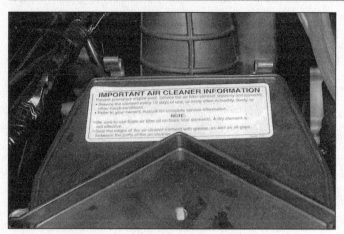

2.1 Decals on the vehicle include maintenance and safety information

2 Introduction to tune-up and routine maintenance

Refer to illustration 2.1

This Chapter covers in detail the checks and procedures necessary for the tune-up and routine maintenance of your vehicle. Section 1 includes the routine maintenance schedule, which is designed to keep the machine in proper running condition and prevent possible problems. The remaining Sections contain detailed procedures for carrying out the items listed on the maintenance schedule, as well as additional maintenance information designed to increase reliability. Maintenance information is also printed on decals, which are mounted in various locations on the vehicle **(see illustration)**. Where information on the decals differs from that presented in this Chapter, use the decal information.

Since routine maintenance plays such an important role in the safe and efficient operation of your vehicle, it is presented here as a comprehensive check list. For the rider who does all of the maintenance, these lists outline the procedures and checks that should be done on a routine basis.

Deciding where to start or plug into the routine maintenance schedule depends on several factors. If you have a vehicle whose warranty has recently expired, and if it has been maintained according to the warranty standards, you may want to pick-up routine maintenance as it coincides with the next mileage or calendar interval. If you have owned the machine for some time but have never performed any maintenance on it, then you may want to start at the nearest interval and include some additional procedures to ensure that nothing important is overlooked. If you have just had a major engine overhaul, then you may

want to start the maintenance routine from the beginning. If you have a used machine and have no knowledge of its history or maintenance record, you may desire to combine all the checks into one large service initially and then settle into the maintenance schedule prescribed.

The Sections which actually outline the inspection and maintenance procedures are written as step-by-step comprehensive guides to the actual performance of the work. They explain in detail each of the routine inspections and maintenance procedures on the check list. References to additional information in applicable Chapters is also included and should not be overlooked.

Before beginning any actual maintenance or repair, the machine should be cleaned thoroughly, especially around the oil filter housing, spark plug, cylinder head covers, side covers, carburetor, etc. Cleaning will help ensure that dirt does not contaminate the engine and will allow you to detect wear and damage that could otherwise easily go unnoticed.

3 Fluid levels - check

Engine oil

Refer to illustrations 3.4 and 3.5

1 Place the vehicle in a level position (front-to-rear and side-to-side).

2 Start the engine and allow it to reach normal operating temperature. **Caution:** *Do not run the engine in an enclosed space such as a garage or shop.*

3 Stop the engine and allow the machine to sit undisturbed in a level position for about five minutes.

4 With the engine off, check the oil level in the window in the right side of the crankcase **(see illustration)**. The oil level should be between the upper and lower level marks on the engine next to the window.

5 If the level is below the lower level line, unscrew the filler cap **(see illustration)**. Add oil through the hole. Add enough oil of the recommended grade and type to bring the level up to the upper level line. Do not overfill.

Brake fluid (hydraulic brakes)

Refer to illustrations 3.8, 3.10 and 3.11

6 In order to ensure the proper operation of the hydraulic front brakes, the fluid lever in the master cylinder reservoir must be properly maintained.

7 With the vehicle supported in a level position, turn the handlebars until the top of the front brake master cylinder is as level as possible.

8 The fluid level is visible through the master cylinder reservoir. Make sure that the fluid level is above the Lower mark on the reservoir **(see illustration)**.

1A

3.4 The oil level in the window should be between the upper and lower lines on the crankcase

3.5 Unscrew the filler cap and check its O-ring; add oil through the filler hole

3.8 The brake fluid level must be above the Lower mark on the reservoir; remove the cover screws (arrows) . . .

3.10 . . . and take off the cover and diaphragm; add fluid . . .

3.11 . . . to bring the level up to the line on the inside of the reservoir (arrow)

3.16a Here's the rear differential filler plug

9   If the level is low, the fluid must be replenished. Before removing the master cylinder cap, place rags beneath the reservoir (to protect the paint from brake fluid spills) and remove all dust and dirt from the area around the cap.

10   Remove the cover screws, then lift off the cover, rubber diaphragm and float (if equipped) **(see illustration)**. **Note:** *Don't operate the brake lever with the cover removed.*

11   Add new, clean brake fluid of the recommended type to bring the level up to the ridge cast on the inside of the reservoir **(see illustration)**. Don't mix different brands of brake fluid in the reservoir, as they may not be compatible. Also, don't mix different specifications (DOT 3 with DOT 4).

12   Reinstall the float (if equipped), rubber diaphragm and cover. Tighten the cover screws securely, but don't overtighten and strip the threads.

13   Wipe any spilled fluid off the reservoir body.

14   If the brake fluid level was low, inspect the front or rear brake system for leaks.

Differential oil

Refer to illustrations 3.16a and 3.16b

15   Park the vehicle on a level surface.

16   Remove the differential filler cap **(see illustrations)**. Feel the oil level inside the differential; it should be up to the bottom of the filler threads.

17   Add oil if necessary of the type recommended in this Chapter's Specifications.

18   Reinstall the filler cap and tighten securely.

4   Brake system - general check

1   A routine general check of the brakes will ensure that any problems are discovered and remedied before the rider's safety is jeopardized.

2   Check the brake levers and pedal for loose connections, excessive play, bends, and other damage. Replace any damaged parts with new ones (see Chapter 6).

3   Make sure all brake fasteners are tight. Check the brake for wear as described below.

4   If you're working on a vehicle with hydraulic brakes, make sure the fluid level in the reservoir is correct (see Section 3). Look for leaks at the hose connections and check for cracks in the hoses. If the lever is spongy, bleed the brakes as described in Chapter 6.

5   Make sure the brake light (if equipped) operates when the front brake lever is depressed. The front brake light switch is not adjustable. If it fails to operate properly, replace it with a new one (see Chapter 8).

6   Operate the rear brake lever and pedal. If operation is rough or sticky, refer to Section 12 and lubricate the cable(s).

3.16b Here's the front differential filler plug (4WD models)

Hydraulic drum brakes (1986 and 1987 300)

7   Securely block the rear wheels so the vehicle won't roll. Jack up the front end and support it securely on jackstands. Remove the front wheels.

8   Remove the rubber plug from the brake drum hole marked SHOE CHECK. Look through the hole to inspect the thickness of the lining material on the brake shoes (use a flashlight if necessary). Turn the drum so you can inspect all of the lining material. If it's worn to near the limit listed in this Chapter's Specifications, refer to Chapter 6 and replace the brake shoes.

9   Remove the rubber plug from the brake drum hole marked SHOE ADJUST. Look through the hole and locate the two adjuster wheels on the adjuster block at the lower ends of the shoes. Turn each of the adjusting wheels evenly upward to expand the shoes until the shoes lock the drum. Then turn the wheels downward until the drum turns with a firm drag, then turn each wheel downward three more clicks to provide running clearance. **Caution:** *Be sure to leave enough running clearance, or the shoes will heat and expand from rubbing until they lock the drum.*

Front disc brakes (1988 and later 300)

Refer to illustration 4.12

10   Raise the front of the vehicle and support it securely on jackstands. Remove the front wheels.

11   If you're working on a 2WD model, look at the friction material on the brake pads through the inspection window in the caliper. If it's worn to or almost to the wear indicator lines, replace the pads (see

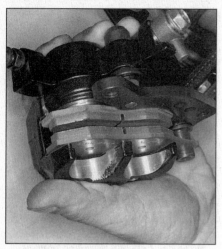

4.12 Check the pad friction material for wear

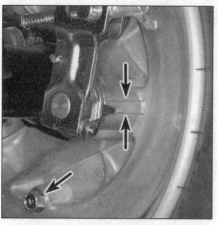

4.13 The wear pointer should be between the upper and lower edges of the raised ridge or the USABLE RANGE mark (arrows); remove the drain bolt (lower arrow) to check for water

5.16 Press the pedal by hand and measure freeplay

1A

Chapter 6). Replace all four pads, even if only one is worn.

12 If you're working on a 4WD model, remove the caliper, leaving the brake hose connected (see Chapter 6). Turn the caliper over and inspect the pad lining material **(see illustration)**. If the friction material is worn to or almost to the limit listed in this Chapter's Specifications, replace the pads. Replace all four pads, even if only one is worn.

Cable-operated drum brakes (all rear; 220 front)

Refer to illustration 4.13

13 To check the linings for wear, have an assistant hold down the pedal while you look at the wear indicator on the brake drum **(see illustration)**. If the pointer is at the limit line (and the cable is properly adjusted), replace the brake shoes (see Chapter 6). There's no shoe adjuster on cable-operated drum brakes.

14 Unscrew the drain bolt **(see illustration 4.13)**. If any water runs out when the bolt is removed, the brake drum seal is worn or damaged. Replace the seal (see Chapter 6).

5 Brake lever and pedal freeplay - check and adjustment

Front brake lever

Cable-operated front drum brakes

1 This procedure applies to the brake lever on the right handlebar on vehicles equipped with cable-operated front drum brakes (Bayou 220 models).

2 Turn the adjuster at the lower end of each front brake cable so the brake lever at the drum has the specified amount of freeplay when the lever is pushed by hand **(see illustration 11.1 in Chapter 6A)**.

3 Loosen the locknut and turn the adjuster at the handlebar to give the specified amount of play at the gap between the lever and the bracket.

4 Remove the cover from the cable equalizer **(see illustration 3.5b in Chapter 5A)**. Operate the front brake lever and make sure the two cables inside the equalizer are pulled evenly. If one side pulls farther than the other, lubricate the cables and check them for fraying. Replace the cables if necessary (see Chapter 6).

5 Finally, check the angle of each brake lever to its cable. The angle should be 80 to 90-degrees. If it's not within this range, remove the cam lever from the spindle and reinstall it on the spindle so it's at the correct angle in relation to the cable (see Chapter 6). **Note:** *If you have to remove and reinstall the cam lever, repeat Steps 2 through 4 above to adjust pedal freeplay.*

Hydraulic front drum brakes

6 This procedure applies to the brake lever on the right handlebar on vehicles equipped with hydraulic front drum brakes (1986 and 1987 Bayou 300 models).

7 Operate the brake lever and note the amount of play from rest until the front brakes are locked (measured at the lever tip). If it's not within the range listed in this Chapter's Specifications, adjust the front brake shoes (see Section 4).

8 If adjusting the brake shoes doesn't bring freeplay into the correct range, there may be air in the brake lines (this is especially likely if the lever feels spongy). Try bleeding the brakes (see Chapter 6).

9 If bleeding the brakes doesn't help, the master or wheel cylinders are probably worn. Inspect them and make necessary repairs (see Chapter 6).

Front disc brakes

10 There's no specified amount of lever freeplay on vehicles with front disc brakes.

11 Operate the lever (on the right handlebar) from rest until it stops. The front brakes should lock firmly. If they don't, bleed the brakes or repair the calipers as necessary (see Chapter 6).

Rear brake pedal

Bayou 220 models

12 Note the position of the brake pedal in relation to the footpeg. The top of the pedal should be even with the top of the footpeg. If not, loosen the locknut, turn the adjusting bolt to adjust pedal height, and tighten the locknut **(see illustration 5.17)**.

13 Press the brake pedal with light hand pressure until it stops. Measure the distance traveled (pedal freeplay) **(see illustration 5.16)**. If it's not within the range listed in this Chapter's Specifications, adjust it by turning the wingnut on the rear brake cable.

Bayou 300 2WD models

Refer to illustrations 5.16 and 5.17

14 Check the rear brakes for wear and replace the shoes if they're worn (Section 4).

15 Jack up the rear end of the vehicle and support it securely on jackstands.

16 Press the brake pedal with light hand pressure until it stops. Measure the distance traveled (pedal freeplay) **(see illustration)**. If it's not within the range listed in this Chapter's Specifications, adjust as described below.

17 Loosen the locknut on the brake pedal adjusting bolt **(see illus-**

5.17 Loosen the locknut (left arrow) and turn the bolt (right arrow) to adjust the brake pedal

5.24 These wingnuts adjust the brake pedal cable (lower arrow) and parking brake cable (upper arrow) (300 models)

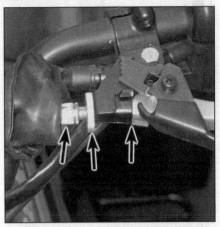

5.26 Measure parking brake lever freeplay at the gap between lever and bracket (right); loosen the locknut (center) and turn the adjuster (left) to change it

tration). Turn the adjusting bolt until the pedal pulls the brake cable equalizer bracket against the stop on the frame.

18   Shift the rear axle into Unlocked mode.

19   Turn the cable wingnut at each of the rear brake levers so the brake on that side of the vehicle drags lightly when you turn the wheel by hand. The drag should be equal at both wheels. **Note:** *If you can't obtain the proper amount of drag by turning the wingnuts at the rear brakes, loosen the locknuts on the adjuster nuts at the cable equalizers. Turn the adjuster nuts to obtain the correct freeplay and tighten the locknuts.*

20   Adjust pedal height to your preferred setting, using the adjusting bolt (there's no specified pedal height). Tighten the adjusting bolt locknut.

21   Check freeplay at the brake pedal. If it's not within the range listed in this Chapter's Specifications, adjust it by turning the wingnut on each brake lever at the drum.

22   Finally, check the angle of each brake lever to its cable. The angle should be 80 to 90-degrees. If it's not within this range, remove the cam lever from the spindle and reinstall it on the spindle so it's at the correct angle in relation to the cable (see Chapter 6). **Note:** *If you have to remove and reinstall the cam lever, repeat Steps 16 through 21 above to adjust pedal freeplay.*

4WD models

Refer to illustration 5.24

23   With the brake released, measure brake pedal height above the top of the footpeg **(see illustration 5.16)**. If it's not within the range listed in this Chapter's Specifications, loosen the adjusting bolt locknut, turn the adjusting bolt to set pedal height and tighten the locknut.

24   Measure pedal freeplay as described in Step 16 above. If it's not within the range listed in this Chapter's Specifications, adjust it by turning the wingnut at the brake drum **(see illustration)**.

Parking brake lever

Refer to illustration 5.26

25   Since the parking brake lever and brake pedal adjustments affect each other, the parking brake lever should be adjusted whenever the brake pedal is adjusted.

26   Operate the parking brake lever and measure its freeplay at the gap between the lever and its bracket **(see illustration)**. If it's not within the range listed in this Chapter's Specifications, adjust it as described below.

Bayou 220 models

27   Loosen the locknut on the adjuster at the lever **(see illustration 5.26)**. Turn the adjuster to change the freeplay, then tighten the locknut.

Bayou 300 4WD models

28   Loosen the locknut on the parking brake cable adjuster **(see illustration 5.26)**. Turn the adjuster all the way in and tighten the locknut.

29   Turn the adjuster wingnut at the brake drum to bring lever play within the specified range **(see illustration 5.24)**.

6   Tires/wheels - general check

Refer to illustration 6.4

1   Routine tire and wheel checks should be made with the realization that your safety depends to a great extent on their condition.

2   Check the tires carefully for cuts, tears, embedded nails or other sharp objects and excessive wear. Operation of the vehicle with excessively worn tires is extremely hazardous, as traction and handling are directly affected. Measure the tread depth at the center of the tire and replace worn tires with new ones when the tread depth is less than that listed in this Chapter's Specifications.

3   Repair or replace punctured tires as soon as damage is noted. Do not try to patch a torn tire, as wheel balance and tire reliability may be impaired.

4   Check the tire pressures when the tires are cold and keep them properly inflated **(see illustration)**. Proper air pressure will increase tire life and provide maximum stability and ride comfort. Keep in mind that low tire pressures may cause the tire to slip on the rim or come off, while high tire pressures will cause abnormal tread wear and unsafe handling.

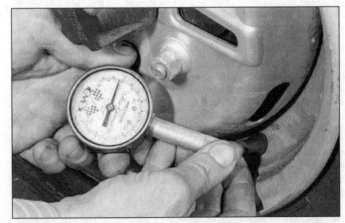

6.4 Check tire pressure with a gauge that will read accurately at the low pressures used in ATV tires

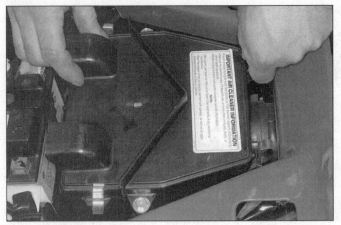

7.2 Pull back the cover clips and lift off the cover . . .

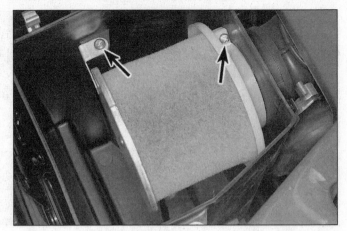

7.3 . . . remove the mounting screws (arrows) and lift out the air filter . . .

5   The steel wheels used on this machine are virtually maintenance free, but they should be kept clean and checked periodically for cracks, bending and rust. Never attempt to repair damaged wheels; they must be replaced with new ones.

6   Check the valve stem locknuts to make sure they're tight. Also, make sure the valve stem cap is in place and tight. If it is missing, install a new one made of metal or hard plastic.

7   Air cleaner - filter element and drain tube cleaning

Element cleaning

Refer to illustrations 7.2, 7.3, 7.4a and 7.4b

1   Remove the seat (see Chapter 7).

2   Release the filter cover clips and lift the cover off **(see illustration)**.

3   Detach the element from the case and lift it out **(see illustration)**.

4   Remove the center screw and take the ends off the metal core **(see illustration)**. Pull the foam element off the metal core and separate the core from the holder **(see illustrations)**.

5   Clean the element and core in a high flash point solvent, squeeze the solvent out of the foam and let the core and element dry completely.

6   Soak the foam element in the amount and type of foam filter oil listed in this Chapter's Specifications, then squeeze it firmly to remove the excess oil. Don't wring it out or the foam may be damaged. The element should be wet through with oil, but no oil should drip from it.

7   Place the element on the core, then assemble the core and end caps on the holder and install the center screw.

7.4a . . . remove the center screw . . .

8   Install the element in the case, secure it with the retaining screws and install the cover.

9   Install the seat (see Chapter 7).

Drain tube cleaning

Refer to illustration 7.10

10   Squeeze the drain tube to let any accumulated water and oil run out **(see illustration)**. **Note:** *A drain tube that's full indicates the need to clean the filter element and the inside of the case.*

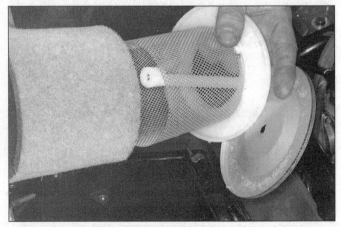

7.4b . . . and separate the element and core from the holder

7.10 Squeeze the drain tube to let out accumulated oil and water

1A

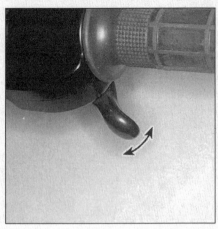

8.2 Remove the screws and take off the clutch release cover (4WD shown; 2WD similar)

8.3 Loosen the locknut, then hold it with a wrench while you turn the adjusting screw; on 4WD models, adjust the upper screw only

9.2 Measure throttle lever freeplay at the lever tip

8   Clutch - check and freeplay adjustment

Refer to illustrations 8.2 and 8.3

1   The clutch release mechanism on these models disengages the secondary clutch automatically when the shift lever is operated, so there is no clutch lever. If shifting gears becomes difficult, the clutch may be in need of adjustment.

2   Remove the clutch release cover on the right side of the engine **(see illustration)**.

3   Hold the adjusting screw with a screwdriver and loosen the locknut **(see illustration)**. **Note:** *On 4WD models, adjust the upper screw only.*

4   Carefully turn the adjusting screw clockwise with a screwdriver until you feel resistance, then turn it counterclockwise until you feel resistance again. Hold the screw in this position and tighten the locknut.

9   Throttle freeplay and speed limiter - check and adjustment

Throttle check

Refer to illustration 9.2

1   Make sure the throttle lever moves easily from fully closed to fully

open with the front wheel turned at various angles. The grip should return automatically from fully open to fully closed when released. If the throttle sticks, check the throttle cable for cracks or kinks in the housings. Also, make sure the inner cable is clean and well-lubricated.

2   Check for a small amount of freeplay at the lever **(see illustration)**. Compare the freeplay to the value listed in this Chapter's Specifications.

Throttle adjustment

Refer to illustrations 9.4 and 9.5

3   Before making adjustments, check and adjust idle speed (see Section 17).

4   Slide the rubber boot back from the adjuster at the throttle lever **(see illustration)**. Loosen the locknut and turn the adjuster until the desired freeplay is obtained, then tighten the locknut.

5   If you can't obtain the correct freeplay at the throttle lever, adjust the cable at the carburetor end.

a) *If you're working on a 220 model, pull back the rubber cap from the top of the carburetor* **(see illustration 8.2 in Chapter 3A)**. *Loosen the locknut and turn the cable adjuster to set freeplay, then tighten the locknut and reposition the cap.*

b) *If you're working on a 300 model, loosen the cable locknuts* **(see illustration)**, *reposition them on the cable to obtain the correct freeplay, then tighten the locknuts.*

9.4 Loosen the locknut (right arrow) and turn the adjuster (left arrow) to adjust freeplay

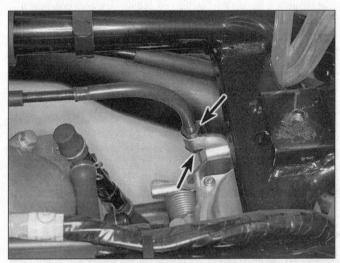

9.5 Loosen the cable locknuts to reposition the cable (Bayou 300 models)

9.6 Loosen the locknut (arrow) and turn the adjusting screw to change the throttle limiter setting

11.1 Adjust the reverse lever (lower arrow) with the cable locknuts (upper arrows) (300 shown; 220 similar)

Speed limiter adjustment

Refer to illustration 9.6

6   The speed limiter can be used to restrict maximum throttle opening (see illustration). Turning the screw in reduces the maximum throttle opening; turning it out allows maximum throttle opening.

7   To make adjustments, loosen the locknut, turn the screw in or out as necessary and tighten the locknut.

10   Choke - operation check

1   Operate the choke lever while you feel for smooth operation.

2   If the lever doesn't move smoothly, try lubricating the choke cable (Section 15). If that doesn't help, refer to Chapter 3 and remove the choke cable and plunger for inspection.

11   Reverse cable – check and adjustment

Refer to illustrations 11.1 and 11.2

1   Locate the reverse lever at the lower end of the reverse cable on the side of the engine (see illustration).

2   Twist the reverse knob until the reverse lever just starts to move and measure the freeplay at the knob (see illustration). If it's not within the range listed in this Chapter's Specifications, loosen the cable locknuts at the reverse lever and reposition them to change the freeplay. Once freeplay is correctly set, tighten the locknuts.

12   Fasteners - check

1   Since vibration of the machine tends to loosen fasteners, all nuts, bolts, screws, etc. should be periodically checked for proper tightness. Also make sure all cotter pins or other safety fasteners are correctly installed.

2   Pay particular attention to the following:

   Spark plug
   Engine oil, transfer case and differential drain plugs
   Oil filter cover bolts
   Gearshift lever
   Brake pedal
   Footpegs
   Engine mount bolts
   Shock absorber mount bolts
   Front axle nuts
   Rear axle nuts
   Skid plate bolts

3   If a torque wrench is available, use it along with the torque specifications at the beginning of this, or other, Chapters.

13   Driveaxle and driveshaft boots – inspection

Refer to illustration 13.1

1   There's a rubber boot at each end of the front driveaxles on 4WD

11.2 Rotate the reverse knob and measure freeplay (300 shown; 220 similar)

13.1 Inspect the rubber boot at each end of the rear driveshaft (all models) and front driveshaft and driveaxles (4WD models)

14.3 Battery electrolyte should be between the horizontal lines on the battery (battery removed for clarity)

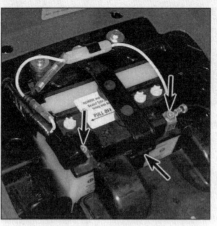

14.4a Disconnect the negative cable (right arrow), then uncover and disconnect the positive cable (left arrow); remove the rubber strap (and retaining bar on later models) (center arrow) . . .

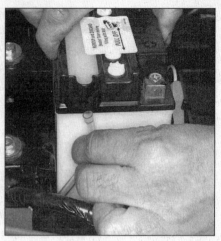

14.4b . . . lift the battery, disconnect the vent tube and take the battery out

models **(see illustration)**, as well as at each end of the front and rear driveshafts on all models.

2   Check the boots for cracks, cuts, tears or deterioration. If any problems are found, remove the driveaxles for boot replacement (see Chapter 5).

3   Check the boot clamp screws to make sure they're tight.

14   Battery electrolyte level/specific gravity - check

Refer to illustrations 14.3, 14.4a, 14.4b, 14.7 and 14.13

Warning: *Be extremely careful when handling or working around the battery. The electrolyte is very caustic and an explosive gas (hydrogen) is given off when the battery is charging.*

1   This procedure applies to batteries that have removable filler caps, which can be removed to add water to the battery. If the original equipment battery has been replaced by a sealed maintenance-free battery, the electrolyte can't be topped up.

2   Remove the seat (see Chapter 7).

3   The electrolyte level is visible through the translucent battery case - it should be between the Upper and Lower level marks **(see illustration)**.

4   Disconnect the negative cable, then the positive cable, then unhook the battery retaining strap or unbolt the retaining bar **(see illustration)**. **Warning:** *Always disconnect the negative cable first and reconnect it last to avoid sparks which could cause a battery explosion.* Lift the battery partway out, disconnect the vent hose and lift the bat-

tery all the way out **(see illustration)**.

5   If the electrolyte is low, remove the cell caps and fill each cell to the upper level mark with distilled water. Do not use tap water (except in an emergency) and do not overfill. The cell holes are quite small, so it may help to use a plastic squeeze bottle with a small spout to add the water. If the level is within the marks on the case, additional water is not necessary.

6   Next, check the specific gravity of the electrolyte in each cell with a small hydrometer made especially for motorcycle batteries. These are available from most dealer parts departments or motorcycle accessory stores.

7   Remove the caps, draw some electrolyte from the first cell into the hydrometer **(see illustration)**, then note the specific gravity. Compare the reading to the value listed in this Chapter's Specifications. **Note:** *Add 0.004 points to the reading for every 10-degrees F above 68-degrees F (20-degrees C) - subtract 0.004 points from the reading for every 10-degrees below 68-degrees F (20-degrees C).*

8   Return the electrolyte to the appropriate cell and repeat the check for the remaining cells. When the check is complete, rinse the hydrometer thoroughly with clean water.

9   If the specific gravity of the electrolyte in each cell is as specified, the battery is in good condition and is apparently being charged by the machine's charging system.

10   If the specific gravity is low, the battery is not fully charged. This may be due to corroded battery terminals, a dirty battery case, a malfunctioning charging system, or loose or corroded wiring connections. On the other hand, it may be that the battery is worn out, especially if

14.7 Check the specific gravity with a hydrometer

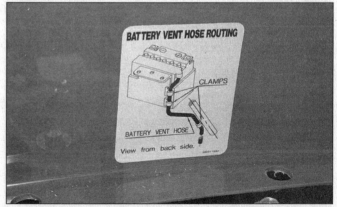

14.13 Be sure to route the battery vent tube according to the decal (this is a typical 4WD model)

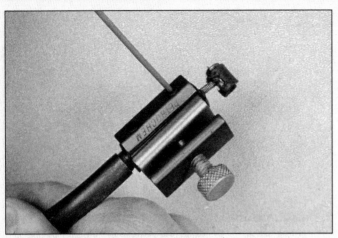

15.3 Lubricating a cable with a pressure lube adapter (make sure the tool seats around the inner cable)

17.3 Turn this knob to set idle speed (300 models)

the machine is old, or that infrequent use of the machine prevents normal charging from taking place.

11   Be sure to correct any problems and charge the battery if necessary. Refer to Chapter 4 for additional battery maintenance and charging procedures.

12   Install the battery cell caps, tightening them securely. Reconnect the cables to the battery, attaching the positive cable first and the negative cable last. Make sure to install the insulating boots over the terminals.

13   Install all components removed for access and route the battery vent tube correctly **(see illustration)**. Be very careful not to pinch or otherwise restrict the tube, as the battery may build up enough internal pressure during normal charging system operation to explode.

14   If the vehicle will be stored for an extended time, fully charge the battery, then disconnect the negative cable before storage.

15   Lubrication - general

Refer to illustration 15.3

1   Since the controls, cables and various other components of a vehicle are exposed to the elements, they should be lubricated periodically to ensure safe and trouble-free operation.

2   The throttle and brake levers and brake pedal, should be lubricated frequently. In order for the lubricant to be applied where it will do the most good, the component should be disassembled. However, if chain and cable lubricant is being used, it can be applied to the pivot joint gaps and will usually work its way into the areas where friction occurs. If motor oil or light grease is being used, apply it sparingly as it may attract dirt (which could cause the controls to bind or wear at an accelerated rate). **Note:** *One of the best lubricants for the control lever pivots is a dry-film lubricant (available from many sources by different names).*

3   The throttle, brake and reverse cables should be removed and treated with a commercially available cable lubricant which is specially formulated for use on ATV control cables. Small adapters for pressure lubricating the cables with spray can lubricants are available and ensure that the cable is lubricated along its entire length **(see illustration)**. When attaching the cable to the lever, be sure to lubricate the barrel-shaped fitting at the end with multi-purpose grease.

4   To lubricate the cables, disconnect them at the lower end, then lubricate the cable with a pressure lube adapter **(see illustration 15.3)**. See Chapter 2A (reverse cable), Chapter 3A (throttle cable) or Chapter 6A (brake cables).

5   Refer to Chapter 5A to access the following components for lubrication:

   a) *Driveaxle splines (4WD models)*
   b) *Rear axle shaft splines*

6   Refer to Chapter 6A for brake pedal removal procedures.

16   Exhaust system - inspection

1   Periodically check the exhaust system for leaks and loose fasteners. If tightening the holder nuts at the cylinder head fails to stop any leaks, replace the gasket with a new one (a procedure which requires removal of the system).

2   The exhaust pipe flange nuts at the cylinder head are especially prone to loosening, which could cause damage to the head. Check them frequently and keep them tight.

17   Idle speed - check and adjustment

Refer to illustration 17.3

1   Before adjusting the idle speed, make sure the valve clearances and spark plug gap are correct. Also, turn the handlebars back-and-forth and see if the idle speed changes as this is done. If it does, the throttle cable may not be adjusted correctly, or it may be worn out. Be sure to correct this problem before proceeding.

2   The engine should be at normal operating temperature, which is usually reached after 10 to 15 minutes of stop and go riding. Make sure the transmission is in Neutral.

3   Turn the idle speed screw **(see illustration 8.2 in Chapter 3A for 220 models or the accompanying illustration for 300 models)** until the idle speed listed in this Chapter's Specifications is obtained.

4   Snap the throttle open and shut a few times, then recheck the idle speed. If necessary, repeat the adjustment procedure.

5   If a smooth, steady idle can't be achieved, the fuel/air mixture may be incorrect. Refer to Chapter 3 for pilot screw adjustment and additional carburetor information.

18   Suspension - check

1   The suspension components must be maintained in top operating condition to ensure rider safety. Loose, worn or damaged suspension parts decrease the vehicle's stability and control.

2   Lock the front brake and push on the handlebars to compress the front shock absorbers several times. See if they move up-and-down smoothly without binding. If binding is felt, the shocks should be inspected as described in Chapter 6.

3   Check the tightness of all front suspension nuts and bolts to be sure none have worked loose.

4   Inspect the rear shock absorber for fluid leakage and tightness of the mounting nuts and bolts. If leakage is found, the shock should be replaced.

5   Support the vehicle securely upright with its rear wheel off the

1A

19.5 The engine oil drain plug (arrow) is accessible from the rear or through a hole in the skid pate

19.6a Unscrew the bolts and remove the oil filter cover and O-ring . . .

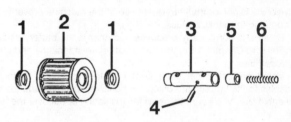

19.6b . . . and pull out the pin and filter element; the narrow end of the relief valve body faces out

1	Gaskets	4	Pin
2	Filter element	5	Relief valve
3	Relief valve body	6	Spring

ground. Grab the rear axle on each side. Rock the axle from side to side - there should be no discernible movement at the rear. If there's a little movement or a slight clicking can be heard, make sure the trailing link pivot bolts are tight. If the pivot bolts are tight but movement is still noticeable, the trailing links will have to be removed and the pivot points inspected as described in Chapter 5.

6   Inspect the tightness of the rear suspension nuts and bolts.

19   Engine oil and filter - change

Refer to illustrations 19.5, 19.6a and 19.6b

1   Consistent routine oil and filter changes are the single most important maintenance procedure you can perform on a vehicle. The oil not only lubricates the internal parts of the engine, transmission, clutch and bevel drive or sub-transmission, but it also acts as a coolant, a cleaner, a sealant, and a protectant. Because of these demands, the oil takes a terrific amount of abuse and should be replaced often with new oil of the recommended grade and type. Saving a little money on the difference in cost between a good oil and a cheap oil won't pay off if the engine is damaged.

2   Before changing the oil and filter, warm up the engine so the oil will drain easily. Be careful when draining the oil, as the exhaust pipe, the engine and the oil itself can cause severe burns.

3   Park the vehicle over a clean drain pan.

4   Remove the oil filler cap to vent the crankcase and act as a reminder that there is no oil in the engine.

5   Next, remove the drain plug from the engine **(see illustration)** and allow the oil to drain into the pan.

6   Remove the oil filter cover bolts, then remove the cover, O-ring and filter element **(see illustrations)**. If additional maintenance is planned for this time period, check or service another component while the oil is allowed to drain completely.

7   Wipe any remaining oil out of the filter housing area of the crankcase and make sure the oil passage in the filter housing is clear. Clean the oil strainer with solvent and let it dry completely.

8   Check the condition of the drain plug threads and the O-rings.

9   Make sure the O-ring is installed on each end of the filter element, then install it. Install the relief valve in the element, with the narrow end facing out. **Caution:** *The valve must be installed facing the correct direction or oil starvation may cause severe engine damage.*

10   Install a new O-ring on the filter cover. Install the cover. Install the cover bolts and tighten them to the torque listed in this Chapter's Specifications.

11   Install the engine drain plug, using a new O-ring if the old one is worn or damaged. Tighten the plug to the torque listed in this Chapter's Specifications. Avoid overtightening, as damage to the engine case will result.

12   Before refilling the engine, check the old oil carefully. If the oil was

drained into a clean pan, small pieces of metal or other material can be easily detected. If the oil is very metallic colored, then the engine is experiencing wear from break-in (new engine) or from insufficient lubrication. If there are flakes or chips of metal in the oil, then something is drastically wrong internally and the engine will have to be disassembled for inspection and repair.

13   If there are pieces of fiber-like material in the oil, the secondary clutch is experiencing excessive wear and should be checked.

14   If the inspection of the oil turns up nothing unusual, refill the crankcase to the proper level with the recommended oil and install the filler cap. Start the engine and let it run for two or three minutes. Shut it off, wait a few minutes, then check the oil level in the oil window on the side of the engine. If necessary, add more oil to bring the level up to the upper level mark on the engine next to the window. Check around the drain plug and filter cover for leaks.

15   The old oil drained from the engine cannot be reused in its present state and should be disposed of. Check with your local refuse disposal company, disposal facility or environmental agency to see whether they will accept the oil for recycling. Don't pour used oil into drains or onto the ground. After the oil has cooled, it can be drained into a suitable container (capped plastic jugs, topped bottles, milk cartons, etc.) for transport to one of these disposal sites.

20   Fuel system - check and filter cleaning

Refer to illustrations 20.5 and 20.9

Warning: *Gasoline is extremely flammable, so take extra precautions when you work on any part of the fuel system. Don't smoke or allow open flames or bare light bulbs near the work area, and don't work in a garage where a natural gas-type appliance (such as a water heater or clothes dryer) with a pilot light is present. Since gasoline is carcino-*

20.5 Slide back the clamp, disconnect the hose and remove the tap screws (arrows)

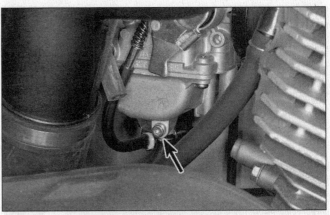

20.9 Here's the Bayou 300 float chamber drain screw (Bayou 220 similar)

genic, wear latex gloves when there's a possibility of being exposed to fuel, and, if you spill any fuel on your skin, rinse it off immediately with soap and water. Mop up any spills immediately and do not store fuel-soaked rags where they could ignite. When you perform any kind of work on the fuel system, wear safety glasses and have a fire extinguisher suitable for a class B type fire (flammable liquids) on hand.

1   Check the carburetor, fuel tank, the fuel tap and the line for leaks and evidence of damage.

2   If carburetor gaskets are leaking, the carburetor should be disassembled and rebuilt by referring to Chapter 3.

3   If the fuel tap is leaking, tightening the screws may help. If leakage persists, the tap should be disassembled and repaired or replaced with a new one.

4   If the fuel line is cracked or otherwise deteriorated, replace it with a new one.

5   Place the fuel tap lever in the Off position. Slide the clamp back from the fuel line fitting, disconnect the fuel line from the tap, remove the tap mounting screws and take it off the fuel tank **(see illustration)**.

6   Clean the strainer with solvent and let it dry.

7   Installation is the reverse of the removal steps, with the following additions:

 a) Use a new gasket.
 b) Hand-tighten the screws firmly, but don't overtighten or the gasket will be squashed, resulting in fuel leaks.

8   After installation, run the engine and check for fuel leaks.

9   If the vehicle will be stored for a month or more, remove and drain the fuel tank. Also loosen the float chamber drain screw and drain the fuel from the carburetor **(see illustration)**.

21 Spark plug - replacement

Refer to illustrations 21.2, 21.6a and 21.6b

1   This vehicle is equipped with a spark plug that has an 18 mm wrench hex.

2   Twist the spark plug cap to break it free from the plug, then pull it off. If available, use compressed air to blow any accumulated debris from around the spark plug. Remove the plug **(see illustration)**.

3   Inspect the electrodes for wear. Both the center and side electrodes should have square edges and the side electrode should be of uniform thickness. Look for excessive deposits and evidence of a cracked or chipped insulator around the center electrode. Compare your spark plug to the color spark plug reading chart on the inside of the back cover. Check the threads, the washer and the ceramic insulator body for cracks and other damage.

4   If the electrodes are not excessively worn, and if the deposits can be easily removed with a wire brush, the plug can be regapped and reused (if no cracks or chips are visible in the insulator). If in doubt concerning the condition of the plug, replace it with a new one, as the expense is minimal.

5   Cleaning the spark plug by sandblasting is permitted, provided you clean the plug with a high flash-point solvent afterwards.

6   Before installing a new plug, make sure it is the correct type and heat range. Check the gap between the electrodes, as it is not preset. For best results, use a wire-type gauge rather than a flat gauge to check the gap **(see illustration)**. If the gap must be adjusted, bend the side electrode only and be very careful not to chip or crack the insula-

1A

21.2 Twist the boot to free it, pull it off and unscrew the plug with a spark plug socket

21.6a Spark plug manufacturers recommend using a wire type gauge when checking the gap - if the wire doesn't slide between the electrodes with a slight drag, adjustment is required

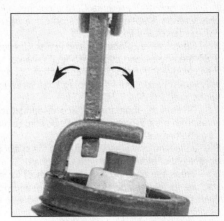

21.6b To change the gap, bend the side electrode only, as indicated by the arrows, and be very careful not to crack or chip the ceramic insulator surrounding the center electrode

22.5 A compression gauge with a threaded fitting for the spark plug hole is preferred over the type that requires hand pressure to maintain the seal

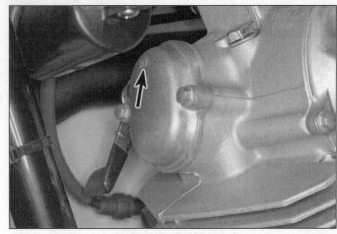

23.6a Note the position of the UP mark (arrow) and remove the cover mounting bolts . . .

tor nose **(see illustration)**. Make sure the washer is in place before installing the plug.

7   Since the cylinder head is made of aluminum, which is soft and easily damaged, thread the plug into the head by hand. Slip a short length of hose over the end of the plug to use as a tool to thread it into place. The hose will grip the plug well enough to turn it, but will start to slip if the plug begins to cross-thread in the hole - this will prevent damaged threads and the accompanying repair costs.

8   Once the plug is finger tight, the job can be finished with a socket. If a torque wrench is available, tighten the spark plug to the torque listed in this Chapter's Specifications. If you do not have a torque wrench, tighten the plug finger tight (until the washer bottoms on the cylinder head) then use a spark plug socket to tighten it an additional 1/4 turn. Regardless of the method used, do not overtighten it.

9   Reconnect the spark plug cap.

22 Cylinder compression - check

Refer to illustration 22.5

1   Among other things, poor engine performance may be caused by leaking valves, incorrect valve clearances, a leaking head gasket, or a worn piston, rings and/or cylinder wall. A cylinder compression check will help pinpoint these conditions and can also indicate the presence of excessive carbon deposits in the cylinder head.

2   The only tools required are a compression gauge and a spark plug wrench. Depending on the outcome of the initial test, a squirt-type oil can may also be needed.

3   Check valve clearances and adjust if necessary (see Section 23). Start the engine and allow it to reach normal operating temperature, then remove the spark plug (see Section 21, if necessary). Work carefully - don't strip the spark plug hole threads and don't burn your hands.

4   Disable the ignition by disconnecting the primary (low tension) wires from the coil (see Chapter 4). Be sure to mark the locations of the wires before detaching them.

5   Install the compression gauge in the spark plug hole **(see illustration)**. Hold or block the throttle wide open.

6   Crank the engine over a minimum of four or five revolutions (or until the gauge reading stops increasing) and observe the initial movement of the compression gauge needle as well as the final total gauge reading. Compare the results to the value listed in this Chapter's Specifications.

7   If the compression built up quickly and evenly to the specified amount, you can assume the engine upper end is in reasonably good mechanical condition. Worn or sticking piston rings and a worn cylinder will produce very little initial movement of the gauge needle, but

compression will tend to build up gradually as the engine spins over. Valve and valve seat leakage, or head gasket leakage, is indicated by low initial compression which does not tend to build up.

8   To further confirm your findings, add a small amount of engine oil to the cylinder by inserting the nozzle of a squirt-type oil can through the spark plug hole. The oil will tend to seal the piston rings if they are leaking.

9   If the compression increases significantly after the addition of the oil, the piston rings and/or cylinder are definitely worn. If the compression does not increase, the pressure is leaking past the valves or the head gasket. Leakage past the valves may be due to insufficient valve clearances, burned, warped or cracked valves or valve seats or valves that are hanging up in the guides.

10   If compression readings are considerably higher than specified, the combustion chamber is probably coated with excessive carbon deposits. It is possible (but not very likely) for carbon deposits to raise the compression enough to compensate for the effects of leakage past rings or valves. Refer to Chapter 2, remove the cylinder head and carefully decarbonize the combustion chamber.

23 Valve clearances - check and adjustment

Refer to illustrations 23.6a, 23.6b, 23.7, 23.8 and 23.10

1   The engine must be cool to the touch for this maintenance procedure, so if possible let the machine sit overnight before beginning.

2   Remove the seat and front fender unit (see Chapter 7).

3   Remove the fuel tank (see Chapter 4)

4   Disconnect the cable from the negative terminal of the battery (see Section 14, if necessary).

5   Refer to Section 21 and remove the spark plug. This will make it easier to turn the engine.

6   Remove the valve adjusting hole covers (there's one on each side of the cylinder head **(see illustrations)**.

7   Remove the timing hole plug **(see illustration)**.

8   Position the piston at Top Dead Center (TDC) on the compression stroke. Do this by turning the crankshaft until the mark on the rotor is aligned with the timing notch on the crankcase **(see illustration)**. You should be able to wiggle both rocker arms - if not (if the exhaust valve is open), the engine is positioned at TDC on the exhaust stroke; turn the crankshaft one complete revolution and realign the marks.

9   With the engine in this position, both of the valves can be checked.

10   To check, insert a feeler gauge of the thickness listed in this Chapter's Specifications between the valve stem and rocker arm **(see illustration)**. Pull the feeler gauge out slowly - you should feel a slight drag. If there's no drag, the clearance is too loose. If there's a heavy

23.6b . . . take off the cover and inspect the O-ring

23.7 Remove the timing hole plug (locations vary slightly, but all models are similar to this)

23.8 Align the T mark on the rotor (arrow) with the groove in the edge of the timing plug hole (crankcase cover removed for clarity)

drag, the clearance is too tight.

11   If the clearance is incorrect, loosen the adjuster locknut with a box-end wrench. Turn the adjusting screw with a screwdriver until the correct clearance is achieved, then tighten the locknut **(see illustration 23.10).**

12   After adjusting, recheck the clearance with the feeler gauge to make sure it wasn't changed when the locknut was tightened.

13   Now measure the other valve, following the same procedure you used for the first valve. Make sure to use a feeler gauge of the specified thickness.

14   With both of the clearances within the Specifications, install the valve adjusting hole covers and timing hole plug. Use new O-rings on the covers and plug if the old ones are hardened, deteriorated or damaged.

15   Install all components removed for access.

24 Steering system - inspection and toe-in adjustment

Inspection

Refer to illustration 24.5

1   This vehicle is equipped with a ball bearing at the lower end of the steering shaft and plastic bushings at the upper end. These can become dented, rough or loose during normal use of the machine. In extreme cases, worn or loose parts can cause steering wobble that is potentially dangerous.

2   To check, block the rear wheels so the vehicle can't roll, jack up the front end and support it securely on jackstands.

3   Point the wheel straight ahead and slowly move the handlebar from side-to-side. Dents or roughness in the bearing or bushing will be felt and the bars will not move smoothly. **Note:** *Make sure any hesitation in movement is not being caused by the cables and wiring harnesses that run to the handlebar.*

4   If the handlebar doesn't move smoothly, or if it moves horizontally, refer to Chapter 5 to remove and inspect the steering shaft bushings and bearing.

5   Look at the tie-rod ends (inner and outer) while slowly turning the handlebar from side-to-side **(see illustration).** If there's any vertical movement in the tie-rod ball-joints, refer to Chapter 5 and replace them.

Toe-in adjustment

Refer to illustrations 24.10 and 24.11

6   Roll the vehicle forward onto a level surface and stop it with the front wheels pointing straight ahead.

7   Make a mark at the front and center of each tire, even with the centerline of the front hub.

8   Measure the distance between the marks with a toe-in gauge or steel tape measure.

9   Have an assistant push the vehicle backward while you watch the marks on the tires. Stop pushing when the tires have rotated exactly one-half turn, so the marks are at the backs of the tires.

10   Again, measure the distance between the marks. Subtract the

1A

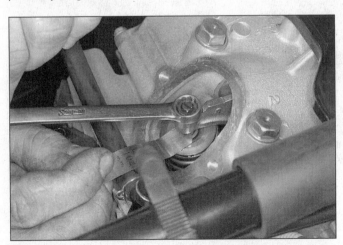

23.10 Measure valve clearance with a feeler gauge; to adjust it, loosen the locknut and turn the adjusting screw

24.5 Inspect the steering shaft bearing (right arrow) and tie-rod ends (left arrows)

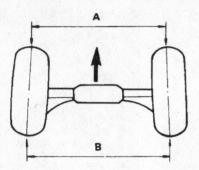

24.10 Toe-in measurement (B minus A = toe-in)

24.11 Place an open-end wrench on the flat (center arrow); loosen the locknuts (outer arrows) and turn the tie-rod with the wrench to change toe-in

front measurement from the rear measurement to get toe-in (see illustration).

11   If toe-in is not as specified in this Chapter's Specifications, hold each tie-rod with a wrench on the flat and loosen the locknuts (see illustration). Turn the tie-rods an equal amount to change toe-in. When toe-in is set correctly, tighten the locknuts to the torque listed in this Chapter's Specifications.

25   Differential oil – change

Refer to illustrations 25.2a and 25.2b

1   Place a drain pan beneath the differential being drained.

2   Remove the oil filler plug, then the drain bolt and sealing washer (see illustrations 3.16a, 3.16b and the accompanying illustrations). Let the oil drain for several minutes, until it stops dripping.

3   Clean the drain bolt and sealing washer. If the sealing washer is in good condition, it can be reused; otherwise, replace it.

4   Install the drain bolt and tighten it to the torque listed in this Chapter's Specifications.

5   Add oil of the type and amount listed in this Chapter's Specifications, then install the filler plug and tighten it to the torque listed in this Chapter's Specifications.

6   Refer to Step 15 of Section 19 to dispose of the drained oil.

26   Spark arrester – cleaning

Warning: The muffler will get hot during this procedure if it isn't already. Don't touch the muffler or spark arrester with bare hands or you could be burned.

Refer to illustration 26.1

1   Unscrew the drain plug from the underside of the muffler (see illustration).

2   Place the transmission in Neutral, then start the engine and let it idle.

3   Rev the engine several times while tapping on the muffler with a rubber mallet to free carbon particles trapped in the muffler.

4   Shut the engine off and reinstall the drain plug.

5   Remove the spark arrester retaining bolt (see illustration 26.1) and pull the spark arrester out of the muffler.

6   Clean the spark arrester with a wire brush and solvent to remove carbon deposits, then let it dry.

7   Slip the spark arrester back into the muffler and reinstall the retaining bolt.

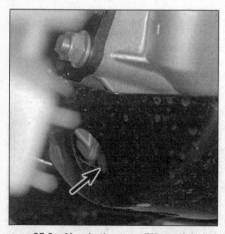

25.2a Here's the rear differential drain bolt . . .

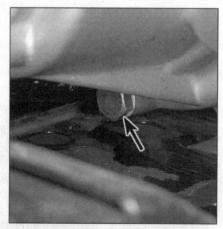

25.2b . . . and here's the front differential drain bolt (4WD models)

26.1 Remove the drain plug (lower arrow) and the spark arrester bolt (upper arrow)

Chapter 1 Part B
Tune-up and routine maintenance
(Prairie models)

Contents

	Section
Air cleaner - filter element and drain tube cleaning	7
Battery electrolyte level/specific gravity - check	12
Brake lever and pedal freeplay - check and adjustment	5
Brake system - general check	4
Choke - operation check	9
Cylinder compression - check	20
Differential oil – change	23
Driveaxle and driveshaft boots – inspection	11
Engine oil and filter - change	17
Exhaust system - inspection	14
Fasteners - check	10
Fluid levels - check	3

	Section
Fuel system - check and filter cleaning	18
Idle speed - check and adjustment	15
Introduction to tune-up and routine maintenance	2
Lubrication - general	13
Spark arrester – cleaning	24
Spark plug - replacement	19
Steering system - inspection and toe-in adjustment	22
Suspension - check	16
Throttle freeplay and speed limiter - check and adjustment	8
Tires/wheels - general check	6
Valve clearances - check and adjustment	21

Specifications

Engine

Compression pressure (at sea level, using electric starter	855 to 1295 kPa (215 to 188 psi)
Spark plug type	
US	NGK D8EA
Except US	NGK DR8ES-L
Gap	0.7 to 0.8 mm (0.028 to 0.031 inch)
Engine idle speed	Lowest stable speed
Valve clearance (COLD engine)	
Intake	0.08 to 0.13 mm (0.003 to 0.005 inch)
Exhaust	0.15 to 0.20 mm (0.006 to 0.008 inch)
Battery specific gravity	1.280 at 20-degrees C (68-degrees F)

Miscellaneous

Front brake pad lining thickness	
New	4.5 mm (3/16 inch)
Limit	1 mm (3/64 inch)
Rear brake shoe lining thickness	
New	5.0 to 5.6 mm (13/64 to 7/32 inch)
Limit	2.6 mm (7/32 inch)

Miscellaneous (continued)

Front brake lever freeplay	Not specified
Rear brake pedal freeplay	15 to 25 mm (39/64 to 1 inch)
Rear brake pedal height	58.5 to 63.5 mm (2 to 2-1/2 inches) above floorboard
Parking brake lever freeplay (at lever gap)	1 to 2 mm (1/32 to 1/16 inch)
Throttle lever freeplay	2 to 3 mm (3/32 to 1/8 inch)
Choke freeplay	Not adjustable
Minimum tire tread depth	Not specified
Tire pressures (cold)	
Front	5 psi
Rear	4 psi
Front wheel toe-in	
2WD models	25 to 40 mm (1 to 1-19/32 inch)
4WD models	5 to 20 mm (13/64 to 25/32 inch)

Torque specifications

Oil drain plug	20 Nm (14.5 ft-lbs)
Valve adjuster cover bolts	8.8 Nm (78 inch-lbs)
Valve adjusting screw locknuts	12 Nm (104 in-lbs)
Spark plug	14 Nm (10 ft-lbs)
Differential filler plug (front and rear)	29 Nm (22 ft-lbs)
Differential drain plug (front and rear)	20 Nm (174 in-lbs)
Tie-rod locknuts	27 Nm (20 ft-lbs)

Recommended lubricants and fluids

Engine/transmission oil	
Type	API grade SE, SF or SG
Viscosity	10W-30, 10W-40, 10W-50, 20W-40 or 20W-50
Capacity	
Without filter change	2.4 liters (2.5 US qt)
With filter change	2.6 liters (2.7 US qt)
Engine overhaul	2.8 liters (2.9 US qt)
Rear differential oil	
Type	Hypoid gear oil, API GL-5
Viscosity	
Below 5-degrees C/41-degrees F	SAE 80
Above 5-degrees C/41-degrees F	SAE 90
Capacity	200 cc (7 US fl oz)
Front differential oil (4WD models)	
Type	Hypoid gear oil for limited slip differentials, API GL-5
Viscosity	SAE 90, 140 or 85W-140
Capacity	200 cc (7 US fl oz)
Brake fluid	DOT 3 or DOT 4

Miscellaneous

Wheel bearings	Medium weight, lithium-based multi-purpose grease (NLGI no. 3)
Swingarm pivot	Medium weight, lithium-based multi-purpose grease (NLGI no. 3)
Cables and lever pivots	Chain and cable lubricant or 10W-30 motor oil
Brake pedal/shift pedal/throttle lever pivots	Chain and cable lubricant or 10W-30 motor oil

Kawasaki Prairie
Routine maintenance intervals

Note: *The pre-ride inspection outlined in the owner's manual covers checks and maintenance that should be carried out on a daily basis. It's condensed and included here to remind you of its importance. Always perform the pre-ride inspection at every maintenance interval (in addition to the procedures listed). The intervals listed below are the shortest intervals recommended by the manufacturer for each particular operation during the model years covered in this manual. Your owner's manual may have different intervals for your model.*

Daily or before riding

Check the engine oil level
Check the fuel level and inspect for leaks
Check the operation of both brakes - check the front brake fluid level and look for leakage (hydraulic brakes); check the front brake lever (drum brakes), rear brake pedal and lever (all models) for correct freeplay
Check the tires for damage, the presence of foreign objects and correct air pressure
Check the rear final drive (and front differential on 4WD models) for visible oil leaks
Check the throttle for smooth operation and correct freeplay
Make sure the steering operates smoothly
Check for proper operation of the headlight, tail light, brake light (if equipped) and indicator lights
Make sure the engine kill switch works properly
Check the driveaxle boots (4WD models) and driveshaft boots for damage or deterioration
Check the air cleaner drain tube and clean it if necessary
Check all fasteners, including wheel nuts and axle nuts, for tightness; make sure axle nut cotter pins are in place
Check the underbody for mud or debris that could start a fire or interfere with vehicle operation
Make sure any cargo is properly loaded and securely fastened

Every 10 operating days

Perform all of the daily checks plus:
Clean the air filter element (1)
Clean the air cleaner housing drain tube (1)
Check clutch adjustment
Check throttle cable adjustment
Check reverse cable adjustment
Check the rear brake lining wear and cable adjustment
Inspect the driveaxle boots (4WD models)

Every 30 operating days

Perform all of the daily checks plus:
Check/adjust the idle speed
Check/adjust the throttle lever freeplay
Check choke operation
Check battery condition and specific gravity
Inspect the suspension
Check the skid plates for looseness or damage
Check the exhaust system for leaks and check fastener tightness
Inspect the wheels and tires
Check disc brake pad wear
Check brake fluid level
Check the wheel bearings for looseness or damage
Lubricate cables and pivot points

Every 90 operating days

Check the cleanliness of the fuel system and the condition of the fuel line
Clean the fuel tap strainer screen
Clean and gap the spark plug
Check and adjust the valve clearances
Change the engine oil and oil filter
Change the final drive oil and front differential oil
Inspect the steering system and steering shaft bearing
Inspect the automatic transmission belt and pulleys (1)

Every year

Change the differential oil
Replace the brake fluid
Clean the spark arrester

Every two years

Overhaul the brake master cylinder
Overhaul the wheel cylinders (drum brakes) or calipers (disc brakes)
Replace the brake fluid hoses (2)
Replace the fuel line

(1) More often in dusty or wet conditions.
(2) Or whenever cracks or damage are visible.

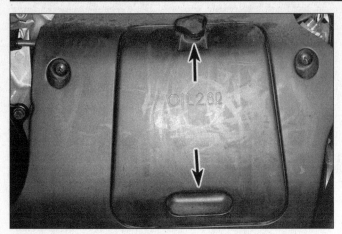

3.3 Unscrew the knob (upper arrow) and lift the handle (lower arrow) for access to the oil filler cap

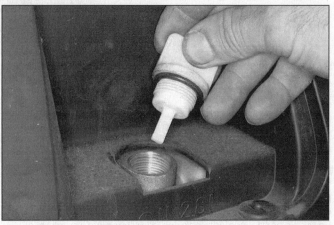

3.4 Unscrew the filler cap and check oil level on the dipstick; add oil through the filler hole

2   Introduction to tune-up and routine maintenance

This Chapter covers in detail the checks and procedures necessary for the tune-up and routine maintenance of your vehicle. Section 1 includes the routine maintenance schedule, which is designed to keep the machine in proper running condition and prevent possible problems. The remaining Sections contain detailed procedures for carrying out the items listed on the maintenance schedule, as well as additional maintenance information designed to increase reliability. Maintenance information is also printed on decals, which are mounted in various locations on the vehicle **(see illustration 2.1 in Chapter 1A)**. Where information on the decals differs from that presented in this Chapter, use the decal information.

Since routine maintenance plays such an important role in the safe and efficient operation of your vehicle, it is presented here as a comprehensive check list. For the rider who does all of the maintenance, these lists outline the procedures and checks that should be done on a routine basis.

Deciding where to start or plug into the routine maintenance schedule depends on several factors. If you have a vehicle whose warranty has recently expired, and if it has been maintained according to the warranty standards, you may want to pick-up routine maintenance as it coincides with the next mileage or calendar interval. If you have owned the machine for some time but have never performed any maintenance on it, then you may want to start at the nearest interval and include some additional procedures to ensure that nothing important is overlooked. If you have just had a major engine overhaul, then you may want to start the maintenance routine from the beginning. If you have a used machine and have no knowledge of its history or maintenance

record, you may desire to combine all the checks into one large service initially and then settle into the maintenance schedule prescribed.

The Sections which actually outline the inspection and maintenance procedures are written as step-by-step comprehensive guides to the actual performance of the work. They explain in detail each of the routine inspections and maintenance procedures on the check list. References to additional information in applicable Chapters is also included and should not be overlooked.

Before beginning any actual maintenance or repair, the machine should be cleaned thoroughly, especially around the oil filter housing, spark plug, cylinder head covers, side covers, carburetor, etc. Cleaning will help ensure that dirt does not contaminate the engine and will allow you to detect wear and damage that could otherwise easily go unnoticed.

3   Fluid levels - check

Engine oil

Refer to illustrations 3.3, 3.4 and 3.5

1   Place the vehicle in a level position (front-to-rear and side-to-side).

2   Start the engine and allow it to reach normal operating temperature. **Warning:** *Do not run the engine in an enclosed space such as a garage or shop.*

3   Stop the engine and allow the machine to sit undisturbed in a level position for about five minutes. During this time, unscrew the knob and lift off the dipstick cover **(see illustration)**.

4   With the engine off, unscrew the filler cap/dipstick and check the oil level **(see illustration)**. The oil level should be between the upper and lower level marks on the dipstick. Also inspect the filler cap/dipstick O-ring and replace it if it's worn or deteriorated.

5   If the level is below the lower level line, add oil through the hole. Add enough oil of the recommended grade and type to bring the level up to the upper level line. Do not overfill. Once the oil level is correct, screw the filler cap/dipstick back into the engine. Install the cover, making sure both its posts fit into the grommets in the left crankcase cover **(see illustration)**.

Brake fluid (hydraulic brakes)

6   In order to ensure the proper operation of the hydraulic front brakes, the fluid lever in the master cylinder reservoir must be properly maintained.

7   With the vehicle supported in a level position, turn the handlebars until the top of the front brake master cylinder is as level as possible.

8   The fluid level is visible through the master cylinder reservoir. Make sure that the fluid level is above the Lower mark on the reservoir **(see illustration 3.8 in Chapter 1A)**.

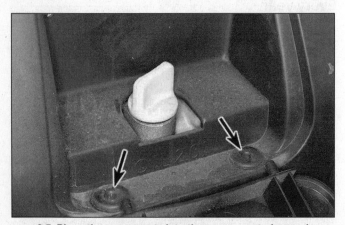

3.5 Place the cover posts into these grommets (arrows) on installation

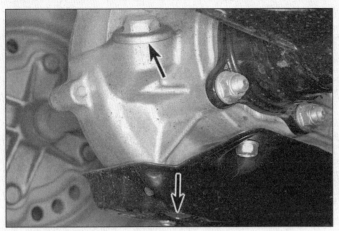

3.16a Here are the rear differential filler and drain plugs

3.16b Here are the front differential filler and drain plugs (4WD models)

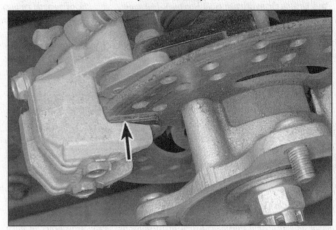

4.8 Replace the pads if the friction material is worn near the line (arrow)

9   If the level is low, the fluid must be replenished. Before removing the master cylinder cap, place rags beneath the reservoir (to protect the paint from brake fluid spills) and remove all dust and dirt from the area around the cap.

10   Remove the cover screws, then lift off the cover, rubber diaphragm and float (if equipped) **(see illustration 3.10 in Chapter 1A)**. Note: *Don't operate the brake lever with the cover removed.*

11   Add new, clean brake fluid of the recommended type to bring the level up to the ridge cast on the inside of the reservoir **(see illustration 3.11 in Chapter 1A)**. Don't mix different brands of brake fluid in the reservoir, as they may not be compatible. Also, don't mix different specifications (DOT 3 with DOT 4).

12   Reinstall the float (if equipped), rubber diaphragm and cover. Tighten the cover screws securely, but don't overtighten and strip the threads.

13   Wipe any spilled fluid off the reservoir body.

14   If the brake fluid level was low, inspect the front or rear brake system for leaks.

Differential oil

Refer to illustrations 3.16a and 3.16b

15   Park the vehicle on a level surface.

16   Remove the differential filler cap **(see illustrations)**. Feel the oil level inside the differential; it should be up to the bottom of the filler threads.

17   Add oil if necessary of the type recommended in this Chapter's Specifications.

18   Reinstall the filler cap and tighten securely.

---

4   Brake system - general check

---

1   A routine general check of the brakes will ensure that any problems are discovered and remedied before the rider's safety is jeopardized.

2   Check the brake levers and pedal for loose connections, excessive play, bends, and other damage. Replace any damaged parts with new ones (see Chapter 7).

3   Make sure all brake fasteners are tight. Check the brake for wear as described below.

4   If you're working on a vehicle with hydraulic brakes, make sure the fluid level in the reservoir is correct (see Section 3). Look for leaks at the hose connections and check for cracks in the hoses. If the lever is spongy, bleed the brakes as described in Chapter 6.

5   Make sure the brake light (if equipped) operates when the front brake lever is depressed. The front brake light switch is not adjustable. If it fails to operate properly, replace it with a new one (see Chapter 8).

6   Operate the rear brake lever and pedal. If operation is rough or sticky, refer to Section 12 and lubricate the cables.

Front brakes

Refer to illustration 4.8

7   Raise the front of the vehicle and support it securely on jackstands. Remove the front wheels.

8   Look at the friction material on the brake pads **(see illustration)**. If it's worn to or almost to the wear indicator lines, replace the pads (see Chapter 6). Replace all four pads, even if only one is worn.

Rear drum brake

Refer to illustrations 4.9 and 4.10

9   To check the linings for wear, have an assistant hold down the

4.9 The wear pointer should be between the upper and lower edges of the scale

4.10 If water runs out when you remove the brake drum drain bolt (arrow), remove the drum and inspect its seal

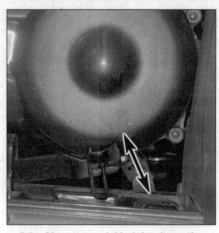

5.6a Measure pedal height above the floorboard; press the pedal by hand to measure freeplay

5.6b Loosen the locknut (lower arrow) and turn the bolt (upper arrow) to adjust the brake pedal

pedal while you look at the wear indicator on the brake drum **(see illustration)**. If the pointer is at the limit line (and the cable is properly adjusted), replace the brake shoes (see Chapter 6). There's no shoe adjuster as on front drum brakes.

10   Unscrew the drain bolt **(see illustration)**. If any water runs out when the bolt is removed, the brake drum seal is worn or damaged. Replace the seal (see Chapter 6).

5   Brake lever and pedal freeplay - check and adjustment

Front brake lever

1   There's no specified amount of lever freeplay on vehicles with front disc brakes.

2   Operate the lever (on the right handlebar) from rest until it stops. The front brakes should lock firmly. If they don't, bleed the brakes or repair the calipers as necessary (see Chapter 6).

Rear brake pedal and parking brake lever

Refer to illustrations 5.6a, 5.6b, 5.7 and 5.10

3   Since the parking brake lever and brake pedal adjustments affect each other, the parking brake lever should be adjusted whenever the brake pedal is adjusted.

4   Check the rear brakes for wear and replace the shoes if they're worn (Section 4).

5   Jack up the rear end of the vehicle and support it securely on jackstands.

6   Measure the brake pedal height above the floorboard **(see illustration)**. If it's not within the range listed in this Chapter's Specifications, loosen the locknut and turn the adjusting bolt to change it, then tighten the locknut **(see illustration)**.

7   Pull the rear brake lever (on the left handlebar) until it stops. Measure the freeplay at the lever gap **(see illustration)**. If it's not within the range listed in this Chapter's Specifications, adjust as described below.

8   Press the brake pedal with light hand pressure until it stops. Measure the distance traveled (pedal freeplay). If it's not within the range listed in this Chapter's Specifications, adjust as described below.

9   Loosen the locknut on the brake lever adjuster at the left handlebar, tighten the adjusting nut all the way and tighten the locknut.

10   At the rear wheel, turn the cable wingnut at the lower rear brake lever so the brake lever has the specified amount of freeplay **(see illustration)**.

11   Adjust brake pedal freeplay by turning the wingnut on the upper brake lever at the drum **(see illustration 5.10)**.

6   Tires/wheels - general check

1   Routine tire and wheel checks should be made with the realization that your safety depends to a great extent on their condition.

2   Check the tires carefully for cuts, tears, embedded nails or other sharp objects and excessive wear. Operation of the vehicle with exces-

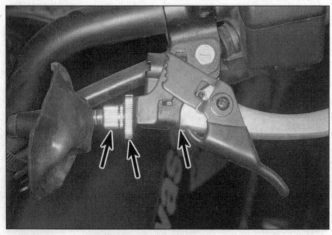

5.7 Measure parking brake lever freeplay at the gap (arrow)

5.10 These wingnuts adjust the brake pedal cable (upper arrow) and parking brake cable (lower arrow)

7.2 Release the clips and lift off the cover . . .

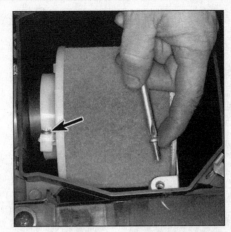

7.3a . . . remove the bracket screw and the clamp screw (arrow) . . .

7.3b and lift out the element

sively worn tires is extremely hazardous, as traction and handling are directly affected. Measure the tread depth at the center of the tire and replace worn tires with new ones when the tread depth is less than that listed in this Chapter's Specifications.

3   Repair or replace punctured tires as soon as damage is noted. Do not try to patch a torn tire, as wheel balance and tire reliability may be impaired.

4   Check the tire pressures when the tires are cold and keep them properly inflated **(see illustration 6.4 in Chapter 1B)**. Proper air pressure will increase tire life and provide maximum stability and ride comfort. Keep in mind that low tire pressures may cause the tire to slip on the rim or come off, while high tire pressures will cause abnormal tread wear and unsafe handling.

5   The steel wheels used on this machine are virtually maintenance free, but they should be kept clean and checked periodically for cracks, bending and rust. Never attempt to repair damaged wheels; they must be replaced with new ones.

6   Check the valve stem locknuts to make sure they're tight. Also, make sure the valve stem cap is in place and tight. If it is missing, install a new one made of metal or hard plastic.

7   Air cleaner - filter element and drain tube cleaning

Element cleaning

Refer to illustrations 7.2, 7.3a, 7.3b and 7.8

1   Remove the seat (see Chapter 7).

2   Release the filter cover clips and lift the cover off **(see illustration)**.

3   Detach the element from the case and lift it out **(see illustrations)**.

4   Remove the center screw and take the ends off the metal core **(see illustration 7.4a in Chapter 1A)**. Pull the foam element off the metal core and separate the core from the holder **(see illustration 7.4b in Chapter 1A)**.

5   Clean the element and core in a high flash point solvent, squeeze the solvent out of the foam and let the core and element dry completely.

6   Soak the foam element in the amount and type of foam filter oil listed in this Chapter's Specifications, then squeeze it firmly to remove the excess oil. Don't wring it out or the foam may be damaged. The element should be wet through with oil, but no oil should drip from it.

7   Place the element on the core, then assemble the core and end caps on the holder and install the center screw.

8   Make sure the seal is in place on the intake tube **(see illustration)**. Install the element in the case, secure it with the retaining screws and install the cover.

9   Install the seat (see Chapter 7).

Drain tube cleaning

Refer to illustrations 7.10a and 7.10b

10   Squeeze the drain tubes, one on the air cleaner housing and one on the inlet duct, to let any accumulated water and oil run out **(see illustrations)**. **Note:** *A drain tube that's full indicates the need to clean the filter element and the inside of the case or inlet duct.*

7.8 replace the intake tube gasket if it's deteriorated

7.10a Squeeze the drain tube on the air cleaner housing (arrow) . . .

7.10b . . . and the one on the air cleaner inlet duct (arrow) to let out accumulated oil and water

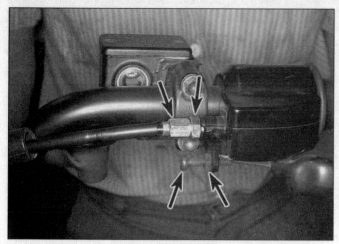

8.4 Here are the throttle cable locknut and adjuster (upper arrows) and speed limiter locknut and adjusting screw (lower arrows)

8.5a If you can't obtain the correct freeplay with the throttle lever adjuster, remove the screw (arrow) and pull off the cover . . .

8   Throttle freeplay and speed limiter - check and adjustment

Throttle check

1   Make sure the throttle lever moves easily from fully closed to fully open with the front wheel turned at various angles. The grip should return automatically from fully open to fully closed when released. If the throttle sticks, check the throttle cable for cracks or kinks in the housings. Also, make sure the inner cable is clean and well-lubricated.

2   Check for a small amount of freeplay at the lever **(see illustration 9.2 in Chapter 1A)**. Compare the freeplay to the value listed in this Chapter's Specifications.

Throttle adjustment

Refer to illustrations 8.4, 8.5a and 8.5b

3   Before making adjustments, check and adjust idle speed (see Section 15).

4   Slide the rubber boot back from the adjuster at the throttle lever **(see illustration)**. Loosen the locknut and turn the adjuster until the desired freeplay is obtained, then tighten the locknut.

5   If you can't obtain the correct freeplay at the throttle lever, adjust the cable at the carburetor end. Remove the cable cover **(see illustration)**. Loosen the cable locknuts **(see illustration)**, reposition them on the cable to obtain the correct freeplay, then tighten the locknuts and reinstall the cover.

Speed limiter adjustment

6   The speed limiter can be used to restrict maximum throttle opening **(see illustration 8.4)**. Turning the screw in reduces the maximum throttle opening; turning it out allows maximum throttle opening.

7   To make adjustments, loosen the locknut, turn the screw in or out as necessary and tighten the locknut.

9   Choke - operation check

1   Operate the choke knob while you feel for smooth operation.

2   If the knob doesn't move smoothly, try lubricating the choke cable (Section 13). If that doesn't help, refer to Chapter 3 and remove the choke cable and plunger for inspection.

10   Fasteners - check

1   Since vibration of the machine tends to loosen fasteners, all nuts,

8.5b . . . then use the cable locknuts (arrows) to change the position of the cable

bolts, screws, etc. should be periodically checked for proper tightness. Also make sure all cotter pins or other safety fasteners are correctly installed.

2   Pay particular attention to the following:

   Spark plug
   Engine oil, transfer case and differential drain plugs
   Oil filter cover bolts
   Gearshift lever
   Brake pedal
   Footpegs
   Engine mount bolts
   Shock absorber mount bolts
   Front axle nuts
   Rear axle nuts
   Skid plate bolts

3   If a torque wrench is available, use it along with the torque specifications at the beginning of this, or other, Chapters.

11   Driveaxle and driveshaft boots – inspection

Refer to illustration 11.1

1   There's a rubber boot at each end of the front driveaxles on 4WD models **(see illustration)**, as well as at each end of the front and rear driveshafts on all models.

11.1 Inspect the rubber boot at each end of the rear driveshaft (all models) and front driveshaft and driveaxles (4WD models)

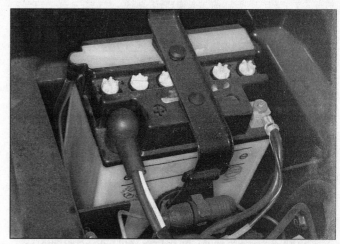

12.3 Battery electrolyte should be between the horizontal lines on the battery

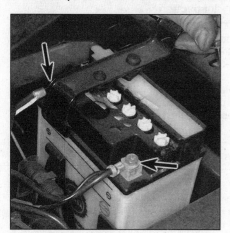

12.4a Disconnect the negative cable (right arrow), then uncover and disconnect the positive cable (left arrow); remove the retainer . . .

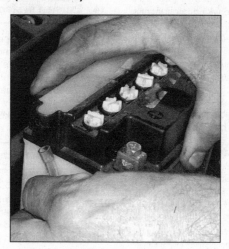

12.4b . . . lift the battery, disconnect the vent tube and take the battery out

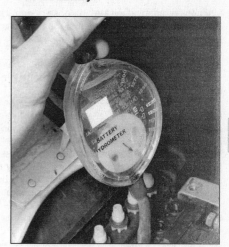

12.7 Check the specific gravity with a hydrometer

2   Check the boots for cracks, cuts, tears or deterioration. If any problems are found, remove the driveaxles for boot replacement (see Chapter 5).

3   Check the boot clamp screws to make sure they're tight.

12 Battery electrolyte level/specific gravity - check

Refer to illustrations 12.3, 12.4a, 12.4b, 12.7 and 12.13

Warning: *Be extremely careful when handling or working around the battery. The electrolyte is very caustic and an explosive gas (hydrogen) is given off when the battery is charging.*

1   This procedure applies to batteries that have removable filler caps, which can be removed to add water to the battery. If the original equipment battery has been replaced by a sealed maintenance-free battery, the electrolyte can't be topped up.

2   Remove the seat (see Chapter 7).

3   The electrolyte level is visible through the translucent battery case - it should be between the Upper and Lower level marks **(see illustration)**.

4   Disconnect the negative cable, then the positive cable, then remove the retainer screw and lift the retainer off the battery **(see illustration 12.3 and the accompanying illustration)**. **Warning:** *Always disconnect the negative cable first and reconnect it last to avoid sparks which could cause a battery explosion.* Lift the battery partway out,

disconnect the vent hose and lift the battery all the way out **(see illustration)**.

5   If the electrolyte is low, remove the cell caps and fill each cell to the upper level mark with distilled water. Do not use tap water (except in an emergency) and do not overfill. The cell holes are quite small, so it may help to use a plastic squeeze bottle with a small spout to add the water. If the level is within the marks on the case, additional water is not necessary.

6   Next, check the specific gravity of the electrolyte in each cell with a small hydrometer made especially for motorcycle batteries. These are available from most dealer parts departments or motorcycle accessory stores.

7   Remove the caps, draw some electrolyte from the first cell into the hydrometer **(see illustration)**, then note the specific gravity. Compare the reading to the value listed in this Chapter's Specifications. **Note:** *Add 0.004 points to the reading for every 10-degrees F above 68-degrees F (20-degrees C) - subtract 0.004 points from the reading for every 10-degrees below 68-degrees F (20-degrees C).*

8   Return the electrolyte to the appropriate cell and repeat the check for the remaining cells. When the check is complete, rinse the hydrometer thoroughly with clean water.

9   If the specific gravity of the electrolyte in each cell is as specified, the battery is in good condition and is apparently being charged by the machine's charging system.

10   If the specific gravity is low, the battery is not fully charged. This may be due to corroded battery terminals, a dirty battery case, a mal-

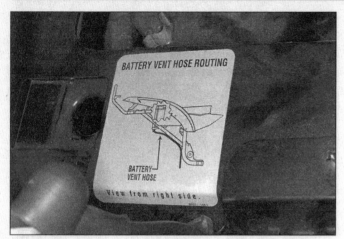

12.13 Be sure to route the battery vent tube according to the decal

15.3 Turn this knob to set idle speed

functioning charging system, or loose or corroded wiring connections. On the other hand, it may be that the battery is worn out, especially if the machine is old, or that infrequent use of the machine prevents normal charging from taking place.

11   Be sure to correct any problems and charge the battery if necessary. Refer to Chapter 4 for additional battery maintenance and charging procedures.

12   Install the battery cell caps, tightening them securely. Reconnect the cables to the battery, attaching the positive cable first and the negative cable last. Make sure to install the insulating boots over the terminals.

13   Install all components removed for access and route the battery vent tube correctly **(see illustration)**. Be very careful not to pinch or otherwise restrict the tube, as the battery may build up enough internal pressure during normal charging system operation to explode.

14   If the vehicle will be stored for an extended time, fully charge the battery, then disconnect the negative cable before storage.

13   Lubrication - general

1   Since the controls, cables and various other components of a vehicle are exposed to the elements, they should be lubricated periodically to ensure safe and trouble-free operation.

2   The throttle and brake levers and brake pedal, should be lubricated frequently. In order for the lubricant to be applied where it will do the most good, the component should be disassembled. However, if chain and cable lubricant is being used, it can be applied to the pivot joint gaps and will usually work its way into the areas where friction occurs. If motor oil or light grease is being used, apply it sparingly as it may attract dirt (which could cause the controls to bind or wear at an accelerated rate). **Note:** *One of the best lubricants for the control lever pivots is a dry-film lubricant (available from many sources by different names).*

3   The throttle, brake and reverse cables should be removed and treated with a commercially available cable lubricant which is specially formulated for use on ATV control cables. Small adapters for pressure lubricating the cables with spray can lubricants are available and ensure that the cable is lubricated along its entire length **(see illustration 15.3 in Chapter 1A)**. When attaching the cable to the lever, be sure to lubricate the barrel-shaped fitting at the end with multi-purpose grease.

4   To lubricate the cables, disconnect them at the lower end, then lubricate the cable with a pressure lube adapter. See Chapter 3B (throttle cable) or Chapter 6B (brake cables).

5   Refer to Chapter 6A to access the following components:

  a) *Driveaxle splines (4WD models)*
  b) *Rear axle shaft splines*

6   Refer to Chapter 6B for brake pedal removal procedures.

14   Exhaust system - inspection

1   Periodically check the exhaust system for leaks and loose fasteners. If tightening the holder nuts at the cylinder head fails to stop any leaks, replace the gasket with a new one (a procedure which requires removal of the system).

2   The exhaust pipe flange nuts at the cylinder head are especially prone to loosening, which could cause damage to the head. Check them frequently and keep them tight.

15   Idle speed - check and adjustment

Refer to illustration 15.3

1   Before adjusting the idle speed, make sure the valve clearances and spark plug gap are correct. Also, turn the handlebars back-and-forth and see if the idle speed changes as this is done. If it does, the throttle cable may not be adjusted correctly, or it may be worn out. Be sure to correct this problem before proceeding.

2   The engine should be at normal operating temperature, which is usually reached after 10 to 15 minutes of stop and go riding. Make sure the transmission is in Neutral.

3   Turn the idle speed screw **(see illustration)** until the idle speed listed in this Chapter's Specifications is obtained.

4   Snap the throttle open and shut a few times, then recheck the idle speed. If necessary, repeat the adjustment procedure.

5   If a smooth, steady idle can't be achieved, the fuel/air mixture may be incorrect. Refer to Chapter 3 for additional carburetor information.

16   Suspension - check

1   The suspension components must be maintained in top operating condition to ensure rider safety. Loose, worn or damaged suspension parts decrease the vehicle's stability and control.

2   Lock the front brake and push on the handlebars to compress the front shock absorbers several times. See if they move up-and-down smoothly without binding. If binding is felt, the shocks should be inspected as described in Chapter 6.

3   Check the tightness of all front suspension nuts and bolts to be sure none have worked loose.

4   Inspect the rear shock absorber for fluid leakage and tightness of the mounting nuts and bolts. If leakage is found, the shock should be replaced.

5   Support the vehicle securely upright with its rear wheel off the ground. Grab the rear axle on each side. Rock the axle from side to side - there should be no discernible movement at the rear. If there's a

17.5 The engine oil drain plug is accessible through this hole in the skid plate

17.6a Remove the screws and the crankcase cover . . .

little movement or a slight clicking can be heard, make sure the trailing link pivot bolts are tight. If the pivot bolts are tight but movement is still noticeable, the trailing links will have to be removed and the pivot points inspected as described in Chapter 5.

6   Inspect the tightness of the rear suspension nuts and bolts.

17   Engine oil and filter - change

Refer to illustrations 17.5, 17.6a, 17.6b, 17.6c and 17.9

1   Consistent routine oil and filter changes are the single most important maintenance procedure you can perform on a vehicle. The oil not only lubricates the internal parts of the engine, transmission, clutch and bevel drive or sub-transmission, but it also acts as a coolant, a cleaner, a sealant, and a protectant. Because of these demands, the oil takes a terrific amount of abuse and should be replaced often with new oil of the recommended grade and type. Saving a little money on the difference in cost between a good oil and a cheap oil won't pay off if the engine is damaged.

2   Before changing the oil and filter, warm up the engine so the oil will drain easily. Be careful when draining the oil, as the exhaust pipe, the engine and the oil itself can cause severe burns.

3   Park the vehicle over a clean drain pan.

4   Remove the oil filler cap/dipstick cover (see Section 3). Remove the oil filler cap to vent the crankcase and act as a reminder that there is no oil in the engine.

5   Next, remove the drain plug from the engine **(see illustration)** and allow the oil to drain into the pan.

6   Remove the left crankcase cover screws **(see illustration)**. Remove the cover, then unscrew the filter, using an oil filter socket if it's tight **(see illustrations)**. If additional maintenance is planned for this time period, check or service another component while the oil is allowed to drain completely.

7   Wipe any remaining oil out of the filter housing area of the crankcase and make sure the oil passage is clear.

8   Check the condition of the drain plug threads and the O-rings.

9   Coat the gasket on the new filter element with a thin layer of clean engine oil, then thread the filter onto the engine **(see illustration)**. Tighten the filter, using the filter socket, to the torque listed in this Chapter's Specifications. Don't overtighten the filter or the gasket will leak.

10   Install the engine drain plug, using a new O-ring if the old one is worn or damaged. Tighten the plug to the torque listed in this Chapter's Specifications. Avoid overtightening, as damage to the engine case will result.

11   Before refilling the engine, check the old oil carefully. If the oil was drained into a clean pan, small pieces of metal or other material can be easily detected. If the oil is very metallic colored, then the engine is experiencing wear from break-in (new engine) or from insufficient lubrication. If there are flakes or chips of metal in the oil, then something is drastically wrong internally and the engine will have to be disassembled for inspection and repair.

12   If the inspection of the oil turns up nothing unusual, refill the crankcase to the proper level with the recommended oil and install the filler cap. Start the engine and let it run for two or three minutes. Shut it off, wait a few minutes, then check the oil level with the dipstick on the

1B

17.6b . . . place a rag beneath the filter . . .

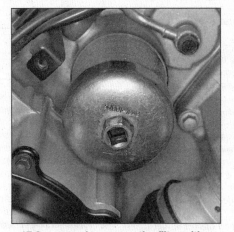

17.6c . . . and unscrew the filter with a filter socket like this one

17.9 Smear a thin coat of clean engine oil on the filter gasket

18.5a Remove the screws (arrows) and detach the tap from the bracket . . .

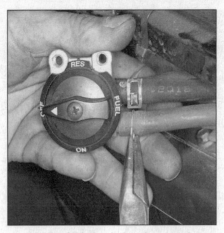

18.5b Slide back the clamp and disconnect the hose . . .

18.6 . . . then turn the tap over and disconnect the remaining hoses

filler cap. If necessary, add more oil to bring the level up to the upper level mark on the dipstick. Check around the drain plug and filter for leaks.

13   Once oil level is correct and you're satisfied that there are no leaks, reinstall the left crankcase cover and the filler cap cover.

14   The old oil drained from the engine cannot be reused in its present state and should be disposed of. Check with your local refuse disposal company, disposal facility or environmental agency to see whether they will accept the oil for recycling. Don't pour used oil into drains or onto the ground. After the oil has cooled, it can be drained into a suitable container (capped plastic jugs, topped bottles, milk cartons, etc.) for transport to one of these disposal sites.

18 Fuel system - check and filter cleaning

Refer to illustrations 18.5a, 18.5b, 18.6 and 18.11

Warning: *Gasoline (petrol) is extremely flammable, so take extra precautions when you work on any part of the fuel system. Don't smoke or allow open flames or bare light bulbs near the work area, and don't work in a garage where a natural gas-type appliance (such as a water heater or clothes dryer) with a pilot light is present. Since gasoline is carcinogenic, wear latex gloves when there's a possibility of being exposed to fuel, and, if you spill any fuel on your skin, rinse it off immediately with soap and water. Mop up any spills immediately and do not store fuel-soaked rags where they could ignite. When you perform any kind of work on the fuel system, wear safety glasses and have a fire extinguisher suitable for a class B type fire (flammable liquids) on hand.*

1   Check the carburetor, fuel tank, the fuel tap and the line for leaks and evidence of damage.

2   If carburetor gaskets are leaking, the carburetor should be disassembled and rebuilt by referring to Chapter 3.

3   These models have a separate fuel tap and strainer. If the fuel tap or strainer is leaking, tightening the screws may help. If leakage from the tap persists, the tap should be disassembled and repaired or replaced with a new one (see Chapter 3B). If strainer leakage persists, remove it from the tank and install a new O-ring.

4   If the fuel lines are cracked or otherwise deteriorated, replace them with new ones.

5   Place the fuel tap lever in the Off position. Remove the tap mounting screws and take it off the mounting bracket **(see illustration)**. Slide the clamp back from the fuel line fitting and disconnect the fuel line from the tap **(see illustration)**.

6   If you're removing only the tap, turn it over and disconnect the remaining fuel lines **(see illustration)**. Plug the lines so they won't leak gasoline.

7   Before removing the fuel strainer, remove and drain the fuel tank (see Chapter 3B). Remove the strainer mounting screws and pull it out of the underside of the tank.

18.11 If the vehicle will be stored more than a month, loosen the float chamber drain screw (arrow) and drain the fuel through the drain hose

8   Clean the strainer with solvent and let it dry.

9   Installation is the reverse of the removal steps, with the following additions:

   a) *Use a new O-ring.*
   b) *Hand-tighten the screws firmly, but don't overtighten or the O-ring will be squashed, resulting in fuel leaks.*

10   After installation, run the engine and check for fuel leaks.

11   If the vehicle will be stored for a month or more, remove and drain the fuel tank. Also loosen the float chamber drain screw and drain the fuel from the carburetor **(see illustration)**.

19 Spark plug - replacement

Refer to illustrations 19.2 and 19.3

1   This vehicle is equipped with a spark plug that has an 18 mm wrench hex.

2   Remove the inner fender cover from the vehicle **(see illustration)**.

3   Twist the spark plug cap to break it free from the plug, then pull it off **(see illustration)**. If available, use compressed air to blow any accumulated debris from around the spark plug. Remove the plug with an 18 mm spark plug socket.

4   Inspect the electrodes for wear. Both the center and side electrodes should have square edges and the side electrode should be of uniform thickness. Look for excessive deposits and evidence of a cracked or chipped insulator around the center electrode. Compare your spark plug to the color spark plug reading chart on the inside of

19.2 Remove the inner fender cover for access to the spark plug

19.3 Twist the boot to free it, pull it off and unscrew the plug with a spark plug socket

21.7 Unscrew the timing hole plug (arrow)

the back cover. Check the threads, the washer and the ceramic insulator body for cracks and other damage.

5   If the electrodes are not excessively worn, and if the deposits can be easily removed with a wire brush, the plug can be regapped and reused (if no cracks or chips are visible in the insulator). If in doubt concerning the condition of the plug, replace it with a new one, as the expense is minimal.

6   Cleaning the spark plug by sandblasting is permitted, provided you clean the plug with a high flash-point solvent afterwards.

7   Before installing a new plug, make sure it is the correct type and heat range. Check the gap between the electrodes, as it is not preset. For best results, use a wire-type gauge rather than a flat gauge to check the gap **(see illustration 21.6a in Chapter 1A)**. If the gap must be adjusted, bend the side electrode only and be very careful not to chip or crack the insulator nose **(see illustration 21.6b in Chapter 1A)**. Make sure the washer is in place before installing the plug.

8   Since the cylinder head is made of aluminum, which is soft and easily damaged, thread the plug into the head by hand. Slip a short length of hose over the end of the plug to use as a tool to thread it into place. The hose will grip the plug well enough to turn it, but will start to slip if the plug begins to cross-thread in the hole - this will prevent damaged threads and the accompanying repair costs.

9   Once the plug is finger tight, the job can be finished with a socket. If a torque wrench is available, tighten the spark plug to the torque listed in this Chapter's Specifications. If you do not have a torque wrench, tighten the plug finger tight (until the washer bottoms on the cylinder head) then use a spark plug socket to tighten it an additional 1/4 turn. Regardless of the method used, do not overtighten it.

10   Reconnect the spark plug cap.

20 Cylinder compression - check

1   Among other things, poor engine performance may be caused by leaking valves, incorrect valve clearances, a leaking head gasket, or a worn piston, rings and/or cylinder wall. A cylinder compression check will help pinpoint these conditions and can also indicate the presence of excessive carbon deposits in the cylinder head.

2   The only tools required are a compression gauge and a spark plug wrench. Depending on the outcome of the initial test, a squirt-type oil can may also be needed.

3   Check valve clearances and adjust if necessary (see Section 21). Start the engine and allow it to reach normal operating temperature, then remove the spark plug (see Section 19, if necessary). Work carefully - don't strip the spark plug hole threads and don't burn your hands.

4   Disable the ignition by disconnecting the primary (low tension) wires from the coil (see Chapter 4B). Be sure to mark the locations of the wires before detaching them.

5   Install the compression gauge in the spark plug hole **(see illustra-**

tion 22.5 in Chapter 1A). Hold or block the throttle wide open.

6   Crank the engine over a minimum of four or five revolutions (or until the gauge reading stops increasing) and observe the initial movement of the compression gauge needle as well as the final total gauge reading. Compare the results to the value listed in this Chapter's Specifications.

7   If the compression built up quickly and evenly to the specified amount, you can assume the engine upper end is in reasonably good mechanical condition. Worn or sticking piston rings and a worn cylinder will produce very little initial movement of the gauge needle, but compression will tend to build up gradually as the engine spins over. Valve and valve seat leakage, or head gasket leakage, is indicated by low initial compression which does not tend to build up.

8   To further confirm your findings, add a small amount of engine oil to the cylinder by inserting the nozzle of a squirt-type oil can through the spark plug hole. The oil will tend to seal the piston rings if they are leaking.

9   If the compression increases significantly after the addition of the oil, the piston rings and/or cylinder are definitely worn. If the compression does not increase, the pressure is leaking past the valves or the head gasket. Leakage past the valves may be due to insufficient valve clearances, burned, warped or cracked valves or valve seats or valves that are hanging up in the guides.

10   If compression readings are considerably higher than specified, the combustion chamber is probably coated with excessive carbon deposits. It is possible (but not very likely) for carbon deposits to raise the compression enough to compensate for the effects of leakage past rings or valves. Refer to Chapter 2, remove the cylinder head and carefully decarbonize the combustion chamber.

21 Valve clearances - check and adjustment

Refer to illustrations 21.7 and 21.8

1   The engine must be cool to the touch for this maintenance procedure, so if possible let the machine sit overnight before beginning.

2   Remove the seat and front fender unit (see Chapter 7).

3   Remove the fuel tank (see Chapter 4)

4   Disconnect the cable from the negative terminal of the battery (see Section 12, if necessary).

5   Refer to Section 19 and remove the spark plug. This will make it easier to turn the engine.

6   Remove the valve adjusting hole covers (there's one on each side of the cylinder head **(see illustrations 23.6a and 23.6b in Chapter 1A)**.

7   Remove the timing hole plug **(see illustration)**.

8   Position the piston at Top Dead Center (TDC) on the compression stroke. Do this by turning the crankshaft until the T mark on the rotor is aligned with the timing notch on the crankcase **(see illustration)**. You

21.8 Align the T mark on the rotor (inside the hole) with the groove in the edge of the timing plug hole (arrow)

22.5 Inspect the bearing at the lower end of the steering column (arrow)

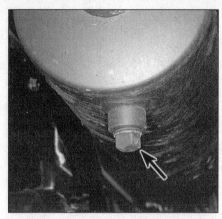

24.1 Unscrew the muffler drain plug (arrow)

should be able to wiggle both rocker arms - if not (if the exhaust valve is open), the engine is positioned at TDC on the exhaust stroke; turn the crankshaft one complete revolution and realign the marks.

9   With the engine in this position, both of the valves can be checked.

10   To check, insert a feeler gauge of the thickness listed in this Chapter's Specifications between the valve stem and rocker arm **(see illustration 23.10 in Chapter 1A)**. Pull the feeler gauge out slowly - you should feel a slight drag. If there's no drag, the clearance is too loose. If there's a heavy drag, the clearance is too tight.

11   If the clearance is incorrect, loosen the adjuster locknut with a box-end wrench. Turn the adjusting screw with a screwdriver until the correct clearance is achieved, then tighten the locknut **(see illustration 23.10 in Chapter 1A)**.

12   After adjusting, recheck the clearance with the feeler gauge to make sure it wasn't changed when the locknut was tightened.

13   Now measure the other valve, following the same procedure you used for the first valve. Make sure to use a feeler gauge of the specified thickness.

14   With both of the clearances within the Specifications, install the valve adjusting hole covers and timing hole plug. Use new O-rings on the covers and plug if the old ones are hardened, deteriorated or damaged.

15   Install all components removed for access.

---

22   Steering system - inspection and toe-in adjustment

Inspection

Refer to illustration 22.5

1   This vehicle is equipped with a ball bearing at the lower end of the steering shaft and plastic bushings at the upper end. These can become dented, rough or loose during normal use of the machine. In extreme cases, worn or loose parts can cause steering wobble that is potentially dangerous.

2   To check, block the rear wheels so the vehicle can't roll, jack up the front end and support it securely on jackstands.

3   Point the wheel straight ahead and slowly move the handlebar from side-to-side. Dents or roughness in the bearing or bushing will be felt and the bars will not move smoothly. **Note:** *Make sure any hesitation in movement is not being caused by the cables and wiring harnesses that run to the handlebar.*

4   If the handlebar doesn't move smoothly, or if it moves horizontally, refer to Chapter 5 to remove and inspect the steering shaft bushings and bearing.

5   Look at the tie-rod ends (inner and outer) while slowly turning the handlebar from side-to-side **(see illustration)**. If there's any vertical movement in the tie-rod ball-joints, refer to Chapter 5B and replace them.

Toe-in adjustment

6   Jack up the vehicle and support it securely with the front tires off the ground.

7   Make a mark at the front and center of each tire, even with the centerline of the front hub.

8   Measure the distance between the marks with a toe-in gauge or steel tape measure.

9   Rotate the tires one-half turn, so the marks are at the rear of the tires, again even with the wheel hubs.

10   Again, measure the distance between the marks. Subtract the front measurement from the rear measurement to get toe-in **(see illustration 22.10 in Chapter 1A)**.

11   If toe-in is not as specified in this Chapter's Specifications, hold each tie-rod with a wrench on the flat and loosen the locknuts **(see illustration 22.11 in Chapter 1A)**. Turn the tie-rods an equal amount to change toe-in. When toe-in is set correctly, tighten the locknuts to the torque listed in this Chapter's Specifications.

---

23   Differential oil – change

1   Place a drain pan beneath the differential being drained.

2   Remove the oil filler plug, then the drain bolt and sealing washer **(see illustrations 3.16a and 3.16b)**. Let the oil drain for several minutes, until it stops dripping.

3   Clean the drain bolt and sealing washer. If the sealing washer is in good condition, it can be reused; otherwise, replace it.

4   Install the drain bolt and tighten it to the torque listed in this Chapter's Specifications.

5   Add oil of the type and amount listed in this Chapter's Specifications, then install the filler plug and tighten it to the torque listed in this Chapter's Specifications.

6   Refer to Step 14 of Section 17 to dispose of the drained oil.

---

24   Spark arrester – cleaning

Warning: *The muffler will get hot during this procedure if it isn't already. Don't touch the muffler or spark arrester with bare hands or you could be burned.*

Refer to illustration 24.1

1   Unscrew the drain plug from the underside of the muffler **(see illustration)**.

2   Place the transmission in Neutral, then start the engine and let it idle.

3   Rev the engine several times while tapping on the muffler with a rubber mallet to free carbon particles trapped in the muffler.

4   Shut the engine off and reinstall the drain plug.

Chapter 2 Part A
Engine, clutch and transmission (Bayou models)

Contents

	Section
Balancer gears - removal, inspection and installation	20
Cam chain tensioner - removal and installation	7
Crankcase - disassembly and reassembly	22
Crankcase components - inspection and servicing	23
Crankshaft and connecting rod - removal, inspection and installation	25
Cylinder - removal, inspection and installation	11
Cylinder head and valves - disassembly, inspection and reassembly	10
Cylinder head, decompression lever, camshaft and rocker arms - removal, inspection and installation	8
Engine - removal and installation	5
Engine disassembly and reassembly - general information	6
External oil pipes - removal and installation	14
External shift mechanism - removal, inspection and installation	18
General information	1

	Section
Initial start-up after overhaul	26
Major engine repair - general note	4
Oil screen and pump - removal, inspection and installation	19
Operations possible with the engine in the frame	2
Operations requiring engine removal	3
Piston - removal, inspection and installation	12
Piston rings - installation	13
Primary clutch - removal, inspection and installation	15
Recoil starter - removal, inspection and installation	21
Recommended break-in procedure	27
Reverse shift mechanism and reverse-neutral switch - removal, inspection and installation	17
Secondary clutch and release mechanism - removal, inspection and installation	16
Transmission shafts, balancer shaft and shift drum - removal, inspection and installation	24
Valves/valve seats/valve guides - servicing	9

2A

Specifications

220 models

General
Bore	67 mm (2.638 inches)
Stroke	61 mm (2.402 inches)
Displacement	215 cc (13.119 cubic inches)

Rocker arms
Rocker arm inside diameter
Standard	10.000 to 10.015 mm (0.393 to 0.394 inch)
Limit	10.05 mm (0.395 inch)

Rocker shaft outside diameter
Standard	9.970 to 9.995 mm (0.392 to 0.393 inch)
Limit	9.95 mm (0.391 inch)

Camshaft
Lobe height

Intake
Standard	40.395 to 40.503 mm (1.590 to 1.594 inches)
Limit	40.30 mm (1.586 inches)

Exhaust
Standard	39.720 to 39.828 mm (1.563 to 1.568 inches)
Limit	39.62 mm (1.559 inches)

220 models (continued)

Cylinder head, valves and valve springs

Cylinder head warpage limit	0.05 mm (0.002 inch)
Valve stem runout limit	0.05 mm (0.002 inch)
Valve stem diameter	
Intake	
Standard	5.495 to 5.510 mm (0.216 to 0.217 inch)
Limit	5.48 mm (0.215 inch)
Exhaust	
Standard	5.480 to 5.495 mm (0.215 to 0.216 inch)
Limit	5.47 mm (0.215 inch)
Valve guide inside diameter	
Standard	5.520 to 5.532 mm (0.217 to 0.218 inch)
Limit	5.60 mm (0.220 inch)
Valve seat width	0.5 to 1.0 mm (0.019 to 0.039inch)
Valve head edge thickness	
Intake	
Standard	0.8 mm (0.031 inch)
Limit	0.4 mm (0.016 inch)
Exhaust	
Standard	1.08 mm (0.039 inch)
Limit	0.5 mm (0.019 inch)
Valve spring free length	
Inner spring	
Standard	37.8 mm (1.488 inch)
Limit	36.2 mm (1.425 inch)
Outer spring	
Standard	40.4 mm (1.590 inch)
Limit	38.7 mm (1.524 inch)
Valve spring bend limit	Not specified

Cylinder

Bore diameter	
Standard	67.000 to 67.012 mm (2.637 to 2.638 inches)
Limit	67.10 mm (2.641 inches)
Out-of-round and taper limits	0.05 mm (0.002 inch)
Measuring points	
Upper	10 mm (0.394 inch) from top of bore
Center	40 mm (1.57 inches) from top of bore
Lower	20 mm (0.787 inch) from bottom of bore

Piston and rings

Diameter	
Standard	66.960 to 66.975 mm (2.636 to 2.637 inch)
Limit	66.81 mm (2.630 inch)
Measuring point	5 mm (0.197 inch) from bottom of skirt
Piston-to-cylinder clearance	0.025 to 0.052 mm (0.001 to 0.002 inch)
Oversize pistons and rings	
First oversize	0.5 mm (0.002 inch)
Second oversize	1.0 mm (0.004 inches)
Ring side clearance	
Standard	0.02 to 0.06 mm (0.0008 to 0.0024 inch)
Limit	0.16 mm (0.0063 inch)
Ring end gap	
Top	
Standard	0.15 to 0.35 mm (0.0059 to 0.0137 inch)
Limit	0.7 mm (0.027 inch)
Second	
Standard	0.30 to 0.45 mm (0.0118 to 0.0177 inch)
Limit	0.8 mm (0.031 inch)

Primary (centrifugal) clutch

Weight lining thickness (groove depth)	
Standard	1.0 to 1.3 mm (0.039 to 0.051 inch)
Limit	0.5 mm (0.019 inch)
Clutch drum inside diameter	
Standard	116.0 to 116.2 mm (4.566 to 4.574 inches)
Limit	116.5 mm (4.586 inches)

Primary gear inside diameter
    Standard... 27.000 to 27.021 mm (1.062 to 1.063 inches)
    Limit.. 27.03 mm (1.064 inches)

Secondary clutch

Spring free length
    Standard... 37.2 mm (1.464 inches)
    Limit.. 35.7 mm (1.405 inches)
Metal plate thickness... Not specified
Friction plate thickness
    Standard... 2.9 to 3.1 mm (0.114 to 0.122 inch)
    Limit.. 2.6 mm (0.102 inch)
Friction plate warp
    Standard... 0.2 mm (0.008 inch) or less
    Limit.. 0.3 mm (0.012 inch)
Steel plate warp
    Standard... 0.1 mm (0.004 inch) or less
    Limit.. 0.3 mm (0.012 inch)
Clutch housing inside diameter
    Standard... 25.000 to 25.021 mm (0.984 to 0.985 inch)
    Limit.. 25.03 mm (0.9854 inch)
Clutch housing bushing diameter
    Standard... 24.970 to 24.985 mm (0.983 to 0.984 inch)
    Limit.. 24.95 mm (0.982 inch)

Transmission

Shift fork finger thickness
    Standard... 4.9 to 5.0 mm (0.193 to 0.196 inch)
    Limit.. 4.8 mm (0.189 inch)
Shift fork pin diameter
    Standard... 5.9 to 6.0 mm (0.232 to 0.236 inch)
    Limit.. 5.8 mm (0.228 inch)
Shift fork groove width in gears
    Standard... 5.05 to 5.15 mm (0.199 to 0.202 inch)
    Limit.. 5.3 mm (0.208 inch)
Pin groove width in shift drum
    Standard... 6.05 to 6.20 mm (0.238 to 0.244 inches)

Crankshaft and connecting rod

Runout (total indicator reading)
    Standard... 0.04 mm (0.0016 inch) or less
    Limit.. 0.01 mm (0.0004 inch)
Connecting rod big-end side clearance
    Standard... 0.4 to 0.5 mm (0.016 to 0.020 inch)
    Limit.. 0.7 mm (0.027 inch)
Connecting rod big-end radial clearance
    Standard... 0.008 to 0.020 mm (0.0003 to 0.0008 inch)
    Limit.. 0.07 mm (0.0027 inch)

Torque specifications (1)

Engine mounting bolts and nuts
    Upper bracket to engine and frame .... 25 Nm (18 ft-lbs)
    Front bracket forward bolts/nuts.. 25 Nm (18 ft-lbs)
    Front bracket rearward bolts/nuts.. 34 Nm (25 ft-lbs)
    Rear bolts/nuts .... 34 Nm (27 ft-lbs)
Cylinder head bolts (2)
    First stage
        Main bolts .... 13 Nm (113 inch-lbs)
        Small bolts .... 5.9 Nm (52 inch-lbs)
    Second stage
        Main bolts .... 34 Nm (25 ft-lbs)
        Small bolts .... 12 Nm (104 inch-lbs)
Cam chain guide bolt.. 8.8 Nm (78 inch-lbs)
Camshaft sprocket bolt .... 34 Nm (25 ft-lbs)
Oil pipe union bolts... 15 Nm (132 inch-lbs)
Primary clutch nut
    1988 models... 83 Nm (61 ft-lbs)
    1989 and later models.. 125 Nm (94 ft-lbs) (3)

220 models (continued)

Torque specifications (1) (continued)

Secondary clutch nut
    1988 models... 78 Nm (58 ft-lbs) (3)
    1989 and later models... 120 Nm (87 ft-lbs) (3)
Secondary clutch spring plate bolts... 12 Nm (104 inch-lbs)
Shift drum stopper bolt.. Not specified
Shift drum pin plate bolt.. 12 Nm (104 inch-lbs)
Shift shaft return spring pins.. 25 Nm (18 ft-lbs) (4)
Clutch release cam pin.. Not specified
Balancer shaft and driven gear nut
    1988 models... 78 Nm (58 ft-lbs) (3)
    1989 models... 120 Nm (87 ft-lbs) (3)
Balancer and oil pump drive gear nut
    1988 models... 78 Nm (58 ft-lbs) (3)
    1989 and later models... 120 Nm (87 ft-lbs) (3)
Oil pressure relief valve... 15 Nm (132 inch-lbs) (4)
Crankcase bearing retainers
    Four-hole retainer.. 8.8 Nm (78 inch-lbs) (4)
    Two-hole retainer .... 3.9 Nm (35 inch-lbs)
Crankcase bolts... 8.8 Nm (78 inch-lbs)
Recoil starter reel nut... 12 Nm (104 inch-lbs)
Recoil starter pulley bolt.. 59 Nm (43 ft-lbs)

1   For fasteners not listed here, refer to the General Specifications at the front of this manual.
2   Apply silicone sealant to the threads of the right front main head bolt. Apply engine oil to the threads and bolt seating surface of the other head bolts.
3   Apply engine oil to the threads.
4   Apply non-permanent thread locking agent to the threads.

300 models

General

Bore .... 76 mm (2.994 inches)
Stroke .... 64 mm (2.519 inches)
Displacement... 290 cc (17.696 cubic inches)

Rocker arms

Rocker arm inside diameter
    Standard... 13.000 to 13.018 mm (0.512 to 0.513 inch)
    Limit... 13.05 mm (0.514 inch)
Rocker shaft outside diameter
    Standard... 12.976 to 12.994 mm (0.511 to 0.512 inch)
    Limit... 12.95 mm (0.510 inch)

Camshaft

Lobe height
    2WD models
        Standard .... 40.876 to 40.984 mm (1.609 to 1.613 inches)
        Limit .... 40.78 mm (1.605 inches)
    4WD models
        Standard .... 40.642 to 40.782 mm (1.600 to 1.605 inches)
        Limit .... 40.78 mm (1.596 inches)

Cylinder head, valves and valve springs

Cylinder head warpage limit .... 0.05 mm (0.002 inch)
Valve stem runout
    Standard... 0.02 mm (0.0008 inch)
    Limit... 0.05 mm (0.002 inch)
Valve stem diameter
    Intake
        Standard .... 6.965 to 6.980 mm (0.274 to 0.275 inch)
        Limit .... 6.95 mm (0.274 inch)
    Exhaust
        Standard .... 6.950 to 6.970 mm (0.273 to 0.274 inch)
        Limit .... 6.94 mm (0.273 inch)

Valve guide inside diameter

    Standard... 7.000 to 7.015 mm (0.275 to 0.276 inch)

    Limit... 7.08 mm (0.278 inch)

Valve seat width... 0.5 to 1.0 mm (0.019 to 0.039 inch)

Valve head edge thickness

    Intake

        Standard... 0.8 to 1.2 mm (0.031 to 0.047 inch)

        Limit... 0.5 mm (0.019 inch)

    Exhaust

        Standard... 0.8 to 1.2 mm (0.031 to 0.047 inch)

        Limit... 0.7 mm (0.027 inch)

Valve spring free length

    Inner spring

        Standard... 32.4 mm (1.276 inch)

        Limit... 31.1 mm (1.224 inch)

    Outer spring

        Standard... 37.3 mm (1.469 inch)

        Limit... 35.8 mm (1.409 inch)

Valve spring bend limit .... 0.1 mm (0.004 inch)

Cylinder

Bore diameter

    Standard... 76.000 to 76.012 mm (2.992 to 2.993 inches)

    Limit... 76.10 mm (2.996 inches)

Out-of-round and taper limits.. 0.05 mm (0.002 inch)

Measuring points

    Upper .... 10 mm (0.394 inch) from top of bore

    Center... 40 mm (1.57 inches) from top of bore

    Lower .... 20 mm (0.787 inch) from bottom of bore

Piston and rings

Diameter

    2WD models

        Standard... 75.950 to 75.965 mm (2.990 to 2.991 inch)

        Limit... 75.81 mm (2.984 inch)

    4WD models

        Standard... 75.960 to 75.975 mm (2.990 to 2.991 inch)

        Limit... 75.81 mm (2.984 inch)

Measuring point... 5 mm (0.197 inch) from bottom of skirt

Piston-to-cylinder clearance

    2WD models.. 0.035 to 0.062 mm (0.0013 to 0.0024 inches)

    4WD models.. 0.025 to 0.052 mm (0.001 to 0.002 inch)

Oversize pistons and rings

    First oversize .... 0.5 mm (0.002 inch)

    Second oversize.. 1.0 mm (0.004 inches)

Ring side clearance

    Top

        Standard... 0.03 to 0.07 mm (0.0012 to 0.0027 inch)

        Limit... 0.17 mm (0.0067 inch)

    Second

        Standard... 0.02 to 0.06 mm (0.0008 to 0.0024 inch)

        Limit... 0.16 mm (0.0063 inch)

Ring end gap (top and second)

    Standard... 0.20 to 0.35 mm (0.0078 to 0.0137 inch)

    Limit .... 0.7 mm (0.014 inch)

Primary (centrifugal) clutch

Weight lining thickness (groove depth)

    Standard... 1.0 mm (0.039 inch)

    Limit... 0.5 mm (0.019 inch)

Clutch drum inside diameter

    Standard... 125.0 to 125.2 mm (4.921 inches)

    Limit... 125.5 mm (4.940 inches)

Primary gear inside diameter

    Standard... 27.000 to 27.021 mm (1.062 to 1.063 inches)

    Limit... 27.03 mm (1.064 inches)

2A

300 models (continued)

Secondary clutch

Spring free length
    Standard... 30.38 mm (1.196 inches)
    Limit... 28.8 mm (1.134 inches)
Metal plate thickness.. Not specified
Friction plate thickness
    Standard... 2.92 to 3.08 mm (0.115 to 0.121 inch)
    Limit... 2.8 mm (0.110 inch)
Friction plate warp
    Standard... 0.15 mm (0.006 inch) or less
    Limit... 0.3 mm (0.012 inch)
Steel plate warp
    Standard... 0.2 mm (0.008 inch) or less
    Limit... 0.3 mm (0.012 inch)
Clutch housing inside diameter
    Standard... 25.000 to 25.021 mm (0.984 to 0.985 inch)
    Limit... 25.03 mm (0.9854 inch)
Clutch housing bushing diameter
    Standard... 24.970 to 24.985 mm (0.983 to 0.984 inch)
    Limit... 24.95 mm (0.982 inch)

Transmission

Shift fork finger thickness
    Standard... 4.4 to 4.5 mm (0.173 to 0.177 inch)
    Limit... 4.3 mm (0.169 inch)
Shift fork pin diameter
    Standard... 5.9 to 6.0 mm (0.232 to 0.236 inch)
    Limit... 5.8 mm (0.228 inch)
Shift fork groove width in gears
    Standard... 4.55 to 4.65 mm (0.179 to 0.183 inch)
    Limit... 4.8 mm (0.188 inch)
Pin groove width in shift drum
    Standard... 6.05 to 6.20 mm (0.238 to 0.244 inches)

Crankshaft and connecting rod

Runout (total indicator reading)
    At left end
        Standard .... 0.03 mm (0.0012 inch) or less
        Limit .... 0.08 mm (0.0031 inch)
    At right end
        Standard .... 0.004 mm (0.0001 inch) or less
        Limit .... 0.10 mm (0.0039 inch)
Connecting rod big-end side clearance
    Standard... 0.25 to 0.35 mm (0.010 to 0.014 inch)
    Limit... 0.6 mm (0.024 inch)
Connecting rod big-end radial clearance
    Standard... 0.008 to 0.020 mm (0.0003 to 0.0008 inch)
    Limit... 0.07 mm (0.0027 inch)

Torque specifications (1)

Engine mounting bolts
    8mm diameter .... 25 Nm (18 ft-lbs)
    10 mm diameter
        2WD models .... 34 Nm (25 ft-lbs)
        4WD models .... 37 Nm (27 ft-lbs)
Cylinder head bolts (3)
    First stage
        Main bolts .... 15 Nm (11 ft-lbs)
        Small bolts .... 5.9 Nm (52 inch-lbs)
    Second stage
        Main bolts
            Used bolts .... 29 Nm (22 ft-lbs)
            New bolts .... 34 Nm (25 ft-lbs)
        Small bolts .... 12 Nm (104 inch-lbs)
Cylinder base bolt.. 12 Nm (104 in-lbs)
Cam chain guide bolt.. 9.8 Nm (87 inch-lbs)
Camshaft sprocket bolt .... 41 Nm (30 ft-lbs)

Oil pipe union bolts	20 Nm (174 inch-lbs)
Primary clutch nut	125 Nm (94 ft-lbs) (2)
Secondary clutch nut	78 Nm (58 ft-lbs) (2)
Secondary clutch spring plate bolts	
Used bolts	12 Nm (104 inch-lbs)
New bolts	15 Nm (123 inch-lbs)
Shift drum stopper bolt	12 Nm (104 inch-lbs)
Shift drum pin plate bolt	12 Nm (104 inch-lbs)
Shift shaft return spring pin	17 Nm (144 inch-lbs) (3)
Clutch release cam pin	17 Nm (144 inch-lbs) (3)
Balancer shaft and driven gear nut	
1986 and 1987 models	83 Nm (61 ft-lbs) (2)
1988 and later models	120 Nm (87 ft-lbs) (2)
Balancer and oil pump drive gear nut	
1986 and 1987 models	78 Nm (58 ft-lbs) (2)
1988 and later models	145 Nm (110 ft-lbs) (2)
Recoil starter reel nut	8.3 Nm (74 inch-lbs)

1   For fasteners not listed here, refer to the General Specifications at the front of this manual.
2   Apply engine oil to the threads and nut or bolt seating surface.
3   Apply non-permanent thread locking agent to the threads.

1   General information

The engine/transmission unit is of the air-cooled, single-cylinder four-stroke design. The two valves are operated by an overhead camshaft which is chain driven off the crankshaft. A manually operated decompression lever is used on 1988 and later models to ease starting. The engine/transmission assembly is constructed from aluminum alloy. The crankcase is divided vertically.

The crankcase incorporates a wet sump, pressure-fed lubrication system which uses a gear-driven rotor-type oil pump, an oil filter and separate strainer screen.

Power from the crankshaft is routed to the transmission via two clutches. The primary (centrifugal) clutch, which engages as engine speed is increased, connects the crankshaft to the secondary clutch, which is of the wet, multi-plate type. The secondary clutch transmits power to the transmission; it's engaged and disengaged automatically when the shift lever is moved from one gear position to another. The transmission has five forward gears and one reverse gear.

2   Operations possible with the engine in the frame

The components and assemblies listed below can be removed without having to remove the engine from the frame. If, however, a number of areas require attention at the same time, removal of the engine is recommended.

Recoil starter (if equipped)
Starter motor
Starter chain and recoil limiter
Starter clutch
Alternator rotor and stator
Primary and secondary clutches
External shift mechanism
Cam chain tensioner
Camshaft
Rocker arms and shafts
Cylinder head
Cylinder and piston
Oil pump
Balancer gears

3   Operations requiring engine removal

It is necessary to remove the engine/transmission assembly from the frame and separate the crankcase halves to gain access to the fol-

lowing components:

Crankshaft and connecting rod
Transmission shafts
Shift drums and forks

4   Major engine repair - general note

1   It is not always easy to determine when or if an engine should be completely overhauled, as a number of factors must be considered.
2   High mileage is not necessarily an indication that an overhaul is needed, while low mileage, on the other hand, does not preclude the need for an overhaul. Frequency of servicing is probably the single most important consideration. An engine that has regular and frequent oil and filter changes, as well as other required maintenance, will most likely give many miles of reliable service. Conversely, a neglected engine, or one which has not been broken in properly, may require an overhaul very early in its life.
3   Exhaust smoke and excessive oil consumption are both indications that piston rings and/or valve guides are in need of attention. Make sure oil leaks are not responsible before deciding that the rings and guides are bad. Refer to Chapter 1 and perform a cylinder compression check to determine for certain the nature and extent of the work required.
4   If the engine is making obvious knocking or rumbling noises, the connecting rod and/or main bearings are probably at fault.
5   Loss of power, rough running, excessive valve train noise and high fuel consumption rates may also point to the need for an overhaul, especially if they are all present at the same time. If a complete tune-up does not remedy the situation, major mechanical work is the only solution.
6   An engine overhaul generally involves restoring the internal parts to the specifications of a new engine. During an overhaul the piston rings are replaced and the cylinder walls are bored and/or honed. If a rebore is done, then a new piston is also required. Generally the valves are serviced as well, since they are usually in less than perfect condition at this point. While the engine is being overhauled, other components such as the carburetor and the starter motor can be rebuilt also. The end result should be a like-new engine that will give as many trouble-free miles as the original.
7   Before beginning the engine overhaul, read through all of the related procedures to familiarize yourself with the scope and requirements of the job. Overhauling an engine is not all that difficult, but it is time consuming. Plan on the vehicle being tied up for a minimum of two (2) weeks. Check on the availability of parts and make sure that any necessary special tools, equipment and supplies are obtained in advance.

2A

5.3 Disconnect the engine ground cable (arrow) (4WD shown)

5.9 Disconnect the breather hose from the cam sprocket cover

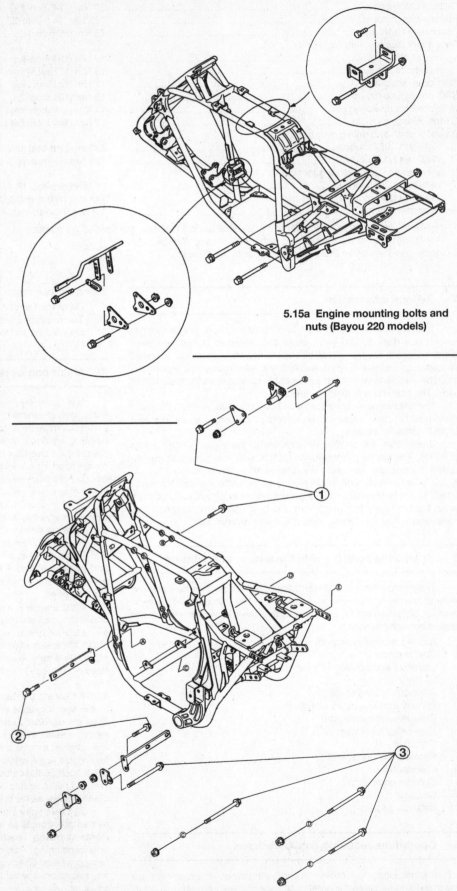

5.15a Engine mounting bolts and nuts (Bayou 220 models)

5.15b Engine mounting bolts and nuts (1986 and 1987 Bayou 300 models)

1. *Upper bracket and bolts*
2. *Lower front bracket and bolts*
3. *Through-bolts*

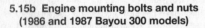

5.15d On 4WD models, remove the upper bracket-to-engine bolt and nut . . .

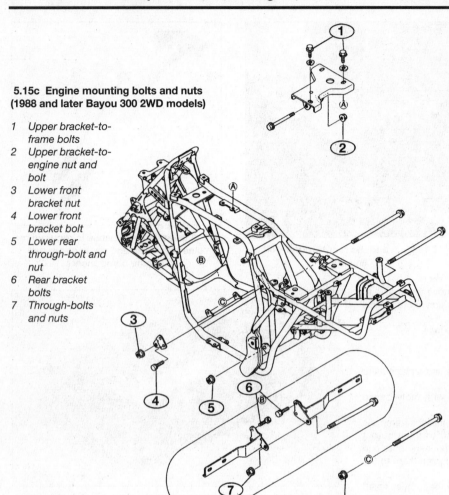

5.15c Engine mounting bolts and nuts (1988 and later Bayou 300 2WD models)

1   *Upper bracket-to-frame bolts*
2   *Upper bracket-to-engine nut and bolt*
3   *Lower front bracket nut*
4   *Lower front bracket bolt*
5   *Lower rear through-bolt and nut*
6   *Rear bracket bolts*
7   *Through-bolts and nuts*

5.15e . . . and unbolt the bracket from the frame

2A

8   Most work can be done with typical shop hand tools, although a number of precision measuring tools are required for inspecting parts to determine if they must be replaced. Often a dealer service department or repair shop will handle the inspection of parts and offer advice concerning reconditioning and replacement. As a general rule, time is the primary cost of an overhaul so it doesn't pay to install worn or sub-standard parts.

9   As a final note, to ensure maximum life and minimum trouble from a rebuilt engine, everything must be assembled with care in a spot-lessly clean environment.

5   Engine - removal and installation

Note: *Engine removal and installation should be done with the aid of an assistant to avoid damage or injury that could occur if the engine is dropped.*

Removal

Refer to illustrations 5.3, 5.9 and 5.15a through 5.15g

1   Drain the engine oil (see Chapter 1).
2   Remove the seat and the front and rear fenders (see Chapter 7).
3   Disconnect the ground cable from the engine **(see illustration)** and disconnect the negative battery cable (see Chapter 1).
4   Remove the fuel tank, carburetor, air cleaner air duct, intake manifold and exhaust system (see Chapter 3).
5   Disconnect the reverse cable (see Section 17).

6   If you're working on a 2WD model, remove the shift pedal (Section 18). If you're working on a 300 2WD model, remove the differential shift lever (see Chapter 5).
7   If you're working on a 4WD model, disconnect the parking brake cable (see Chapter 6).
8   Disconnect the odometer/speedometer cable (if equipped).
9   Disconnect the crankcase breather hose from the camshaft cover **(see illustration)**. If you're working on a 4WD model, disconnect the oil cooler hoses from the engine (Section 14).
10   Disconnect the spark plug wire (see Chapter 1).
11   Label and disconnect the following wires (see Chapter 4 for component locations if necessary):
   CDI magneto and alternator
   Reverse and neutral switches
   Starter
12   If you're working on a 4WD model, you can either remove the sub-transmission or not, whichever seems easier. **Note:** *If you don't remove the sub-transmission, you may need an assistant to help you align the splines of the rear driveshaft with the sub-transmission when you install the engine.*

   a) *Remove the sub-transmission (Chapter 5), OR*
   b) *Remove the left footpeg (Chapter 7) and the front driveshaft (see Chapter 5).*

13   Loosen the clamp that secures the forward end of the rear drive-shaft.
14   Support the engine securely from below.
15   Remove the engine mounting bolts, nuts and brackets **(see illustrations)**.

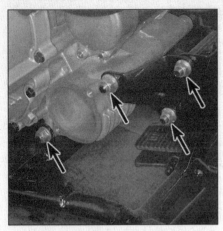

5.15f Remove the front bracket nuts and through-bolts . . .

5.15g . . . and the rear through-bolt and nut

6.2 A selection of brushes is required for cleaning holes and passages in the engine components

16   Have an assistant help you lift the engine. Remove the engine to the right side of the vehicle (2WD models) or the left side of the vehicle (4WD models).

17   Carefully lower the engine to a suitable work surface.

Installation

18   Check the engine supports for wear or damage and replace them if necessary before installing the engine.

19   Lubricate the splines of the rear driveshaft with moly-based grease.

20   With the help of an assistant, lift the engine up into the frame. As you position the engine, engage the rear driveshaft with the output gear (2WD) or sub-transmission (4WD). Install the mounting nuts and bolts. Finger-tighten the mounting bolts, but don't tighten them to the specified torque yet.

21   Tighten the engine mounting bolts and nuts to the torques listed in this Chapter's Specifications. Tighten the upper bracket bolts and nuts first, then tighten the lower brackets.

22   The remainder of installation is the reverse of the removal steps, with the following additions:

   a) *Use new gaskets at all exhaust pipe connections.*
   b) *Adjust the throttle cable, reverse cable and parking brake cable (4WD) following the procedures in Chapter 1.*
   c) *Fill the engine with oil, also following the procedures in Chapter 1. Run the engine and check for leaks.*

---

6   Engine disassembly and reassembly - general information

Refer to illustrations 6.2 and 6.3

1   Before disassembling the engine, clean the exterior with a degreaser and rinse it with water. A clean engine will make the job easier and prevent the possibility of getting dirt into the internal areas of the engine.

2   In addition to the precision measuring tools mentioned earlier, you will need a torque wrench, a valve spring compressor, oil gallery brushes **(see illustration)**, a piston ring removal and installation tool and, ideally, a piston ring compressor (which is described in Section 8). Some new, clean engine oil of the correct grade and type, some engine assembly lube (or moly-based grease) and a tube of RTV (silicone) sealant will also be required.

3   An engine support stand made from short lengths of 2 x 4's bolted together will facilitate the disassembly and reassembly procedures **(see illustration)**. If you have an automotive-type engine stand, an adapter plate can be made from a piece of plate, some angle iron and some nuts and bolts.

4   When disassembling the engine, keep "mated" parts together

6.3 An engine stand can be made from short lengths of lumber and lag bolts or nails

(including gears, rocker arms and shafts, etc.) that have been in contact with each other during engine operation. These "mated" parts must be reused or replaced as an assembly.

5   Engine/transmission disassembly should be done in the following general order with reference to the appropriate Sections.

   Remove the cam chain tensioner
   Remove the cylinder head, rocker arms and camshaft
   Remove the cylinder
   Remove the piston
   Remove the primary and secondary clutches
   Remove the balancer gears
   Remove the oil pump
   Remove the external shift mechanism
   Remove the alternator rotor and starter reduction gears
   Separate the crankcase halves
   Remove the shift drums and forks
   Remove the transmission gears and shafts
   Remove the balancer shaft
   Remove the crankshaft and connecting rod

6   Reassembly is accomplished by reversing the general disassembly sequence.

---

7   Cam chain tensioner - removal and installation

Removal

Refer to illustrations 7.1, 7.2 and 7.3

Caution: *Once you start to remove the tensioner bolts you must remove the tensioner all the way and reset it before tightening the*

7.1 Loosen but don't remove the lockbolt (upper arrow), unscrew the mounting bolts (lower arrows). . .

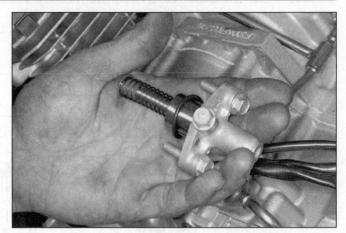

7.2 . . . and take the tensioner out of the engine

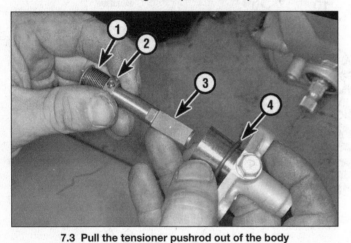

7.3 Pull the tensioner pushrod out of the body

1 Spring	2 Retainer	3 Pushrod	4 O-ring

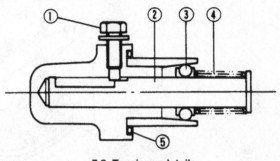

7.8 Tensioner details

1	Lockbolt	3	Retainer	5	O-ring
2	Pushrod	4	Spring		

bolts. *The tensioner extends and locks in place, so if you loosen the bolts partway and then tighten them, the tensioner or cam chain will be damaged.*

1   Loosen the tensioner lockbolt, but don't remove it yet **(see illustration)**.
2   Remove the tensioner mounting bolts and detach it from the cylinder **(see illustration)**.
3   Unscrew the lockbolt and pull the tensioner pushrod out of the tensioner body **(see illustration)**. Slide the retainer ring and spring off the pushrod and remove the O-ring from the tensioner body.

Installation

Refer to illustration 7.8

4   Clean all old gasket material from the tensioner body and engine.
5   Lubricate the friction surfaces of the components with moly-based grease.
6   Install a new O-ring on the tensioner body.
7   Slide the spring onto the tensioner pushrod. Compress it all the way to expose the hole in the tensioner pushrod, then slip a short length of wire into the hole to hold the spring in the compressed position.
8   Slide the retainer ring onto the tensioner pushrod, then install the pushrod in the tensioner body **(see illustration)**. Push the pushrod in as far as it will go, then tighten the lockbolt to hold it in place and pull out the length of wire.
9   Position the tensioner body on the cylinder and install the bolts, tightening them securely but don't overtighten and strip the threads.
10   Loosen the lockbolt to let the tensioner pushrod extend, then tighten the lockbolt.

8   Cylinder head, decompression lever, camshaft and rocker arms - removal, inspection and installation

Decompression lever

Removal

Refer to illustrations 8.3a, 8.3b, 8.4a and 8.4b

1   A decompression lever is used on 1988 and later models.
2   If the engine is still in the vehicle, remove the front fender for access (see Chapter 7).
3   Note how the ends of the spring engage the decompression lever and the post cast into the cylinder head **(see illustrations)**.

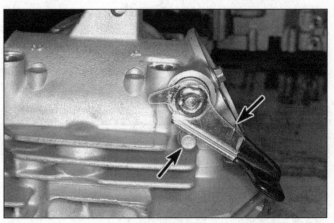

8.3a Note how the spring ends are hooked to the lever and the post (arrows) . . .

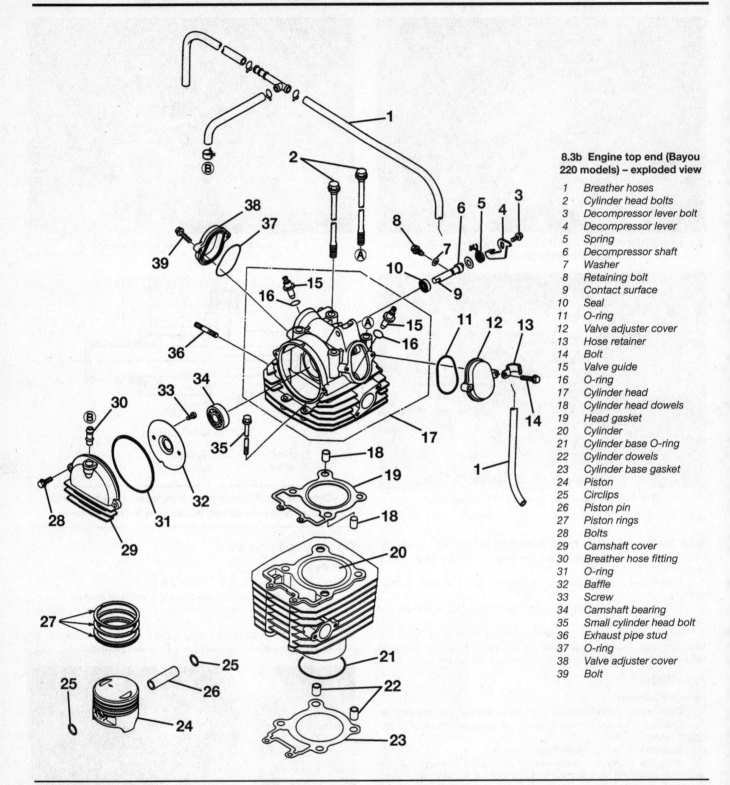

8.3b Engine top end (Bayou 220 models) – exploded view

1	Breather hoses
2	Cylinder head bolts
3	Decompressor lever bolt
4	Decompressor lever
5	Spring
6	Decompressor shaft
7	Washer
8	Retaining bolt
9	Contact surface
10	Seal
11	O-ring
12	Valve adjuster cover
13	Hose retainer
14	Bolt
15	Valve guide
16	O-ring
17	Cylinder head
18	Cylinder head dowels
19	Head gasket
20	Cylinder
21	Cylinder base O-ring
22	Cylinder dowels
23	Cylinder base gasket
24	Piston
25	Circlips
26	Piston pin
27	Piston rings
28	Bolts
29	Camshaft cover
30	Breather hose fitting
31	O-ring
32	Baffle
33	Screw
34	Camshaft bearing
35	Small cylinder head bolt
36	Exhaust pipe stud
37	O-ring
38	Valve adjuster cover
39	Bolt

4   Remove the lockbolt and washer, then pull the decompression lever shaft out of the cylinder head **(see illustrations)**.

Inspection

Refer to illustration 8.6

5   Check the shaft seal for wear **(see illustration 8.4b)**. If it's worn, or if oil has been leaking past it, pry the seal out of the cylinder head. Push in a new one, using a bearing driver or socket the same diameter as the seal.

6   Check the friction surface on the end of the shaft for wear **(see illustration)**. If there's noticeable wear, replace the lever.

Installation

7   Installation is the reverse of the removal steps. Coat the shaft with clean engine oil before inserting it through the seal. Engage the spring ends with the lever and the post on the cylinder head **(see illustration 8.3b)**.

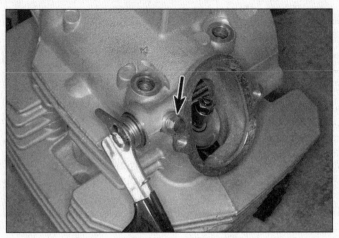

8.4a ... then unscrew the lockbolt ...

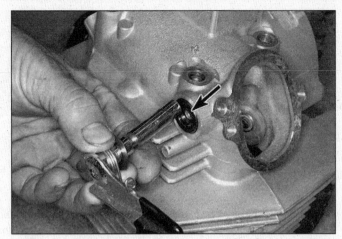

8.4b ... pull the shaft out of its bore and inspect the seal (arrow)

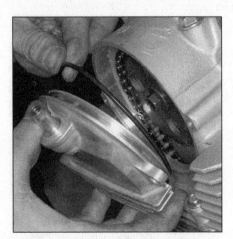

8.6 Check the shaft for wear where it contacts the rocker arm (arrow)

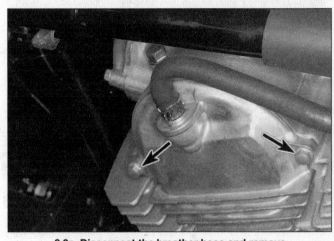

8.9a Disconnect the breather hose and remove the bolts (arrows) ...

2A

Camshaft removal

Refer to illustrations 8.9a, 8.9b, 8.10a, 8.10b, 8.11a, 8.11b, 8.12a and 8.12b

Note: *Either the camshaft or the rocker arms can be removed first.*

8   Remove the valve adjusting hole covers (see Chapter 1).

9   Disconnect the crankcase breather hose from the cam sprocket cover. Unbolt the cover and take it off **(see illustrations)**. If it's stuck,

carefully pry it off, using the pry point behind each bolt boss.

10   Refer to *Valve clearances - check and adjustment* in Chapter 1 and place the engine at top dead center on the compression stroke. The cam sprocket mark will align with the indicator cast into the cylinder head **(see illustrations)** and the rocker arms will be loose when the cylinder is at TDC compression.

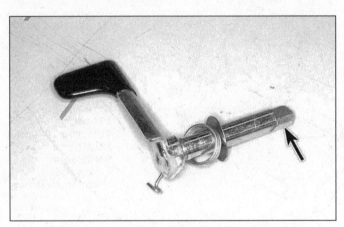

8.9b ... then remove the cover and its O-ring

8.10a On Bayou 300 models, the line next to the "LF300" mark on the sprocket (arrow) ...

8.10b ... should align with the ridge next to the TOP mark (arrow) (sprocket removed for clarity)

8.11a Unbolt the sprocket and pull it off the camshaft

8.11b Remove the camshaft retainer

8.12a Thread the sprocket bolt into the camshaft . . .

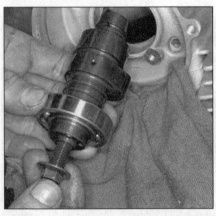

8.12b . . . and use it as a handle to pull the camshaft out

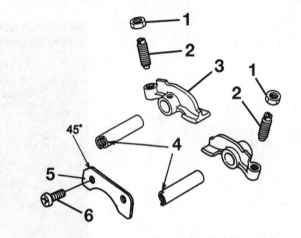

8.13a Rocker arm details (Bayou 220 models)

1   *Valve adjusting screw locknuts*
2   *Valve adjusting screws*
3   *Rocker arms*
4   *Rocker shaft indentations*
5   *Rocker shaft retainer*
6   *Screw*

11   Unbolt the cam sprocket and take it off the camshaft **(see illustration)**. Disengage the sprocket from the chain and support the chain with wire so it doesn't fall down off the crankshaft sprocket. Remove the screws and detach the camshaft retainer from the head **(see illustration)**.

12   Thread the sprocket bolt into the end of the camshaft and use it as a handle to pull the camshaft out of the cylinder head **(see illustrations)**. **Caution:** *The camshaft should come out easily. If it seems stuck, make sure it isn't caught on the rocker arms. You can remove the rocker arms first, if necessary, to make camshaft removal easier.*

Rocker arm removal

Refer to illustrations 8.13a, 8.13b, 8.14, 8.15a and 8.15b

13   Remove the screw(s) and detach the rocker shaft retainer from the head **(see illustrations)**.

14   Thread a 6 mm bolt into the end of each rocker arm shaft **(see illustration)**. Support the rocker and use the bolt as a handle to pull out the shaft. **Note:** *If the shaft is stuck, it may be necessary to use a slide hammer. These can be rented from equipment rental yards (some auto parts stores also rent tools).*

8.13b On 300 models, remove the screw (arrow) and the rocker shaft retainer

8.14 Thread a bolt into the rocker shafts and pull them out . . .

8.15a . . . then remove the rocker arms through the valve adjusting hole . . .

8.15b . . . and the camshaft bore

8.16 Remove these two small cylinder head bolts first and install them last

8.17 Main head bolt TIGHTENING sequence

15   Remove the rocker arms through the valve adjusting holes and the camshaft bearing bore **(see illustrations)**.

Cylinder head removal

Refer to illustrations 8.16, 8.17 and 8.18

16   Remove the two small cylinder head bolts **(see illustration)**.

17   Loosen the main cylinder head bolts in several stages, in the reverse order of the tightening sequence **(see illustration)**.

18   Lift the cylinder head off the cylinder **(see illustration)**. If it's stuck, don't attempt to pry it off - tap around the sides of it with a plastic hammer to dislodge it. Be careful not to tap against the cooling fins; they're easily broken.

19   Locate the dowels **(see illustration 8.3a or 8.18)**. They may be in the cylinder or they may have come off with the head.

Cam chain and guide removal

Front chain guide

Refer to illustration 8.20

20   Lift the front cam chain guide out of the cylinder **(see illustration)**.

21   Stuff clean rags into the cam chain openings so dirt, small parts or tools can't fall into them.

Rear chain guide and chain

Refer to illustrations 8.23 and 8.24

22 The rear guide is bolted at the bottom, so the primary clutch will have to be removed for access if the guide or the cam chain needs to

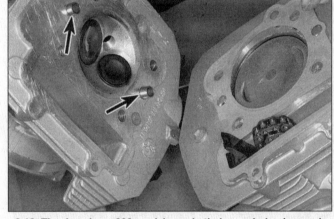

8.18 The dowels on 300 models are in their own holes (arrows); the dowels on 220 models are in the right front and left rear bolt holes

be removed (Section 15).

23   With the primary clutch removed, remove the bolt and bushing that secure the lower end of the rear chain guide **(see illustration)**.

24   To remove the cam chain, remove the chain retainer screw, take off the retainer and disengage the chain from the sprocket on the crankshaft **(see illustration)**.

2A

8.20 Pull the chain guide out; on installation, place its hook in the notch (arrow)

8.23 Remove the chain guide bolt and bushing; on assembly, install the bushing with its wide side outward

8.24 Cam chain and guide details

A   Exhaust side chain guide lower pocket
B   Chain retainer and screw
C   Intake side chain guide bolt

8.26a Check the cam lobes for wear – here's a good example of damage which will require replacement (or repair) of the camshaft

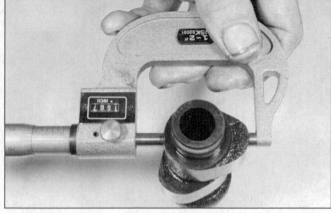

8.26b Measure the height of the cam lobes with a micrometer

Inspection

Camshaft, chain and guides

Refer to illustrations 8.26a and 8.26b

Note: *Before replacing camshafts or the cylinder head because of damage, check with local machine shops specializing in ATV or motorcycle engine work. In the case of the camshaft, it may be possible for cam lobes to be welded, reground and hardened, at a cost far lower than that of a new camshaft. If the bearing surfaces in the cylinder head are damaged, it may be possible for them to be bored out to accept bearing inserts. Due to the cost of a new cylinder head it is recommended that all options be explored before condemning it as trash!*

25   Rotate the cam bearing and check for roughness, looseness or noise. Replace the bearing(s) if problems are found.

26   Check the camshaft lobes for heat discoloration (blue appearance), score marks, chipped areas, flat spots and spalling **(see illustration)**. Measure the height of each lobe with a micrometer **(see illustration)** and compare the results to the minimum lobe height listed in this Chapter's Specifications. If damage is noted or wear is excessive, the camshaft must be replaced. Check the bearing surfaces for scoring or wear. Also, be sure to check the condition of the rocker arms, as described below.

27   Except in cases of oil starvation, the camshaft chain wears very little. If the chain has stretched excessively, which makes it difficult to maintain proper tension, replace it with a new one.

28   Check the sprocket for wear, cracks and other damage, replacing it if necessary. If the sprocket is worn, the chain is also worn, and possibly the sprocket on the crankshaft. If wear this severe is apparent, the entire engine should be disassembled for inspection.

29   Check the chain guides for wear or damage, especially along the surfaces that contact the chain. If they are worn or damaged, replace them.

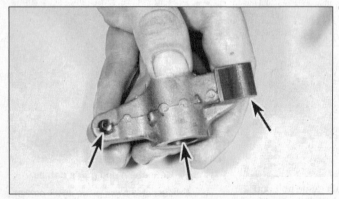

8.30 Check rocker arms for wear on the adjuster surface, inside the bore and on the cam contact surface (arrows)

Rocker arms, shafts and decompression lever

Refer to illustration 8.30

30   Check the rocker arms for wear at the cam contact surfaces, inside the shaft bores and at the tips of the valve adjusting screws **(see illustration)**. Try to twist the rocker arms from side-to-side on the shafts. If they're loose on the shafts or if there's visible wear, measure the rocker arm shaft diameter and bore diameter with a micrometer and hole gauge. If the parts are worn beyond the limits listed in this Chapter's Specifications, replace them. Replace the rocker arm and shaft as a set.

31   Check the decompression lever (if equipped) and its shaft for wear, damage or a broken spring **(see illustration 8.3a or 8.6)**. If any problems are found, pull the lever/shaft out of the cover, together with the spring. Pry the shaft oil seal out of its bore.

Cylinder head

32   Check the cylinder head gasket and the mating surfaces on the cylinder head and cylinder for leakage, which could indicate warpage. Refer to Section 10 and check the flatness of the cylinder head.

33   Clean all traces of old gasket material from the cylinder head and cylinder. Be careful not to let any of the gasket material fall into the crankcase, the cylinder bore or the bolt holes.

Installation

Refer to illustration 8.44

34   If the decompression lever/shaft was removed, press a new oil seal into the bore with a seal driver or a socket the same diameter as the seal. Install the shaft and engage its spring with the cover and the lever, then install the retaining bolt in the cover **(see illustrations 8.3b and 8.4a)**.

35   Coat the rocker shafts and rocker arm bores with moly-based grease. Install the rocker shafts and rocker arms in the cylinder head. Be sure to install the intake and exhaust rocker arms and shafts in the correct sides of the head. Install the rocker shaft retainer. If you're working on a 220 model, be sure to engage the rocker shaft indentations with the retainer and position the 45-degree notch in the correct location **(see illustration 8.13a)**.

36   Install the bearing on the camshaft (if it was removed). Lubricate the camshaft bearing with engine oil.

37   Install the camshaft in the cylinder head with its lobes pointing down.

38   Install the camshaft retainer and tighten the screws securely **(see illustration 8.11b)**.

39   Install the dowels, then place the new head gasket on the cylinder **(see illustration 8.18)**. Never reuse the old gasket and don't use any type of gasket sealant.

40   Install the exhaust side cam chain damper, fitting the lower end into its notch and engaging the upper end with the notch in the cylinder **(see illustrations 8.20 and 8.24)**.

41   Carefully lower the cylinder head over the dowels, guiding the

8.44 Place the sprocket dowel in the camshaft hole (arrows)

cam chain through the slot in the cylinder head. It's helpful to have an assistant support the cam chain with a piece of wire so it doesn't fall and become kinked. When the head is resting on the cylinder, wire the cam chain to another component to keep tension on it.

42   If you're working on a Bayou 220, coat the threads of the right front head bolt with silicone sealant and lubricate the threads of the other head bolts with engine oil. If you're working on a Bayou 300 model, lubricate the threads of all of the cylinder head bolts with engine oil. Install the head bolts finger-tight. Tighten the four main bolts in the correct sequence **(see illustration 8.17)**, followed by the two small bolts **(see illustration 8.16)**. Tighten the six bolts in two stages. There's a specific torque for each stage, listed in this Chapter's Specifications.

43   Refer to the valve adjustment procedure in Chapter 1 and make sure the timing mark with the T next to it is aligned with the notch in the timing hole. If it's necessary to turn the crankshaft, hold the cam chain up so it doesn't fall off the crankshaft sprocket and become jammed.

44   Engage the camshaft sprocket with the timing chain so its dowel hole aligns with the dowel **(see illustration)**. Slip the sprocket onto the camshaft over the dowel, then install the sprocket bolt finger-tight. On Bayou 220 models, the punch mark on the camshaft sprocket aligns with the raised projection on the top of the cylinder head. On Bayou 300 models, the line on the cam sprocket should be aligned with the cast indicator in the cylinder head **(see illustrations 8.10a and 8.10b)**.

45   Twist the cam sprocket in both directions to remove the slack from the cam chain. Insert a screwdriver in the cam chain tensioner hole and push against the cam chain guide. With the guide pushed in, the cam sprocket line and cast indicator should line up **(see illustrations 8.10a and 8.10b)**. If they don't, remove the cam sprocket from the chain, reposition it and try again. Don't continue with assembly until the marks are lined up correctly.

46   Tighten the cam sprocket bolt to the torque listed in this Chapter's Specifications.

47   Apply engine oil to a new O-ring for the cam sprocket cover. Install the O-ring and cover and tighten the bolts.

48   Install the cam chain tensioner (see Section 7).

49   Change the engine oil (see Chapter 1).

50   Adjust the valve clearances (see Chapter 1).

51   The remainder of installation is the reverse of removal.

9   Valves/valve seats/valve guides - servicing

1   Because of the complex nature of this job and the special tools and equipment required, servicing of the valves, the valve seats and the valve guides (commonly known as a valve job) is best left to a professional.

2   The home mechanic can, however, remove and disassemble the head, do the initial cleaning and inspection, then reassemble and deliver the head to a dealer service department or properly equipped vehicle repair shop for the actual valve servicing. Refer to Section 10 for those procedures.

3   The dealer service department will remove the valves and springs,

recondition or replace the valves and valve seats, replace the valve guides, check and replace the valve springs, spring retainers and keepers (as necessary), replace the valve seals with new ones and reassemble the valve components.

4   After the valve job has been performed, the head will be in like-new condition. When the head is returned, be sure to clean it again very thoroughly before installation on the engine to remove any metal particles or abrasive grit that may still be present from the valve service operations. Use compressed air, if available, to blow out all the holes and passages.

10   Cylinder head and valves - disassembly, inspection and reassembly

1   As mentioned in the previous Section, valve servicing and valve guide replacement should be left to a dealer service department or other repair shop. However, disassembly, cleaning and inspection of the valves and related components can be done (if the necessary special tools are available) by the home mechanic. This way no expense is incurred if the inspection reveals that service work is not required at this time.

2   To properly disassemble the valve components without the risk of damaging them, a valve spring compressor is absolutely necessary. If the special tool is not available, have a dealer service department or vehicle repair shop handle the entire process of disassembly, inspection, service or repair (if required) and reassembly of the valves.

Disassembly

Refer to illustrations 10.7a and 10.7b

3   Remove the carburetor intake tube from the cylinder head (see Chapter 3).

4   Before the valves are removed, scrape away any traces of gasket material from the head gasket sealing surface. Work slowly and do not nick or gouge the soft aluminum of the head. Gasket removing solvents, which work very well, are available at most ATV shops and auto parts stores.

5   Carefully scrape all carbon deposits out of the combustion chamber area. A hand held wire brush or a piece of fine emery cloth can be used once most of the deposits have been scraped away. Do not use a wire brush mounted in a drill motor, or one with extremely stiff bristles, as the head material is soft and may be eroded away or scratched by the wire brush.

6   Before proceeding, arrange to label and store the valves along with their related components so they can be kept separate and reinstalled in the same valve guides they are removed from (again, plastic bags work well for this).

7   Compress the valve spring(s) on the first valve with a spring compressor, then remove the keepers and the retainer from the valve assembly **(see illustration)**. Do not compress the spring(s) any more than is absolutely necessary. Carefully release the valve spring com-

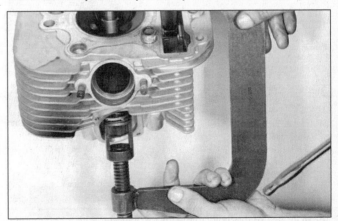

10.7a Compress the valve springs with a valve spring compressor

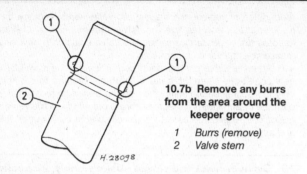

10.7b Remove any burrs from the area around the keeper groove

1   Burrs (remove)
2   Valve stem

10.14 Check the gasket surface for flatness with a straightedge and feeler gauge in the directions shown

pressor and remove the spring(s), spring seat and valve from the head. If the valve binds in the guide (won't pull through), push it back into the head and deburr the area around the keeper groove with a very fine file or whetstone **(see illustration)**.

8   Repeat the procedure for the remaining valve. Remember to keep the parts for each valve together so they can be reinstalled in the same location.

9   Once the valves have been removed and labeled, pull off the valve stem seals with pliers and discard them (the old seals should never be reused).

10   Next, clean the cylinder head with solvent and dry it thoroughly. Compressed air will speed the drying process and ensure that all holes and recessed areas are clean.

11   Clean all of the valve springs, keepers, retainers and spring seats with solvent and dry them thoroughly. Do the parts from one valve at a time so that no mixing of parts between valves occurs.

12   Scrape off any deposits that may have formed on the valve, then use a motorized wire brush to remove deposits from the valve heads and stems. Again, make sure the valves do not get mixed up.

Inspection

Refer to illustrations 10.14, 10.16, 10.17, 10.18a, 10.18b, 10.19a and 10.19b

13   Inspect the head very carefully for cracks and other damage. If cracks are found, a new head will be required. Check the cam bearing surfaces for wear and evidence of seizure. Check the camshaft for wear as well (see Section 8).

14   Using a precision straightedge and a feeler gauge, check the head gasket mating surface for warpage. Lay the straightedge lengthwise, across the head and diagonally (corner-to-corner), intersecting the head bolt holes, and try to slip a feeler gauge under it, on either side of each combustion chamber **(see illustration)**. The feeler gauge thickness should be the same as the cylinder head warpage limit listed in this Chapter's Specifications. If the feeler gauge can be inserted between the head and the straightedge, the head is warped and must either be machined or, if warpage is excessive, replaced with a new

one. Using the same method, measure the flatness of the head mating surface on top of the cylinder.

15   Examine the valve seats in each of the combustion chambers. If they are pitted, cracked or burned, the head will require valve service that is beyond the scope of the home mechanic. Measure the valve seat width and compare it to this Chapter's Specifications. If it is not within the specified range, or if it varies around its circumference, valve service work is required.

16   Clean the valve guides to remove any carbon buildup, then measure the inside diameters of the guides (at both ends and the center of the guide) with a small hole gauge and a micrometer **(see illustration)**. If they're worn beyond the limit listed in this Chapter's Specifications, they must be replaced. The guides are measured at the ends and at the center to determine if they are worn in a bell-mouth pattern (more wear at the ends). If they are, guide replacement is an absolute must.

17   Carefully inspect each valve face for cracks, pits and burned spots. Check the valve stem and the keeper groove area for cracks **(see illustration)**. Rotate the valve and check for any obvious indication that it is bent. Check the end of the stem for pitting and excessive wear and make sure the bevel is not worn away. The presence of any of the above conditions indicates the need for valve servicing.

18   Measure the valve stem diameter **(see illustration)**. If the diameter is less than listed in this Chapter's Specifications, the valves will have to be replaced with new ones. Also check the valve stem for bending. Set the valve in a V-block with a dial indicator touching the middle of the stem **(see illustration)**. Rotate the valve and look for a reading on the gauge (which indicates a bent stem). If the stem is bent, replace the valve.

19   Check the end of each valve spring for wear and pitting. Measure the free length **(see illustration)** and compare it to this Chapter's Specifications. Any springs that are shorter than specified have

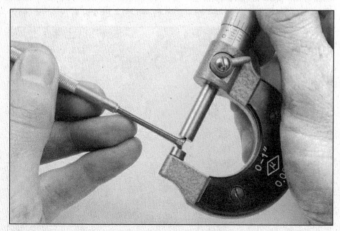

10.16 Measure the valve guide inside diameter with a hole gauge, then measure the gauge with a micrometer

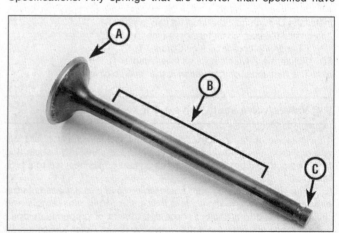

10.17 Check the valve face (A), stem (B) and keeper groove (C) for wear and damage

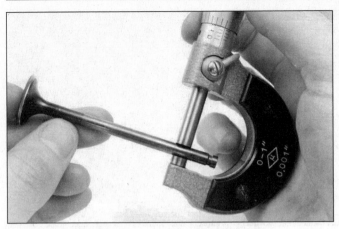

10.18a Measuring valve stem diameter

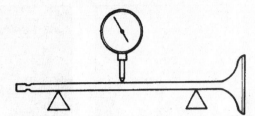

10.18b Check the valve stem for bends with a V-block (or V-blocks, as shown here) and a dial indicator

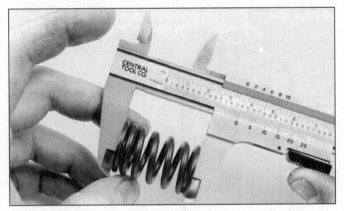

10.19a Measuring the free length of the valve springs

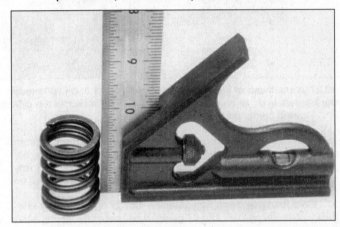

10.19b Checking the valve springs for squareness

2A

sagged and should not be reused. Stand the spring on a flat surface and check it for squareness **(see illustration)**.

20　Check the spring retainers and keepers for obvious wear and cracks. Any questionable parts should not be reused, as extensive damage will occur in the event of failure during engine operation.

21　If the inspection indicates that no service work is required, the valve components can be reinstalled in the head.

Reassembly

Refer to illustrations 10.23, 10.24, 10.26 and 10.27

22　If the valve seats have been ground, the valves and seats should be lapped before installing the valves in the head to ensure a positive seal between the valves and seats. This procedure requires coarse and fine valve lapping compound (available at auto parts stores) and a

valve lapping tool. If a lapping tool is not available, a piece of rubber or plastic hose can be slipped over the valve stem (after the valve has been installed in the guide) and used to turn the valve.

23　Apply a small amount of coarse lapping compound to the valve face **(see illustration)**, then slip the valve into the guide. **Note:** *Make sure the valve is installed in the correct guide and be careful not to get any lapping compound on the valve stem.*

24　Attach the lapping tool (or hose) to the valve and rotate the tool between the palms of your hands. Use a back-and-forth motion rather than a circular motion. Lift the valve off the seat and turn it at regular intervals to distribute the lapping compound properly. Continue the lapping procedure until the valve face and seat contact area is of uniform width and unbroken around the entire circumference of the valve face and seat **(see illustration)**. Once this is accomplished, lap the valves again with fine lapping compound.

25　Carefully remove the valve from the guide and wipe off all traces of lapping compound. Use solvent to clean the valve and wipe the seat area thoroughly with a solvent soaked cloth. Repeat the procedure for the remaining valves.

26　Lay the spring seat in place in the cylinder head, then install new

10.23 Apply the lapping compound very sparingly, in small dabs, to the valve face only

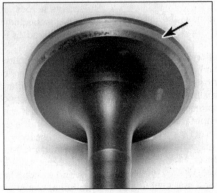

10.24 After lapping, the valve face should exhibit a uniform, unbroken contact pattern (arrow)

10.26 Push the oil seal onto the valve guide (arrow)

10.27 A small dab of grease will help hold the keepers in place on the valve while the spring compressor is released

11.3 On 300 models, remove the bolt that attaches the cylinder to the crankcase

11.4 Lift the cylinder off and locate the dowels (300 dowels shown; both 220 dowels are on the right side)

valve stem seals on both of the guides **(see illustration)**. Use an appropriate size deep socket to push the seals into place until they are properly seated. Don't twist or cock them, or they will not seal properly against the valve stems. Also, don't remove them again or they will be damaged.

27   Coat the valve stems with assembly lube or moly-based grease, then install one of them into its guide. Next, install the spring seat, springs and retainers, compress the springs and install the keepers. **Note:** *Install the springs with the tightly wound coils at the bottom (next to the spring seat).* When compressing the springs with the valve spring compressor, depress them only as far as is absolutely necessary to slip the keepers into place. Apply a small amount of grease to the keepers **(see illustration)** to help hold them in place as the pressure is released from the springs. Make certain that the keepers are securely locked in their retaining grooves.

28   Support the cylinder head on blocks so the valves can't contact the workbench top, then very gently tap each of the valve stems with a soft-faced hammer. This will help seat the keepers in their grooves.

29   Once all of the valves have been installed in the head, check for proper valve sealing by pouring a small amount of solvent into each of the valve ports. If the solvent leaks past the valve(s) into the combustion chamber area, disassemble the valve(s) and repeat the lapping procedure, then reinstall the valve(s) and repeat the check. Repeat the procedure until a satisfactory seal is obtained.

11   Cylinder - removal, inspection and installation

Removal

Refer to illustrations 11.3 and 11.4

1   Following the procedure given in Section 8, remove the cylinder head. Make sure the crankshaft is positioned at Top Dead Center (TDC).
2   Lift out the cam chain front guide **(see illustration 8.20)**.
3   If you're working on a Bayou 300, remove the bolt that secures the base of the cylinder to the crankcase **(see illustration)**.
4   Lift the cylinder straight up to remove it **(see illustration)**. If it's stuck, tap around its perimeter with a soft-faced hammer (but don't tap on the cooling fins or they may break). Don't attempt to pry between the cylinder and the crankcase, as you'll ruin the sealing surfaces.
5   Locate the dowel pins (they may have come off with the cylinder or still be in the crankcase) **(see illustration 8.3a or 11.4)**. On 220 models, the dowels are in the two right side bolt holes. On 300 models, the dowels are in their own holes, at front center and rear center. Be careful not to let the dowels drop into the engine. Stuff rags around the piston and remove the gasket and all traces of old gasket material from the surfaces of the cylinder and the crankcase.

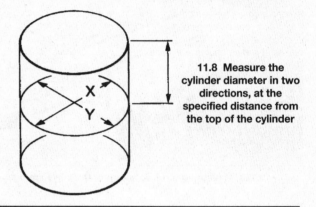

11.8 Measure the cylinder diameter in two directions, at the specified distance from the top of the cylinder

Inspection

Refer to illustration 11.8

6   Don't attempt to separate the liner from the cylinder.
7   Check the cylinder walls carefully for scratches and score marks.
8   Using the appropriate precision measuring tools, check the cylinder's diameter. Measure parallel to the crankshaft axis and across the crankshaft axis, at the depths from the top, center and bottom of the cylinder listed in this Chapter's Specifications **(see illustration)**. Compare the results to this Chapter's Specifications. If the cylinder walls are worn beyond the specified limits, or badly scuffed or scored, have the cylinder rebored and honed by a dealer service department or an ATV repair shop. This will also be necessary if the measurements at top, center and bottom vary more than the taper limit, or if the measurements across and parallel to the crankshaft axis differ more than the out-of-round limit. If a rebore is done, an oversize piston and rings will be required as well. **Note:** *Kawasaki supplies pistons in two oversizes.*
9   As an alternative, if the precision measuring tools are not available, a dealer service department or repair shop will make the measurements and offer advice concerning servicing of the cylinder.
10   If it's in reasonably good condition and not worn to the outside of the limits, and if the piston-to-cylinder clearance can be maintained properly, then the cylinder does not have to be rebored; honing is all that is necessary.
11   To perform the honing operation you will need the proper size flexible hone with fine stones as shown in Maintenance techniques, tools and working facilities at the front of this book, or a "bottle brush" type hone, plenty of light oil or honing oil, some shop towels and an electric drill motor. Hold the cylinder block in a vise (cushioned with soft jaws or wood blocks) when performing the honing operation. Mount the hone in the drill motor, compress the stones and slip the

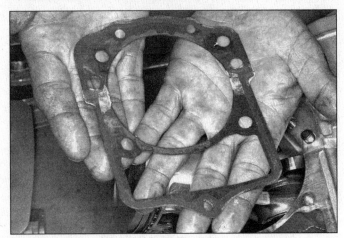

11.14 Install a new base gasket over the dowels

11.16 If you're experienced and very careful, the cylinder can be installed over the rings without a ring compressor, but a compressor is recommended

hone into the cylinder. Lubricate the cylinder thoroughly, turn on the drill and move the hone up and down in the cylinder at a pace which will produce a fine crosshatch pattern on the cylinder wall with the crosshatch lines intersecting at approximately a 60-degree angle. Be sure to use plenty of lubricant and do not take off any more material than is absolutely necessary to produce the desired effect. Do not withdraw the hone from the cylinder while it is running. Instead, shut off the drill and continue moving the hone up and down in the cylinder until it comes to a complete stop, then compress the stones and withdraw the hone. Wipe the oil out of the cylinder and repeat the procedure on the remaining cylinder. Remember, do not remove too much material from the cylinder wall. If you do not have the tools, or do not desire to perform the honing operation, a dealer service department or vehicle repair shop will generally do it for a reasonable fee.

12   Next, the cylinder must be thoroughly washed with warm soapy water to remove all traces of the abrasive grit produced during the honing operation. Be sure to run a brush through the bolt holes and flush them with running water. After rinsing, dry the cylinder thoroughly and apply a coat of light, rust-preventative oil to all machined surfaces.

Installation

Refer to illustrations 11.14 and 11.16

13   Lubricate the cylinder bore with plenty of clean engine oil. Apply a thin film of moly-based grease to the piston skirt.

14   Install the dowel pins, then lower a new cylinder base gasket over them **(see illustration 8.3a, 11.4 and the accompanying illustration)**.

15   Attach a piston ring compressor to the piston and compress the piston rings. A large hose clamp can be used instead - just make sure it doesn't scratch the piston, and don't tighten it too much.

16   Install the cylinder and carefully lower it down until the piston crown fits into the cylinder liner **(see illustration)**. While doing this, pull the camshaft chain up, using a hooked tool or a piece of stiff wire. Push down on the cylinder, making sure the piston doesn't get cocked sideways, until the bottom of the cylinder liner slides down past the piston rings. A wood or plastic hammer handle can be used to gently tap the cylinder down, but don't use too much force or the piston will be damaged.

17   Remove the piston ring compressor or hose clamp, being careful not to scratch the piston.

18   The remainder of installation is the reverse of the removal steps.

12   Piston - removal, inspection and installation

1   The piston is attached to the connecting rod with a piston pin that's a slip fit in the piston and rod.

2   Before removing the piston from the rod, stuff a clean shop towel into the crankcase hole, around the connecting rod. This will prevent the snap-rings from falling into the crankcase if they are inadvertently dropped.

Removal

Refer to illustrations 12.3a, 12.3b and 12.4

3   The piston should have an arrow or arrowhead mark on its crown that points toward the exhaust (front) side of the engine **(see illustration)**. If this mark is not visible due to carbon buildup, scribe an arrow into the piston crown before removal. Support the piston and pry the snap-ring out with a pointed tool **(see illustration)**.

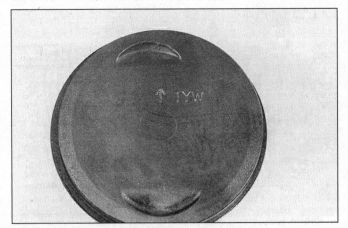

12.3a The arrow or arrowhead mark on top of the piston faces the exhaust (front) side of the engine

12.3b Wear eye protection and pry the snap-ring out of its groove with a pointed tool

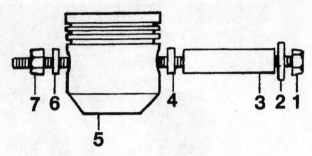

12.4 The piston pin should come out with hand pressure - if it doesn't, this removal tool can be fabricated from readily available parts

1	Bolt	7	Nut (B)
2	Washer	A	Large enough for piston
3	Pipe (A)		pin to fit inside
4	Padding (A)	B	Small enough to fit
5	Piston		through piston pin bore
6	Washer (B)		

4   Push the piston pin out from the opposite end to free the piston from the rod. You may have to deburr the area around the groove to enable the pin to slide out (use a triangular file for this procedure). If the pin won't come out, you can fabricate a piston pin removal tool from a long bolt, a nut, a piece of tubing and washers **(see illustration)**.

Inspection

Refer to illustrations 12.6, 12.11, 12.13, 12.14, 12.15 and 12.16

5   Before the inspection process can be carried out, the piston must be cleaned and the old piston rings removed.
6   Using a piston ring removal and installation tool, carefully remove the rings from the piston **(see illustration)**. Do not nick or gouge the piston in the process.
7   Scrape all traces of carbon from the top of the piston. A hand-held wire brush or a piece of fine emery cloth can be used once the majority of the deposits have been scraped away. Do not, under any circumstances, use a wire brush mounted in a drill motor to remove deposits from the piston; the piston material is soft and will be eroded away by the wire brush.
8   Use a piston ring groove cleaning tool to remove any carbon deposits from the ring grooves. If a tool is not available, a piece broken off the old ring will do the job. Be very careful to remove only the carbon deposits. Do not remove any metal and do not nick or gouge the sides of the ring grooves.
9   Once the deposits have been removed, clean the piston with solvent and dry them thoroughly. Make sure the oil return holes below the

12.6 Remove the piston rings with a ring removal and installation tool

oil ring grooves are clear.
10   If the piston is not damaged or worn excessively and if the cylinder is not rebored, a new piston will not be necessary. Normal piston wear appears as even, vertical wear on the thrust surfaces of the piston and slight looseness of the top ring in its groove. New piston rings, on the other hand, should always be used when an engine is rebuilt.
11   Carefully inspect each piston for cracks around the skirt, at the pin bosses and at the ring lands **(see illustration)**.
12   Look for scoring and scuffing on the thrust faces of the skirt, holes in the piston crown and burned areas at the edge of the crown. If the skirt is scored or scuffed, the engine may have been suffering from overheating and/or abnormal combustion, which caused excessively high operating temperatures. The oil pump should be checked thoroughly. A hole in the piston crown, an extreme to be sure, is an indication that abnormal combustion (pre-ignition) was occurring. Burned areas at the edge of the piston crown are usually evidence of spark knock (detonation). If any of the above problems exist, the causes must be corrected or the damage will occur again.
13   Measure the piston ring-to-groove clearance (side clearance) by laying a new piston ring in the ring groove and slipping a feeler gauge in beside it **(see illustration)**. Check the clearance at three or four locations around the groove. Be sure to use the correct ring for each groove; they are different. If the clearance is greater then specified, a new piston will have to be used when the engine is reassembled.
14   Check the piston-to-bore clearance by measuring the bore (see Section 11) and the piston diameter **(see illustration)**. Measure the piston across the skirt on the thrust faces at a 90-degree angle to the piston pin, at the specified distance up from the bottom of the skirt. Subtract the piston diameter from the bore diameter to obtain the

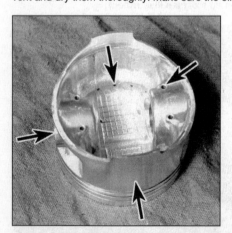

12.11 Check the piston pin bore and the piston skirt for wear, and make sure the internal holes are clear (arrows)

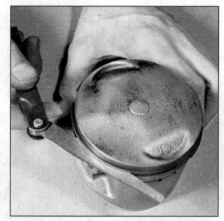

12.13 Measure the piston ring-to-groove clearance with a feeler gauge

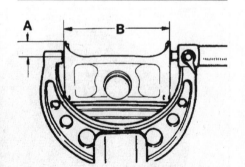

12.14 Measure the piston diameter with a micrometer

A   Specified distance from bottom of piston
B   Piston diameter

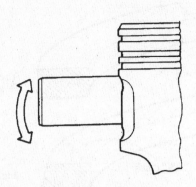

12.15 Slip the pin into the piston and try to wiggle it back-and-forth to check for looseness

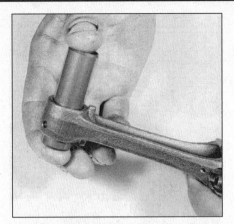

12.16 Slip the piston pin into the rod and try to rock it back-and-forth to check for looseness

12.18 Make sure both piston pin snap-rings are securely seated in the piston grooves

clearance. If it is greater than specified, the cylinder will have to be rebored and a new oversized piston and rings installed. If the appropriate precision measuring tools are not available, the piston-to-cylinder clearance can be obtained, though not quite as accurately, using feeler gauge stock. Feeler gauge stock comes in 12-inch lengths and various thicknesses and is generally available at auto parts stores. To check the clearance, slip a piece of feeler gauge stock of the same thickness as the specified piston clearance into the cylinder along with appropriate piston. The cylinder should be upside down and the piston must be positioned exactly as it normally would be. Place the feeler gauge between the piston and cylinder on one of the thrust faces (90-degrees to the piston pin bore). The piston should slip through the cylinder (with the feeler gauge in place) with moderate pressure. If it falls through, or slides through easily, the clearance is excessive and a new piston will be required. If the piston binds at the lower end of the cylinder and is loose toward the top, the cylinder is tapered, and if tight spots are encountered as the piston/feeler gauge is rotated in the cylinder, the cylinder is out-of-round. Be sure to have the cylinder and piston checked by a dealer service department or a repair shop to confirm your findings before purchasing new parts.

15   Apply clean engine oil to the pin, insert it into the piston and check for freeplay by rocking the pin back-and-forth **(see illustration)**. If the pin is loose, a new piston and possibly new pin must be installed.
16   Repeat Step 15, this time inserting the piston pin into the connecting rod **(see illustration)**. If the pin is loose, check the pin and the pin bore in the rod for visible wear. A worn pin can be replaced separately; if the rod bore is worn, the rod can be replaced, but this requires disassembly of the crankshaft. Check with a dealer service department or other qualified shop; it may be less expensive to buy a new crankshaft (which includes a connecting rod) than to have the

crankshaft rebuilt.
17   Refer to Section 13 and install the rings on the piston.

Installation

Refer to illustration 12.18
18   Install the piston with its arrow mark toward the exhaust side (front) of the engine. Lubricate the pin and the rod bore with moly-based grease. Install a new snap-rings in the groove in one side of the piston (don't reuse the old snap-rings). Push the pin into position from the opposite side and install another new snap-ring. Compress the snap-rings only enough for them to fit in the piston. Make sure the clips are properly seated in the grooves **(see illustration)**.

13   Piston rings - installation

Refer to illustrations 13.2, 13.4, 13.7a, 13.7b, 13.9a, 13.9b, 13.9c and 13.9d
1   Before installing the new piston rings, the ring end gaps must be checked.
2   Insert the top (No. 1) ring into the bottom of the first cylinder and square it up with the cylinder walls by pushing it in with the top of the piston. The ring should be about one-half inch above the bottom edge of the cylinder. To measure the end gap, slip a feeler gauge between the ends of the ring **(see illustration)** and compare the measurement to the Specifications.
3   If the gap is larger or smaller than specified, double check to make sure that you have the correct rings before proceeding.
4   If the gap is too small, it must be enlarged or the ring ends may come in contact with each other during engine operation, which can

2A

13.2 Check the piston ring end gap with a feeler gauge at the bottom of the cylinder

13.4 If the end gap is too small, clamp a file in a vise and file the ring ends (from the outside in only) to enlarge the gap slightly

13.7a Installing the oil ring expander - make sure the ends don't overlap

13.7b Installing an oil ring side rail - don't use a ring installation tool to do this

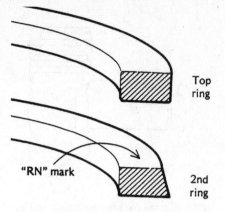

13.9a Compression ring identification – Bayou 220 models

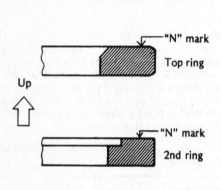

13.9b Compression ring identification – Bayou 300 2WD models

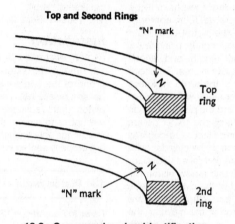

13.9c Compression ring identification – Bayou 300 4WD models

13.9d Install the middle ring with its identification mark up

cause serious damage. The end gap can be increased by filing the ring ends very carefully with a fine file **(see illustration)**. When performing this operation, file only from the outside in.

5   Repeat the procedure for the second compression ring (ring gap is not specified for the oil ring rails or spacer).

6   Once the ring end gaps have been checked/corrected, the rings can be installed on the piston.

7   The oil control ring (lowest on the piston) is installed first. It is composed of three separate components. Slip the spacer into the groove first, butting its ends together (don't overlap the ends). Then install the upper side rail **(see illustrations)**. Do not use a piston ring installation tool on the oil ring side rails as they may be damaged. Instead, place one end of the side rail into the groove between the spacer expander and the ring land. Hold it firmly in place and slide a finger around the piston while pushing the rail into the groove (taking care not to cut your fingers on the sharp edges). Next, install the lower side rail in the same manner.

8   After the three oil ring components have been installed, check to make sure that both the upper and lower side rails can be turned smoothly in the ring groove.

9   Install the no. 2 (middle) ring next with its identification mark facing up **(see illustrations)**. Do not mix the top and middle rings; they can be identified by their profiles.

10   To avoid breaking the ring, use a piston ring installation tool and make sure that the identification mark is facing up **(see illustration 13.9a, 13.9b, 13.9c or 13.9d)**. Fit the ring into the middle groove on the piston. Do not expand the ring any more than is necessary to slide it into place.

11   Finally, install the no. 1 (top) ring in the same manner. Make sure the identifying mark is facing up. Be very careful not to confuse the top and second rings.

12   Once the rings have been properly installed, stagger the end gaps, including those of the oil ring side rails, as follows:

a) Top compression ring: gap forward
b) Second compression ring: gap rearward
c) Oil ring expander: gap forward
d) Oil ring top rail: gap 30-degrees left of forward
e) Oil ring bottom rail: gap 30-degrees right of forward

14   External oil pipes - removal and installation

Removal

Oil pipes

Refer to illustrations 14.1a, 14.1b, 14.1c, 14.2a and 14.2b

1   On 220 models, remove the union bolts and sealing washers **(see illustration)**. On 300 models without an oil cooler, remove the union bolt and sealing washers from the pipe on the right side of the engine **(see illustration)**. On all 300 models, remove the union bolts and sealing washers from the pipe that crosses over the back of the engine **(see illustration)**. Note that the union bolts are different colors; don't mix them up, as the different color bolts have different size oil passages.

2   On 4WD models, remove the union bolt and washers from the pipe on the left side of the engine. The forward union bolt is on top of

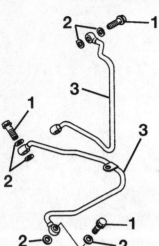

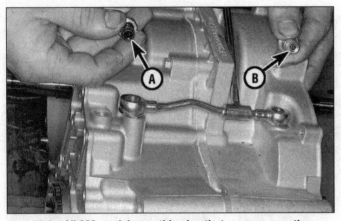

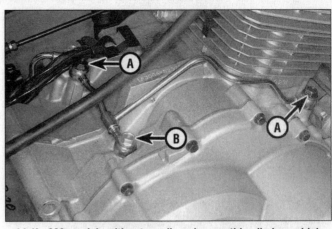

14.1a External oil line details (220 models)

1　Union bolts
2　Sealing washers
3　Oil pipes

14.1b 300 models without an oil cooler use this oil pipe, which runs to the right front of the engine

A　Dark colored union bolts　　B　Silver union bolt

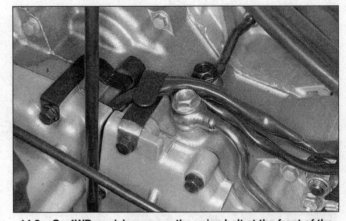

14.1c All 300 models use this pipe that crosses over the back of the engine

A　Dark colored union bolt　　B　Silver union bolt

14.2a On 4WD models, remove the union bolt at the front of the left oil pipe . . .

the engine **(see illustration)**. The rearward union bolt is at the back of the sub-transmission **(see illustration)**.

Oil cooler

Refer to illustration 14.3

3　Hold the fitting at one of the oil cooler hoses with a wrench and

loosen the nut with a second wrench **(see illustration)**. Unscrew the nut from the oil cooler.

4　Remove the oil cooler mounting nuts, lower the oil cooler so the top post clears its grommet and take the oil cooler out of the vehicle.

5　To remove the oil cooler hoses from the vehicle, remove the hose retainer. Detach the hoses from the engine in the same way they were disconnected from the oil cooler.

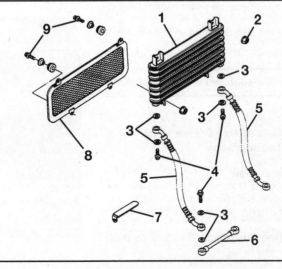

14.3 Oil cooler details (300 models)

1　Oil cooler
2　Mounting nuts
3　Sealing washers
4　Union bolts
5　Oil cooler hoses
6　Oil pipe
7　Retainer
8　Screen
9　Mounting bolts, collars and grommets

14.2b . . . and at the rear, at the sub-transmission

2A

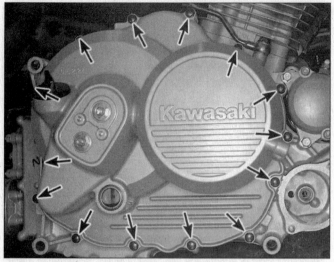

15.4 Here are the 300 right crankcase cover bolts (220 similar)

15.5 Here are the 300 cover dowels (A) (220 models similar); on 4WD models, note how the release lever points to the center of the secondary clutch (B)

15.6a Wedge the gears (right arrow); align the cutout (left arrow) with the gear before you pull the primary clutch off

15.6b Unscrew the locknut . . .

15.7a . . . align the gear with the secondary clutch cutout (arrow), pull the primary clutch off . . .

Installation

6   Installation is the reverse of the removal steps, with the following additions:

a) *Be sure to install the correct color (dark or silver) union bolts in the correct holes.*

b) *Replace the sealing washers whenever the union bolts or hose fittings are loosened.*

c) *Tighten the union bolts to the torques listed in this Chapter's Specifications.*

15   Primary clutch - removal, inspection and installation

Removal

Refer to illustrations 15.4, 15.5, 15.6a, 15.6b, 15.7a and 15.7b

1   Place the shift pedal in the Neutral position.

2   Drain the engine oil (see Chapter 1).

3   Remove the right footrest (see Chapter 7).

4   Unbolt the right crankcase cover from the engine **(see illustration)**. Pull the cover off. If the cover is stuck, tap it gently with a soft hammer to free it - don't pry it loose or the gasket surfaces will be damaged.

5   Locate the cover dowels **(see illustration)**. Set them aside for safekeeping.

6   Wedge a copper washer or penny between the gears of the primary clutch and the secondary clutch to prevent the primary clutch from turning **(see illustration)**, then unscrew the locknut **(see illustration)**.

7   Pull the primary clutch off the crankshaft and remove the washer **(see illustrations)**.

15.7b . . . and remove the washer

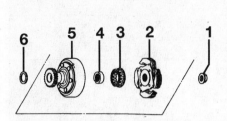

15.8 Primary clutch details

1	Locknut	4	Bushing
2	Weight	5	Drum
	assembly	6	Washer
3	One-way clutch		

15.10 Measure the thickness of the friction material (arrow)

15.13 Inspect the ball bearing and on 4WD models, take a look at the clutch release mechanism

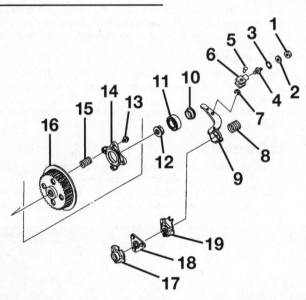

16.2 Release mechanism details (220 and 300 2WD models)

1	Locknut	11	Bearing
2	Washer	12	Secondary clutch locknut
3	O-ring	13	Spring retainer bolts
4	Adjusting screw	14	Spring retainer
5	Clevis pin	15	Pressure plate spring
6	Clevis	16	Secondary clutch
7	Circlip		pressure plate
8	Spring	17	Release cam
9	Release lever	18	Ball retainer
10	Push piece	19	Release cam

2A

Inspection

Refer to illustrations 15.8, 15.10 and 15.13

8   Take the weight assembly out of the drum **(see illustration)**. Turn the one-way clutch clockwise and take it out.

9   Check the one-way clutch rollers for signs of wear or scoring. The rotors should be unmarked with no signs of wear such as pitting or flat spots. Replace the one-way clutch if it's worn.

10   Measure the thickness of the lining material on the weights **(see illustration)**. If the depth from the lining material surface to the bottom of its grooves is less than the minimum listed in this Chapter's Specifications, replace the weights as a set.

11   Check the springs for breakage and the weights for wear or damage. Replace the weight assembly if problems are found.

12   Check the inside of the drum and replace it if it's worn or damaged. Measure the drum inside diameter and compare it with the value listed in this Chapter's Specifications. Replace the drum if it's worn beyond the limit.

13   Check the bearing inside the cover. If it's loose, rough or noisy when you turn it with a finger, replace it. If you're working on a 4WD model, give a quick visual inspection to the secondary clutch release mechanism as well **(see illustration)**.

Installation

14   Slip the washer onto the crankshaft **(see illustration 15.7b)**, then install the primary clutch **(see illustration 15.7a)**.

15   Install the nut. Wedge a copper penny or washer between the gears of the primary and secondary clutches to prevent the primary clutch from turning (similar to Step 6 above, but insert the washer or penny from below this time), then tighten the nut to the torque listed in this Chapter's Specifications.

16   Make sure the dowels are in position and install a new gasket **(see illustration 15.5)**.

17   Thread the cover bolts into their holes. Tighten the cover bolts in two or three stages, in a criss-cross pattern.

18   The remainder of installation is the reverse of the removal steps.

19   Refill the engine with oil (see Chapter 1).

16   Secondary clutch and release mechanism - removal, inspection and installation

Release mechanism

Removal

1   Remove the right crankcase cover (see Section 15).

2WD models

Refer to illustration 16.2

2   Remove the cover from the clutch adjusting screw, then remove the locknut and screw from the cover (see Chapter 1). Remove the washer and O-ring from the adjusting screw **(see illustration)**.

16.5a   On 4WD models, unscrew the locknut from the upper adjusting screw (arrow) . . .

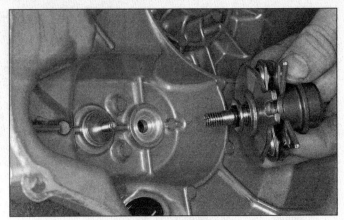

16.5b   . . . take the release mechanism out of the right crankcase cover . . .

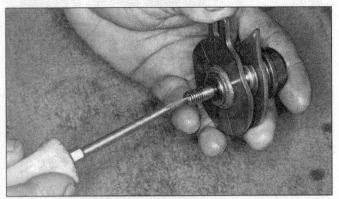

16.5c   . . . unscrew the adjusting screw from the release cam and remove its O-ring . . .

3   Pull the release lever and clevis out of the right crankcase cover, then remove the release lever spring from the cover.
4   Slide the release cam and ball assembly off of the shift shaft.

4WD models

Refer to illustrations 16.5a through 16.5g, 16.6a and 6.6b
5   Remove the release mechanism components from the cover **(see illustrations).**
6   Remove the washer and release lever from the shift shaft **(see illustrations).**

Inspection

7   Check for visible wear or damage at the contact points of the lever and the friction points of the cam and ball assembly. Check the spring for bending or distortion. Replace any parts that show problems. Replace the adjusting screw O-ring whenever it's removed.

16.5d   . . . remove the spring . . .

16.5e   . . . the push piece . . .

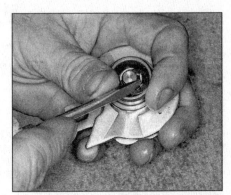

16.5f   . . . the circlip . . .

16.5g   . . . the release cam, ball retainer and second release cam

16.6a   Take the washer off the shift shaft . . .

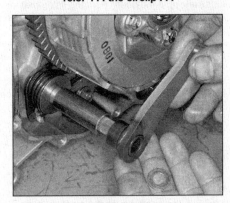

16.6b   . . . and slide the release lever off

16.9 Turn the lower adjusting screw so its pin (arrow) is as close as possible to the release mechanism hole in the cover . . .

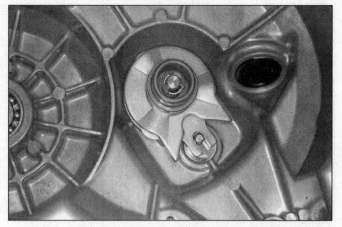

16.10 . . . then install the release mechanism with its fork over the pin

Installation

2WD models

8   Installation is the reverse of the removal steps. Fill the engine with oil and adjust the clutch (see Chapter 1).

4WD models

Refer to illustrations 16.9 and 16.10

9   Position the pin of the lower adjusting screw as far toward the upper adjusting screw hole as it will go **(see illustration),** then tighten the locknut on the lower adjusting screw.

10   Reverse the disassembly steps to reassemble the release mechanism. Thread the adjusting screw all the way in when you install it in the release cam. Install the mechanism in the cover with the adjusting fork over the lower adjusting screw pin **(see illustration).**

11   Lubricate the release lever splines with multi-purpose grease, then slide the lever onto the shift shaft so its upper end is centered on the spring retainer of the secondary clutch **(see illustration 15.5).** Slip the washer on after the release lever.

12   Install the right crankcase cover (Section 15).

13   Thread the locknut onto the upper adjusting screw, but don't tighten it yet.

14   Turn the upper adjusting screw clockwise until it becomes hard to turn, then mark this point with a pencil on the cover. Turn the screw counterclockwise, again until it becomes hard to turn, and mark this point with a pencil. Turn the screw halfway between the pencil marks, hold the screw with a screwdriver and tighten the locknut.

15   Refill the engine oil and adjust the lower clutch adjusting screw (see Chapter 1).

16.17a Remove the spring retainer bolts . . .

Secondary clutch

Removal

Refer to illustrations 16.17a through 16.17g

16   Remove the right crankcase cover and the primary clutch (see Section 15).

17   Refer to the accompanying illustrations to remove the clutch components **(see illustration 15.8a and the accompanying illustrations).** To prevent the clutch from turning while the nut is loosened,

2A

16.17b . . . take off the spring retainer and remove the springs . . .

16.17c . . . hold the clutch from turning and unscrew the locknut . . .

16.17d . . . remove the pressure plate and note how the friction plate tabs fit in the clutch housing notches (arrow) . . .

16.17e . . . remove the friction plates and metal plates . . .

16.17f . . . slide off the bushing and remove the clutch housing . . .

16.17g . . . and remove the thrust washer

temporarily reinstall the primary clutch on the end of the crankshaft. Wedge the gears on the primary clutch and secondary clutch from below **(see illustration 15.6a)**.

Inspection

Refer to illustrations 16.21, 16.22 and 16.23

18   Check the bolt posts and the friction surface on the pressure plate for damaged threads, scoring or wear. Replace the pressure plate if any defects are found.

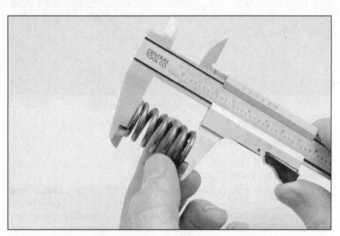

16.21 Measure the clutch spring free length

19   Check the edges of the slots in the clutch housing for indentations made by the friction plate tabs. If the indentations are deep they can prevent clutch release, so the housing should be replaced with a new one. If the indentations can be removed easily with a file, the life of the housing can be prolonged to an extent. Also, check the driven gear teeth for cracks, chips and excessive wear and the springs on the back side for breakage. If the gear is worn or damaged or the springs are broken, the clutch housing must be replaced with a new one. Check the bearing surface in the center of the clutch housing for score marks, scratches and excessive wear.

20   Check the splines of the clutch boss for indentations made by the tabs on the metal plates. Check the clutch boss friction surface for wear or scoring. Replace the clutch boss if problems are found.

21   Measure the free length of the clutch springs **(see illustration)** and compare the results to this Chapter's Specifications. If the springs have sagged, or if cracks are noted, replace them with new ones as a set.

22   If the lining material of the friction plates smells burnt or if it is glazed, new parts are required. If the metal clutch plates are scored or discolored, they must be replaced with new ones. Measure the thickness of the friction plates **(see illustration)** and replace with new parts any friction plates that are worn.

23   Lay the metal plates, one at a time, on a perfectly flat surface (such as a piece of plate glass) and check for warpage by trying to slip a feeler gauge between the flat surface and the plate **(see illustration)**. The feeler gauge should be the same thickness as the maximum warp listed in this Chapter's Specifications. Do this at several places around the plate's circumference. If the feeler gauge can be slipped under the plate, it is warped and should be replaced with a new one.

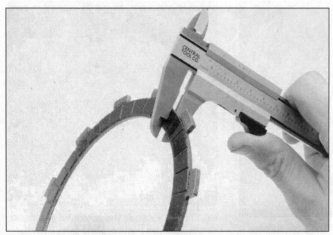

16.22 Measure the thickness of the friction plates

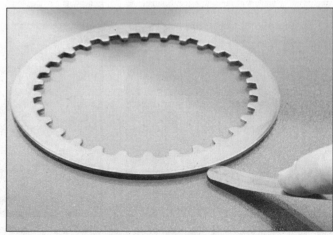

16.23 Check the metal plates for warpage

17.2a Loosen the upper locknut (arrow) and take the cable out of the bracket . . .

17.2b . . . then grip the cable with pliers and slip its end plug out of the lever

24 Check the tabs on the friction plates for excessive wear and mushroomed edges. They can be cleaned up with a file if the deformation is not severe. Check the friction plates for warpage as described in Step 13.

25 Check the clutch collar for score marks, heat discoloration and evidence of excessive wear.

26 Check the clutch spring plate for wear and damage. Rotate the inner race of the bearing and check for roughness, looseness or excessive noise.

Installation

27 Lubricate the inner and outer surfaces of the clutch collar with moly-based grease and install it on the crankshaft.

28 Install the clutch housing, thrust washer and bushing **(see illustrations 16.17g and 16.17f)**.

29 Coat the friction plates with engine oil, then install the friction plates and metal plates on the clutch boss. Be sure to install them in the correct order **(see illustrations 16.17e and 16.17d)**.

30 Install the pressure plate on the last friction plate **(see illustration 16.17d)**.

31 Install the clutch locknut on the mainshaft. Hold the clutch as described in Step 8 and tighten the locknut to the torque listed in this Chapter's Specifications.

32 Install the clutch springs and the spring plate **(see illustrations 16.17b and 16.17a)**. Tighten the bolts to the torque listed in this Chapter's Specifications in two or three stages, in a criss-cross pattern.

33 The remainder of installation is the reverse of the removal steps. Be sure to fill the engine with oil as described in Chapter 1.

---

17 Reverse shift mechanism and reverse-neutral switch - removal, inspection and installation

Removal

1 The reverse lockout lever and switch are accessible from outside the engine after removing the bevel drive unit (2WD) or sub-transmission (4WD). The crankcase must be disassembled for access to the transmission reverse gears and shift fork.

Cable and lever

Refer to illustrations 17.2a, 17.2b, 17.4 and 17.5

2 Detach the reverse cable from the bracket, then slip its end plug out of the lever **(see illustrations)**.

3 Remove the left crankcase cover (see Chapter 4).

4 If you're working on a 300 2WD model, note the position of the lever on the shaft **(see illustration)**. The lever should point straight down. The split in the lever that the pinch bolt passes through should

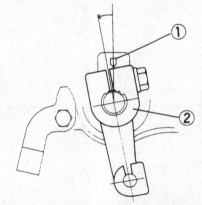

17.4 On 300 2WD models, align the mark (1) with the split (2), or move the lever one notch counterclockwise if necessary

be straight up, aligned with a protrusion on the left crankcase cover. Remove the lever pinch bolt and slide the lever off the shaft.

5 If you're working on a 220 or a 300 4WD model, mark the installed position of the lever on the crankcase cover with a felt pen or scribe **(see illustration)**. Unscrew the bolt, remove the washer and take the lever off the shaft.

6 To remove the cable from the vehicle, disconnect the upper end from the underside of the reverse knob **(see illustration 11.2 in Chapter 1)**.

7 Installation is the reverse of the removal steps. Adjust the cable (see Chapter 1).

17.5 On all 220 and 300 4WD models, mark the position of the lever on the crankcase

2A

17.10a The spring end fits in a hole in the crankcase (4WD shown)

17.10b Pull the lever out of the crankcase

17.12 Disengage the grommets (upper arrows) and remove the switch screws (lower arrows)

18.1 Mark the position of the shift pedal on the shaft and remove the pinch bolt (arrow)

18.3 Replace the shift pedal seal if it has been leaking

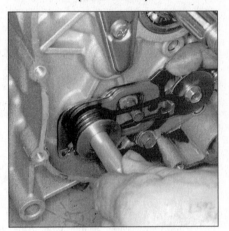

18.7a Lift the shift pawls clear of the drum . . .

Lockout lever and switch

Refer to illustrations 17.10a, 17.10b and 17.12

8   Remove the reverse lever as described above.

9   Remove the bevel drive unit (2WD) or sub-transmission (4WD) (see Chapter 5).

10   Unhook the lever spring from its hole in the crankcase, then pull the lever out **(see illustrations)**.

11   Check all parts for wear and damage and replace any that show problems.

12   Follow the wiring harness from the switch to the connectors and disconnect them. Detach the grommets from their notches in the crankcase **(see illustration)**. Remove the switch mounting screws and take the switch out.

---

18   External shift mechanism - removal, inspection and installation

Shift pedal

Removal

Refer to illustration 18.1

1   Look for alignment marks on the end of the shift pedal and shift shaft **(see illustration)**. If they aren't visible, make your own marks with a sharp punch. Remove the shift pedal pinch bolt and slide the pedal off the shaft.

Inspection

Refer to illustration 18.3

2   Check the shift pedal for wear or damage such as bending. Check the splines on the shift pedal and shaft for stripping or step wear. Replace the pedal or shaft if these problems are found.

3   Check the shift shaft seal for signs of leakage **(see illustration)**. If the seal has been leaking, pry it out of the cover, then tap in a new one with a seal driver or socket the same diameter as the seal.

Installation

4   Install the shift pedal. Line up its punch marks and tighten the pinch bolt.

External shift linkage

Removal

Refer to illustrations 18.7a, 18.7b, 18.8, 18.9, 18.10, 18.11 and 18.12

5   Remove the right crankcase cover (see Section 15).

6   If you plan to remove any components except the shift drum stopper arm, remove the primary and secondary clutches (Sections 15 and 16).

7   Lift the shift shaft pawls free of the shift drum segment, then pull the shift shaft out of the crankcase **(see illustrations)**.

8   Check the return spring pin for wear and damage **(see illustration)**. If it's worn, damaged or loose, unscrew it from the crankcase.

9   Remove the bolt and pin plate from the shift drum **(see illustration)**.

18.7b ... and pull the shift shaft out
of the engine

18.8 Remove the return spring pin (arrow)
if it's worn, damaged or loose

18.9 Unbolt the pin plate from the
shift drum

18.10 Remove the shift drum segment;
on installation, place the dowel in
the hole (arrows)

18.11 Unbolt the stopper arm and remove
it together with the spring

18.12 Remove the screws (arrows), take
off the bearing retainer and pull out the
shift drum bearing (300 4WD shown;
others similar)

10   Take the shift drum segment off the shift drum, making sure not to lose its dowel pin **(see illustration)**.

11   Unbolt the stopper arm, then remove the arm and its spring **(see illustration)**.

12   Remove the retainer plate from the shift drum bearing **(see illustration)**. Pull the bearing out, using a magnet if necessary.

Inspection

13   Check the shift shaft for bends and damage to the splines **(see illustration 18.7b)**. If the shaft is bent, you can attempt to straighten it, but if the splines are damaged it will have to be replaced. Check the condition of the return spring, shift arm and the pawl spring. Replace the shift shaft if they're worn, cracked or distorted.

14   Check the shift drum bearing for rough, loose or noisy movement and replace it if any of these problems are found.

15   Check the shift drum segment for wear on the friction surfaces and replace it if it's worn.

16   Check the roller on the stopper arm for wear and replace it if it's worn.

Installation

17   If you removed the return spring post, clean its threads, apply non-permanent thread locking agent and tighten the post to the torque listed in this Chapter's Specifications.

18   Position the spring on the stopper arm, then install the stopper arm on the engine and tighten its bolt to the torque listed in this Chap-

ter's Specifications.

19   Pull down the stopper arm and install the drum segment on the shift drum, making sure its dowel is located in the drum segment notch **(see illustration 18.10)**.

20   Install the pin plate on the shift drum segment and tighten its bolt to the torque listed in this Chapter's Specifications. Make sure the stopper arm spring is correctly installed and that the roller end of the stopper arm engages a notch in the drum segment.

21   Place the washer on the shift shaft and slide it into the engine **(see illustration 18.7b)**. Slide the shaft all the way in, making sure the return spring fits over the post and the pawls engage the drum segment pins **(see illustration 18.7a)**.

22   The remainder of installation is the reverse of the removal steps.

23   Check the engine oil level and add some, if necessary (see Chapter 1).

19   Oil screen and pump - removal, inspection and installation

Removal

Refer to illustrations 19.2, 19.3, 19.4, 19.5a and 19.5b

1   Remove the right crankcase cover and primary clutch (see Section 15).

2A

19.2 Pull the oil screen out of its bore in the crankcase (300 shown; 220 similar)

19.3 On 300 models, loosen the screws (arrows) with an impact driver and remove the cover

19.4 It's easier to loosen the single assembly screw (arrow) while the pump is on the engine

19.5a Turn the driven gear to expose the mounting screws

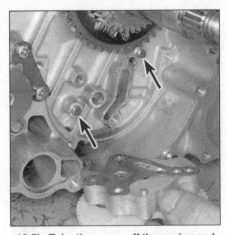

19.5b Take the pump off the engine and locate the dowels (arrows)

2   Pull the oil screen out of its bore in the crankcase (see illustration).

3   Loosen the oil pump cover screws with an impact driver and remove the cover (see illustration).

4   If you're planning to disassemble the pump, loosen the assembly screw now while the pump is secured to the engine (see illustration).

5   Rotate the oil pump driven gear for access to the mounting screws (see illustration). Remove the mounting screws and take the pump and gasket off (see illustration).

Inspection

Refer to illustration 19.6

6   Remove the assembly screw and take off the pump cover (see illustration).

7   Remove the pump rotors and drive pin from the pump body, then pull out the driven gear and shaft.

8   Wash all the components in solvent, then dry them off. Check the pump body, the rotors and the cover for scoring and wear. If any damage or uneven or excessive wear is evident, replace the pump. If you are rebuilding the engine, it's a good idea to install a new oil pump.

9   Check the pump driven gear for wear or damage.

10   Reassemble the pump by reversing the disassembly steps, with the following additions:

a) *Before installing the cover, pack the cavities between the rotors with petroleum jelly - this will ensure the pump develops suction quickly and begins oil circulation as soon as the engine is started.*

b) *Make sure the cover dowels and drive pin are in position (see illustration 19.6).*

Installation

11   Installation is the reverse of removal, with the following additions:

a) *Use a new O-ring on the oil screen if the old one is flattened or deteriorated*

b) *Install a new oil pump gasket (see illustration 19.5b).*

c) *Tighten the oil pump mounting and cover screws securely, but don't overtighten them and strip the threads.*

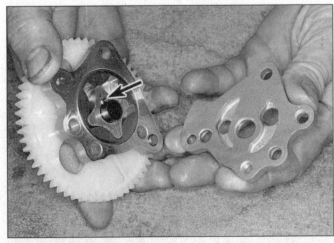

19.6 Remove the drive pin (arrow), rotors and shaft

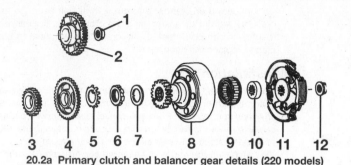

20.2a Primary clutch and balancer gear details (220 models)

1 Balancer driven gear
2 Driven gear locknut
3 Oil pump drive gear
4 Balancer drive gear
5 Lockwasher
6 Drive gear locknut
7 Thrust washer
8 Primary clutch housing
9 One-way clutch
10 Spacer
11 Primary clutch weight assembly
12 Primary clutch locknut

20.2b Align the marks on the drive and driven gears (300 shown; 220 similar)

20.3 Bend back the lockwasher tab

20.4 Wedge the gears from the right to loosen the drive gear nut, and from the left to loosen the driven gear nut

20.5 Remove the locknut, washer (300 models), lockwasher and oil pump drive gear (arrow)

2A

20 Balancer gears - removal, inspection and installation

Removal

Refer to illustrations 20.2a, 20.2b, 20.3, 20.4, 20.5, 20.6a and 20.6b

1   Remove the primary and secondary clutches (see Sections 15 and 16).

2   Turn the crankshaft so the match marks on the balancer drive and driven gears align (**see illustrations**).

3   Bend back the tab on the balancer gear lockwasher (**see illustration**).

4   Wedge the balancer drive and driven gears to prevent them from turning and loosen the locknuts (**see illustration**).

5   Unscrew the drive gear nut with the special tool (you can also use a hammer and punch) and remove the washer and lockwasher (**see illustration**).

6   Slide off the drive gear and remove its Woodruff key (**see illustrations**).

20.6a Be sure the Woodruff key (arrow) is in its groove on installation

20.6b The drive gear boss (arrow) faces the engine

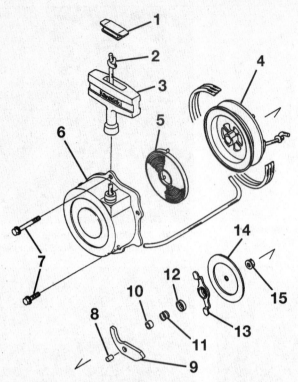

21.1a Recoil starter (220 models) – exploded view

1	Cap	6	Cover	11	Spring
2	Rope	7	Bolts	12	Cover
3	Handle	8	Pin	13	Recoil guide
4	Pulley	9	Pawl	14	Friction plate
5	Recoil spring	10	Recoil shaft	15	Nut

7   Unscrew the driven gear nut **(see illustration 20.4)**. Slide off the driven gear and remove its Woodruff key.

Inspection

8   Check the gears for worn or damaged teeth and replace them as a set if problems are found.
9   Check the springs for distortion or fatigue. Replace the drive gear as a unit if problems are found.
10   Check the remaining components for wear and damage and replace any worn or damaged parts. Replace the lockwasher with a new one whenever it's removed.

11   Inspect the balancer and crankshaft ball bearings to the extent possible without disassembling the crankcase. If wear, looseness or roughness can be detected, the crankcase will have to be disassembled to replace the bearings.

Installation

Note: *Kawasaki makes a special tool for tightening the balancer drive gear nut (part no. 57001-1214). You may be able to order the tool or an aftermarket equivalent from a Kawasaki dealer service department. You can also make the tool by grinding square notches in the end of a piece of pipe the same diameter as the nut (leaving teeth standing out to grip the notches in the nut) and welding a socket onto the other end of the pipe so you can attach a torque wrench.*
12   Installation is the reverse of the removal steps, with the following additions:
  a) *Make sure the alignment marks on the drive gear and driven gear are lined up (see illustration 20.2b).*
  b) *Use a new drive gear lockwasher and make sure its tab fits in the slot in the balancer shaft **(see illustration 20.3)**. Tighten the drive gear and driven gear nuts to the torque listed in this Chapter's Specifications.*

---

21   Recoil starter - removal, inspection and installation

Warning: *Rewinding the recoil spring can be potentially dangerous. If you don't have experience with recoil starters, read through the procedure before starting. Most repairs can be done without removing the recoil spring, but if it is necessary, consider taking the job to a Kawasaki dealer or other qualified shop. If you do the job yourself, wear eye protection and heavy gloves in case the recoil spring flies out.*

Removal

Refer to illustration 21.1a, 21.1b, 21.2, 21.3a, 21.3b, 21.4a, 21.4b, 21.5a, 21.5b, 21.6a, 21.6b and 21.7
1   Unbolt the recoil starter case from the left side of the engine **(see illustrations)**. Take the recoil starter off.
2   Pull the rope partway out and tie a knot or squeeze it with locking pliers so it won't be pulled into the case **(see illustration)**.
3   Pry the cap out of the rope handle, then pull out the knot and untie it **(see illustrations)**.
4   Hold the reel so it can't turn and pull the rope back through the cover hole, then place the rope in the removal notch **(see illustrations)**. **Note:** *Don't let the rope wedge between the reel and cover.* Hold the end of the rope with one hand and slowly release the reel, letting it unwind to relieve the spring tension. Keep the rope positioned in the removal notch while the reel unwinds. You'll need to move the rope in a circle around the edge of the cover.

21.1b Remove the cover bolts (arrows) and take the recoil starter off the engine

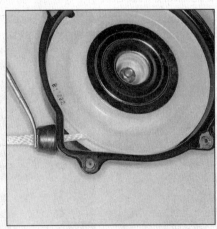

21.2 Pull the rope out partway and clamp it

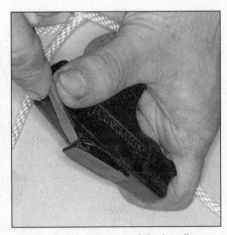

21.3a Pry the cap out of the handle . . .

21.3b . . . then pull the knot out of the handle and untie it

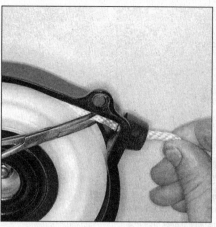

21.4a While holding the reel so it can't turn, pull the rope back through the cover hole . . .

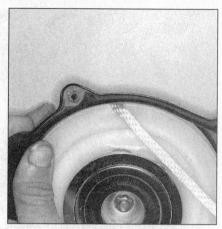

21.4b . . . position the rope in the notch, then "walk" it around the cover until the recoil spring unwinds

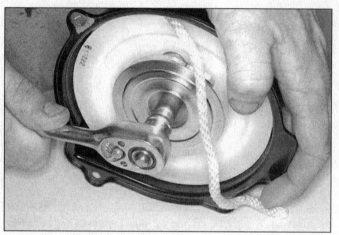

21.5a Unscrew the reel nut and lift out the reel . . .

21.5b . . . note the positions of the clip (A), friction surface (B), pawl (C) and inner knot (D) (300 models)

5   Once the reel has unwound, let go of the rope.
a) If you're working on a 220 model, remove the ratchet cover nut (see illustration 21.1a). Lift out the ratchet cover with the recoil guide and collar, then remove the ratchet cover spring, pawl and pin.
b) If you're working on a 300 model, unscrew the friction plate nut (see illustration). Turn the reel 1/4-turn counterclockwise from the point where it stopped by itself, then lift out the friction plate and clip (see illustration).

6   If you're working on a 300 model, note how the pawl spring fits into the notch in the pawl, then disengage the pawl spring and lift the pawl out (see illustration). Note how the other end of the pawl spring fits in the reel, then remove the pawl spring (see illustration).

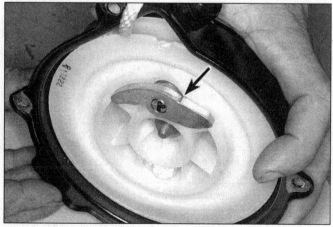

21.6a Note how the spring hooks into the notch, then remove the pawl . . .

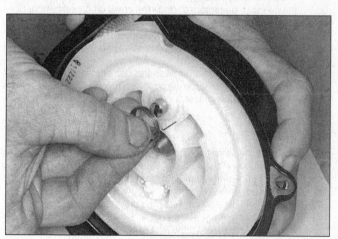

21.6b . . . note how the other end of the spring fits into the hole in the reel, then remove it from the pivot post

2A

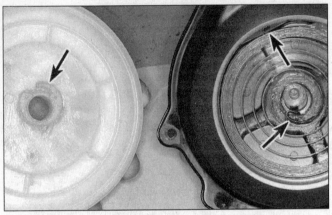

21.7 Lift off the reel; the reel's hook engages the inner spring hook, while the outer spring hook engages the tab in the cover (arrows)

21.10a Remove the pulley bolt . . .

21.10b . . . note the location of the Woodruff key and be sure to reinstall it . . .

21.10c . . . pry the pulley off the crankshaft . . .

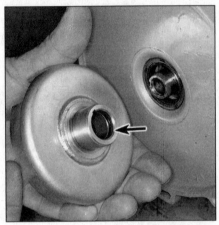

21.10d . . . then pry the O-ring out of its groove and install a new one

7   Lift the reel out of the cover **(see illustration)**. **Warning:** *Don't remove the recoil spring unless necessary.*

Inspection

Refer to illustrations 21.10a, 21.10b, 21.10c and 21.10d

8   Check for obvious wear or damage, such as a broken rope. Replace worn or damaged parts.

9   Inspect the recoil spring. If it's in good condition, leave it in the cover. If it needs to be replaced, place the cover on a workbench, open side down. Tap on the bench around the cover (DO NOT tap on the cover itself) to shake the spring loose. Let the spring fall out and unwind, then lift the cover off the bench and remove the spring the rest of the way.

10   Check the starter pulley for wear and damage **(see illustration)**. If problems can be seen, remove the pulley bolt and pry the pulley off the engine **(see illustrations)**. Use a new O-ring on installation **(see illustration)**.

Installation

11   If the spring was removed, hook its outer hook into the tab in the outer circumference of the cover **(see illustration 21.7)**. Coil the spring clockwise to tighten it, installing it from outside to inside. Once the spring is installed, grease it lightly.

12   Place the reel on a bench with the spring post upward. If the rope was removed completely, tie a knot in its inner end. Pull the rope through the hole in the reel so the knot ends up in the cavity in the center of the reel **(see illustration 21.5b)**.

13   Turn the reel counterclockwise to wind the rope onto it in a clock-

wise direction (this prevents the rope from twisting, which would happen if you wound the rope around the reel instead of turning the reel). Turn the reel until the rope winds four turns around the small diameter of the reel and one-half turn around the large diameter.

14   Place the reel over the spring, making sure the hook molded on the inside of the reel engages the hook in the center of the spring **(see illustration 21.7)**.

15   Grease the pawl spring and pawl, then install them on the reel **(see illustrations 21.6b and 21.6a)**.

16   Grease the friction surface of the friction plate, then install the friction plate and clip on the reel **(see illustration 21.5b)**. Be sure the ends of the clip don't jam on the pawl. Install the reel nut and tighten it to the torque listed in this Chapter's Specifications.

17   Turn the reel four turns clockwise to preload the spring, then pull the rope through the hole and clamp it so it won't pull back in. There should be about 14 inches (350 mm) of rope protruding from the hole.

18   Slip the starter handle into the rope and tie a knot in its end, then install the cap.

19   Unclamp the rope and let it back into the case.

20   Install the recoil starter on the engine, engaging it with the rotor. Install the case bolts and tighten them securely, but don't overtighten them and strip the threads.

22 Crankcase - disassembly and reassembly

1   To examine and repair or replace the crankshaft, connecting rod, bearings and transmission components, the crankcase must be split into two parts.

22.14 Loosen the case bolts (arrows) evenly, then remove them all (300 4WD shown; others similar)

22.15a Pry only between the pry points; there's one at each end of the case

Disassembly

Refer to illustrations 22.14, 22.15a and 22.15b

2   Remove the engine from the vehicle (see Section 5).

3   Remove the recoil starter (Section 21).

4   Remove the alternator rotor and the starter motor (see Chapter 4).

5   Remove the bevel drive unit (2WD models) or sub-transmission (4WD models). Remove the output shaft bevel gear and bearing housing from the left side of the crankcase (see Chapter 5).

6   Remove the external oil pipes (Section 14)

7   Remove the primary and secondary clutches (see Sections 15 and 16).

8   Remove the reverse lockout lever and switch (Section 17).

9   Remove the external shift mechanism (see Section 18).

10   Remove the oil pump (see Section 19).

11   Remove the balancer gears (Section 20).

12   Remove the cam chain tensioner, cylinder head, cam chain, cylinder and piston (see Sections 7, 8, 11 and 12).

13   Check carefully to make sure there aren't any remaining components that attach the upper and lower halves of the crankcase together.

14   Loosen the crankcase bolts in two or three stages, in a criss-cross pattern **(see illustration)**. Remove the bolts and label them; they are different lengths.

15   Tap gently on the ends of the transmission shafts, balancer shaft and crankshaft as the case halves are being separated. Carefully pry the crankcase apart at the pry points and lift the left half off the right half **(see illustrations)**. Don't pry against the mating surfaces or they'll develop leaks.

16   Locate the crankcase dowels **(see illustration 22.15b)**. If they aren't secure in their holes, remove them and set them aside for safekeeping.

17   Refer to Sections 23 through 25 for information on the internal components of the crankcase.

Reassembly

18   Remove all traces of old gasket and sealant from the crankcase mating surfaces with a sharpening stone or similar tool. Be careful not to let any fall into the case as this is done and be careful not to damage the mating surfaces.

18   Check to make sure the dowel pins are in place in their holes in the mating surface of the crankcase **(see illustration 22.14b)**.

19   Coat both crankcase mating surfaces with silicone sealant.

20   Pour some engine oil over the transmission gears, balancer shaft and crankshaft bearing surfaces and the shift drum. Don't get any oil on the crankcase mating surfaces.

21   Carefully place the left crankcase half onto the right crankcase

22.15b Lift the left case half off the right case half and locate the dowels (arrows)

half. While doing this, make sure the transmission shafts, shift drum, crankshaft and balancer fit into their ball bearings in the left crankcase half.

22   Install the crankcase half bolts in the correct holes and tighten them so they are just snug. Then tighten them in two or three stages, in a criss-cross pattern, to the torque listed in this Chapter's Specifications.

23   Turn the transmission shafts to make sure they turn freely. Also make sure the crankshaft and balancer shaft turn freely.

24   The remainder of installation is the reverse of removal.

23   Crankcase components - inspection and servicing

Refer to illustrations 23.3a, 23.3b, 23.3c and 23.3d

1   Separate the crankcase and remove the following:

a) *Transmission shafts and gears*

b) *Balancer shaft*

c) *Crankshaft and main bearings*

d) *Shift drum and forks*

2   Clean the crankcase halves thoroughly with new solvent and dry them with compressed air. All oil passages should be blown out with compressed air and all traces of old gasket sealant should be removed from the mating surfaces. **Caution:** *Be very careful not to nick or gouge the crankcase mating surfaces or leaks will result. Check both crankcase sections very carefully for cracks and other damage.*

2A

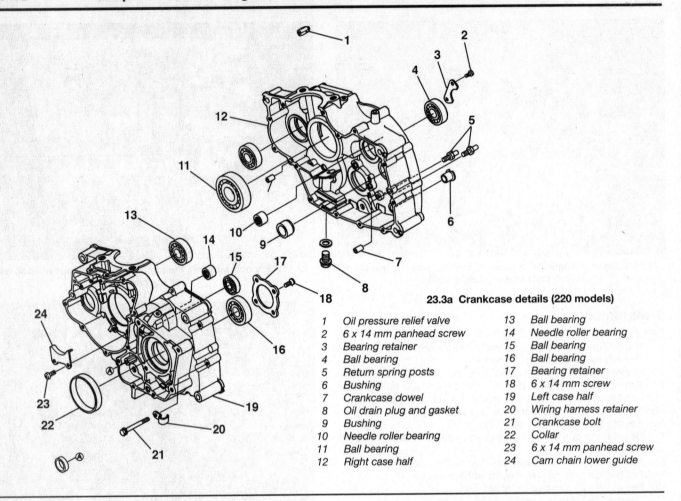

23.3a Crankcase details (220 models)

1	Oil pressure relief valve	13	Ball bearing
2	6 x 14 mm panhead screw	14	Needle roller bearing
3	Bearing retainer	15	Ball bearing
4	Ball bearing	16	Ball bearing
5	Return spring posts	17	Bearing retainer
6	Bushing	18	6 x 14 mm screw
7	Crankcase dowel	19	Left case half
8	Oil drain plug and gasket	20	Wiring harness retainer
9	Bushing	21	Crankcase bolt
10	Needle roller bearing	22	Collar
11	Ball bearing	23	6 x 14 mm panhead screw
12	Right case half	24	Cam chain lower guide

3   Check the bearings in the case halves **(see illustrations)**. If they don't turn smoothly, replace them. You'll need to remove the retainers **(see illustration)**. For bearings that aren't accessible from the outside, a blind hole puller will be needed for removal. Drive the remaining bearings out with a bearing driver or a socket having an outside diameter slightly smaller than that of the bearing outer race. Before installing the bearings, allow them to sit in the freezer overnight, and about fifteen-minutes before installation, place the case half in an oven, set to about 200-degrees F, and allow it to heat up. The bearings are an interference fit, and this will ease installation. **Warning:** *Before heating the case, wash it thoroughly with soap and water so no explosive fumes are present. Also, don't use a flame to heat the case. Install the bearings with a socket or bearing driver that bears against the bearing outer race.*

4   If any damage is found that can't be repaired, replace the crankcase halves as a set.

5   Assemble the case halves (see Section 22) and check to make sure the crankshaft and the transmission shafts turn freely.

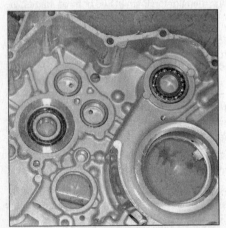

23.3b Inspect the bearings in the left case half . . .

23.3c . . . and those in the right case half . . .

23.3d . . . in some cases you'll need to remove retainers to remove the bearings

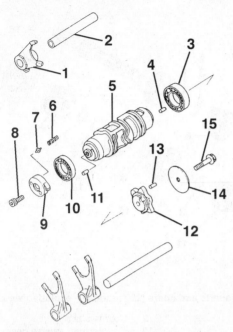

24.4b 4WD models use a single shift fork guide bar

24.4a Shift drum and forks (2WD models)

1	Shift fork	9	Neutral switch holder
2	Short guide bar	10	Bearing
3	Shift drum bearing	11	Pin
4	Pin	12	Shift drum segment
5	Shift drum	13	Pin
6	Spring	14	Pin plate
7	Pin	15	Bolt
8	Bolt		

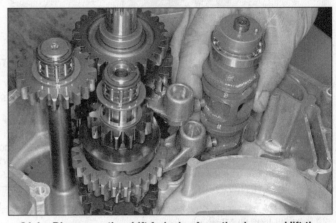

24.4c Disengage the shift fork pins from the drum and lift the shift drum out

24 Transmission shafts, balancer shaft and shift drum - removal, inspection and installation

Note: *When disassembling the transmission shafts, place the parts on a long rod or thread a wire through them to keep them in order and facing the proper direction.*

Removal

Refer to illustrations 24.4a, 24.4b, 24.4c, 24.5a, 24.5b, 24.5c, 24.5d and 24.6

1   Remove the engine, then separate the case halves (see Sections 5 and 22).

2   The transmission components and shift drum remain in the right case half when the case is separated.

3   Pull the balancer out of its bearing in the top of the right case half **(see illustration 22.15b)**.

4   Pull out the two shift fork guide bars (2WD) or single guide bar (4WD) **(see illustrations)**. Lift the shift drum out, disengaging the shift fork pins from the grooves in the drum **(see illustration)**.

5   Remove the shift forks from their gears. As you do this, note the numbers on the forks **(see illustrations)**. These will tell you where to reinstall the forks, and which side to place upward. Assemble the forks onto the shaft(s) to remind you how they go **(see illustration)**.

24.5a Lift out the shift forks, noting their numbers; this one's numbered 74 . . .

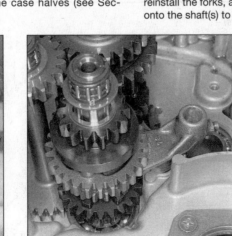

24.5b . . . the center fork is numbered 73 . . .

24.5c . . . and the lower fork is numbered 72

2A

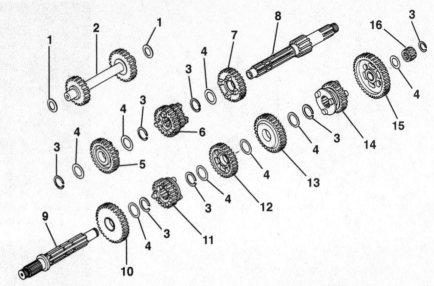

24.5d Assemble the forks onto the guide
bar (both guide bars on 2WD models) so
you'll remember how they go

24.6 Lift the transmission shafts
out together

24.13a Transmission shafts and gears (220 models) – exploded view

1	Thrust washer	9	Countershaft
2	Reverse idler gears	10	Countershaft reverse gear
3	Snap-ring	11	Countershaft fifth gear
4	Thrust washer	12	Countershaft third gear
5	Mainshaft fifth gear	13	Countershaft second gear
6	Mainshaft second-third gear	14	Countershaft fourth gear
7	Mainshaft fourth gear	15	Countershaft first gear
8	Mainshaft		

6   Grasp the mainshaft, countershaft and reverse shaft and lift them
out together **(see illustration)**.

Inspection

Refer to illustration 24.13a, 24.13b and 24.13c

7   Wash all of the components in clean solvent and dry them off.
8   Inspect the shift fork grooves in the gears. If a groove is worn or
scored, replace the gear and inspect its corresponding shift fork.
9   Check the shift forks for distortion and wear, especially at the fork
ears **(see illustration 24.5d)**. If they are discolored or severely worn
they are probably bent. Inspect the guide pins for excessive wear and
distortion and replace any defective parts with new ones.
10   Check the shift fork guide bars evidence of wear, galling and

other damage. Make sure the shift forks move smoothly on the guide
bars. If the shafts are worn or bent, replace them with new ones.
11   Check the edges of the grooves in the shift drums for signs of
excessive wear.
12   Hold the inner race of the shift drum bearing with fingers and spin
the outer race. Replace the bearing if it's rough, loose or noisy. Replace
the shift drum segment if it's worn or damaged (see Section 18).
13   Disassemble the transmission shafts so you can inspect their
components. Remove the snap-rings with snap-ring pliers and slide
the gears, thrust washers and snap-rings off the shafts **(see illustrations)**. As you remove each part, place them in order on a piece of
dowel or a straightened coat hanger to keep them in order. Check the
gear teeth for cracking and other obvious damage. Check the bushing

24.13b Mainshaft and countershaft (300 models) –
exploded view

1	Snap-ring	17	Countershaft first gear
2	Bearing	18	Countershaft fourth gear
3	Thrust washer		
4	Snap-ring	19	Snap-ring
5	Thrust washer	20	Thrust washer
6	Mainshaft second gear	21	Countershaft third gear
7	Thrust washer	22	Thrust washer
8	Snap-ring	23	Countershaft fifth gear
9	Mainshaft third-fifth gear	24	Thrust washer
10	Snap-ring	25	Snap-ring
11	Thrust washer	26	Countershaft second gear
12	Mainshaft fourth gear	27	Snap-ring
13	Mainshaft	28	Thrust washer
14	Snap-ring	29	Countershaft reverse gear
15	Bearing	30	Countershaft
16	Thrust washer		

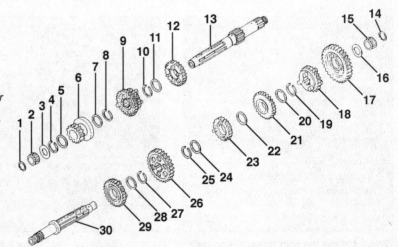

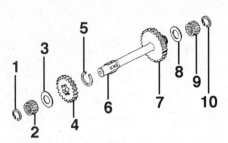

24.13c Reverse gear and shaft details

1	Snap-ring	6	Reverse gear shaft
2	Bearing	7	Reverse gear (fixed)
3	Thrust washer	8	Thrust washer
4	Reverse gear (removable)	9	Bearing
5	Snap-ring	10	Snap-ring

24.16a The mainshaft and countershaft mesh like this when they're installed in the crankcase (300 shown; 220 similar)

24.16b The reverse shaft meshes like this

24.16c With the shift drum on your right as you face the crankcase, the square hole (arrow) should be toward you

24.16d With the shift drum on your left as you face the crankcase, the round hole (arrow) should be toward you

surface in the inner diameter of the freewheeling gears for scoring or heat discoloration. Replace damaged parts.

14 Inspect the engagement dogs and dog holes on gears so equipped for excessive wear or rounding off. Replace the paired gears as a set if necessary.

15 Check the transmission shaft bearings in the crankcase for wear or heat discoloration and replace them if necessary (see Section 23).

Installation

Refer to illustration 24.16a, 24.16b, 24.16c and 24.16d

16 Installation is the basically the reverse of the removal procedure, but take note of the following points:

a) *Lubricate the components with engine oil before assembling them.*

b) *Always replace snap-rings with new ones whenever they're removed. When installing a snap-ring on a splined portion of one of the shafts, make sure the snap-ring gap is centered on one of the spline grooves.*

c) *After installation, check the gears and shift drum to make sure they're installed correctly (see illustrations). Rotate the shift drum through the gear positions and rotate the gears to make sure they mesh and shift correctly.*

---

25 Crankshaft and connecting rod - removal, inspection and installation

Note: *The procedures in this section require special tools. If you don't have the necessary equipment or suitable substitutes, have the crankshaft removed and installed by a Kawasaki dealer or other qualified shop.*

Removal

1 Remove the engine and separate the crankcase halves (Sections 5, 22 and 23). The transmission shafts need not be removed.

2 Generally, the crankshaft should stay in the right half of the case when the left half is lifted off **(see illustration 22.15b)**.

3 The crankshaft may be loose enough in its bearing that you can lift it out of the right crankcase half. If not, have it pressed out by a dealer service department or machine shop.

Inspection

Refer to illustrations 25.4, 25.5, 25.6 and 25.7

4 Measure the side clearance between connecting rod and crankshaft with a feeler gauge **(see illustration)**. If it's more than the

25.4 Measure the gap between the connecting rod and crankshaft with a feeler gauge

2A

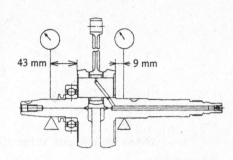

25.5 Pull up-and-down on the connecting rod and measure its big end play with a dial indicator

25.6 Check the cam chain sprocket and the ball bearing on the end of the crankshaft

43 mm   9 mm

25.7 Measure runout with a dial indicator at the specified distances from the counterweights

limit listed in this Chapter's Specifications, replace the crankshaft and connecting rod as an assembly.

5   Set up the crankshaft in V-blocks with a dial indicator contacting the big end of the connecting rod **(see illustration)**. Move the connecting rod up-and-down against the indicator pointer and compare the reading to the value listed in this Chapter's Specifications. If it's beyond the limit, the crankshaft can be disassembled and the crankpin and connecting rod big end bearing replaced. However, this is a specialized job that should be done by a Kawasaki dealer or other qualified shop.

6   Check the crankshaft splines, the cam chain sprocket, the ball bearing at the sprocket end of the crankshaft and the bearing journals for visible wear or damage **(see illustration)**. Kawasaki lists the ball bearing end of the crankshaft as a separately available part, but check with your dealer first; it may be more practical to replace the entire crankshaft if the ball bearing or cam sprocket is worn or damaged. Replace the crankshaft if any of the other conditions are found.

7   Set the crankshaft in a lathe or a pair of V-blocks, with a dial indicator contacting each end at the specified distance from the counterweights **(see illustration)**. Rotate the crankshaft and note the runout. If the runout at either end is beyond the limit listed in this Chapter's Specifications, replace the crankshaft and connecting rod as an assembly.

Installation

Refer to illustration 25.8

8   Start the crankshaft into the right case half. If you finish the installation with a press, support the crankshaft with Kawasaki tool 57001-1174, inserted between the counterweight opposite the crankpin **(see illustration)**. Otherwise the force of the press might collapse the crankshaft. Also use this tool if you press the crankshaft into the left case half.

9   The remainder of installation is the reverse of the removal steps.

26 Initial start-up after overhaul

1   Make sure the engine oil level is correct, then remove the spark plug from the engine. Place the engine kill switch in the Off position and unplug the primary (low tension) wires from the coil.

2   Turn on the key switch and crank the engine over with the starter several times to build up oil pressure. Reinstall the spark plug, connect the wires and turn the switch to On.

3   Make sure there is fuel in the tank, then operate the choke.

4   Start the engine and allow it to run at a moderately fast idle until it reaches operating temperature.

5   Check carefully for oil leaks and make sure the transmission and controls, especially the brakes, function properly before road testing the machine. Refer to Section 27 for the recommended break-in procedure.

6   Upon completion of the road test, and after the engine has cooled down completely, recheck the valve clearances (see Chapter 1).

27 Recommended break-in procedure

1   Any rebuilt engine needs time to break-in, even if parts have been installed in their original locations. For this reason, treat the machine gently for the first few miles to make sure oil has circulated throughout the engine and any new parts installed have started to seat. For new vehicles, Kawasaki recommends using no more than one-half throttle for the first ten hours of operation. This is a good general guide for rebuilt engines as well.

2   Even greater care is necessary if the cylinder has been rebored or a new crankshaft has been installed. In the case of a rebore, the engine will have to be broken in as if the machine were new. This means greater use of the transmission and a restraining hand on the throttle for the first few operating days. There's no point in keeping to any set speed limit - the main idea is to vary the engine speed, keep from lugging the engine and to avoid full-throttle operation. These recommendations can be lessened to an extent when only a new crankshaft is installed. Experience is the best guide, since it's easy to tell when an engine is running freely.

3   If a lubrication failure is suspected, stop the engine immediately and try to find the cause. If an engine is run without oil, even for a short period of time, irreparable damage will occur.

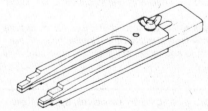

25.8 Slip a support tool between the counterweights to keep the crankshaft from collapsing as it's pressed in

Chapter 2 Part B
Engine, clutch and transmission (Prairie models)

Contents

	Section
Automatic transmission drive belt - width and play check	17
Automatic transmission - general information	13
Automatic transmission air ducts - removal and installation	14
Automatic transmission pulleys - disassembly, inspection and reassembly	19
Automatic transmission pulleys, inner cover and seal - removal and installation	18
Automatic transmission drive belt - removal, inspection and installation	16
Automatic transmission outer cover and seal - removal, inspection and installation	15
Cam chain tensioner - removal and installation	7
Crankcase - disassembly and reassembly	24
Crankcase components - inspection and servicing	25
Crankshaft, connecting rod and balancer - removal, inspection and installation	27
Cylinder head and valves - disassembly, inspection and reassembly	10
Cylinder head, decompression lever, camshaft and rocker arms - removal, inspection and installation	8

	Section
Cylinder, piston and rings - removal, inspection and installation	11
Engine - removal and installation	5
Engine disassembly and reassembly - general information	6
External oil pipe and oil cooler- removal and installation	12
General information	1
High-low and reverse gears, shafts and shift mechanism - removal, inspection and installation	26
High-low and reverse shift mechanism - removal, inspection and installation	21
Initial start-up after overhaul	28
Major engine repair - general note	4
Oil pump - removal, inspection and installation	22
Operations possible with the engine in the frame	2
Operations requiring engine removal	3
Recoil starter - removal, inspection and installation	23
Recommended break-in procedure	29
Shift lever - adjustment	20
Valves/valve seats/valve guides - servicing	9

2B

Specifications

General

Bore	76 mm (2.994 inches)
Stroke	64 mm (2.519 inches)
Displacement	290 cc

Rocker arms

Rocker arm inside diameter
Standard	13.000 to 13.018 mm (0.512 to 0.513 inch)
Limit	13.05 mm (0.514 inch)

Rocker shaft outside diameter
Standard	12.976 to 12.994 mm (0.511 to 0.512 inch)
Limit	12.95 mm (0.510 inch)

Camshaft

Lobe height
Intake
Standard	40.961 to 41.069 mm (1.613 to 1.617 inches)
Limit	40.86 mm (1.609 inches)

Exhaust
Standard	40.671 to 40.779 mm (1.601 to 1.605 inches)
Limit	40.57 mm (1.597 inches)

Cylinder head, valves and valve springs

Cylinder head warpage limit	0.05 mm (0.002 inch)
Valve stem runout	
Standard	0.02 mm (0.0008 inch)
Limit	0.05 mm (0.002 inch)
Valve stem diameter	
Intake	
Standard	6.965 to 6.980 mm (0.274 to 0.275 inch)
Limit	6.95 mm (0.274 inch)
Exhaust	
Standard	6.950 to 6.970 mm (0.273 to 0.274 inch)
Limit	6.94 mm (0.273 inch)
Valve guide inside diameter	
Standard	7.000 to 7.015 mm (0.275 to 0.276 inch)
Limit	7.08 mm (0.278 inch)
Valve seat width	0.5 to 1.0 mm (0.019 to 0.039 inch)
Valve head edge thickness	
Intake	
Standard	0.8 to 1.2 mm (0.031 to 0.047 inch)
Limit	0.5 mm (0.019 inch)
Exhaust	
Standard	0.8 to 1.2 mm (0.031 to 0.047 inch)
Limit	0.7 mm (0.027 inch)
Valve spring free length	
Inner spring	
Standard	32.4 mm (1.276 inch)
Limit	31.1 mm (1.224 inch)
Outer spring	
Standard	37.3 mm (1.469 inch)
Limit	35.8 mm (1.409 inch)
Valve spring bend limit	0.1 mm (0.004 inch)

Cylinder

Bore diameter	
Standard	76.000 to 76.012 mm (2.992 to 2.993 inches)
Limit	76.10 mm (2.996 inches)
Out-of-round and taper limits	0.05 mm (0.002 inch)
Measuring points	
Upper	10 mm (0.394 inch) from top of bore
Center	40 mm (1.57 inches) from top of bore
Lower	20 mm (0.787 inch) from bottom of bore

Piston and rings

Diameter	
Standard	75.960 to 75.975 mm (2.990 to 2.991 inch)
Limit	75.81 mm (2.984 inch)
Measuring point	5 mm (0.197 inch) from bottom of skirt
Piston-to-cylinder clearance	0.025 to 0.052 mm (0.001 to 0.002 inch)
Oversize pistons and rings	
First oversize	0.5 mm (0.002 inch)
Second oversize	1.0 mm (0.004 inches)
Ring side clearance	
Top	
Standard	0.03 to 0.07 mm (0.0012 to 0.0027 inch)
Limit	0.17 mm (0.0067 inch)
Second	
Standard	0.02 to 0.06 mm (0.0008 to 0.0024 inch)
Limit	0.16 mm (0.0063 inch)
Ring end gap (top and second)	
Standard	0.20 to 0.35 mm (0.0078 to 0.0137 inch)
Limit	0.7 mm (0.014 inch)

Transmission

Shift fork finger thickness	
Standard	5.9 to 6.0 mm (0.232 to 0.236 inch)
Limit	5.8 mm (0.228 inch)
Shift fork groove width in gears	
Standard	5.95 to 6.15 mm (0.234 to 0.242 inch)
Limit	6.25 mm (0.246 inch)

Crankshaft and connecting rod

Runout (total indicator reading)
At left end
   Standard .... 0.03 mm (0.0012 inch) or less
   Limit .... 0.08 mm (0.0031 inch)
At right end
   Standard .... 0.004 mm (0.0001 inch) or less
   Limit .... 0.10 mm (0.0039 inch)
Connecting rod big-end side clearance
   Standard... 0.25 to 0.35 mm (0.010 to 0.014 inch)
   Limit .... 0.6 mm (0.024 inch)
Connecting rod big-end radial clearance
   Standard .... 0.008 to 0.020 mm (0.0003 to 0.0008 inch)
   Limit... 0.07 mm (0.0027 inch)

Torque specifications (1)

Engine mounting bolts
   8mm diameter .... 25 Nm (18 ft-lbs)
   10 mm diameter .... 42 ft-lbs (31 Nm)
Valve adjustment cover bolts .... 8.8 Nm (78 inch-lbs)
Cylinder head bolts (2)
   First stage
      Main bolts .... 15 Nm (11 ft-lbs)
      Small bolts .... 5.9 Nm (52 inch-lbs)
   Second stage
      Main bolts
         Used bolts .... 29 Nm (22 ft-lbs)
         New bolts .... 34 Nm (25 ft-lbs)
      Small bolts .... 12 Nm (104 inch-lbs)
Cylinder base bolt... 12 Nm (104 in-lbs)
Cam chain guide bolt... 9.8 Nm (87 inch-lbs)
Camshaft cover bolts .... 8.8 Nm (78 inch-lbs)
Camshaft cover inner plate screws .... 4.4 Nm (39 inch-lbs)
Camshaft sprocket bolt .... 41 Nm (30 ft-lbs)
Oil pipe union bolts... 20 Nm (174 inch-lbs)
Oil pump bearing retainer screws................................ 8.8.Nm (78 inch-lbs)
Oil pump screws .... 4.4 Nm (39 inch-lbs)
Oil pump cover screws .... 25 Nm (18 ft-lbs)
Balancer and oil pump drive gear nut .... 41 Nm (30 ft-lbs)
Recoil starter reel nut... 8.3 Nm (74 inch-lbs)
Automatic transmission outer cover bolts.................... 8.8 Nm (78 inch-lbs)
Automatic transmission drive pulley bolt..................... 76 Nm (56 ft-lbs) (3)
Automatic transmission driven pulley bolt................... 42 Nm (31 ft-lbs) (4)
Automatic transmission inner cover bolts .... 9.8 Nm (87 inch-lbs) (5)
Automatic transmission spider roller nuts .... 6.9 Nm (61 inch-lbs)
Automatic transmission drive pulley cover bolts.......... 13 Nm (113 inch-lbs)
Automatic transmission drive pulley spider................. 275 Nm (205 ft-lbs)
Automatic transmission driven pulley button screws............................ 8.8. Nm (78 inch-lbs)

1   For fasteners not listed here, refer to the General Specifications at the front of this manual.
2   Apply engine oil to the threads and nut or bolt seating surface.
3   Replace the bolt with a new one whenever it's removed.
4   Apply non-permanent thread locking agent to the threads.
5   Apply non-permanent thread locking agent to the threads of the four forward and four rearward bolts, but not to the two center bolts.

2B

1   General information

The engine/transmission unit is of the air-cooled, single-cylinder four-stroke design. The two valves are operated by an overhead camshaft which is chain driven off the crankshaft. A manually operated decompression lever is used to ease starting. The engine/transmission assembly is constructed from aluminum alloy. The crankcase is divided vertically.

The crankcase incorporates a wet sump, pressure-fed lubrication system which uses a gear-driven rotor-type oil pump, an oil filter and separate strainer screen.

Power from the crankshaft is routed to the high-low and reverse gears by a belt-type automatic transmission mounted on the right side of the engine. The high-low and reverse gears are inside the crankcase. Power is transmitted from the crankshaft through the transmission drive-belt to the input shaft for the high-low and reverse gears. Power from the high-low and reverse gears is transmitted through the crankcase to the bevel drive unit on the left side of the engine, and from there to the rear differential (and to the front differential on 4WD models).

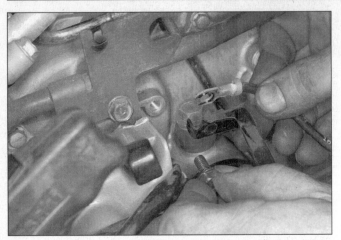

5.3 Disconnect the ground cable from the engine

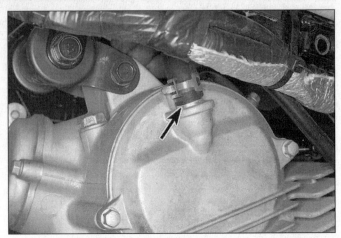

5.7 Disconnect the breather hose from the camshaft sprocket cover (arrow)

2   Operations possible with the engine in the frame

The components and assemblies listed below can be removed without having to remove the engine from the frame. If, however, a number of areas require attention at the same time, removal of the engine is recommended.

Recoil starter (if equipped)
Starter motor
Starter chain and recoil limiter
Starter clutch
Alternator rotor and stator
Automatic transmission
Cam chain tensioner
Camshaft
Rocker arms and shafts
Cylinder head
Cylinder and piston
Oil pump
Balancer gears

3   Operations requiring engine removal

It is necessary to remove the engine/transmission assembly from the frame and separate the crankcase halves to gain access to the following components:

Crankshaft and connecting rod
High-low and reverse gears and shifting forks

4   Major engine repair - general note

1   It is not always easy to determine when or if an engine should be completely overhauled, as a number of factors must be considered.
2   High mileage is not necessarily an indication that an overhaul is needed, while low mileage, on the other hand, does not preclude the need for an overhaul. Frequency of servicing is probably the single most important consideration. An engine that has regular and frequent oil and filter changes, as well as other required maintenance, will most likely give many miles of reliable service. Conversely, a neglected engine, or one which has not been broken in properly, may require an overhaul very early in its life.
3   Exhaust smoke and excessive oil consumption are both indications that piston rings and/or valve guides are in need of attention. Make sure oil leaks are not responsible before deciding that the rings and guides are bad. Refer to Chapter 1 and perform a cylinder compression check to determine for certain the nature and extent of the work required.

4   If the engine is making obvious knocking or rumbling noises, the connecting rod and/or main bearings are probably at fault.
5   Loss of power, rough running, excessive valve train noise and high fuel consumption rates may also point to the need for an overhaul, especially if they are all present at the same time. If a complete tune-up does not remedy the situation, major mechanical work is the only solution.
6   An engine overhaul generally involves restoring the internal parts to the specifications of a new engine. During an overhaul the piston rings are replaced and the cylinder walls are bored and/or honed. If a rebore is done, then a new piston is also required. Generally the valves are serviced as well, since they are usually in less than perfect condition at this point. While the engine is being overhauled, other components such as the carburetor and the starter motor can be rebuilt also. The end result should be a like-new engine that will give as many trouble-free miles as the original.
7   Before beginning the engine overhaul, read through all of the related procedures to familiarize yourself with the scope and requirements of the job. Overhauling an engine is not all that difficult, but it is time consuming. Plan on the vehicle being tied up for a minimum of two (2) weeks. Check on the availability of parts and make sure that any necessary special tools, equipment and supplies are obtained in advance.
8   Most work can be done with typical shop hand tools, although a number of precision measuring tools are required for inspecting parts to determine if they must be replaced. Often a dealer service department or repair shop will handle the inspection of parts and offer advice concerning reconditioning and replacement. As a general rule, time is the primary cost of an overhaul so it doesn't pay to install worn or substandard parts.
9   As a final note, to ensure maximum life and minimum trouble from a rebuilt engine, everything must be assembled with care in a spotlessly clean environment.

5   Engine - removal and installation

Note: *Engine removal and installation should be done with the aid of an assistant to avoid damage or injury that could occur if the engine is dropped.*

Removal

Refer to illustrations 5.3, 5.7, 5.10 and 5.13a through 5.13f
1   Drain the engine oil (see Chapter 1).
2   Remove the seat, front and rear fenders and the front side covers (see Chapter 7).
3   Disconnect the ground cable from the engine **(see illustration)** and disconnect the negative battery cable (see Chapter 1).

5.10 Disconnect the electrical connectors (right), neutral and reverse switches (center) and free the harness from the retainer (left arrow)

4   Remove the fuel tank, carburetor, air cleaner ducts, intake manifold and exhaust system (see Chapter 3).

5   Remove the automatic transmission cover, pulleys and inner cover (see Sections 15, 16 and 18).

6   Disconnect the rear end of the shift lever link rod (see Chapter 5).

7   Disconnect the crankcase breather hose from the camshaft cover **(see illustration)**.

8   Disconnect the oil cooler hoses and external oil pipes from the engine (Section 12).

9   Disconnect the spark plug wire (see Chapter 1).

10   Label and disconnect the following wires **(see illustration)** (see Chapter 4 for component locations if necessary):

CDI magneto and alternator
Reverse and neutral switches
Starter

11   Loosen the clamp that secures the boot at the forward end of the rear driveshaft. If you're working on a 4WD model, remove the front driveshaft (see Chapter 5).

12   Support the engine securely from below.

13   Remove the engine mounting bolts, nuts and brackets **(see illustrations)**.

14   Have an assistant help you lift the engine. Remove the engine to the left side of the vehicle.

15   Carefully lower the engine to a suitable work surface.

Installation

16   Check the engine supports for wear or damage and replace them if necessary before installing the engine.

17   Lubricate the splines of the rear driveshaft with moly-based grease.

18   With the help of an assistant, lift the engine up into the frame. As you position the engine, engage the rear driveshaft with the output gear. Install the mounting nuts and bolts. Finger-tighten the mounting bolts, but don't tighten them to the specified torque yet.

19   Tighten the engine mounting bolts and nuts to the torques listed

2B

5.13a Remove the through-bolt from the upper mount . . .

5.13b . . . and unbolt the mount bracket from the frame

5.13c Undo the harness retainer from the upper rear mounting bolt . . .

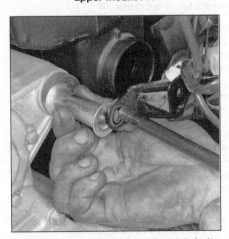

5.13d . . . then remove the through-bolt and spacer

5.13e Remove the lower front through-bolt . . .

5.13f . . . and the lower rear through-bolt

8.1a Unscrew the nut from the decompression cable . . .

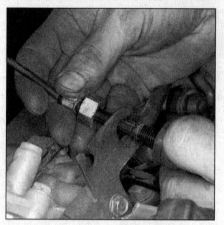

8.1b . . . and free the cable from the bracket

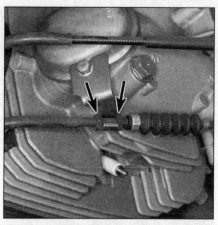

8.2 Loosen the nuts (arrows) and free the cable from the bracket at the cylinder head

in this Chapter's Specifications. Use non-permanent thread locking agent on the threads of the specified bolts.

20   The remainder of installation is the reverse of the removal steps, with the following additions:

   a) *Use new gaskets at all exhaust pipe connections.*
   b) *Adjust the throttle cable following the procedures in Chapter 1.*
   c) *Fill the engine with oil, also following the procedures in Chapter 1. Run the engine and check for leaks.*
   d) *Adjust the idle speed (see Chapter 1).*

6   Engine disassembly and reassembly - general information

1   Before disassembling the engine, clean the exterior with a degreaser and rinse it with water. A clean engine will make the job easier and prevent the possibility of getting dirt into the internal areas of the engine.

2   In addition to the precision measuring tools mentioned earlier, you will need a torque wrench, a valve spring compressor, oil gallery brushes **(see illustration 6.2 in Chapter 2A)**, a piston ring removal and installation tool and a piston ring compressor. Some new, clean engine oil of the correct grade and type, some engine assembly lube (or moly-based grease) and a tube of RTV (silicone) sealant will also be required.

3   An engine support stand made from short lengths of 2 x 4's bolted together will facilitate the disassembly and reassembly procedures **(see illustration 6.3 in Chapter 2A)**. If you have an automotive-type engine stand, an adapter plate can be made from a piece of plate, some angle iron and some nuts and bolts.

4   When disassembling the engine, keep "mated" parts together (including gears, rocker arms and shafts, etc.) that have been in contact with each other during engine operation. These "mated" parts must be reused or replaced as an assembly.

5   Engine/transmission disassembly should be done in the following general order with reference to the appropriate Sections.

   Remove the cam chain tensioner
   Remove the cylinder head, rocker arms and camshaft
   Remove the cylinder
   Remove the piston
   Remove the automatic transmission
   Remove the oil pump
   Remove the alternator rotor and starter chain
   Separate the crankcase halves
   Remove the shift drum and forks
   Remove the balancer shaft
   Remove the high-low and reverse gears and shafts
   Remove the crankshaft and connecting rod

6   Reassembly is accomplished by reversing the general disassembly sequence.

7   Cam chain tensioner - removal and installation

This procedure is the same as for Bayou 300 models. Refer to Chapter 2A.

8   Cylinder head, decompression lever, camshaft and rocker arms - removal, inspection and installation

Decompression lever

Refer to illustrations 8.1a, 8.1b and 8.2

1   Loosen the cable locknuts and detach the cable from the bracket **(see illustrations)**. Rotate the cable to align it with the slot in the lever and slip its end plug out of the lever.

2   Unscrew the locknut from the cable knob and slide the cable out of the bracket **(see illustration)**.

3   The remainder of this procedure is the same as for Bayou models (see Chapter 2A).

Camshaft, cylinder head and rocker arms

4   Removal, inspection and installation procedures for these parts are the same as for Bayou models (see Chapter 2A).

Cam chain and guide removal

Front chain guide

5   Removal, inspection and installation procedures for these parts are the same as for Bayou models (see Chapter 2A).

Rear chain guide and chain

6   The rear guide is bolted at the bottom, so the alternator rotor, starter chain and starter chain sprockets will have to be removed for access if the guide or the cam chain needs to be removed (see Chapter 4).

7   The remaining procedures for the rear chain guide and timing chain are the same as for Bayou models (see Chapter 2A).

9   Valves/valve seats/valve guides - servicing

1   Because of the complex nature of this job and the special tools and equipment required, servicing of the valves, the valve seats and the valve guides (commonly known as a valve job) is best left to a professional.

2   The home mechanic can, however, remove and disassemble the head, do the initial cleaning and inspection, then reassemble and deliver the head to a dealer service department or properly equipped

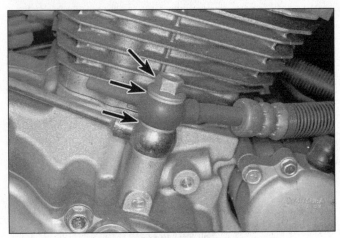

12.1a Remove the union bolt and three sealing washers (arrows) . . .

12.1b . . . and the remaining union bolt and sealing washers next to the oil filter

vehicle repair shop for the actual valve servicing. Refer to Section 10 for those procedures.

3   The dealer service department will remove the valves and springs, recondition or replace the valves and valve seats, replace the valve guides, check and replace the valve springs, spring retainers and keepers (as necessary), replace the valve seals with new ones and reassemble the valve components.

4   After the valve job has been performed, the head will be in like-new condition. When the head is returned, be sure to clean it again very thoroughly before installation on the engine to remove any metal particles or abrasive grit that may still be present from the valve service operations. Use compressed air, if available, to blow out all the holes and passages.

10 Cylinder head and valves - disassembly, inspection and reassembly

These procedures are the same as for Bayou models (see Chapter 2A).

11 Cylinder, piston and rings - removal, inspection and installation

1   Removal and inspection procedures for the cylinder, piston and rings are the same as for Bayou models (see Chapter 2A).

2   Ring profiles are the same as Bayou 4WD models **(see illustration 13.9b in Chapter 2A)**.

12 External oil pipe and oil cooler- removal and installation

Removal

Oil pipe
Refer to illustrations 12.1a and 12.1b

1   Remove the union bolts and sealing washers from the pipe on the outside of the engine **(see illustrations)**. Note that the union bolts are different colors; don't mix them up, as the different color bolts have different size oil passages.

Oil cooler
Refer to illustrations 12.2, 12.3, 12.5a and 12.5b

2   Remove the bolts that secure the oil cooler and screen from the front of the screen **(see illustration)**.

3   Hold the fitting at one of the oil cooler hoses with a wrench and unscrew the union bolt with a second wrench **(see illustration)**. Remove the bolt and sealing washers, then disconnect the other hose in the same way.

4   Lift the oil cooler out of the lower grommets and take it out of the vehicle.

5   To remove the oil cooler hoses from the vehicle, free them from

2B

12.2 Remove the bolts (arrows) and take the screen off the oil cooler

12.3 Remove the union bolt and sealing washers from each of the oil cooler hoses (arrow)

12.5a Free the hose grommets from the retainers near the steering shaft base (arrow)

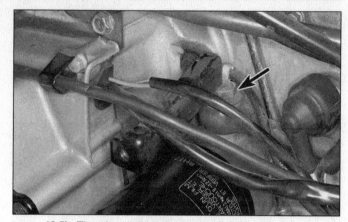

12.5b There's an oil cooler hose fitting just above the oil filter (arrow)

the hose retainer **(see illustration)**. Remove the union bolts and sealing washers that attach the hoses to the engine **(see illustration 12.1a and the accompanying illustration)**.

Installation

6   Installation is the reverse of the removal steps, with the following additions:

a) *Be sure to install the correct color (dark or silver) union bolts in the correct holes.*

b) *Replace the sealing washers whenever the union bolts or hose fittings are loosened.*

c) *Tighten the union bolts to the torques listed in this Chapter's Specifications.*

13   Automatic transmission - general information

All Prairie models covered in this manual use a variable-ratio belt drive automatic transmission. This consists of a drive pulley, drive belt and driven pulley, all mounted in a sealed housing on the right side of the machine. The automatic transmission connects the engine to the high-low and reverse gears inside the crankcase.

The automatic transmission's drive and driven pulleys control variable-diameter pulleys. The drive pulley is mounted on the end of the engine crankshaft. The driven pulley is mounted on the input shaft.

At low engine speeds, the drive pulley has a small diameter and the driven pulley has a large diameter. As engine speed increases, the drive pulley diameter gets larger and the driven pulley diameter gets smaller. This changes the effective gear ratio of the automatic transmission.

The drive pulley changes its pulley diameter in response to changes in engine speed. At idle, the spring in the drive pulley forces the pulley halves apart, so the drive belt is not gripped and no power is transferred to the driven pulley. As engine speed increases, the drive pulley spins faster. This causes the three shift weights (centrifugal levers) in the drive pulley to push the sliding pulley half toward the fixed pulley half. As a result, the drive belt is gripped by the pulley and power is transferred to the driven pulley. As engine speed increases still more, the shift weights push the drive pulley's sliding pulley half closer to the fixed pulley half. This makes the pulley groove narrower, so the drive belt rides higher in the pulley groove (closer to the outer edge of the pulley). This causes the driven pulley to be rotated more times for each rotation of the drive pulley (higher gearing).

Since the drive belt doesn't change length, the driven pulley must become smaller in diameter as the drive pulley becomes larger. To make this happen, the driven pulley changes diameter in response to the load placed on it by the drive belt. At low engine speeds, the spring in the driven pulley pushes the pulley halves together, which causes the drive belt to ride higher in the groove (closer to the outer edge of the pulley). This is the equivalent of a low gear in a conventional transmission. As engine speed increases, more power is applied to the drive

belt. The belt forces the driven pulley halves apart, causing the belt to ride lower in the pulley groove (closer to the center of the pulley). This is the equivalent of a higher gear in a conventional transmission. Two things control the rate at which the driven pulley halves are forced apart; the tension of the driven pulley spring and the angle of the helical cam that connects the centers of the two halves.

The automatic transmission is air cooled. The cooling air is drawn into the housing by fins on the fixed half of the drive pulley pulley. The air enters a duct at the front of the vehicle and exits through two ducts at the rear.

The system is designed so that at full throttle, engine rpm is maintained at a setting that produces peak power output. Springs, shift weights and driven pulley cams are specifically designed for each model. They must be replaced with the exact equivalents if new ones are needed. In addition, the pulley components are balanced as a unit, so installing used parts from another pulley will probably cause vibration.

14   Automatic transmission air ducts - removal and installation

1   There are three ducts that supply and remove cooling air for the transmission components, one at the front and two at the rear.

Removal

2   Remove the seat and fenders (see Chapter 7).

Front duct

Refer to illustrations 14.3 and 14.4

3   Remove the mounting bolt at the top of the front duct **(see illustration)**.

14.3 Remove the bolt that secures the front duct (arrow) . . .

14.4 . . . and loosen the lower duct clamps, then remove the ducts

14.5 Loosen the left rear lower duct's clamps at the transmission housing and at the upper duct . . .

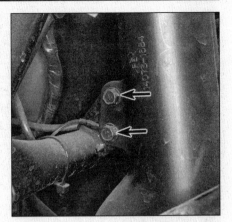

14.6 . . . then remove the upper duct mounting bolts (arrows) and take both ducts out

14.7a Loosen the clamp that secures the right rear lower duct to the housing . . .

14.7b . . . and to the upper duct . . .

14.8 . . then unbolt the upper duct and take both ducts out

2B

4   Loosen the clamps that secure the bottom end of the front duct to the transmission housing and take the duct out **(see illustration)**.

Left (inner) rear duct

Refer to illustrations 14.5 and 14.6

5   Loosen the clamps that secure the lower inner duct to the housing and the upper duct **(see illustration)**.

6   Remove the upper duct's mounting bolts **(see illustration)**, then take out the upper duct and the lower duct.

15.4a Unscrew the cover bolts (four lower bolts hidden) . . .

Right (outer) rear duct

Refer to illustrations 14.7a, 14.7b and 14.8

7   Loosen the clamps that secure the lower duct to the housing and to the upper duct **(see illustrations)**.

8   Remove the upper duct's mounting bolt, then take the upper and lower ducts **(see illustration)**.

Inspection

9   Clean away any debris clogging the ducts. Check the ducts for cracks and the couplings for cracks, brittleness or deteriorated rubber. Replace any parts that have problems.

Installation

10   Installation is the reverse of the removal steps. Make sure the ducts fit completely together and tighten the clamps securely.

---

15   Automatic transmission outer cover and seal - removal, inspection and installation

---

Refer to illustrations 15.4a, 15.4b and 15.5

1   The seals in the outer cover and inner cover are important because they keep water from leaking in and cooling air from leaking out. A wet or overheated automatic transmission belt will slip on the pulleys.

2   Remove the seat, rear fenders and left footrest (see Chapter 7).

3   Remove the outlet air duct (Section 14).

4   Remove the cover bolts, washers and grommets **(see illustrations)**.

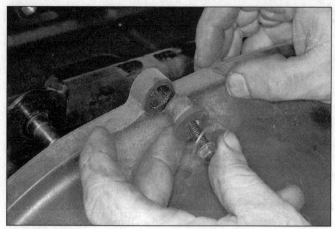

15.4b . . . and remove the washers and grommets

15.5 Pull the seal out of its groove

5   Carefully pull the seal out of its groove **(see illustration)**. Check for cracks, hardening and deterioration of the rubber. Also look for pinched spots caused by the cover being tightened while the seal is out of position. If you find any problems, replace the seal.
6   Installation is the reverse of the removal steps.

16.2 The part number on the belt should be upright when viewed from the right side of the vehicle

16   Automatic transmission drive belt - removal, inspection and installation

Refer to illustrations 16.2, 16.4, 16.5a and 16.5b
1   Remove the outer cover (see Section 15). Lock the front brake by wrapping a bungee cord around the lever.
2   There should be a visible part number on the belt, which should be upright when you're facing the belt from the right side of the vehicle **(see illustration)**. If not, draw an arrow on the belt with chalk or white paint to indicate its direction of rotation.
3   Turn the driven pulley with one hand while operating the shift lever with the other hand. Place the transmission in any gear to prevent the drive pulley from turning.
4   With the engine off, there may be enough slack in the belt to slip it off the driven pulley **(see illustration)**. You can then lift it out of the drive pulley groove and over the drive pulley. If the belt is too tight to just slip off, go to the next Step.
5   **Warning:** *The halves of the driven pulley are strongly spring loaded towards each other. All during this step, be sure to keep your fingers out from between the pulley halves. They can snap together suddenly and will cause injury if your fingers are in the way.*
Note: *This step will be much easier with an assistant.* If the belt is too tight, push the inner half of the driven pulley away from you and turn it counterclockwise at the same time **(see illustration)**. This will separate the pulley halves and create slack in the belt so it can be removed **(see illustration)**.

16.4 If there's enough slack in the belt, slip it off the driven pulley . . .

16.5a . . . if necessary, push the inner driven pulley half away from you and turn it counterclockwise - DO NOT place your fingers between the pulley halves!

16.5b Slip the belt off the driven pulley, then off the drive pulley

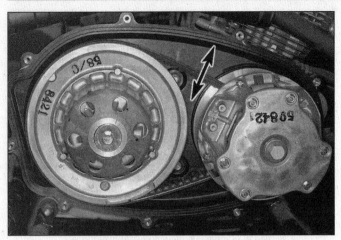

17.3 Check drive belt play between the pulleys

6   Check the belt for worn or broken cogs and for separation of the plies. Check along the surface that contacts the pulleys for wear, especially for cupped spots that indicate severe slippage. Also check for burn marks caused by belt slippage. If you find any problems, replace the belt. If the belt has been slipping, check the outer cover O-ring and the inner cover seal for leaks that could allow the entry of water.
7   Check the friction surface on each pulley for wear, scoring or corrosion. If there's a problem, replace the complete front or rear pulley as a unit (Section 18).
8   Installation is the reverse of removal. If you're reinstalling the old belt, make sure it rotates in the original direction. If you're installing a new belt, place the part number so it's upright when viewed from the right side of the vehicle.
9   Check belt play and adjust if necessary (Section 17).

17 Automatic transmission drive belt - width and play check

Refer to illustration 17.3
1   Remove the outer cover (Section 15).
2   Measure the width of the belt with a steel ruler or vernier caliper and compare it to the value listed in this Chapter's Specifications. Check at several places along the belt. If it's significantly narrower at any one point, or if it's worn to less than the minimum specification, replace it (Section 17).
3   Press down on the belt midway between the pulleys on the top side and measure its play (see illustration). Press with a finger hard enough to tension the belt lightly. If the play is not within the range

18.4b . . . then remove the bolt, lockwasher, washer and collar

18.4a Turn the drive pulley bolt clockwise to loosen it (use a new bolt on installation) . . .

listed in this Chapter's Specifications, add or remove shims between the inner and outer halves of the driven pulley (Section 19). Removing shims (placing the pulley halves closer together) tightens the belt and decreases play. Adding shims (placing the pulley halves farther apart) loosens the belt and increases play.

18 Automatic transmission pulleys, inner cover and seal - removal and installation

1   Remove the outer cover and drive belt (Sections 15 and 16).
2   Remove the recoil starter from the left side of the engine (Section 23).

Drive pulley
Refer to illustrations 18.4a, 18.4b and 18.5
3   Place a bar through the slots of the recoil starter pulley to keep the engine from turning over while you loosen the bolt.
4   The drive pulley bolt has left-hand threads. Turn the drive pulley bolt clockwise to loosen it, then remove the drive pulley bolt, lockwasher, washer and bushing (see illustrations). Note: *The drive pulley bolt must be replaced with a new one whenever it's removed.*
5   Install a removal tool (Kawasaki part no. 57001-1411 or equivalent) in the drive pulley center (see illustration). The tool is a special bolt with 14X1.25 mm right-hand threads. Thread the bolt into the removal threads in the drive pulley center (these are right-hand threads, which tighten clockwise, not the same as the pulley bolt threads, which tighten counterclockwise). Tighten the bolt to break the drive pulley loose from the crankshaft, then pull the drive pulley off and remove the bolt.
6   Installation is the reverse of the removal steps, with the following additions:

a) Clean the taper on the end of the crankshaft and its bore inside the drive pulley before installing the pulley, using a non-residue solvent such as acetone.
b) Tighten the new drive pulley bolt to the torque listed in this Chapter's Specifications.

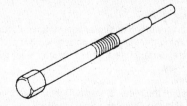

18.5 This tool is used to break the drive pulley free from the crankshaft

2B

18.7a Turn the driven pulley bolt CLOCKWISE to loosen it . . .

18.7b . . . then remove the bolt and collar

18.10a Remove the cover bolts (arrows) . . .

18.10b . . . then take off the reinforcing plate and the inner cover

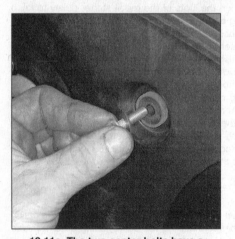

18.11a The two center bolts have a washer on the transmission side of the cover . . .

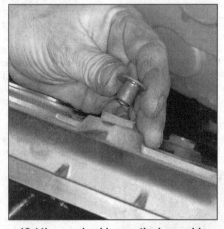

18.11b . . . a bushing on the inner side and a grommet that's centered in the cover

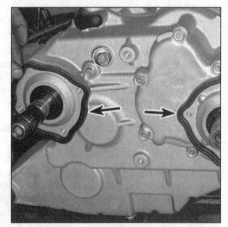

18.12 Peel the seals from around the transmission shaft (left) and crankshaft (right)

Driven pulley

Refer to illustrations 18.7a and 18.7b

7   Hold the pulley with a strap wrench or similar tool so it won't turn. Loosen the pulley bolt by turning it clockwise, then remove the pulley bolt and washer **(see illustrations)**. Note that the washer's smaller diameter faces toward the pulley.

8   Remove the driven pulley.

9   Installation is the reverse of the removal steps. Tighten the driven pulley bolt to the torque listed in this Chapter's Specifications.

Inner cover and seals

Refer to illustrations 18.10a, 18.10b, 18.11a, 18.11b and 18.12

10   Remove the bolts that secure the inner cover and reinforcing plate to the engine **(see illustrations)**.

11   Take the cover off and turn it over. Remove the washer, bushing and grommet from each of the two center bolts **(see illustrations)**.

12   Inspect the inner cover seals on the engine **(see illustration)**. If the seals are deteriorated or damaged, carefully pry them out of the cover. Clean the seal groove in the cover thoroughly, then coat it with

19.2a This driven pulley holding fixture is designed for a slotted workbench or press plate . . .

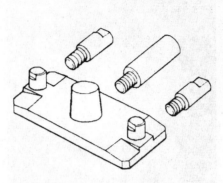

19.2b . . . the Kawasaki factory tool can be mounted in a vise . . .

19.2c . . . the spider adapter has a post to engage each spider arm and a square hole at the top for a torque wrench

19.3 Mark the components so they can be reassembled in the same relative positions

19.4 Loosen the cover bolts in stages, in a criss-cross pattern

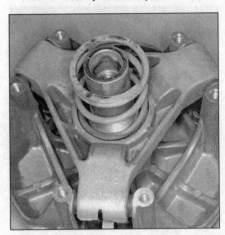

19.5a Remove the spring . . .

silicone sealant and press in a new seal, using a block of wood.

13   Installation is the reverse of the removal steps. Be sure to install a grommet and collar on each of the three bolts.

19 Automatic transmission pulleys - disassembly, inspection and reassembly

1   Remove the pulley you plan to work on (Section 18).

Drive pulley

Disassembly

Refer to illustrations 19.2a, 19.2b, 19.2c, 19.3, 19.4, 19.5a, 19.5b, 19.5c, 19.6a, 19.6b, 19.7, 19.8a, 19.8b, 19.9, 19.10a and 19.10b

2   Disassembly of the drive pulley requires a special holding fixture or its equivalent to secure the unit while the spider is unscrewed (**see illustrations**). Because the spider is tightened to 205 ft-lbs, trying to unscrew it with improvised tools may damage it. You may be able to duplicate the factory tools if you have a well-equipped shop, but read through the procedure before trying it. **Caution:** *Whatever method you use, make sure it doesn't scratch the mild-steel friction surfaces of the pulley. The entire drive pulley must be replaced as a unit if one of the pulley surfaces is damaged.*

3   There should be arrow marks on the cover and spider (**see illus-tration**). Just in case they aren't there, mark the cover, the spider, the moving pulley half and the fixed pulley half with a felt pen so they can

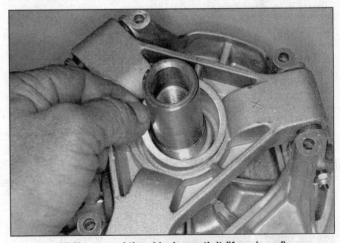

19.5b . . . and the shim beneath it (if equipped)

be reassembled in the same relationship. This is necessary to preserve the unit's balance.

4   Loosen the cover bolts in stages, in a criss-cross pattern, then remove them and take off the cover (**see illustration**).

5   Remove the cover spring and the shim beneath it (if equipped) (**see illustrations**). **Note:** *Before disassembling further, check each of the spider arms for play at the buttons (see illustration). If there's any*

19.5c If there's clearance between the spider buttons and posts (arrows), install new buttons

19.6a Clamp the fixed pulley half and unscrew the spider . . .

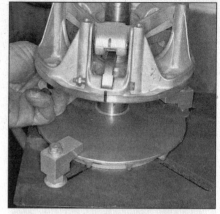

19.6b . . . and lift the clutch components off the fixed pulley half

19.7 Remove the spacer shims

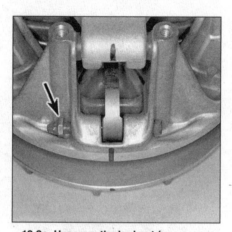

19.8a Unscrew the locknut (use a new one on assembly) . . .

19.8b . . . and pull out the shift weight bolt

clearance between the buttons and the posts next to them, replace the buttons as described later.

6   Place the unit in the holding fixture and unscrew the spider **(see illustration)**. Lift the clutch mechanism and moving pulley half off the fixed pulley half **(see illustration)**.

7   Remove the spacer shim or shims from the clutch mechanism **(see illustration)**. If there's more than one shim, tie them together and place them where they won't be lost; it's important to reinstall the same number and thickness of shims.

8   Remove the nut from each of the shift weight pivot bolts **(see**

illustration). Pull out the bolt and remove the shift weight **(see illustration)**. Mark each of the shift weights with its position in the moving pulley half so it can be returned to its original position.

9   Check to make sure each roller in the spider turns freely **(see illustration)**. If the roller turns roughly or not at all, remove and clean its components, then reassemble it and recheck its movement. Rollers that don't turn freely are a common cause of shift weight wear.

10   Remove the button and O-ring or washer from each end of each spider pivot **(see illustration)**. Push out the roller pivot, then remove the roller and thrust washers **(see illustration)**.

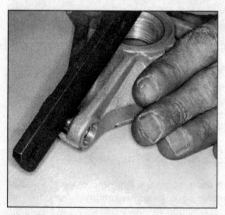

19.9 Roll a flat bar over the spider rollers and check for free movement

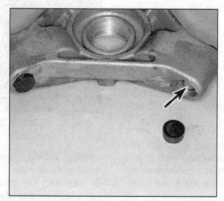

19.10a Remove the spider buttons, the O-ring or rubber washer (if equipped) and the pivot roller shaft (arrow)

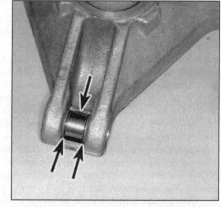

19.10b Remove the roller (upper arrow) and thrust washers (lower arrows)

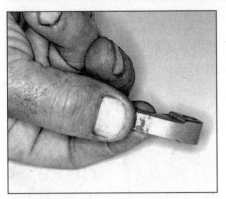

19.11a Replace the shift weights if they're corroded, like this, or cupped

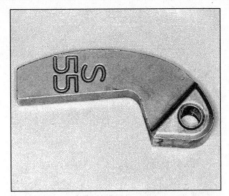

19.11b Replace all three shift weights with weights that have the same markings

19.13a Inspect the bushing in the moving pulley half . . .

19.13b . . . and the bushing in the cover

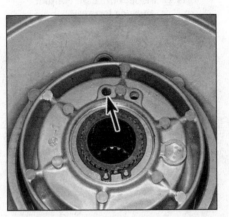

19.15 The cam holes are numbered 1 and 2; look for the end of the spring in the no. 2 hole (arrow)

19.16a Push down on the cam and remove the snap-ring . . .

2B

Inspection

Refer to illustrations 19.11a, 19.11b, 19.13a and 19.13b

11   Check the shift weight friction surfaces for wear, especially for cupping **(see illustration)**. This is usually caused by sticking rollers. Replace all three shift weights, along with their nuts and bolts, if any problem is found with any one of them. Be sure to use new shift weights with the same identification numbers and letters **(see illustration)**. These indicate the weight and the profile of the weights, both of which are specifically tailored to the vehicle. **Note:** *If the vehicle will be consistently operated above 2500 feet, change the shift weights, spring and shim(s). See your Kawasaki dealer parts department for the correct part numbers.*

12   If the shift weights were worn enough to need replacement, replace the rollers as well.

13   Check the bushings in the cover and moving pulley half **(see illustrations)**. Replace them if they're worn or damaged. The bushing in the moving pulley half is Teflon-coated brass. If you can see more exposed brass than Teflon, replace the bushing. Drive or press the bushings out using a bearing driver or socket, then drive or press new ones in using the same tool.

Reassembly

14   Assembly is the reverse of the disassembly steps, with the following additions:

  a) *Don't use any lubricant on any of the parts during assembly. It may fly off and contaminate the belt when the vehicle is operated.*
  b) *Align the felt pen marks and factory arrow marks on the pulley halves, spider and cover with each other when assembling the unit* **(see illustration 19.3)**.
  c) *Be sure the spacer shim(s) are fully seated in their bore* **(see illustration 19.7)**.

19.16b . . . and the washer beneath it (arrow)

  d) *Tighten the spider to 275 Nm (205 ft-lbs), using a holding fixture and a torque wrench. Don't guess at this critical torque setting. If you don't have the necessary tools, have a Kawasaki dealer or qualified ATV repair shop tighten the spider for you.*

Driven pulley

Disassembly

Refer to illustrations 19.15, 19.16a, 19.16b, 19.16c, 19.17 and 19.18

15   Note the location of the spring end in the no. 2 hole of the cam **(see illustration)**. The spring must be positioned in the same hole on assembly.

16   Remove the snap-ring from its groove in the pulley shaft, then lift off the cam **(see illustrations)**. The moving pulley half has three holes

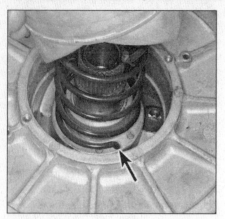

19.16c Lift up the cam and note which hole the other end of the spring is in (arrow)

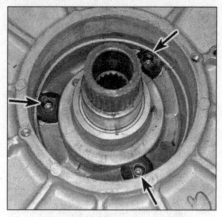

19.17 Inspect the cam contact buttons (arrows)

19.18 These spacer washers adjust drive belt tension

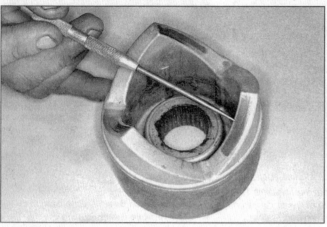

19.20 Check the cam contact surfaces for wear or damage

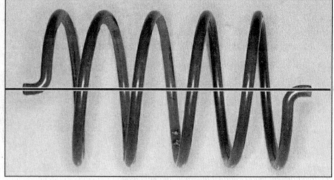

19.21 The ends of the spring should be in a straight line

Inspection

Refer to illustrations 19.20, 19.21, 19.22a and 19.22b

19   Check the cam contact buttons as described in Step 17 if you haven't already done so. Turn them over and reinstall them if they're worn on one side or install new ones of they're worn on both sides.

20   Check the button contact surfaces on the cam **(see illustration)**. Replace the cam if they're worn or damaged.

21   Lay a straightedge across the spring ends, parallel to the center-line of the spring **(see illustration)**. If the ends don't both line up with the straightedge, replace the spring.

22   Check the bushings in the moving pulley half for wear or damage **(see illustrations)**. Replace the Teflon-coated brass bushing if there's more brass than Teflon visible on the surface. Press or drive the bushings out and press new ones in, using a bearing driver or socket.

for the spring. Note which of the holes the spring is in, then lift the spring out. Again, write down the spring position.

17   Inspect the cam contact buttons in the moving pulley half **(see illustration)**. If they're worn on the visible side, undo their Torx screws and remove them. If their undersides are not worn, the buttons can be reused; just reinstall them with the good sides showing. Discard them if both sides are worn.

18   Pull the moving pulley half off the fixed half and remove the shims **(see illustration)**. **Note:** *These are the shims used to adjust belt tension (Section 19). At least one shim must be used when the pulley is reassembled.*

19.22a Check the bushing in the inner side of the moving pulley half . . .

19.22b . . . and the bushing in the outer side

19.23a Position the spring end in the correct cam hole

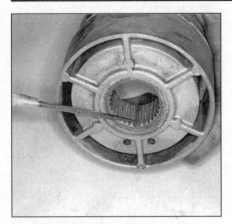

19.23b Align this wide spline in the cam . . .

19.23c . . . with this wide spline on the pulley shaft

20.2 Shift lever mounting nuts (A) and alignment tabs (B)

Reassembly

Refer to illustrations 19.23a, 19.23b and 19.23c

23   Reassembly is the reverse of the disassembly procedure, with the following additions:

a) *Don't use any lubricant during assembly. It may fly off and contaminate the drive belt.*

b) *When you install the spring, position it in the same holes it was removed from* **(see illustration)**. *The standard factory setting is the no. 2 hole at both ends of the spring. Changing the hole at either end will affect the shift characteristics.*

c) *When you install the cam, align its wide spline with the wide spline on the fixed pulley half* **(see illustrations)**. *Push the cam onto the shaft about 1/2 to 3/4-inch, then, while pressing the cam down, turn it counterclockwise 1/3 turn to seat the cam. Install the washer, then the snap-ring, making sure the snap-ring is seated securely in its groove.*

20 Shift lever - adjustment

Refer to illustrations 20.2 and 20.3

1   Place the shift lever in Neutral.

2   Check the alignment of the tabs on the shift lever and bracket **(see illustration)**. They should be perfectly aligned with each other. If they aren't, adjust the linkage.

3   To make the adjustment, loosen the locknuts at each end of the linkage rod (the rear locknut has left-hand threads, so turn it clockwise to loosen it) **(see illustration)**. Turn the tie-rod to align the tabs, then tighten the locknuts.

20.3 The shift lever locknuts; the rear locknut (left arrow) has left-hand threads

2B

21 High-low and reverse shift mechanism - removal, inspection and installation

Refer to illustrations 21.2, 21.4, 21.5a and 21.5b

1   Remove the fuel tank (see Chapter 3).

2   Check the alignment of the shift arm on the shaft **(see illustration)**. The punch mark on the end of the shaft and the slit in the arm should both line up with the cast protrusion on the crankcase.

3   Remove the shift arm pinch bolt (completely, don't just loosen it) and pull the shift arm off the shaft together with the linkage rod.

4   At the shift lever end of the linkage rod, remove the nut and detach the linkage rod's ball-joint stud from the shift lever **(see illustration)**.

5   Remove the shift lever cover screws, mounting bolts and nuts

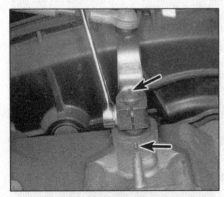

21.2 The shaft punch mark (upper arrow) and crankcase protrusion (lower arrow) should both align with the slit in the shift arm

21.4 Remove the nut (arrow) and detach the stud from the shift lever

21.5a Remove the cover screws (arrows) . . .

21.5b . . . and the shift lever bolts (arrows)

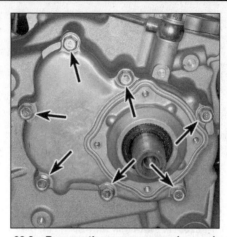

22.2a Remove the cover screws (arrows) and take off the cover . . .

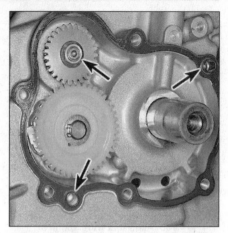

22.2b . . . locate the cover dowels (lower and right arrows); if necessary, loosen the drive gear nut (upper arrow)

22.4a Remove the driven gear snap-ring . . .

22.4b . . . washer and driven gear

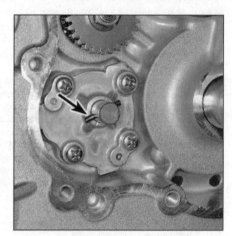

22.4c Remove the drive pin (arrow) and the four oil pump screws . . .

(see illustration 20.2 and the accompanying illustrations). Take the lever off.

6   Installation is the reverse of the removal steps. Check the lever position and adjust it if necessary (Section 20).

22 Oil pump - removal, inspection and installation

Removal

Refer to illustrations 22.2a, 22.2b, 22.4a, 22.4b, 22.4c, 22.5, 22.6 and 22.7

1   Remove the automatic transmission outer cover, drive belt, drive and driven pulleys and inner cover (Sections 15, 16 and 18).
2   Unbolt the oil pump cover from the crankcase **(see illustration)**. Take the cover off and locate the dowels **(see illustration)**.
3   If you plan to remove the oil pump drive gear, wedge the pump gears with a rag and remove the nut from the drive gear **(see illustration 22.2b)**. The pump drive gear need not be removed unless you plan to replace it or to separate the crankcase halves.
4   Remove the snap-ring and washer, then take the driven gear off the oil pump and remove the drive pin **(see illustrations)**.
5   Loosen the oil pump cover screws with an impact driver **(see illustration 22.4c)**. Remove the cover, together with the shaft and inner rotor, and locate the dowels **(see illustration)**.
6   Take the outer rotor out of the crankcase **(see illustration)**.
7   Slide the drive gear off its shaft **(see illustration)**.

Inspection

Refer to illustration 22.10

8   Wash all the components in solvent, then dry them off. Check the pump body, rotors and cover for scoring and wear. If any damage or uneven or excessive wear is evident, replace the pump. If you are

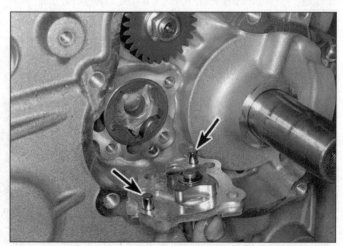

22.5 . . . take off the pump cover, shaft and inner rotor and locate the dowels (arrows) . . .

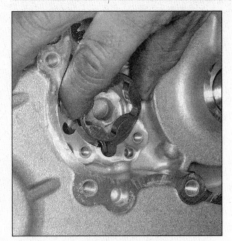

22.6 . . . and remove the outer rotor

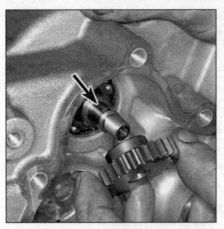

22.7 Slide off the drive gear; make sure its Woodruff key (arrow) is in place before installing the gear

22.10 Remove these screws and the retainer to replace the cover bearing

rebuilding the engine, it's a good idea to install a new oil pump.

9   Check the pump driven gear for wear or damage and replace it if necessary.

10   Inspect the bearing in the pump cover **(see illustration)**. If it's rough, loose or noisy when rotated, replace it. Remove the bearing retainer screws with an impact driver, take out the bearing and install a new one. Install the retainer and tighten its screws to the torque listed in this Chapter's Specifications.

Installation

11   Install the pump by reversing the removal steps, with the following additions:

a)   *Before installing the cover, pack the cavities between the rotors with petroleum jelly - this will ensure the pump develops suction quickly and begins oil circulation as soon as the engine is started.*

b)   *Make sure the pump dowels, drive pin and cover dowels are in position* **(see illustrations 22.5 and 22.2b).**

c)   *Install a new cover gasket* **(see illustration 22.2b).**

d)   *Tighten the oil pump and cover screws to the torques listed in this Chapter's Specifications.*

23   Recoil starter - removal, inspection and installation

Warning: *Rewinding the recoil spring can be dangerous. If you don't have experience with recoil starters, read through the procedure before starting. Most repairs can be done without removing the recoil spring, but if it is necessary, consider taking the job to a Kawasaki dealer or other qualified shop. If you do the job yourself, wear eye protection and heavy gloves in case the recoil spring flies out.*

Removal

Refer to illustration 23.1

1   Unbolt the recoil starter case from the left side of the engine **(see illustration)**. Take the recoil starter off.

2   The remainder of the procedure is the same as for Bayou 300 models (see Chapter 2A).

Inspection

3   Inspection procedures are the same as for Bayou 300 models (see Chapter 2A).

Installation

4   This is the same as for Bayou 300 models, with one difference: In Step 17 of the procedure in Chapter 2A, wind the reel three turns clockwise to preload the spring, rather than four turns.

23.1 Remove the case bolts (arrows) and take the recoil starter off the engine

24   Crankcase - disassembly and reassembly

1   To examine and repair or replace the crankshaft, connecting rod, bearings and transmission components, the crankcase must be split into two parts.

Disassembly

Refer to illustrations 24.12, 24.13a, 24.13b, 24.13c and 24.15

2   Remove the engine from the vehicle (see Section 5).

3   Remove the recoil starter (Section 23).

4   Remove the alternator rotor and the starter motor (see Chapter 4).

5   Remove the bevel drive unit (2WD models) or sub-transmission (4WD models). Remove the output shaft bevel gear and bearing housing from the left side of the crankcase (see Chapter 5).

6   Remove the external oil pipe (Section 12)

7   Remove the automatic transmission outer cover, drive belt, pulleys and inner cover (see Sections 15, 16 and 18).

8   Remove the high-low and reverse shift lever (Section 21).

9   Remove the oil pump (see Section 22).

10   Remove the cam chain tensioner, cylinder head, cam chain, cylinder and piston (see Chapter 2A).

11   Check carefully to make sure there aren't any remaining components that attach the upper and lower halves of the crankcase together.

2B

24.12 Loosen the crankcase bolts (arrows) evenly, then remove them all

24.13a Pry the cases apart at the rear pry point . . .

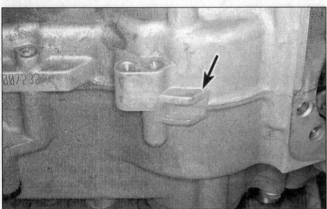

24.13b . . . and at the bottom pry point (arrow) - don't pry between the gasket surfaces

24.13c Separate the case halves and locate the dowels (arrows)

12   Loosen the crankcase bolts in two or three stages, in a criss-cross pattern **(see illustration)**.

13   Tap gently on the ends of the transmission shafts, balancer shaft and crankshaft as the case halves are being separated. Carefully pry the crankcase apart at the pry points and lift the left half off the right half **(see illustrations)**. Don't pry against the mating surfaces or they'll develop leaks.

14   Locate the crankcase dowels **(see illustration 24.13c)**. If they aren't secure in their holes, remove them and set them aside for safe-keeping.

15   Remove the O-ring from the oil passage between the crankcase halves **(see illustration)**.

16   Refer to Sections 25 through 27 for information on the internal components of the crankcase.

Reassembly

17   Remove all traces of old gasket and sealant from the crankcase mating surfaces with a sharpening stone or similar tool. Be careful not to let any fall into the case as this is done and be careful not to damage the mating surfaces.

18   Check to make sure the dowel pins and the oil passage O-ring are in place **(see illustrations 24.13c and 24.15)**.

19   Coat both crankcase mating surfaces with silicone sealant.

20   Pour some engine oil over the transmission gears, balancer shaft and crankshaft bearing surfaces and the shift drum. Don't get any oil on the crankcase mating surfaces.

21   Carefully place the left crankcase half onto the right crankcase half. While doing this, make sure the transmission shafts, shift drum,

crankshaft and balancer fit into their ball bearings in the left crankcase half.

22   Install the crankcase half bolts in the correct holes and tighten them so they are just snug. Then tighten them in two or three stages, in a criss-cross pattern, to the torque listed in this Chapter's Specifications.

23   Turn the transmission shafts to make sure they turn freely. Also make sure the crankshaft and balancer shaft turn freely.

24   The remainder of installation is the reverse of removal.

24.15 DO NOT forget to reinstall this O-ring when you reassemble the case halves!

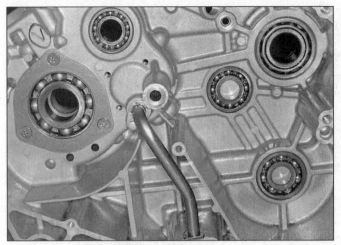

25.3a Right side crankcase bearings

25.3b Left side crankcase bearings

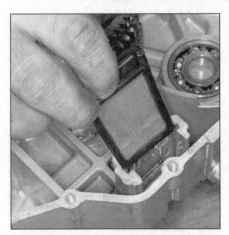

25.4a Slide the oil screen out of its slot

25.4b Remove the oil passage bolt (arrow)

25.5 Unscrew the oil pressure relief valve (arrow); use thread locking agent when you install the new one

2B

25 Crankcase components - inspection and servicing

Refer to illustrations 25.3a, 25.3b, 25.4a, 25.4b, 25.5 and 25.6

1   Separate the crankcase and remove the following:

a) *Transmission shafts and gears*
b) *Balancer shaft*
c) *Crankshaft and main bearings*
d) *Shift mechanism*

2   Clean the crankcase halves thoroughly with new solvent and dry them with compressed air. All oil passages should be blown out with compressed air and all traces of old gasket sealant should be removed from the mating surfaces. **Caution:** *Be very careful not to nick or gouge the crankcase mating surfaces or leaks will result. Check both crankcase sections very carefully for cracks and other damage.*

3   Check the bearings in the case halves **(see illustrations)**. If they don't turn smoothly, replace them. Use an impact driver to remove the retainers from bearings so equipped. For bearings that aren't accessible from the outside, a blind hole puller will be needed for removal. Drive the remaining bearings out with a bearing driver or a socket having an outside diameter slightly smaller than that of the bearing outer race. Before installing the bearings, allow them to sit in the freezer overnight, and about fifteen minutes before installation, place the case half in an oven, set to about 200-degrees F, and allow it to heat up. The bearings are an interference fit, and this will ease installation. **Warning:** *Before heating the case, wash it thoroughly with soap and water so no explosive fumes are present. Also, don't use a flame to heat the case. Install the bearings with a socket or bearing driver that bears against*

the bearing outer race.

4   Slide the oil screen out of its slot in the bottom of the case **(see illustration)**. Unbolt the oil passage from the right case half **(see illustration)**. Clean the oil strainer screen and passage and check them for damage.

5   If the oil pressure relief valve is clogged or damaged, unscrew it from the crankcase **(see illustration)**.

6   Check the engine mounting bushings in the rear of the crankcase

25.6 Replace the engine mounting bushings if they're damaged or deteriorated

26.3a The shift shaft retaining pin (A), shift shaft positioning bolt (B) and shift fork guide bar bolt (C) are accessible from outside the crankcase

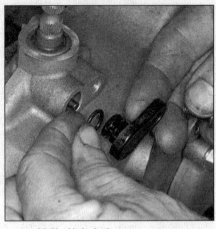

26.3b Unbolt the cap, remove the O-ring . . .

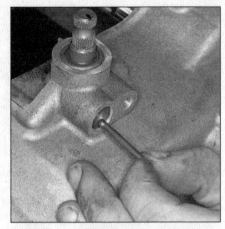

26.3c . . . and pull out the shift shaft retaining pin

26.3d Remove the shift shaft positioning bolt, sealing washer, spring and detent ball

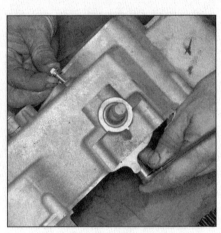

26.3e Unscrew the shift fork guide bar bolt

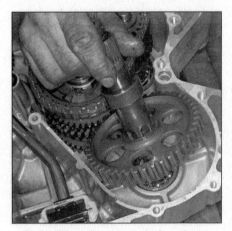

26.4 Lift out the output shaft and gear

castings and replace them if they're damaged or deteriorated **(see illustration)**.

7   If any damage is found that can't be repaired, replace the crankcase halves as a set.

8   Assemble the case halves (see Section 24) and check to make sure the crankshaft and the transmission shafts turn freely.

26 High-low and reverse gears, shafts and shift mechanism - removal, inspection and installation

Removal

Refer to illustrations 26.3a through 26.3e, 26.4, 26.5, 26.6a and 26.6b

1   Remove the engine, then separate the case halves (see Sec-

26.5 Pull the shift shaft all the way up to the top of the case so it clears the bushings on the shift forks . . .

26.6a . . . grasp the reverse chain and gears . . .

26.6b . . . and pull the idler shaft, input shaft and shift forks out of the crankcase

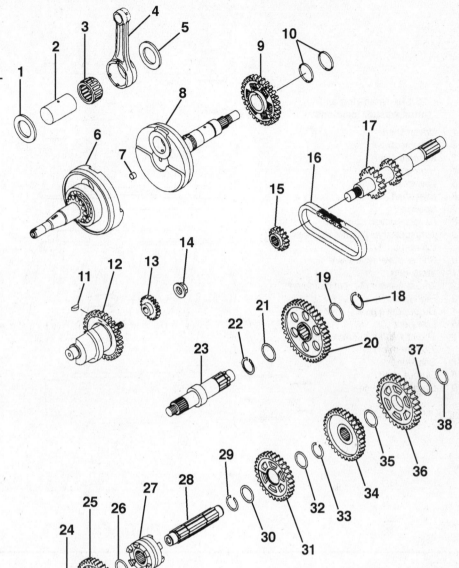

26.11a Crankcase internal components - exploded view

1   Thrust washer
2   Crankpin
3   Connecting rod big end bearing
4   Connecting rod
5   Thrust washer
6   Crankshaft end
7   Dowel pin
8   Crankshaft end
9   Balancer drive gear
10 Crankshaft sealing rings
11 Woodruff key
12 Balancer
13 Oil pump drive gear
14 Drive gear nut
15 Reverse drive gear
16 Reverse chain
17 Input shaft
18 Snap-ring
19 Thrust washer
20 Output gear
21 Thrust washer
22 Snap-ring
23 Output shaft
24 Thrust washer
25 Reverse driven gear
26 Thrust washer
27 Shifter (reverse/forward high range)
28 Idler shaft
29 Snap-ring
30 Thrust washer
31 Forward high gear
32 Thrust washer
33 Snap-ring
34 Idler shaft gear
35 Thrust washer
36 Forward low gear
37 Thrust washer
38 Snap-ring

tions 5 and 24).

2   The high-low transmission components and shift drum remain in the right case half when the case is separated.

3   Remove the shift rod retaining pin, shift shaft positioning bolt and shift fork guide bar bolt **(see illustrations)**.

4   Lift the output shaft out of the crankcase **(see illustration)**.

5   Lift the shift shaft clear of the shift fork bushings **(see illustration)**.

6   Grasp the reverse chain and gears **(see illustration)**. Pull the chain, idler shaft and the driven shaft out of the crankcase, together with the shift forks and guide bar **(see illustration)**.

Inspection

Refer to illustrations 26.11a, 26.11b and 26.13

7   Wash all of the components in clean solvent and dry them off.

8   Inspect the shift fork grooves in the gears. If a groove is worn or scored, replace the gear and inspect its corresponding shift fork.

9   Check the shift forks for distortion and wear, especially at the fork ears. If they are discolored or severely worn they are probably bent.

Inspect the guide pins for excessive wear and distortion and replace any defective parts with new ones.

10   Check the shift fork guide bar evidence of wear, galling and other damage. Make sure the shift forks move smoothly on the guide bar. If the guide bar is worn or bent, replace it with a new ones.

11   Disassemble the transmission shafts so you can inspect their components. Remove the snap-rings with snap-ring pliers and slide the gears, thrust washers and snap-rings off the shafts **(see illustrations)**. As you remove each part, place them in order on a piece of dowel or a straightened coat hanger to keep them in order. Check the gear teeth for cracking and other obvious damage. Check the bushing surface in the inner diameter of the freewheeling gears for scoring or heat discoloration. Replace damaged parts.

12   Inspect the engagement dogs on the shifter and output drive gear and the dog holes on the adjacent gears for excessive wear or rounding off. Replace the shifter, output drive gear and adjacent gears as a set if necessary.

13   Check the transmission shaft bearings in the crankcase for wear or heat discoloration and replace them if necessary (see Section 25).

2B

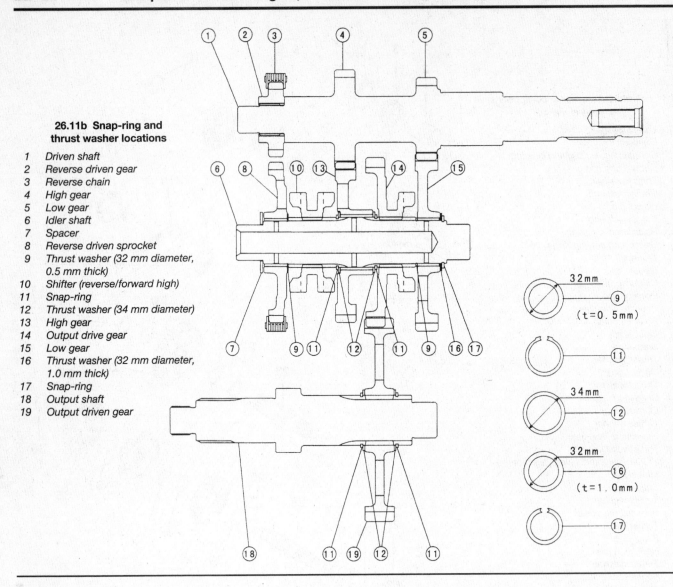

26.11b Snap-ring and thrust washer locations

1   Driven shaft
2   Reverse driven gear
3   Reverse chain
4   High gear
5   Low gear
6   Idler shaft
7   Spacer
8   Reverse driven sprocket
9   Thrust washer (32 mm diameter, 0.5 mm thick)
10   Shifter (reverse/forward high)
11   Snap-ring
12   Thrust washer (34 mm diameter)
13   High gear
14   Output drive gear
15   Low gear
16   Thrust washer (32 mm diameter, 1.0 mm thick)
17   Snap-ring
18   Output shaft
19   Output driven gear

Slip the shift shaft out of the case and check its bearings and seal **(see illustration)**. If they're worn, pry out the seal and pull the bearings with a slide hammer. Push in new bearings with a drift just smaller than the bearing bore. Seat the lower bearing on the ridge at the bottom of the bore and position the upper bearing flush with the top of the bore. Install the new seal on top of the upper bearing.

Installation

Refer to illustrations 26.14a through 26.14e

14   Installation is the basically the reverse of the removal procedure, but take note of the following points:

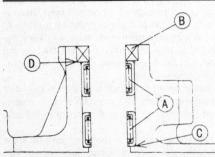

26.13 Shift arm shaft bearings and seal

A   Needle roller bearings
B   Seal
C   Lower bearing seating surface
D   Upper bearing flush with this surface

a)   *Lubricate the components with engine oil before assembling them.*
b)   *Always replace snap-rings with new ones whenever they're removed. When installing a snap-ring on a splined portion of one of the shafts, make sure the snap-ring gap is centered on one of the spline grooves.*

26.14a The idler shaft and input shaft gears mesh like this

26.14b The shift forks engage the gears like this

26.14c Oil and install the needle roller bearings (arrow) then install the bushings

26.14d Install the springs and detent balls in the shift fork pockets . . .

26.14e . . . the detent balls engage the guide bar grooves like this when the guide bar is installed

27.3 A tool like this one can be used to push the crankshaft out of the right case half

c) Check the gears to make sure they mesh correctly and that the shift forks engage the gear grooves **(see illustrations)**.
d) Don't forget to install the needle roller bearings on the shift fork pins before you install the collars **(see illustration)**.
e) Before installing the shift fork guide bar, install the detent balls and springs **(see illustration)**. The guide bar will hold the balls and springs in position.

27 Crankshaft, connecting rod and balancer - removal, inspection and installation

Note: The procedures in this section require special tools. If you don't have the necessary equipment or suitable substitutes, have the crankshaft removed and installed by a Kawasaki dealer or other qualified shop.

Removal

Refer to illustrations 27.3 and 27.4

1   Remove the engine and separate the crankcase halves (Sections 5 and 24). The transmission shafts need not be removed.
2   Generally, the crankshaft should stay in the right half of the case when the left half is lifted off **(see illustration 24.13c)**.
3   The crankshaft may be loose enough in its bearing that you can lift it out of the right crankcase half. If not, either push it out with a three-legged puller **(see illustration)** or have it pressed out by a dealer service department or machine shop.
4   If you haven't already done so, remove the oil pump drive gear from the balancer shaft (see Section 22). Lift the balancer out of the crankcase **(see illustration)**.

Inspection

Refer to illustration 27.5

5   Crankshaft inspection is the same as for Bayou models (see Chapter 2A), with one addition: check the sealing rings for wear **(see**

27.4 Be sure the balancer and crankshaft match marks are lined up

2B

illustration). If they're worn, unhook the ends and remove them from the crankshaft. Install new ones, spreading them just enough to fit over the crankshaft, and hook their ends together.

6   Check the balancer driven gear and its drive gear on the crankshaft for wear or damage. If there's a problem with either one, replace both gears as a set. This means that the balancer must be replaced. Its drive gear on the crankshaft can be replaced separately from the crankshaft, but this is a specialized job that should be done by a dealer service department or other qualified shop.

Installation

7   Installation is the same as for Bayou models (see Chapter 2A), with this addition: be sure the match marks on the balancer and crankshaft are lined up when the crankshaft is installed **(see illustration 27.4).**

6   The remainder of installation is the reverse of the removal steps.

28   Initial start-up after overhaul

1   Make sure the engine oil level is correct, then remove the spark plug from the engine. Place the engine kill switch in the Off position and unplug the primary (low tension) wires from the coil.

2   Turn on the key switch and crank the engine over with the starter several times to build up oil pressure. Reinstall the spark plug, connect the wires and turn the switch to On.

3   Make sure there is fuel in the tank, then operate the choke.

4   Start the engine and allow it to run at a moderately fast idle until it reaches operating temperature.

5   Check carefully for oil leaks and make sure the transmission and controls, especially the brakes, function properly before road testing the machine. Refer to Section 29 for the recommended break-in procedure.

6   Upon completion of the road test, and after the engine has cooled down completely, recheck the valve clearances (see Chapter 1).

29   Recommended break-in procedure

1   Any rebuilt engine needs time to break-in, even if parts have been

27.5 There's a sealing ring on either side of the oil hole; hook the ends together when installing them

installed in their original locations. For this reason, treat the machine gently for the first few miles to make sure oil has circulated throughout the engine and any new parts installed have started to seat. For new vehicles, Kawasaki recommends using no more than one-half throttle for the first ten hours of operation. This is a good general guide for rebuilt engines as well.

2   Even greater care is necessary if the cylinder has been rebored or a new crankshaft has been installed. In the case of a rebore, the engine will have to be broken in as if the machine were new. This means greater use of the transmission and a restraining hand on the throttle for the first few operating days. There's no point in keeping to any set speed limit - the main idea is to vary the engine speed, keep from lugging the engine and to avoid full-throttle operation. These recommendations can be lessened to an extent when only a new crankshaft is installed. Experience is the best guide, since it's easy to tell when an engine is running freely.

3   If a lubrication failure is suspected, stop the engine immediately and try to find the cause. If an engine is run without oil, even for a short period of time, irreparable damage will occur.

Chapter 3 Part A
Fuel and exhaust systems (Bayou models)

Contents

	Section
Air cleaner housing - removal and installation	11
Air filter element - servicing	See Chapter 1
Carburetor - disassembly, cleaning and inspection	8
Carburetor - removal and installation	7
Carburetor overhaul - general information	6
Carburetors - reassembly and float height check	9
Exhaust system - check	See Chapter 1
Exhaust system - removal and installation	13
Fuel level - check and adjustment	10

	Section
Fuel level gauge (1988 and later) – removal, inspection and installation	4
Fuel tank - cleaning and repair	3
Fuel tank and gauge - removal and installation	2
General information	1
Idle fuel/air mixture adjustment	5
Throttle and choke cables - removal, installation and adjustment	12

Specifications

General

Fuel type .... Unleaded gasoline (petrol) subject to local regulations; minimum octane 91 RON (86 pump octane)

Carburetor

220 models

Type	Mikuni VM24SS
Main jet	115
Jet needle	5GN46-2
Needle jet	O-0
Pilot jet	30
Pilot air jet	1.2
Starter (choke) jet	45
Air screw setting (turns out from lightly seated position)	1-1/2
Float height	21.8 mm (55/64 inch)
Fuel level	5 mm (0.20 inch) below lower edge of carburetor body

300 models

Type	Keihin CVK32
Main jet	
1986 and 1987	130
1988 on	
2WD models	128
4WD models	125
Jet needle	
2WD models	N27Q
4WD models	N36W
Needle jet	6
Pilot jet	38
Pilot air jet	140
Starter (choke) jet	
2WD models	55
4WD models	58
Pilot screw setting (turns out from lightly seated position)	2-1/8
Float height	
2WD models	17+/-2 mm (0.669+/-0.079 inch)
4WD models	17+/-1 mm (0.669 +/-0.039 inch)
Fuel level	0.5 mm (0.020 inch) below to 1.5 mm (0.059 inch) above lower edge of carburetor body

3A

1   General information

The fuel system consists of the fuel tank, fuel tap, filter screen, carburetor and connecting lines, hose and control cables. A fuel gauge is built into the fuel tank on 1988 and later models.

220 models use a Mikuni VM carburetor. A single throttle cable operates a piston-type throttle valve and jet needle. 300 models use a Keihin CVK carburetor. A single throttle cable operates a butterfly-type throttle valve, while vacuum through the carburetor venturi lifts the jet needle. On all models, a thumb lever on the right handlebar operates the throttle. A choke lever on the left handlebar operates the enrichment circuit.

The exhaust system consists of a pipe, a pre-muffler (4WD models) and a muffler.

Many of the fuel system service procedures are considered routine maintenance items and for that reason are included in Chapter 1.

2   Fuel tank and gauge - removal and installation

Warning: *Gasoline (petrol) is extremely flammable, so take extra precautions when you work on any part of the fuel system. Don't smoke or allow open flames or bare light bulbs near the work area, and don't work in a garage where a gas-type appliance (such as a water heater or clothes dryer) is present. Since gasoline is carcinogenic, wear fuel-resistant gloves when there's a possibility of being exposed to fuel, and, if you spill any fuel on your skin, rinse it off immediately with soap and water. Mop up any spills immediately and do not store fuel-soaked rags where they could ignite. When you perform any kind of work on the fuel system, wear safety glasses and have a fire extinguisher suitable for a class B type fire (flammable liquids) on hand.*

Removal

Refer to illustrations 2.1a, 2.1b and 2.4

1   The fuel tank on all 220 models, 1986 and 1987 US 300 models, and later UK and European 300 models is secured by a single bolt at the rear and a bolt and rubber grommet on each side at the front **(see illustration)**. On 1988 and later US 300 models, the fuel tank is secured by a single bolt at the front and another single bolt at the rear (see illustration).

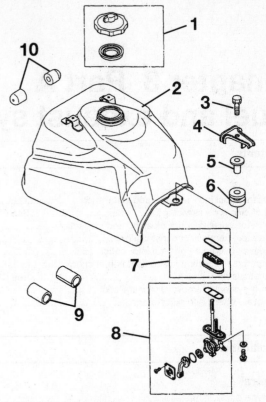

2.1a Fuel tank details, 1986 and 1987 US models (later UK and European models similar)

1	Cap and gasket	7	Fuel tap mounting base
2	Fuel tank		and gasket
3	Mounting bolt	8	Fuel tap
4	Mounting retainer	9	Mounting pads – frame
5	Collar	10	Mounting bushings - front
6	Grommet		

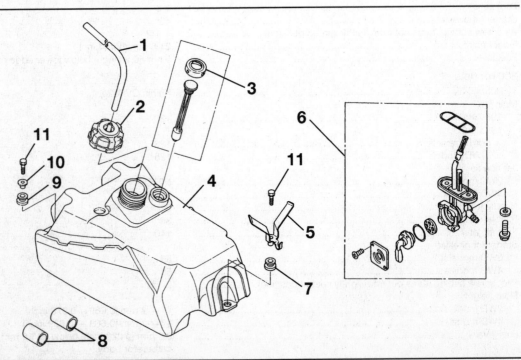

2.1b Fuel tank details, 1988 and later US models (300 shown; 220 similar)

1   Vent hose
2   Fuel tank cap
3   Fuel level gauge
4   Fuel tank
5   Hose retainer
6   Fuel tap
7   Grommet
8   Mounting pads – frame
9   Grommet
10   Collar
11   Bolt

2.4 On later models, the rear mounting bolt secures this hose retainer

2   If you're working on a 1986 or 1987 model, remove the front fender (see Chapter 7). If you're working on a 1988 or later model, remove the seat and the fuel tank top cover. Reinstall the fuel tank cap as soon as the top cover is removed.

3   Turn the fuel tap to Off and disconnect the fuel line that runs to the carburetor (see Chapter 1).

4   If you're working on a 1988 or later model, remove the screw that secures the hose retainer at the rear of the tank **(see illustration)**.

5   Remove the fuel tank mounting bolt(s) **(see illustration 2.1a or 2.1b)**.

6   If you're working on a 1986 or 1987 model, pull the fuel tank backward out of the front mounting brackets. If you're working on a 1988 or later model, lift the tank off.

Installation

7   Before installing the tank, check the condition of the rubber mounting dampers - if they're hardened, cracked, or show any other signs of deterioration, replace them.

8   When installing the tank, reverse the removal procedure. Don't pinch any control cables or wires.

3   Fuel tank - cleaning and repair

1   The fuel tank on some models is plastic and can't be repaired by traditional welding or brazing techniques. In any case, all repairs to the fuel tank – plastic or metal - should be carried out by a professional who has experience in this critical and potentially dangerous work. Even after cleaning and flushing of the fuel system, explosive fumes can remain and ignite during repair of the tank.

2   If the fuel tank is removed from the vehicle, it should not be placed in an area where sparks or open flames could ignite the fumes coming out of the tank. Be especially careful inside garages where a gas-type appliance (such as a water heater or clothes dryer) is present.

4   Fuel level gauge (1988 and later) - removal, inspection and installation

Removal

1   Remove the fuel tank top cover (see Chapter 7).

2   Carefully pry the metal cap off the fuel tank gauge **(see illustration 2.1b)**. **Caution:** *The cap is held in place by tabs that fit into small grooves on the fuel tank. If the tank grooves are damaged, the entire tank will have to be replaced.*

3   Lift the gauge out of the tank.

Inspection

4   Check the gauge for visible damage and replace it if problems can be seen.

5   Turn the gauge upside down and back upright. The gauge float should move smoothly up and down under its own weight. If not, replace the gauge.

Installation

6   Installation is the reverse of the removal steps. Align the notch in the gauge cap with the 1/2 mark on the gauge scale. Replace the gauge retainer with a new one.

5   Idle fuel/air mixture adjustment

1   Idle fuel/air mixture on these vehicles is preset at the factory and should not need adjustment unless a stable idle can't be achieved during the idle speed adjustment procedure described in Chapter 1. The mixture should also be adjusted whenever the carburetor is overhauled or the pilot screw, which controls the mixture adjustment, is replaced.

2   The engine must be properly tuned up before making the adjustment (valve clearances set to specifications, spark plug in good condition and properly gapped).

220 models

3   Locate the air screw on the underside of the carburetor **(see illustration 8.2)**. Turn it in lightly until it bottoms, then back it out the number of turns listed in this Chapter's Specifications. **Caution:** *Turn the screw just far enough to seat it lightly. If it's bottomed hard, the screw or its seat may be damaged, which will make accurate mixture adjustments impossible.*

300 models

4   To gain access to the pilot screw, loosen the carburetor mounting clamps (Section 7). Turn the carburetor bottom toward the right side of the vehicle.

5   To make an initial adjustment, turn the pilot screw clockwise until it seats lightly, then back it out the number of turns listed in this Chapter's Specifications **(see illustration 8.3d in Section 7)**. **Caution:** *Turn the screw just far enough to seat it lightly. If it's bottomed hard, the screw or its seat may be damaged, which will make accurate mixture adjustments impossible.*

6   Turn the carburetor back to its normal installed position and tighten the mounting clamps.

All models

7   Warm up the engine to normal operating temperature.

8   Restart the engine and set the idle to the slowest smooth idle speed (see Chapter 1).

6   Carburetor overhaul - general information

1   Poor engine performance, hesitation, hard starting, stalling, flooding and backfiring are all signs that major carburetor maintenance may be required.

2   Keep in mind that many so-called carburetor problems are really not carburetor problems at all, but mechanical problems within the engine or ignition system malfunctions. Try to establish for certain that the carburetor is in need of maintenance before beginning a major overhaul.

3   Check the fuel tap and its strainer screen, the fuel line, the intake manifold clamps and Allen bolts, the O-ring(s) between the intake manifold and cylinder head, the air filter element, the cylinder compression, the spark plug and the ignition timing before assuming that a carburetor overhaul is required. If the vehicle has been unused for more than a month, refer to Chapter 1, drain the float chamber and refill the tank with fresh fuel.

3A

7.2a Loosen the clamping bands (arrows) on the carburetor air tube . . .

7.2b . . . and lift the tube out

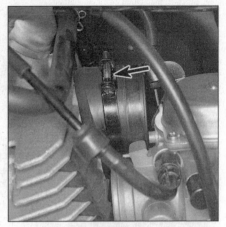

7.3 Loosen the intake manifold clamp (arrow) and slide it down the intake manifold (300 shown; 220 similar)

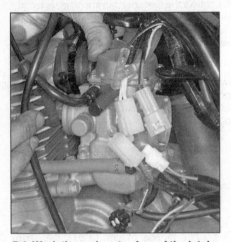

7.4 Work the carburetor free of the intake manifold (300 shown; 220 similar)

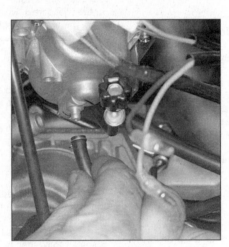

7.6 Disconnect the float chamber drain hose from the bottom (300 shown; 220 similar)

7.7 Remove the Allen bolts to detach the manifold from the head; on 300 models, the right bolt secures a hose clip

4   Most carburetor problems are caused by dirt particles, varnish and other deposits which build up in and block the fuel and air passages. Also, in time, gaskets and O-rings shrink or deteriorate and cause fuel and air leaks which lead to poor performance.

5   When the carburetor is overhauled, it is generally disassembled completely and the parts are cleaned thoroughly with a carburetor cleaning solvent and dried with filtered, unlubricated compressed air. The fuel and air passages are also blown through with compressed air to force out any dirt that may have been loosened but not removed by the solvent. Once the cleaning process is complete, the carburetor is reassembled using new gaskets, O-rings and, generally, a new inlet needle valve and seat.

6   Before disassembling the carburetor, make sure you have all necessary O-rings, gaskets and other parts, some carburetor cleaner, a supply of rags, some means of blowing out the carburetor passages and a clean place to work.

---

7   Carburetor - removal and installation

Warning: *Gasoline (petrol) is extremely flammable, so take extra precautions when you work on any part of the fuel system. Don't smoke or allow open flames or bare light bulbs near the work area, and don't work in a garage where a gas-type appliance (such as a water heater or clothes dryer) is present. Since gasoline is carcinogenic, wear fuel-resistant gloves when there's a possibility of being exposed to fuel,* *and, if you spill any fuel on your skin, rinse it off immediately with soap and water. Mop up any spills immediately and do not store fuel-soaked rags where they could ignite. When you perform any kind of work on the fuel system, wear safety glasses and have a fire extinguisher suitable for a class B type fire (flammable liquids) on hand.*

Removal

Refer to illustrations 7.2a, 7.2b, 7.3, 7.4, 7.6 and 7.7

1   Remove the fuel tank (see Section 2).

2   Loosen the clamps on the air intake duct and remove it from the vehicle **(see illustrations)**.

3   Loosen the clamp on the intake manifold and slide it down the manifold **(see illustration)**.

4   Work the carburetor out of the intake manifold **(see illustration)**.

5   Disconnect the throttle and choke cables from the carburetor (Section 12).

6   Disconnect the float chamber drain hose from the carburetor **(see illustration)**. Take the carburetor out.

7   If you plan to overhaul the carburetor or replace the manifold O-ring, remove the Allen bolts and separate the intake manifold from the cylinder head **(see illustration)**.

Installation

8   Installation is the reverse of the removal steps, with the following additions: Adjust throttle lever freeplay and idle speed (see Chapter 1).

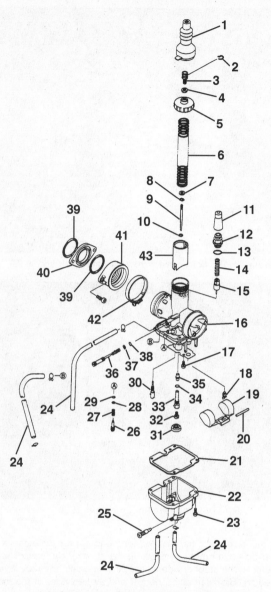

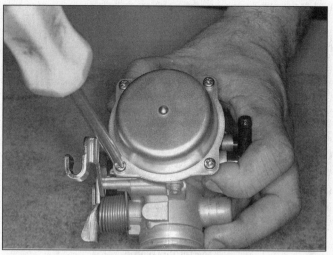

8.3a Remove the screws from the cap . . .

8.3b . . . lift off the cap, then remove the spring, throttle diaphragm and jet needle components

8.2 Carburetor (220 models) – exploded view

1	Rubber cover	23	Screw
2	Snap-ring	24	Hoses
3	Cable adjuster	25	Drain screw
4	Adjuster locknut	26	Air screw
5	Cap	27	Spring
6	Throttle spring	28	Washer
7	Spring seat	29	O-ring
8	Jet needle clip	30	Pilot jet
9	Jet needle	31	Baffle
10	Washer	32	Main jet
11	Rubber cap	33	Air bleed tube
12	Starter (choke) fitting	34	O-ring
13	O-ring	35	Needle jet
14	Spring	36	Idle speed screw
15	Starter (choke) plunger	37	Washer
16	Carburetor body	38	O-ring
17	Pan head screw	39	O-ring
18	Needle valve	40	Spacer
19	Floats	41	Intake manifold
20	Float pivot pin	42	Clamp
21	Gasket	43	Throttle piston
22	Float chamber		

8 Carburetor - disassembly, cleaning and inspection

Warning: *Gasoline (petrol) is extremely flammable, so take extra precautions when you work on any part of the fuel system. Don't smoke or allow open flames or bare light bulbs near the work area, and don't work in a garage where a gas-type appliance (such as a water heater or clothes dryer) is present. Since gasoline is carcinogenic, wear fuel-resistant gloves when there's a possibility of being exposed to fuel, and, if you spill any fuel on your skin, rinse it off immediately with soap and water. Mop up any spills immediately and do not store fuel-soaked rags where they could ignite. When you perform any kind of work on the fuel system, wear safety glasses and have a fire extinguisher suitable for a class B type fire (flammable liquids) on hand.*

Disassembly

Refer to illustrations 8.2 and 8.3a through 8.3m

1   Remove the carburetor from the machine as described in Section 7. Set it on a clean working surface.

2   If you're working on a 220 model, refer to the accompanying illustration to disassemble the carburetor **(see illustration)**.

3   If you're working on a 300 model, refer to the accompanying illustrations to disassemble the carburetor **(see illustrations)**.

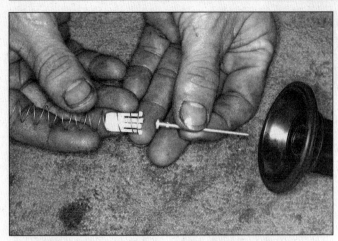

8.3c Remove the spring, retainer and jet needle from the throttle piston

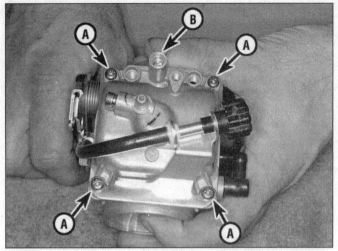

8.3d Here are the float bowl screws (A) and pilot screw (B)

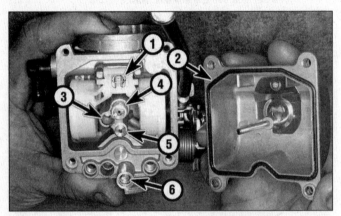

8.3e Carburetor bottom end components

1 Float tang	5 Starter (choke) jet
2 Float bowl O-ring	6 Pilot screw, spring,
3 Pilot jet	washer and O-ring
4 Main jet	

Cleaning

Caution: *Use only a carburetor cleaning solution that is safe for use with plastic parts (be sure to read the label on the container).*

4   Submerge the metal components in the carburetor cleaner for approximately thirty minutes (or longer, if the directions recommend it).

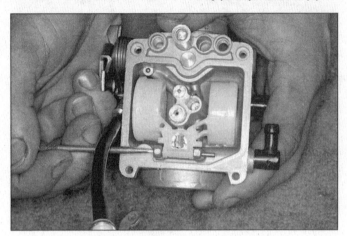

8.3f Push out the float pivot pin . . .

5   After the carburetor has soaked long enough for the cleaner to loosen and dissolve most of the varnish and other deposits, use a brush to remove the stubborn deposits. Rinse it again, then dry it with compressed air. Blow out all of the fuel and air passages in the main and upper body. **Caution:** *Never clean the jets or passages with a piece of wire or a drill bit, as they will be enlarged, causing the fuel and air metering rates to be upset.*

8.3g . . . lift out the floats and unhook the needle valve

8.3h Unscrew the starter (choke) jet . . .

8.3i . . . and the pilot jet

8.3j Hold the air bleed pipe with a wrench and unscrew the main jet . . .

8.3k . . . then unscrew the air bleed pipe and remove the needle jet; the shorter end of the needle jet goes in first

8.3l Remove the pilot screw, spring and washer, then pull out the O-ring with a bent paper clip

8.3m Pilot screw, spring, washer and O-ring

9.2 Don't block the vacuum hole (arrow) when you install the jet needle retainer

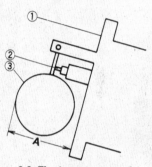

9.6 Float measurement

A   Float height
1   Float bowl mating surface on carburetor body
2   Needle valve rod
3   Float

3A

Inspection

6   Check the operation of the choke plunger. If it doesn't move smoothly, replace it, along with the return spring. If the plunger O-ring is deteriorated or damaged, replace it.

7   Check the tapered portion of the pilot screw for wear or damage. Replace the pilot screw if necessary.

8   Check the carburetor body, float chamber and top cover for cracks, distorted sealing surfaces and other damage. If any defects are found, replace the faulty component, although replacement of the entire carburetor will probably be necessary (check with your parts supplier for the availability of separate components).

9   Check the jet needle for straightness by rolling it on a flat surface (such as a piece of glass). Replace it if it's bent or if the tip is worn.

10   Check the tip of the fuel inlet valve needle. If it has grooves or scratches in it, it must be replaced. Push in on the rod in the other end of the needle, then release it - if it doesn't spring back, replace the valve needle.

11   Check the float chamber O-ring and the drain plug (in the float chamber). Replace them if they're damaged.

12   Operate the throttle shaft to make sure the throttle butterfly valve opens and closes smoothly. If it doesn't, replace the carburetor.

13   Check the floats for damage. This will usually be apparent by the presence of fuel inside one of the floats. If the floats are damaged, they must be replaced.

14   Check the throttle diaphragm for splits, holes and general deterioration. Holding it up to a light will help to reveal problems of this nature.

15   Check the piston valve in the carburetor body for wear or damage. If it's worn or damaged, replace the carburetor.

9   Carburetors - reassembly and float height check

Refer to illustrations 9.2 and 9.6

1   Reassembly is the reverse of disassembly, with the following additions. **Caution:** *When installing the jets, be careful not to over-tighten them - they're made of soft material and can strip or shear easily.*

2   Install the clip on the jet needle if it was removed. Place it in the needle groove listed in this Chapter's Specifications. When you reinstall the jet needle and retainer in the throttle piston on a 300 model, make sure the retainer doesn't block the vacuum hole in the top of the piston **(see illustration).**

3   Install the air screw or pilot screw (if removed) along with its spring, washer and O-ring, turning it in until it seats lightly. Now, turn the screw out the number of turns listed in this Chapter's Specifications.

4   If you're working on a 300 model, install the throttle diaphragm into the carburetor body. Seat the bead of the diaphragm into the groove in the carburetor body, making sure the diaphragm isn't distorted or kinked **(see illustration 8.3b).**

5   Reverse the disassembly steps to install the jets. If you're working on a 220 model, install the needle jet so its long end will face upward when the carburetor is installed on he vehicle.

6   Invert the carburetor. Attach the fuel inlet valve needle to the float. Set the float into position in the carburetor, making sure the valve needle seats correctly. Install the float pivot pin. To check the float height, hold the carburetor so the float hangs down, then tilt it back until the valve needle is just seated. Measure the distance from the float chamber gasket surface to the top of the float and compare your measurement to the float height listed in this Chapter's Specifications **(see**

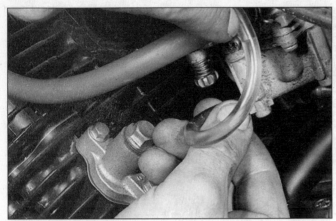

10.2 A ruler and a clear plastic tube like this one can be used to measure fuel level if you don't have the special tool

11.2a   Remove the screws and loosen the clamp (arrows) to remove the duct

11.2b Loosen this clamp at the air cleaner housing

11.4 Disconnect the breather hose from the housing

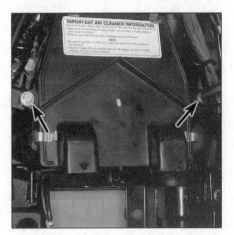

11.5 Remove the housing bolts (arrows)

illustration). If it isn't as specified, bend the tang on the float to change it **(see illustration 8.3e)**.

7   Install the O-ring into the groove in the float chamber. Place the float chamber on the carburetor and install the screws, tightening them securely.

10   Fuel level - check and adjustment

Refer to illustration 10.2

Warning: *Gasoline (petrol) is extremely flammable, so take extra precautions when you work on any part of the fuel system. Don't smoke or allow open flames or bare light bulbs near the work area, and don't work in a garage where a gas-type appliance (such as a water heater or clothes dryer) is present. Since gasoline is carcinogenic, wear fuel-resistant gloves when there's a possibility of being exposed to fuel, and, if you spill any fuel on your skin, rinse it off immediately with soap and water. Mop up any spills immediately and do not store fuel-soaked rags where they could ignite. When you perform any kind of work on the fuel system, wear safety glasses and have a fire extinguisher suitable for a class B type fire (flammable liquids) on hand.*

1   Park the vehicle on a level surface and make sure the carburetor is level. If necessary, adjust its position slightly by placing a floor jack under the engine and raising it.

2   Attach Kawasaki service tool 57001-1017 to the drain fitting on the bottom of the carburetor float bowl. This is a clear plastic tube graduated in millimeters. An alternative is to use a length of clear plastic tubing and an accurate ruler **(see illustration)**. Hold the graduated tube (or the free end of the clear plastic tube) vertically against the float

chamber cover.

3   Unscrew the drain screw at the bottom of the float chamber a couple of turns, then start the engine and let it idle - fuel will flow into the tube. Wait for the fuel level to stabilize, then note how far the fuel level is below the line on the float chamber cover.

4   Measure the distance between the line and the top of the fuel in the tube or gauge. This distance is the fuel level.

5   Compare your reading to the value listed in this Chapter's Specifications. If the fuel level is not correct, remove the float chamber cover and bend the float tang up or down as necessary, then recheck the fuel level.

11   Air cleaner housing - removal and installation

Removal

Refer to illustrations 11.2a, 11.2b, 11.4 and 11.5

1   Refer to Section 2 and remove the fuel tank.

2   Loosen the clamp, unscrew the mounting screws and remove the upper intake duct (if equipped) **(see illustration)**. Loosen the lower duct clamp and detach the lower intake duct from the air cleaner housing **(see illustration)**.

3   Loosen the clamps and detach the carburetor air tube from the air cleaner housing and carburetor **(see illustrations 7.2a and 7.2b)**.

4   Disconnect the breather hose from the housing **(see illustration)**.

5   Remove the air cleaner housing bolts **(see illustration)**. Lift the air cleaner housing out of the frame.

6   Installation is the reverse of the removal steps.

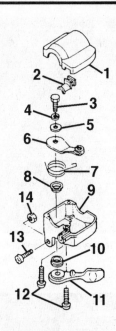

**12.3 Throttle lever housing –
exploded view**

1 *Housing cover*
2 *Cap*
3 *Cable lever screw*
4 *Lockwasher*
5 *Washer*
6 *Cable lever*
7 *Return spring*
8 *Collar*
9 *Throttle housing*
10 *Wave washer*
11 *Throttle lever (thumb lever)*
12 *Screws*
13 *Throttle limiter screw*
14 *Locknut*

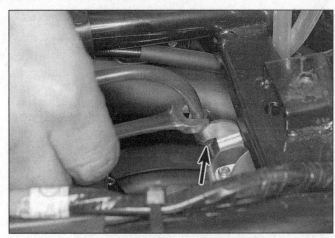

12.5a Loosen the locknuts (arrow) . . .

**12.5b . . . free the cable from the bracket, then rotate its end and
slip the end plug out of the lever**

3A

12 Throttle and choke cables - removal, installation and adjustment

Throttle cable

1   The throttle cable runs from the housing on the right handlebar to the carburetor.

Removal

Refer to illustrations 12.3, 12.5a and 12.5b
2   Remove the front fender (see Chapter 7).
3   Remove the screws and separate the upper and lower halves of the throttle housing **(see illustration)**.
4   Loosen the throttle cable at the handlebar adjuster, then detach the cable end plug from the lever inside the throttle housing.
5   Loosen the locknuts at the lower end of the cable **(see illustration)**. Free the cable from the bracket, then rotate its end and slip the end plug out of the throttle lever on the carburetor **(see illustration)**.
6   Remove the cable from the vehicle, noting how it's routed.

Installation

7   Route the cable into place. Make sure it doesn't interfere with any other components and isn't kinked or bent sharply.
8   Lubricate the ends of the cable with multi-purpose grease and connect them to the throttle housing lever and carburetor lever. Install the cable in the carburetor bracket and assemble the upper and lower halves of the throttle housing.
9   Operate the lever and make sure it returns to the idle position by itself under spring pressure. **Warning:** *If the lever doesn't return by itself, find and solve the problem before continuing with installation. A stuck lever can lead to loss of control of the vehicle.*

Adjustment

10   Follow the procedure outlined in Chapter 1, *Throttle operation/grip freeplay - check and adjustment*, to adjust the cable.
11   Turn the handlebar back and forth to make sure the cable doesn't cause the steering to bind.
12   With the engine idling, turn the handlebar through its full travel (full left lock to full right lock) and note whether idle speed increases. If it does, a cable is routed incorrectly. Correct this dangerous condition before riding the vehicle.
13   Install the front fender.

Choke cable

Removal

Refer to illustrations 12.15a, 12.15b and 12.16
14   Remove the carburetor partway for access to the lower end of the cable (Section 7).
15   Unscrew the plunger cap from the carburetor and pull the choke plunger out **(see illustrations)**. Compress the spring on the choke

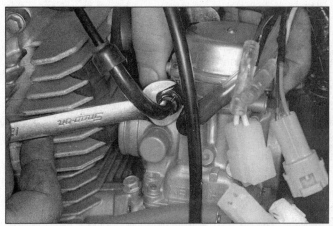

12.15a Unscrew the choke cable fitting from the carburetor . . .

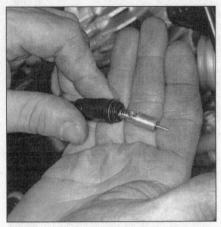

12.15b . . . then compress the spring and slip the cable end out of the choke plunger

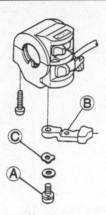

12.16 Choke lever details

A   Screw
B   Choke lever
C   Wave washer

13.1a Remove the holder nuts . . .

13.1b . . . then slide the holder off the studs and the collar out of the exhaust port

13.3 Loosen the clamp and pull the exhaust pipe forward

13.5a Remove the muffler mounting bolts . . .

plunger and slip the cable end sideways out of the plunger.

16   Remove the choke lever pivot screw, washer and choke lever from the housing on the left handlebar **(see illustration)**.

17   Turn the choke lever to align its slot with the cable, then slip the cable end plug out of the lever.

Installation

18   Installation is the reverse of the removal steps. The choke cable is not adjustable.

13   Exhaust system - removal and installation

Refer to illustrations 13.1a, 13.1b, 13.3, 13.5a and 13.5b

1   Remove the exhaust pipe holder nuts and slide the holder off the mounting studs **(see illustrations)**.

2   If necessary, unbolt the heat shield and remove it from the exhaust pipe.

3   Loosen the clamp and separate the muffler from the front exhaust pipe **(see illustration)**.

4   Pull the exhaust pipe forward, separate it from the cylinder head and remove it from the machine.

5   On 4WD models, loosen the clamp between the pre-muffler and

13.5b . . . and the pre-muffler mounting bolts (4WD models)

muffler. Remove the muffler and pre-muffler mounting bolts and remove them from the vehicle **(see illustrations)**.

6   Installation is the reverse of removal, with the following addition: Be sure to install new gaskets at the cylinder head and pipe joint.

Chapter 3 Part B
Fuel and exhaust systems (Prairie models)

Contents

	Section			Section
Air cleaner duct and housing - removal and installation	12		Fuel level - check and adjustment	10
Air filter element - servicing	See Chapter 1		Fuel level gauge – removal, inspection and installation	4
Carburetor - disassembly, cleaning and inspection	8		Fuel tank - cleaning and repair	3
Carburetor - removal and installation	7		Fuel tank and gauge - removal and installation	2
Carburetor heater – removal, inspection and installation	11		General information	1
Carburetor overhaul - general information	6		Idle fuel/air mixture adjustment	5
Carburetors - reassembly and float height check	9		Throttle and choke cables - removal, installation	
Exhaust system - check	See Chapter 1		and adjustment	13
Exhaust system - removal and installation	14			

Specifications

General

Fuel type	Unleaded gasoline (petrol) subject to local regulations; minimum octane 91 RON (86 pump octane)

Carburetor

Type	Keihin CVK32
Main jet	
Sea level (standard)	140
500 to 1500 meters (1650 to 5000 feet)	138
1500 to 2500 meters (5000 to 8000 feet)	132
2500 to 3500 meters (8000 to 11500 feet)	130
3500 to 4500 meters (11500 to 15000 feet)	128
Jet needle	N4YP
Needle jet	6
Pilot jet	35
Pilot air jet	120
Starter (choke) jet	75
Pilot screw setting (turns out from lightly seated position)	2
Float height	17+/-2 mm (0.669+/-0.079 inch)
Fuel level	0.5 mm (0.020 inch) below to 1.5 mm (0.059 inch) above lower edge of carburetor body

1   General information

The fuel system consists of the fuel tank, fuel tap, filter screen, carburetor and connecting lines, hose and control cables. A fuel gauge is built into the fuel tank.

A Keihin CVK carburetor is used on these models. A single throttle cable operates a butterfly-type throttle valve, while vacuum through the carburetor venturi lifts the jet needle. A thumb lever on the right handlebar operates the throttle. A choke lever on the handlebar operates the enrichment circuit. The carburetor is electrically heated to prevent icing during cold-weather operation.

The exhaust system consists of a pipe and a muffler.

Many of the fuel system service procedures are considered routine maintenance items and for that reason are included in Chapter 1.

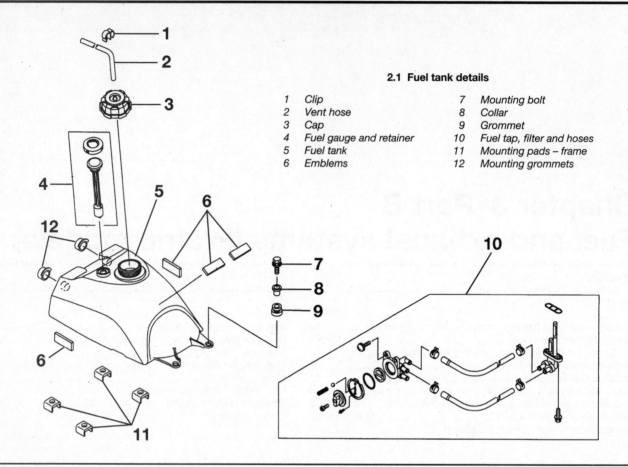

2.1 Fuel tank details

1	Clip	7	Mounting bolt
2	Vent hose	8	Collar
3	Cap	9	Grommet
4	Fuel gauge and retainer	10	Fuel tap, filter and hoses
5	Fuel tank	11	Mounting pads – frame
6	Emblems	12	Mounting grommets

2   Fuel tank and gauge - removal and installation

Warning: *Gasoline (petrol) is extremely flammable, so take extra precautions when you work on any part of the fuel system. Don't smoke or allow open flames or bare light bulbs near the work area, and don't work in a garage where a gas-type appliance (such as a water heater or clothes dryer) is present. Since gasoline is carcinogenic, wear fuel-resistant gloves when there's a possibility of being exposed to fuel, and, if you spill any fuel on your skin, rinse it off immediately with soap and water. Mop up any spills immediately and do not store fuel-soaked rags where they could ignite. When you perform any kind of work on the fuel system, wear safety glasses and have a fire extinguisher suitable for a class B type fire (flammable liquids) on hand.*

Removal

Refer to illustration 2.1

1   The fuel tank is secured by two bolts at the rear. At the front, the tank is supported by a damper on each side **(see illustration)**.
2   Remove the seat and the fuel tank top cover (see Chapter 7). Reinstall the fuel tank cap as soon as the top cover is removed.
3   Turn the fuel tap to Off and disconnect the fuel line that runs to the carburetor (see Chapter 1).
4   Remove the fuel tank mounting bolts **(see illustration 2.1)**.
5   Pull the fuel tank backward out of the front mounting brackets.

Installation

6   Before installing the tank, check the condition of the rubber mounting dampers - if they're hardened, cracked, or show any other signs of deterioration, replace them.
7   When installing the tank, reverse the removal procedure. Don't pinch any control cables or wires.

3   Fuel tank - cleaning and repair

1   The fuel tank on some models is plastic and can't be repaired by traditional welding or brazing techniques. In any case, all repairs to the fuel tank – plastic or metal - should be carried out by a professional who has experience in this critical and potentially dangerous work. Even after cleaning and flushing of the fuel system, explosive fumes can remain and ignite during repair of the tank.
2   If the fuel tank is removed from the vehicle, it should not be placed in an area where sparks or open flames could ignite the fumes coming out of the tank. Be especially careful inside garages where a gas-type appliance (such as a water heater or clothes dryer) is present.

4   Fuel level gauge – removal, inspection and installation

This procedure is the same as for 1988 and later Bayou models (see Chapter 3A).

5   Idle fuel/air mixture adjustment

Refer to illustration 5.4

1   Idle fuel/air mixture on these vehicles is preset at the factory and should not need adjustment unless the carburetor is overhauled or the pilot screw, which controls the mixture adjustment, is replaced.
2   The engine must be properly tuned up before making the adjustment (valve clearances set to specifications, spark plug in good condition and properly gapped).
3   The pilot screw is threaded into the bottom of the carburetor. Kawasaki makes a special angle screwdriver (part no. 57001-1239)

5.4 The pilot screw is inside this bore in the bottom of the carburetor

that can reach the pilot screw with the carburetor installed. To gain access to the pilot screw if you don't have the special tool, loosen the carburetor mounting clamps (Section 7). Turn the carburetor bottom toward the right side of the vehicle.

4   To make an initial adjustment, turn the pilot screw clockwise until it seats lightly, then back it out the number of turns listed in this Chapter's Specifications **(see illustration)**. **Caution:** *Turn the screw just far enough to seat it lightly. If it's bottomed hard, the screw or its seat may be damaged, which will make accurate mixture adjustments impossible.*

5   Turn the carburetor back to its normal installed position and tighten the mounting clamps.

6   Warm up the engine to normal operating temperature.

7   Restart the engine and set the idle to the slowest smooth idle speed (see Chapter 1).

6   Carburetor overhaul - general information

1   Poor engine performance, hesitation, hard starting, stalling, flooding and backfiring are all signs that major carburetor maintenance may be required.

2   Keep in mind that many so-called carburetor problems are really not carburetor problems at all, but mechanical problems within the engine or ignition system malfunctions. Try to establish for certain that the carburetor is in need of maintenance before beginning a major overhaul.

3   Check the fuel tap and its strainer screen, the fuel line, the intake manifold clamps and Allen bolts, the O-ring between the intake manifold and cylinder head, the air filter element, the cylinder compression, the spark plug and the ignition timing before assuming that a carburetor overhaul is required. If the vehicle has been unused for more than a month, refer to Chapter 1, drain the float chamber and refill the tank with fresh fuel.

4   Most carburetor problems are caused by dirt particles, varnish and other deposits which build up in and block the fuel and air passages. Also, in time, gaskets and O-rings shrink or deteriorate and cause fuel and air leaks which lead to poor performance.

5   When the carburetor is overhauled, it is generally disassembled completely and the parts are cleaned thoroughly with a carburetor cleaning solvent and dried with filtered, unlubricated compressed air. The fuel and air passages are also blown through with compressed air to force out any dirt that may have been loosened but not removed by the solvent. Once the cleaning process is complete, the carburetor is reassembled using new gaskets, O-rings and, generally, a new inlet needle valve and seat.

6   Before disassembling the carburetor, make sure you have all necessary O-rings, gaskets and other parts, some carburetor cleaner, a supply of rags, some means of blowing out the carburetor passages and a clean place to work.

7   Carburetor - removal and installation

Warning: *Gasoline (petrol) is extremely flammable, so take extra precautions when you work on any part of the fuel system. Don't smoke or allow open flames or bare light bulbs near the work area, and don't work in a garage where a gas-type appliance (such as a water heater or clothes dryer) is present. Since gasoline is carcinogenic, wear fuel-resistant gloves when there's a possibility of being exposed to fuel, and, if you spill any fuel on your skin, rinse it off immediately with soap and water. Mop up any spills immediately and do not store fuel-soaked rags where they could ignite. When you perform any kind of work on the fuel system, wear safety glasses and have a fire extinguisher suitable for a class B type fire (flammable liquids) on hand.*

Removal

Refer to illustrations 7.2, 7.4, 7.5a, 7.5b, 7.5c and 7.6

1   Remove the fuel tank (see Section 2).

2   Loosen the clamps on the air intake duct and intake manifold **(see illustration)**.

3   Disconnect the throttle cable from the carburetor (Section 12).

4   Pull the vent hose out of its hole in the frame **(see illustration)**.

5   Disconnect the carburetor heater electrical connector and free the harness **(see illustrations)**.

7.2 Loosen the clamps (arrows)

7.4 Pull the vent hose out of its hole

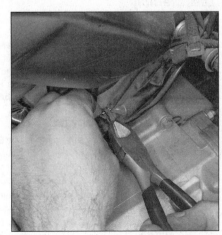

7.5a Cut the wiring harness tie wrap . . .

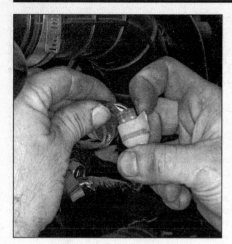

7.5b . . . disconnect the
electrical connector . . .

7.5c . . . and pull the connector out from
behind the decompressor knob bracket

7.6 Work the carburetor out of the
intake manifold

6   Work the carburetor out of the intake manifold **(see illustration)**.
7   Disconnect the choke cable from the carburetor (Section 12).
8   Disconnect the carburetor heater electrical connectors from the underside of the carburetor (Section 11).Take the carburetor out.
9   If you plan to overhaul the carburetor or replace the manifold O-ring, remove the Allen bolts and separate the intake manifold from the cylinder head **(see illustration 7.7 in Chapter 3A)**.

Installation

10   Installation is the reverse of the removal steps, with the following addition: Adjust throttle lever freeplay (see Chapter 1).

8   Carburetor - disassembly, cleaning and inspection

Warning: *Gasoline (petrol) is extremely flammable, so take extra precautions when you work on any part of the fuel system. Don't smoke or allow open flames or bare light bulbs near the work area, and don't work in a garage where a gas-type appliance (such as a water heater or clothes dryer) is present. Since gasoline is carcinogenic, wear fuel-resistant gloves when there's a possibility of being exposed to fuel, and, if you spill any fuel on your skin, rinse it off immediately with soap and water. Mop up any spills immediately and do not store fuel-soaked rags where they could ignite. When you perform any kind of work on the fuel system, wear safety glasses and have a fire extinguisher suitable for a class B type fire (flammable liquids) on hand.*

Disassembly

1   Remove the carburetor from the machine as described in Section 7. Set it on a clean working surface.
2   If necessary, remove the carburetor heater components from the float bowl (Section 11).
3   Carburetor disassembly, except for removing the heater components and idle speed screw, is the same as for Bayou models **(see illustrations 8.2a through 8.2m in Chapter 3A)**.

Cleaning and inspection

4   These procedures are the same as for Bayou 300 models (see Chapter 3A).

9   Carburetors - reassembly and float height check

These procedures are the same as for Bayou 300 models (see Chapter 3A). Refer to this Chapter's Specifications for the correct float height.

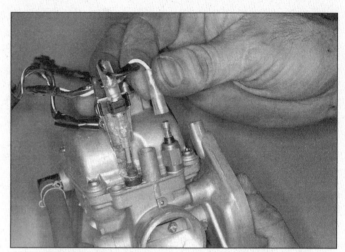

11.3 Disconnect the wire from the temperature sensor and
unscrew the sensor from the carburetor

10   Fuel level - check and adjustment

These procedures are the same as for Bayou 300 models (see Chapter 3A). Refer to this Chapter's Specifications for the correct fuel level.

11   Carburetor heater – removal, inspection and installation

1   The carburetor heater consists of a temperature sensor and heater unit installed in the float bowl on the bottom of the carburetor. A control unit and relay direct current to the system.

Removal

Heater and temperature sensor
Refer to illustrations 11.3, 11.4a, 11.4b and 11.4c
2   Remove the carburetor (Section 7).
3   Disconnect the electrical connector from the temperature sensor **(see illustration)**. Unscrew the temperature sensor from the carburetor.
4   Remove the screw, wire terminal and retainer, then pull the heater out of the carburetor **(see illustrations)**.

11.4a Remove the wiring harness screw . . .

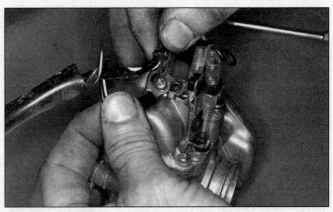

11.4b . . . the wire and the retainer . . .

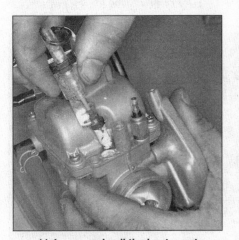

11.4c . . . and pull the heater out of the carburetor

11.5 Here are the heater relay (right arrow) and control unit (left arrow)

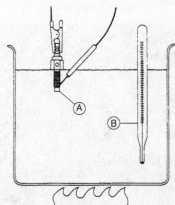

11.7 Connect an ohmmeter (A) to the sensor and read the temperature on the thermostat (B)

Control unit and relay

Refer to illustration 11.5

5   Locate the carburetor control unit and relay **(see illustration)**. Follow the unit's wiring harness to the connector and disconnect it. Remove the mounting bolt to remove the control unit or slip the relay out of its band.

6   Installation is the reverse of the removal steps.

Inspection

Temperature sensor

Refer to illustration 11.7

7   Remove the temperature sensor as described above. Place it in a pan of water with a thermometer **(see illustration)**. **Note:** *The initial temperature for this test is 48-degrees F (9-degrees C) so you may need to put some ice in the water to cool it.*

8   Connect an ohmmeter to the temperature sensor. Heat the water and note the ohmmeter readings at different temperatures as it warms up. Readings and temperatures should be as follows:

a) *9-degrees C (48-degrees F) – 2900 ohms*
b) *10-degrees C (50-degrees F) – 2200 to 5200 ohms*
c) *12-degrees C (54-degrees F) – 3000 to 7200 ohms*
d) *25-degrees C (77-degrees F) – 4300 ohms*

9   If the readings are not as specified, replace the temperature sensor.

Carburetor heater

10   Remove the engine cover (see Chapter 7).

11   Follow the harness from the carburetor heater to its electrical connector and disconnect it.

12   Connect an ohmmeter to the black wire's terminal in the heater

side of the harness. Connect the other ohmmeter terminal to ground (bare metal on the carburetor). The ohmmeter should read 11 to 20 ohms. If not, replace the heater.

Heater relay

Refer to illustration 11.14

13   Remove the relay from the vehicle as described above.

14   Connect an ohmmeter between relay terminals 3 and 4 **(see illustration)**. The ohmmeter should indicate infinite resistance.

15   Leave the ohmmeter connected to terminals 3 and 4. Connect the positive terminal of a 12-volt battery to terminal 1 and the battery negative terminal to terminal 2. The ohmmeter should now indicate continuity (zero ohms).

16   If the relay doesn't perform as described, replace it.

Heater control unit

17   The heater control unit can be tested for resistance between its various terminals, but this requires a special Kawasaki tester (part no. 57001-1394). Because the resistance of a semiconductor varies with

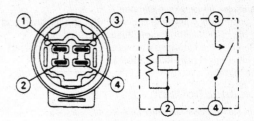

11.14 Heater relay terminal numbers

3B

12.2 Loosen the clamps on the breather hose (left) and duct (right)

12.3a Remove the air duct center screw . . .

12.3b . . . and front screw

12.6 Loosen this clamp at the bottom left of the air cleaner housing

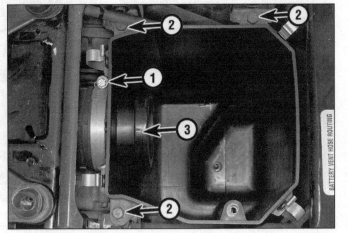

12.7 Loosen the duct clamp (1) and remove the mounting bolts (2); align the notch and ridge (3) on installation

the amount of current passing through it, other testers will produce different readings than the Kawasaki tester, in some cases very different.
18   If the other system components are good, and the wiring harness is in good condition and all the connections are clean and tight, the control unit may be defective. Have it tested by a dealer service department or substitute a known good unit before replacing it.

Installation

19   Installation is the reverse of the removal steps, with the following addition: Use electrically conductive sealer on the temperature sensor and heater.

12   Air cleaner duct and housing - removal and installation

Intake duct

Refer to illustrations 12.2, 12.3a and 12.3b
1   Remove the seat, fuel tank cover, left front side cover and the front and rear fenders (see Chapter 7).
2   Loosen the clamps and disconnect the air hose and breather hose from the intake duct **(see illustration)**.
3   Remove the mounting screws at center and front and remove the upper intake duct **(see illustrations)**.
4   Installation is the reverse of the removal steps.

Air cleaner housing

Refer to illustrations 12.6 and 12.7
5   Remove the seat (see Chapter 7).
6   Loosen the clamp and detach the air intake duct tube from the air

cleaner housing **(see illustration)**.
7   Loosen the clamp that secures the carburetor air duct to the housing **(see illustration)**. Remove the air cleaner housing bolts and lift the air cleaner housing out of the frame.
8   Installation is the reverse of the removal steps, with the following addition: Align the notch in the carburetor air tube with the ridge on the air cleaner housing.

13   Throttle and choke cables - removal, installation and adjustment

Throttle cable

Removal

Refer to illustrations 13.1, 13.2, 13.5a, 13.5b and 13.5c
1   Remove the single screw and take the side cover off the carburetor **(see illustration)**.
2   Loosen the locknuts and detach the cable housing from the bracket on the carburetor **(see illustration)**. Turn the cable to align it with the slot in the pulley, then slip the cable end plug out of the pulley.
3   Follow the cable up to the throttle housing on the handlebar. Note how the cable is routed and free it from any retainers.
4   Remove the screws and take the cover off the throttle housing **(see illustration 12.3 in Chapter 3A)**.
5   Loosen the locknut on the throttle cable adjuster, then unscrew the adjuster from the throttle housing and detach the cable end plug from the lever inside the throttle housing **(see illustrations)**.
6   Remove the cable from the vehicle.

13.1 Take the side cover off the carburetor . . .

13.2 . . . loosen the locknuts and free the cable from the bracket

13.5a Note how the cable fits in the throttle arm and loosen the locknut (arrow) . . .

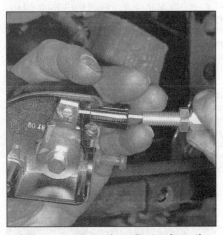

13.5b . . . unscrew the adjuster from the throttle housing . . .

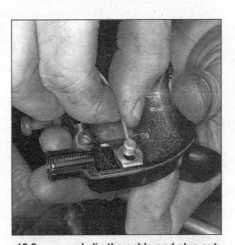

13.5c . . . and slip the cable end plug out of the throttle arm

13.15a Note how the choke lever fits in the housing . . .

3B

Installation

7   Route the cable into place. Make sure it doesn't interfere with any other components and isn't kinked or bent sharply.

8   Lubricate the ends of the cable with multi-purpose grease and connect them to the throttle housing lever and carburetor lever. Install the cable in the carburetor bracket and assemble the upper and lower halves of the throttle housing.

9   Operate the lever and make sure it returns to the idle position by itself under spring pressure. **Warning:** *If the lever doesn't return by itself, find and solve the problem before continuing with installation. A stuck lever can lead to loss of control of the vehicle.*

Adjustment

10   Follow the procedure outlined in Chapter 1, *Throttle operation/grip freeplay - check and adjustment*, to adjust the cable.

11   Turn the handlebar back and forth to make sure the cable doesn't cause the steering to bind.

12   With the engine idling, turn the handlebar through its full travel (full left lock to full right lock) and note whether idle speed increases. If it does, a cable is routed incorrectly. Correct this dangerous condition before riding the vehicle.

Choke cable

Removal

Refer to illustrations 13.15a, 13.15b, 13.15c, 13.16 and 13.17

13   Remove the carburetor partway for access to the lower end of the

13.15b . . . remove the screw, lockwasher and washer . . .

cable (Section 7).

14   Pull back the cover from the plunger cap, then unscrew the plunger cap from the carburetor and pull the choke plunger out **(see illustrations 12.15a and 12.15b in Chapter 3A)**. Compress the spring on the choke plunger and slip the cable end sideways out of the plunger.

15   Remove the choke lever pivot screw, lockwasher and washer from the choke lever housing on the left handlebar **(see illustrations)**.

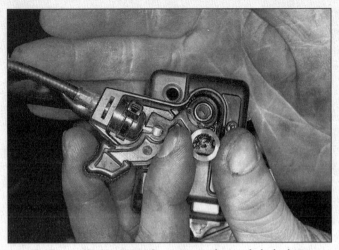

13.16 Slip the cable end plug out of the lever . . .

13.15c . . . then remove the wave washer and choke lever

14 Exhaust system - removal and installation

Remove the choke lever and its wave washer (see illustration).

16   Turn the choke lever to align its slot with the cable, then slip the cable end plug out of the lever (see illustration).

17   Pull out the cable retaining clip, then slip the cable out of the housing (see illustration).

Installation

18   Installation is the reverse of the removal steps. The choke cable is not adjustable.

Refer to illustrations 14.1a, 14.1b, 14.2, 14.3 and 14.4

1   Remove the exhaust pipe holder nuts and slide the holder off the mounting studs (see illustrations).

2   If necessary, unbolt the heat shield and remove it from the exhaust pipe (see illustration).

3   Remove the muffler mounting bolts (see illustration). Loosen the clamp and separate the muffler from the front exhaust pipe (see illustration 14.2).

4   Pull the exhaust pipe forward, separate the pipe from the cylinder head and remove the gasket (see illustration).

5   Installation is the reverse of removal, with the following addition: Be sure to install new gaskets at the cylinder head and pipe joint.

13.17 . . . pull off the clip and slip the cable end out of the housing

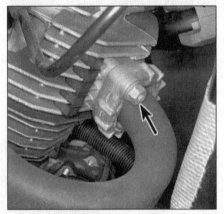

14.1a Remove the holder nuts (one nut hidden) . . .

14.1b . . . and slide the holder and retainer down the pipe

14.2 Remove the heat shield screws (aright arrows) and loosen the clamp (left arrow)

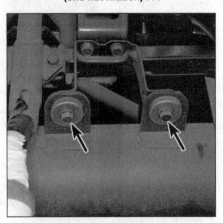

14.3 Remove the muffler mounting bolts (arrows)

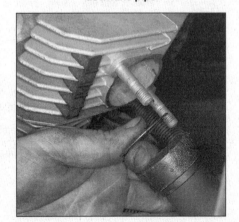

14.4 Use a new gasket on installation

Chapter 4 Part A
Ignition and electrical systems (Bayou models)

Contents

	Section
Alternator stator coils and rotor - check and replacement	18
Battery - charging	4
Battery - inspection and maintenance	3
Brake switch - check and replacement	10
CDI unit - check, removal and installation	23
Charging system - output test	17
Charging system testing - general information and precautions	16
Cooling fan (UK 300 models) – check, removal and installation	15
Electrical troubleshooting	2
Fuse - check and replacement	5
General information	1
Handlebar switches - check	13
Handlebar switches - removal and installation	14
Headlight aim - check and adjustment	8
Headlight bulb - replacement	7

	Section
Ignition coil - check, removal and installation	21
Ignition main (key) switch - check and replacement	12
Ignition system - check	20
Ignition timing - general information and check	24
Indicator bulbs - replacement	11
Lighting system - check	6
Pickup coil – check and replacement	22
Regulator/rectifier - check and replacement	19
Spark plug replacement	See Chapter 1
Starter circuit - check and component replacement	25
Starter drive – removal, inspection and installation	27
Starter motor - removal and installation	26
Tail light and brake light bulbs - replacement	9
Wiring diagrams	28

Specifications

Fuses

Main fuse

220 models	20 amps
300 models	30 amps
Cooling fan fuse (UK 300 models)	10 amps

Battery

Type

220 models

US

1988 through 1995	12V 12Ah
1996 on	12V 11Ah

Except US

1988 through 1995	12V 12Ah
1996 on	12V 11Ah (1)
300 models	12V 14 Ah
Specific gravity	1.28 at 20-degrees C (68-degrees F)

Bulbs

220 models

Headlights	25/25 watts
Taillights	8 watts
Speedometer light	3.4 watts
Indicator lights	3 watts

300 models

Headlights	65/60 watts
Tail lights	8 watts
Indicator lights	Not specified

Charging system
Charging output voltage
    220 models
        1988 through 1994 (unrectified AC) .... 31 volts minimum
        1995 on (unrectified AC) .... 38 volts minimum
    300 models (rectified DC)... Battery voltage to 15 volts
Stator coil resistance
    220 models
        1988 through 1994.. 0.2 to 0.8 ohms
        1995 on .... 0.4 to 1.1 ohms
    300 models
        1986 and 1987 .... 0.2 to 0.8 ohms
        1988 through 1999.. 0.1 to 0.7 ohms
        2000 on .... 0.33 to 0.49 ohms

Ignition system
Spark plug cap resistance
    220 models... Not specified
    300 models
        1986 and 1987 .... Not specified
        1988 on .... 3750 to 6250 ohms
Ignition coil resistance
    220 models
        Primary resistance .... 0.09 to 0.13 ohms
        Secondary resistance .... 3800 to 5800 ohms
    300 models...
        Primary resistance .... 1.8 to 2.8 ohms
        Secondary resistance .... 10,000 to 16,000 ohms
Pick-up coil resistance
    220 models
        1988 through 1994.. 83 to 150 ohms
        1995 on .... 100 to 150 ohms
    300 models... 390 to 590 ohms
Pickup coil air gap
    1988 through 1994 220 models .... 0.7+/-0.25 mm (0.027+/-0.010 inch)
    300 2WD models... Not specified
    300 4WD models... 0.9 mm (0.035 inch)
Exciter coil resistance (1988 through 1994 220 models)........................ 100 to 190 ohms

Starting system
Starter chain length, 20 links (300 models)
    Standard.. 155.8 to 156.1 mm (6.133 to 6.145 inches)
    Limit.. 158.0 mm (6.220 inches)

Torque specifications
Alternator rotor bolt .... 59 Nm (43 ft-lbs)
Starter clutch Allen bolts
    220 models... 34 Nm (25 ft-lbs) (2)
    300 models... 49 Nm (36 ft-lbs) (2)

1 *Late 1995 European models (KLF220-A8A) use a 12V 11Ah battery.*
2 *Apply non-permanent thread locking agent to the threads.*

1   General information

These vehicles use a 12-volt electrical system with a battery. The components include a crankshaft-mounted permanent-magnet alternator and a solid state voltage regulator/rectifier unit. The alternator consists of a multi-coil stator mounted inside the left engine cover and a permanent magnet rotor mounted on the end of the crankshaft. The regulator maintains the charging system output within the specified range to prevent overcharging. The rectifier converts the AC output of the alternator to direct current (DC) to power the lights and other components and to charge the battery.

All models use an electric starter, mounted behind the engine case. A recoil (pull rope) starter, also standard equipment, is covered in Chapter 2.

Bayou models are equipped with a battery operated, fully transis-torized, breakerless ignition system. The system consists of the following components:

    CDI magneto
    CDI unit
    Battery and fuse
    Ignition coil
    Spark plug
    Engine kill (stop) and main (key) switches
    Primary and secondary (HT) circuit wiring

The transistorized ignition system functions on the same principle as a DC ignition system with the CDI magneto and CDI unit performing the tasks previously associated with the breaker points and mechanical advance system. As a result, adjustment and maintenance of ignition components is eliminated (with the exception of spark plug replacement).

Because of their nature, individual electrical components can be checked but not repaired. If ignition system troubles occur, and the faulty component can be isolated, the only cure for the problem is to replace the part with a new one. **Note:** *Keep in mind that most electrical parts, once purchased, can't be returned. To avoid unnecessary expense, make very sure the faulty component has been positively identified before buying a replacement part.*

2 Electrical troubleshooting

A typical electrical circuit consists of an electrical component, the switches, relays, etc. related to that component and the wiring and connectors that hook the component to both the battery and the frame. To aid in locating a problem in any electrical circuit, wiring diagrams are included at the end of this manual.

Before tackling any troublesome electrical circuit, first study the appropriate diagrams thoroughly to get a complete picture of what makes up that individual circuit. Trouble spots, for instance, can often be narrowed down by noting if other components related to that circuit are operating properly or not. If several components or circuits fail at one time, chances are the fault lies in the fuse or ground/earth connection, as several circuits often are routed through the same fuse and ground/earth connections.

Electrical problems often stem from simple causes, such as loose or corroded connections or a blown fuse. Prior to any electrical troubleshooting, always visually check the condition of the fuse, wires and connections in the problem circuit.

If testing instruments are going to be utilized, use the diagrams to plan where you will make the necessary connections in order to accurately pinpoint the trouble spot.

The basic tools needed for electrical troubleshooting include a test light or voltmeter, a continuity tester (which includes a bulb, battery and set of test leads) and a jumper wire, preferably with a circuit breaker incorporated, which can be used to bypass electrical components. Specific checks described later in this Chapter may also require an ammeter or ohmmeter.

Voltage checks should be performed if a circuit is not functioning properly. Connect one lead of a test light or voltmeter to either the negative battery terminal or a known good ground/earth. Connect the other lead to a connector in the circuit being tested, preferably nearest to the battery or fuse. If the bulb lights, voltage is reaching that point, which means the part of the circuit between that connector and the battery is problem-free. Continue checking the remainder of the circuit in the same manner. When you reach a point where no voltage is present, the problem lies between there and the last good test point. Most of the time the problem is due to a loose connection. Since these vehicles are designed for off-road use, the problem may also be water or corrosion in a connector. Keep in mind that some circuits only receive voltage when the ignition key is in the On position.

One method of finding short circuits is to remove the fuse and connect a test light or voltmeter in its place to the fuse terminals. There should be no load in the circuit. Move the wiring harness from side-to-side while watching the test light. If the bulb lights, there is a short to ground/earth somewhere in that area, probably where insulation has rubbed off a wire. The same test can be performed on other components in the circuit, including the switch.

A ground check should be done to see if a component is grounded properly. Disconnect the battery and connect one lead of a self-powered test light (such as a continuity tester) to a known good ground. Connect the other lead to the wire or ground connection being tested. If the bulb lights, the ground is good. If the bulb does not light, the ground is not good.

A continuity check is performed to see if a circuit, section of circuit or individual component is capable of passing electricity through it. Disconnect the battery and connect one lead of a self-powered test light (such as a continuity tester) to one end of the circuit being tested and the other lead to the other end of the circuit. If the bulb lights, there is continuity, which means the circuit is passing electricity through it

properly. Switches can be checked in the same way.

Remember that all electrical circuits are designed to conduct electricity from the battery, through the wires, switches, relays, etc. to the electrical component (light bulb, motor, etc.). From there it is directed to the frame (ground) where it is passed back to the battery. Electrical problems are basically an interruption in the flow of electricity from the battery or back to it.

3 Battery - inspection and maintenance

1   Most battery damage is caused by heat, vibration, and/or low electrolyte levels, so keep the battery securely mounted, check the electrolyte level frequently and make sure the charging system is functioning properly. **Warning:** *Always disconnect the negative cable first and connect it last to prevent sparks which could the battery to explode.*
2   Refer to Chapter 1 for electrolyte level and specific gravity checking procedures.
3   Check around the base inside of the battery for sediment, which is the result of sulfation caused by low electrolyte levels. These deposits will cause internal short circuits, which can quickly discharge the battery. Look for cracks in the case and replace the battery if either of these conditions is found.
4   Check the battery terminals and cable ends for tightness and corrosion. If corrosion is evident, disconnect the cables from the battery, disconnecting the negative (-) terminal first, and clean the terminals and cable ends with a wire brush or knife and emery paper. Reconnect the cables, connecting the negative cable last, and apply a thin coat of petroleum jelly to the cables to slow further corrosion.
5   The battery case should be kept clean to prevent current leakage, which can discharge the battery over a period of time (especially when it sits unused). Wash the outside of the case with a solution of baking soda and water. Do not get any baking soda solution in the battery cells. Rinse the battery thoroughly, then dry it.
6   If acid has been spilled on the frame or battery box, neutralize it with a baking soda and water solution, then touch up any damaged paint. Make sure the battery vent tube (if equipped) is directed away from the frame and is not kinked or pinched **(see illustration 4.13 in Chapter 1A)**.
7   If the vehicle sits unused for long periods of time, disconnect the cables from the battery terminals. Refer to Section 4 and charge the battery approximately once every month.

4 Battery - charging

1   If the machine sits idle for extended periods or if the charging system malfunctions, the battery can be charged from an external source.
2   To properly charge the battery, you will need a charger of the correct rating, a hydrometer, a clean rag and a syringe for adding distilled water to the battery cells.
3   The maximum charging rate for any battery is 1/10th of the rated amp-hour capacity. As an example, the maximum charge rate for a 14 amp/hour battery would be 1.4 amps. If the battery is charged at a higher rate, it could overheat, causing the plates inside the battery to buckle.
4   Do not allow the battery to be subjected to a so-called quick charge (high charge rate over a short period of time) unless you are prepared to buy a new battery. The excess heat will warp the plates inside the battery until they touch each other, causing a short that ruins the battery.
5   When charging the battery, always remove it from the machine and be sure to check the electrolyte level before hooking up the charger. Add distilled water to any cells that are low.
6   Loosen the cell caps, hook up the battery charger leads (positive lead to battery positive terminal, negative lead to battery negative terminal), cover the top of the battery with a clean rag, then, and only then, plug in the battery charger. **Warning:** *The hydrogen gas escaping*

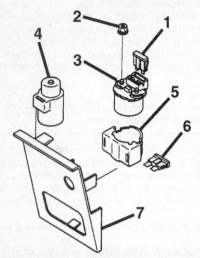
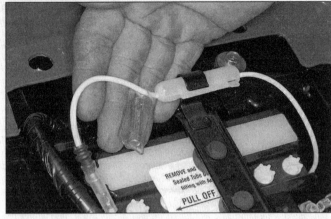

5.1a Fuse, starter relay and starter circuit relay (220 models)

1   *Fuse*
2   *Terminal nut*
3   *Starter relay*
4   *Starter circuit relay*
5   *Starter relay rubber mount*
6   *Spare fuse*
7   *Mounting bracket*

5.1b On 300 models, the main fuse and a spare fuse are located near the battery. . .

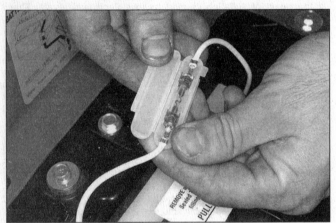

5.2 . . . open the holder for access to the fuse

from a charging battery is explosive, so keep open flames and sparks well away from the area. Also, the electrolyte is extremely corrosive and will damage anything it comes in contact with.

7   Allow the battery to charge until the specific gravity is as specified (refer to Chapter 1 for the specific gravity checking procedure). The charger must be unplugged and disconnected from the battery when making specific gravity checks. If the battery overheats or gases excessively, the charging rate is too high. Either disconnect the charger or lower the charging rate to prevent damage to the battery.

8   If one or more of the cells do not show an increase in specific gravity after a long slow charge, or if the battery as a whole does not seem to want to take a charge, it's time for a new battery.

9   When the battery is fully charged, unplug the charger first, then disconnect the leads from the battery. Install the cell caps and wipe any electrolyte off the outside of the battery case.

10   If the recharged battery discharges rapidly when left disconnected, it's likely that an internal short caused by physical damage or sulfation has occurred. A new battery will be required. A sound battery will tend to lose its charge at about 1-percent per day.

5   Fuse - check and replacement

Refer to illustration 5.1a, 5.1b and 5.2

1   These models use a single main fuse. On 220 models, it's located on the starter relay **(see illustration)**. On 300 models, it's under the seat near the battery **(see illustration)**. The fuse on 300 models is mounted in a plastic holder. A spare fuse is contained in a holder next to the main fuse.

2   The fuse can be removed and checked visually. On 220 models, pull it out. On 300 models, open the plastic cover and pull the fuse out **(see illustration)**. A blown fuse is easily identified by a break in the element.

3   UK models equipped with a cooling fan also use a 10 amp fuse mounted in the black-red wire between the main fuse and the fan switch.

6   Lighting system - check

1   The battery provides power for operation of the headlights, tail light, brake light (if equipped) and instrument cluster lights. If none of the lights operate, always check battery voltage before proceeding. Low battery voltage indicates either a faulty battery, low battery electrolyte level or a defective charging system. Refer to Chapter 1 and Section 3 of this Chapter for battery checks and Sections 16 and 17 for charging system tests. Also, check the condition of the fuse and replace it with a new one if it's blown.

Headlights

2   If both of the headlight bulbs are out with the headlight switch in Lo or Hi and the main key switch On, check the fuse (see Section 5).

3   If only one headlight is out, try installing the bulb from the working headlight. If this solves the problem, replace the defective bulb. If not, test further as described below.

4   Disconnect the electrical connector from the bulb that doesn't light. Connect the positive lead of a voltmeter to the black-red wire terminal in the wiring harness. Turn the main key switch On and connect the negative lead to the black-yellow wire. The voltmeter should indicate 12 volts or more.

a) *If there's voltage at the terminals, the bulb is burned out or the bulb socket is corroded.*

b) *If there's no voltage, the problem lies in the wiring or one of the switches in the circuit. Refer to Sections 12 and 13 for the switch testing procedures, and also the wiring diagrams at the end of this manual.*

Tail light

5   If the tail light fails to work, check the bulb and the bulb terminals first.

6   If the bulb and terminals are good, disconnect the tail light electrical connector. Connect a voltmeter negative lead to the black-yellow wire in the wiring harness and the positive lead to the red wire. With the main key switch and lighting switch On, the voltmeter should indicate 12 volts or more.

a) *If there's voltage at the terminals, the bulb is burned out or the bulb socket is corroded.*

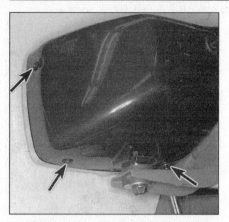

7.1 Remove the screws (arrows) and take the reflector out of the housing . . .

7.2a . . . pull off the rubber cover . . .

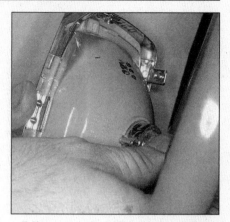

7.2b . . . turn the bulb socket counter-clockwise and remove it from the case . . .

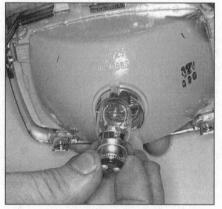

7.3 . . . then pull the bulb out of the socket without touching the glass

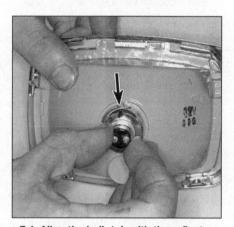

7.4 Align the bulb tab with the reflector slot (arrow) when installing the bulb

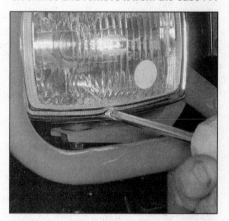

8.4 The headlight adjusting screw on later models is mounted below each headlight

b) If there's no voltage, the problem lies in the wiring or one of the switches in the circuit. Refer to Sections 12 and 13 for the switch testing procedures, and also the wiring diagrams at the end of this manual.

7   If no voltage is indicated, check the ground wire and the wiring between the tail light and the lighting switch, then check the switch.

Brake light

8   If the machine is equipped with a brake light, see Section 10 for the brake light circuit checking procedure.

Neutral indicator light

9   If the neutral light fails to operate when the transmission is in Neutral, check the fuse and the bulb (see Section 11 for bulb removal procedures). If the bulb and fuse are in good condition, check for battery voltage at the wire attached to the neutral switch on the left side of the engine. If battery voltage is present, refer to Chapter 2A for the neutral switch check and replacement procedures.

10   If no voltage is indicated, check the wiring to the bulb, to the switch and between the switch and the bulb for open circuits and poor connections.

7   Headlight bulb - replacement

Refer to illustrations 7.1, 7.2a, 7.2b, 7.3 and 7.4
Warning: *If the headlight has just burned out, give the bulb time to cool before changing the bulb to avoid burning your fingers.*

1   Remove the headlight reflector side knobs (1986 and 1987 300 models) or screws (all 1988 and later models) and take the reflector out of the headlight assembly **(see illustration)**.

2   Pull the rubber cover off the bulb **(see illustration)**. Push the bulb retainer in and turn counterclockwise, then remove it from the socket **(see illustration)**.
3   Pull the bulb out without touching the glass **(see illustration)**.
4   Installation is the reverse of the removal procedure, with the following additions:
   a) *Be sure not to touch the bulb with your fingers - oil from your skin will cause the bulb to overheat and fail prematurely. If you do touch the bulb, wipe it off with a clean rag dampened with rubbing alcohol.*
   b) *Align the tab on the metal bulb flange with the slot in the headlight case* **(see illustration)**.
   c) *Make sure the arrow mark on the headlight cover is facing up.*

8   Headlight aim - check and adjustment

Refer to illustration 8.4
1   An improperly adjusted headlight may cause problems for oncoming traffic or provide poor, unsafe illumination of the terrain ahead. Before adjusting the headlight, be sure to consult with local traffic laws and regulations.
2   The headlight beam can be adjusted vertically. Before performing the adjustment, make sure the fuel tank is at least half full, and have an assistant sit on the seat.
3   If the vehicle has mounting knobs on each side of the headlight housing, loosen them. Turn the housing up or down to align the beam, then tighten the mounting knobs.
4   If the vehicle has a vertical adjuster screw, insert a Phillips screwdriver into it **(see illustration)**, then turn the adjuster as necessary to raise or lower the beam.

4A

9.1 Remove the lens screws and take off the lens . . .

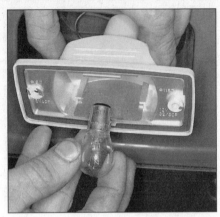

9.2 . . . press the bulb into the socket, turn it counterclockwise and pull it out

10.1a Remove the screw (arrow) and remove the front brake switch

9   Tail light and brake light bulbs - replacement

Tail light

Refer to illustrations 9.1 and 9.2

1   Remove the tail light lens screws and take off the lens **(see illustration)**.

2   Press the bulb into its socket and turn it counterclockwise to remove **(see illustration)**.

3   Check the socket terminals for corrosion and clean them if necessary.

4   Press the bulb into its socket, turn counterclockwise to engage the pins, then release the bulb.

5   Install the lens and tighten the screws securely, but not enough to crack the plastic.

Brake light

6   The brake light bulbs, used on later models, are combined with the tail light bulbs. Note that the retaining pins on the bulb are offset so the bulb can only go in one way.

10   Brake switch - check and replacement

Check

Refer to illustrations 10.1a and 10.1b

1   Models equipped with brake lights use electrical switches at the brake pedal and right brake lever **(see illustrations)**.

2   Before checking any electrical circuit, check the fuses (see Section 5).

3   Using a test light connected to a good ground, check for voltage to the wire at the brake light switch. If there's no voltage present, check the wire between the switch and the ignition switch (see the wiring diagrams at the end of the book).

4   If voltage is available, touch the probe of the test light to the other terminal of the switch, then depress the brake pedal - if the test light doesn't light up, replace the switch.

5   If the test light does light, check the wiring between the switch and the brake lights (see the wiring diagrams at the end of the book).

Replacement

Front brake switch

6   Remove the mounting screw and pull the switch out of the brake lever **(see illustration 10.1a)**.

7   Installation is the reverse of the removal steps.

Rear brake switch

8   Disconnect the electrical connector in the switch harness.

9   Disconnect the spring from the brake pedal switch.

10   Hold the adjuster nut from turning and rotate the switch body all the way up until it clears the nut threads, then lift it out **(see illustration 10.1b)**.

9   Install the switch by reversing the removal procedure.

11   Indicator bulbs - replacement

Refer to illustration 11.1

1   Reach under the handlebar cover and pull the rubber socket out **(see illustration)**.

2   If the socket contacts are dirty or corroded, they should be scraped clean and sprayed with electrical contact cleaner before new

10.1b Hold the nut and unscrew the rear brake switch

11.1 Pull the bulb sockets (arrow) out of the cover and pull out the bulb

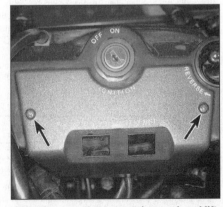

12.6 Remove the screws (arrows) and lift off the cover

14.1 Remove these screws to separate the handlebar switch housing

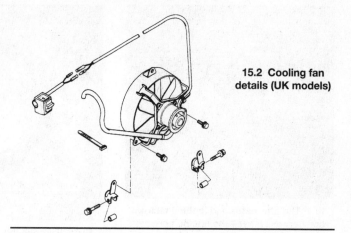

15.2 Cooling fan details (UK models)

bulbs are installed.

3   Push the new bulb into its socket and push the socket back into the handlebar cover.

12   Ignition main (key) switch - check and replacement

Check

1   Follow the wiring harness from the ignition switch to the connector and disconnect the connector.

2   Using an ohmmeter, check the continuity of the terminal pairs indicated in the wiring diagrams at the end of the book. Continuity should exist between the terminals connected by a solid line when the switch is in the indicated position.

3   If the switch fails any of the tests, replace it.

Replacement

Refer to illustration 12.6

4   The ignition switch is secured by a plastic nut.

5   If you haven't already done so, disconnect the switch electrical connector.

6   On 300 models, remove the screw and lift off the handlebar cover to expose the switch **(see illustration)**.

7   Unscrew the nut. Remove the switch from the side panel (220 models) or lower the switch out of the bracket (300 models).

8   Installation is the reverse of the removal procedure.

13   Handlebar switches - check

1   Generally speaking, the switches are reliable and trouble-free. Most problems, when they do occur, are caused by dirty or corroded contacts, but wear and breakage of internal parts is a possibility that should not be overlooked. If breakage does occur, the entire switch and related wiring harness will have to be replaced with a new one, since individual parts are not usually available.

2   The switches can be checked for continuity with an ohmmeter or a continuity test light. Always disconnect the battery negative cable, which will prevent the possibility of a short circuit, before making the checks.

3   Follow the wiring harness of the switch in question and disconnect the electrical connectors.

4   Using the ohmmeter or test light, check for continuity between the terminals of the switch harness with the switch in the various positions. Refer to the continuity diagrams contained in the wiring diagrams at the end of the book. Continuity should exist between the terminals connected by a solid line when the switch is in the indicated position.

5   If the continuity check indicates a problem exists, refer to Section 14, disassemble the switch and spray the switch contacts with

electrical contact cleaner. If they are accessible, the contacts can be scraped clean with a knife or polished with crocus cloth. If switch components are damaged or broken, it will be obvious when the switch is disassembled.

14   Handlebar switches - removal and installation

Refer to illustration 14.1

1   The handlebar switches are composed of two halves that clamp around the bar. They are easily removed for cleaning or inspection by taking out the clamp screws and pulling the switch halves away from the handlebars **(see illustration)**.

2   To completely remove the switches, the electrical connectors in the wiring harness must be unplugged and the harness separated from the tie wraps and retainers.

3   When installing the switches, make sure the wiring harness is properly routed to avoid pinching or stretching the wires.

15   Cooling fan (UK 300 models) – check, removal and installation

Check

Refer to illustration 15.2

1   If the fan doesn't rotate, check the fuse (10 amps, located in the black-red wire between the main fuse and the fan switch) and replace it if necessary.

2   Follow the fan wires to the connectors and disconnect them **(see illustration)**. Using jumper wires, connect the battery positive terminal to the black wire and the battery negative terminal to the black-yellow wire. The fan should rotate counterclockwise when viewed from the rear. If not, replace it.

3   Disconnect the fan switch electrical connector. Connect an ohmmeter between the terminals of the wiring harness that leads to the switch. With the switch in the On position, the ohmmeter should indicate continuity (zero ohms). With the switch in the Off position, the ohmmeter should indicate no continuity (infinite resistance). If the switch doesn't perform as described, replace it.

16   Charging system testing - general information and precautions

1   If the performance of the charging system is suspect, the system as a whole should be checked first, followed by testing of the individual components (the alternator and the regulator/rectifier). **Note:** *Before beginning the checks, make sure the battery is fully charged and that all system connections are clean and tight.*

2   Checking the output of the charging system and the performance

4A

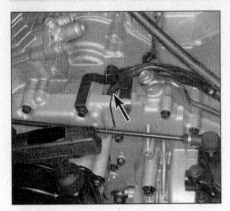

18.1 The alternator and ignition pick-up coil harness leaves the engine between the left crankcase cover and crankcase (arrow) (300 shown)

18.6a Remove the left crankcase cover bolts (arrows) . . .

18.6b . . . pull the cover off against the resistance of the rotor magnets, but don't force it . . .

of the various components within the charging system requires the use of an ohmmeter, voltmeter or the equivalent multimeter.

3   When making the checks, follow the procedures carefully to prevent incorrect connections or short circuits, as irreparable damage to electrical system components may result if short circuits occur.

4   If the necessary test equipment is not available, it is recommended that charging system tests be left to a dealer service department or a reputable ATV repair shop.

17 Charging system - output test

1   If a charging system problem is suspected, perform the following checks. Start by checking the fuse (see Section 5) and battery (see Section 3 and Chapter 1). If necessary, charge the battery (see Section 4).

2   With the battery fully charged, connect a voltmeter between the battery terminals and note the reading.

3   Start the engine and let it warm up to normal operating temperature.

4   With the engine idling, attach the positive lead of a 0 to 20 volt voltmeter to the positive (+) battery terminal and the negative lead to the battery negative (-) terminal. The voltmeter should indicate approximately the same reading as in Step 2.

5   Slowly increase the engine speed and read the voltmeter. It should increase to approximately 15 volts.

6   If the output is as specified, the alternator is functioning properly.

7   Low voltage may be the result of damaged windings in the alternator stator coils or wiring problems. Make sure all electrical connections are clean and tight, then refer to the following Sections to check the alternator stator coils and the regulator/rectifier.

8   Output above the specified range indicates a defective voltage regulator/rectifier. Refer to Section 19 for regulator testing and replacement procedures.

9   Disconnect the test equipment.

18 Alternator stator coils and rotor - check and replacement

Stator coil check

Refer to illustration 18.1

1   Follow the stator coil wiring harness from the point where it leaves the left crankcase cover to its connector. On 1988 through 1994 220 models, the connector has two yellow wires. On 1995 and later 220 models and all 300 models, the connector has three yellow wires **(see illustration)**.

18.6c . . . and locate the cover dowels (arrows) (300 shown)

2   Measure stator coil resistance with an ohmmeter as follows:

a)   *On 1988 through 1994 220 models, connect the ohmmeter between the two yellow wires in the harness side of the connector.*

b)   *On 1995 and later 220 models and all 300 models, connect an ohmmeter between each of the terminals in the side of the connector that runs back to the engine (connect the positive lead to one of the terminals and the negative lead to each of the two remaining terminals in turn).*

If the readings are outside the range listed in this Chapter's Specifications, replace the stator as described below.

3   Connect the ohmmeter between a good ground on the vehicle and each of the connector terminals in turn. The meter should indicate infinite resistance (no continuity). If not, replace the stator.

Stator replacement

Refer to illustrations 18.6a, 18.6b, 18.6c, 18.7a, 18.7b and 18.8

4   Drain the engine oil (see Chapter 1).

5   Remove the recoil starter and its pulley (see Chapter 2).

6   Remove the left crankcase cover **(see illustrations)**. You may need to pull firmly to overcome the resistance of the rotor magnets, but don't use excessive force. If the cover seems to be stuck, check to make sure all fasteners have been removed.

7   Remove the stator coil screws **(see illustrations)**, then remove the stator coils.

8   Check the seal in the cover for wear or damage. Spin the rotor bearing with a finger and check for roughness, looseness or noise (see

18.7a Stator and pick-up coil details (1988 through 1994 220 models)

1   *Pick-up coil*
2   *Rotor*
3   *Stator*

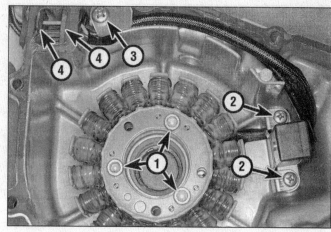

18.7b Stator and pick-up coil details (300 models shown; 1995 and later 220 models similar)

1   *Stator coil screws*   3   *Harness retainer screw*
2   *Pick-up coil screws*   4   *Harness grommets*

18.8 Replace the rotor bearing if it's rough, loose or noisy

18.12a Thread the rotor puller counterclockwise onto the threaded portion of the rotor . . .

18.12b . . . and hold the flats with a wrench while turning the puller bolt to free the rotor

4A

illustration). Slip it off the crankshaft and install a new one if problems are found.

9   Installation is the reverse of the removal steps, with the following additions:

a) *Apply non-permanent thread locking agent to the threads of the stator coil and pick-up coil screws, then tighten them securely.*

b) *Remove all old gasket material from the alternator cover and crankcase. Use a new gasket on the alternator cover.*

c) *Make sure the cover dowels are in position (see illustration 18.6c).*

d) *Tighten the cover bolts evenly, in a criss-cross pattern.*

Rotor replacement

Removal

Refer to illustrations 18.12a, 18.12b, 18.12c and 18.13

Note: *To remove the alternator rotor, the special Kawasaki puller (part no. 57001-1099) or an aftermarket equivalent will be required. Don't try to remove the rotor without the proper puller, as it's almost sure to be damaged. Pullers are readily available from ATV dealers and aftermarket tool suppliers.*

10   Remove the recoil starter (Chapter 2).

11   Remove the alternator cover as described above for access to the rotor.

12   Thread the outer portion of the puller onto the rotor **(see illustra-**

18.12c Rap the puller bolt with a hammer if the rotor is stuck

tion). Hold the flats of the outer portion with a wrench and turn the bolt with another wrench to separate the rotor from the crankshaft **(see illustration).** If the rotor is stuck, tap on the puller bolt with a hammer **(see illustration).**

18.13 Pull off the rotor and starter clutch and locate the Woodruff key (arrow)

18.19 Make sure there's nothing stuck to the rotor magnets; even a small object like this circlip can ruin the stator

19.4 The regulator/rectifier is at the left rear of the vehicle (300 shown)

20.5 Unscrew the spark plug cap from the plug wire and measure its resistance with an ohmmeter

20.13 A simple spark gap testing fixture can be made from a block of wood, two nails, a large alligator clip, a screw and a piece of wire

13   Pull the rotor off, together with the starter clutch **(see illustration)**.

14   Check the rotor Woodruff key; if it's not secure in its slot, pull it out and set it aside for safekeeping. A convenient method is to stick the Woodruff key to the magnets inside the rotor, but be certain not to forget it's there, as serious damage to the rotor and charging coils will occur if the engine is run with anything stuck to the magnets.

Inspection

15   Check the rotor for physical damage, such as separated magnets. If metal objects don't stick firmly to the rotor, the magnets may be weak. Damaged or weak magnets will cause low charging system output. Replace the rotor if these problems are found.

Installation

Refer to illustration 18.19

16   Degrease the center of the rotor and the end of the crankshaft.

17   Make sure the Woodruff key is positioned securely in its slot.

18   Align the rotor slot with the Woodruff key. Place the rotor, together with the starter clutch, on the crankshaft.

19   Take a look to make sure there isn't anything stuck to the inside of the rotor **(see illustration)**.

20   The remainder of installation is the reverse of the removal steps.

---

19   Regulator/rectifier - check and replacement

Check

1   The regulator/rectifier should be suspected if the alternator output was significantly too high during the charging system output test or if

charging system output never rises and the stator coils are good.

2   Regulator/rectifier testing is a complicated procedure that requires special equipment for complete accuracy. If the regulator/rectifier is suspect, have it tested by a dealer service department or substitute a known good unit.

Replacement

Refer to illustration 19.4

3   Remove the seat (220 models) or rear fender (300 models) (see Chapter 7).

4   Disconnect the rectifier/regulator electrical connector(s) **(see illustration)**. Remove the mounting bolts and lift it off the frame.

5   Installation is the reverse of the removal steps.

---

20   Ignition system - check

Refer to illustrations 20.5 and 20.13

Warning: *Because of the very high voltage generated by the ignition system, extreme care should be taken when these checks are performed.*

1   If the ignition system is the suspected cause of poor engine performance or failure to start, a number of checks can be made to isolate the problem.

2   Make sure the ignition kill (stop) switch is in the Run or On position.

Engine will not start

3   Disconnect the spark plug wire from the spark plug (refer to Chapter 1 if necessary). Connect the wire to a spare spark plug and lay the plug on the engine with the threads contacting the engine. If neces-

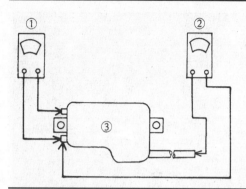

21.4 Ignition coil test setup

1   *Primary resistance measurement*
2   *Secondary resistance measurement*
3   *Ignition coil*

21.9 Ignition coil mounting details (300 shown; others similar)

sary, hold the spark plug with an insulated tool. Crank the engine over and make sure a well-defined, blue spark occurs between the spark plug electrodes. **Warning:** *Don't remove the spark plug from the engine to perform this check - atomized fuel being pumped out of the open spark plug hole could ignite, causing severe injury!*

4   If no spark occurs, the following checks should be made:

5   Unscrew the spark plug cap from the plug wire and check the cap resistance with an ohmmeter **(see illustration)**. If the resistance is infinite, replace it with a new one.

6   Make sure all electrical connectors are clean and tight. Check all wires for shorts, opens and correct installation.

7   Check the battery voltage with a voltmeter. If the voltage is less than 12-volts, recharge the battery.

8   Check the fuse and the fuse connections (see Section 5). If the fuse is blown, replace it with a new one; if the connections are loose or corroded, clean or repair them.

9   Refer to Section 21 and check the ignition coil primary and secondary resistance.

10   Refer to Section 22 and check the pick-up coil resistance.

11   If the preceding checks produce positive results but there is still no spark at the plug, refer to Section 23 for information on the CDI unit.

Engine starts but misfires

12   If the engine starts but misfires, make the following checks before deciding that the ignition system is at fault.

13   The ignition system must be able to produce a spark across a six millimeter (1/4-inch) gap (minimum). A simple test fixture **(see illustration)** can be constructed to make sure the minimum spark gap can be jumped. Make sure the fixture electrodes are positioned six millimeters apart.

14   Connect one of the spark plug wires to the protruding test fixture electrode, then attach the fixture's alligator clip to a good engine ground (earth).

15   Crank the engine over with the key in the On position and see if well-defined, blue sparks occur between the test fixture electrodes. If the minimum spark gap test is positive, the ignition coil is functioning properly. If the spark will not jump the gap, or if it is weak (orange colored), refer to Steps 5 through 11 of this Section and perform the component checks described.

21   Ignition coil - check, removal and installation

Check

Refer to illustration 21.4

1   In order to determine conclusively that the ignition coil is defective, it should be tested by an authorized Kawasaki dealer service department which is equipped with the special electrical tester required for this check.

2   However, the coil can be checked visually (for cracks and other damage) and the primary and secondary coil resistances can be measured with an ohmmeter. If the coil is undamaged, and if the resistances are as specified, it is probably capable of proper operation.

3   To check the coil for physical damage, it must be removed (see

Step 9). To check the resistance, remove the fuel tank on 300 models (see Chapter 3). On all models, disconnect the primary circuit electrical connectors from the coil and remove the spark plug wire from the spark plug. Mark the locations of all wires before disconnecting them.

4   To check the coil primary resistance, attach one ohmmeter lead to a primary terminal and the other ohmmeter lead to the other primary terminal **(see illustration)**.

5   Place the ohmmeter selector switch in the Rx1 position and compare the measured resistance to the value listed in this Chapter's Specifications.

6   If the coil primary resistance is as specified, check the coil secondary resistance by disconnecting the meter leads and attaching them between the spark plug wire terminal and the primary terminal **(see illustration 21.4)**.

7   Place the ohmmeter selector switch in the Rx1000 position and compare the measured resistance to the values listed in this Chapter's Specifications.

8   If the resistances are not as specified, unscrew the spark plug cap from the plug wire and check the resistance between the primary terminal and the end of the spark plug wire. If it is now within specifications, the spark plug cap is bad. If it's still not as specified, the coil is probably defective and should be replaced with a new one.

Removal and installation

Refer to illustration 21.9

9   The coil on 220 models is accessible from below. On 300 models, refer to Chapter 3 and remove the fuel tank. Disconnect the spark plug wire from the plug and disconnect the coil primary circuit electrical connector **(see illustration)**.

10   Support the coil with one hand and remove the coil mounting screw(s), then lift the coil out.

11   Installation is the reverse of removal.

22   Pick-up and exciter coils – check and replacement

Pick-up coil check

1   Follow the wiring harness from the engine cover on the left side of the vehicle to the electrical connectors **(see illustration 18.1)**. Disconnect the connector.

2   Set the ohmmeter to Rx100. **Note:** *During the next steps, connect the ohmmeter to the side of the connector that leads back to the engine, not to the wiring harness side.*

3   Connect the ohmmeter between the black and blue wire terminals in the connector. These are the pick-up coil wires. Compare the readings with the value listed in this Chapter's Specifications.

4   If the reading is incorrect, the pick-up coil must be replaced.

Replacement

5   Remove the left crankcase cover (Section 18).

4A

6   Remove the pick-up coil mounting screws and the wiring harness retainer screw **(see illustration 18.7a or 18.7b)**. Take the pick-up coil and its harness out of the cover.

7   Installation is the reverse of the removal steps. Route the harness through its groove in the top of the cover, reinstall the retainer and position the grommets in their notches in the cover **(see illustration 18.7b)**.

Exciter coil check

8   An exciter coil is used on 1988 through 1994 220 models.

9   Remove the front fuel tank cover (see Chapter 7).

10   Follow the wiring harness from the crankcase cover on the left side of the vehicle to the electrical connectors inside the left side of the rear fuel tank cover. Disconnect the connector.

11   Set the ohmmeter to Rx10. **Note:** *During the next step, connect the ohmmeter to the side of the connector that leads back to the engine, not to the wiring harness side.*

12   Connect the ohmmeter between the red/black and red wire terminals in the connector. These are the exciter coil wires. Compare the readings with the value listed in this Chapter's Specifications.

13   If the reading is incorrect, the alternator stator must be replaced.

23   CDI unit - check, removal and installation

Check

1   The CDI unit is checked by process of elimination (when all other possible causes have been checked and eliminated, the CDI unit is at fault). Because the CDI unit is expensive and can't be returned once purchased, consider having a Kawasaki dealer test the system before you buy a new CDI unit.

Replacement

Refer to illustration 23.3

2   Refer to Chapter 7 and remove the rear fender.

3   Disconnect the electrical connector(s) from the CDI unit **(see illustration)**. Remove its mounting screws and take it off the frame.

4   Installation is the reverse of the removal steps.

24   Ignition timing - general information and check

General information

1   Ignition timing need be checked only if you're troubleshooting a problem such as loss of power. Since the ignition timing can't be adjusted and since none of the ignition system parts is subject to mechanical wear, there's no need for regular checks.

2   The ignition timing is checked with the engine running, both at idle and at higher speeds listed in Step 7 of this Section. Inexpensive neon timing lights should be adequate in theory, but in practice may produce such dim pulses that the timing marks are hard to see. If possible, one of the more precise xenon timing lights should be used, powered by an external source of the appropriate voltage. **Note:** *Don't use the vehicle's own battery as an incorrect reading may result from stray impulses within the electrical system.*

Check

3   Warm the engine to normal operating temperature, make sure the transmission is in Neutral, then shut the engine off.

4   Refer to *Valve clearance - check and adjustment* in Chapter 1 and remove the timing hole plug.

5   Connect the timing light and a tune-up tachometer to the engine, following manufacturer's instructions.

6   Start the engine and let it idle. Adjust if necessary to the lowest stable idle speed (see Chapter 1).

7   Point the timing light into the timing window. At 2100 rpm, the notch at the top of the timing window should be even with the line next to the F mark on the alternator rotor **(see illustration 23.8 in Chapter 1A)**. At 4200 rpm, the notch should be between the two advanced

23.3 On 300 models, the starter relay (left), CDI unit (center) and starter circuit relay (right) are mounted behind the battery

timing marks on the rotor.

8   If the timing is incorrect and all other ignition components have tested as good, the CDI unit may be defective. Have it tested by a Kawasaki dealer.

9   When the check is complete, grease the timing hole plug O-ring, then install the O-ring and plug and disconnect the test equipment.

25   Starter circuit - check and component replacement

1   Depending on the procedure, it may be necessary to remove the seat, rear cargo rack or rear fender for access to other parts (see Chapter 7).

2   Start by taking a good look at all of the wires and connections in the circuit. Disconnect and clean the battery cables and both ends of the heavy cables that run to the starter relay. A common cause of starter problems is corrosion of these terminals. Corrosion that isn't obvious can still be enough to prevent the starter from working. Make sure all wiring is clean, in good condition and tightly connected before you start testing or you won't get accurate results.

Starter relay

Check

Warning: *Make sure the transmission is in Neutral before performing this test.*

3   Locate the starter relay. On 220 models, it's on a bracket next to the battery **(see illustration 5.1a)**. On 300 models, it's at the rear of the vehicle **(see illustration 23.3)**.

4   Disconnect the electrical connector for the two thin wires connected to the relay.

5   Connect a length of wire from the black wire terminal in the connector to the battery positive terminal (the side of the connector that runs to the relay, not the harness side). Connect another length of wire from the battery negative terminal to the yellow/black wire terminal in the connector. The starter should crank the engine. If it doesn't, the problem may be in the starter itself, in the electrical cables between the battery and starter relay, or in the starter relay. If the starter is good and the cables are in good condition and properly connected, the relay is probably at fault.

6   To test the relay further, disconnect its heavy cables. Repeat the test in Step 5 and listen for a clicking sound from the relay when the wires are connected. If there is no sound, the relay is probably bad. To confirm this, connect an ohmmeter between the cable terminals, then repeat Step 5. The ohmmeter should indicate zero ohms when power is applied to the small relay terminals. If not, the relay is bad. Replace it.

7   As a final check on the relay, disconnect all of its cables and connect an ohmmeter between the terminals for the small wires. It should read close to zero ohms. If it reads higher, replace the relay.

Replacement

8   Disconnect the negative cable from the battery.

9   Pull back the rubber covers from the terminal nuts, remove the nuts and disconnect the starter relay cables **(see illustration 5.1a, 220 models or 23.3, 300 models)**. Disconnect the remaining electrical connector from the starter relay.

10   Pull the relay's rubber mount off the metal bracket and pull the relay out of the mount.

11   Installation is the reverse of removal. Reconnect the negative battery cable after all the other electrical connections are made.

Starting circuit relay
Check

Refer to illustration 25.13

12   Locate the relay **(see illustration 5.1a, 220 models, or 23.3, 300 models)**. Disconnect the connector from the relay.

13   Connect an ohmmeter between relay terminals 3 and 4 **(see illustration)**. The ohmmeter should indicate no continuity (infinite resistance).

14   Connect a 12-volt battery (the vehicle's battery will work if it's fully charged) between relay terminals 1 and 2. With the battery connected, the ohmmeter should indicate 0 ohms. With the battery disconnected, the ohmmeter should indicate infinite resistance. If the relay doesn't perform as described, replace it.

Replacement

15   If you haven't already done so, disconnect the relay's electrical connector. Pull the relay out of its mounting band and install a new one, then connect the wiring harness.

Starter switch

16   The starter switch is part of the switch assembly on the left handlebar. Refer to Section 14 for checking and replacement procedures.

---

26   Starter motor - removal and installation

1   On 300 models, the starter motor drive sprocket will fall out of position when the starter is removed. For this reason, the left crankcase cover must be removed so the starter motor can be guided into the drive sprocket during installation.

Removal

Refer to illustrations 26.4a and 26.4b

2   Disconnect the cable from the negative terminal of the battery.

3   If you're working on a 300 model, remove the left crankcase cover (Section 18).

4   Pull back the rubber boot and disconnect the starter cable, then remove the starter mounting bolts **(see illustrations)**.

5   Slide the starter out of the engine case. **Caution:** *Don't drop or strike the starter - its magnets may be demagnetized, which will ruin it.*

6   Check the condition of the O-ring on the end of the starter that fits into the engine and replace it if necessary.

Installation

Refer to illustration 26.9

7   Remove any corrosion or dirt from the mounting lugs on the starter and the mounting points on the crankcase.

8   Apply a little engine oil to the O-ring and install the starter by reversing the removal procedure.

9   If you're working on a 300 model, guide the starter splines into the drive sprocket **(see illustration)**.

10   Refer to Section 18 and reinstall the left crankcase cover.

---

27   Starter drive – removal, inspection and installation

1   On 220 models, the starter motor turns the crankshaft through an idler gear, starter clutch gear and starter clutch. On 300 models, the starter motor drives a sprocket which turns the crankshaft through a chain, driven sprocket and starter clutch. The starter clutch on all models is bolted to the alternator rotor, which is secured to the crankshaft by a bolt and Woodruff key.

2   Remove the left crankcase cover and alternator rotor (see Section 18).

Removal
220 models

Refer to illustration 27.3

3   Slide off the idler gear and starter clutch gear **(see illustration on following page)**.

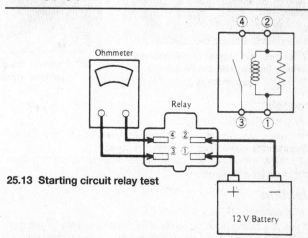

25.13 Starting circuit relay test

4A

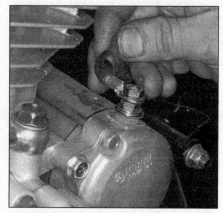

26.4a Remove the nut and washer and disconnect the cable . . .

26.4b . . . then remove the starter mounting bolts (arrows) to detach the starter (300 shown)

26.9 On 300 models, engage the starter splines with the drive sprocket during installation

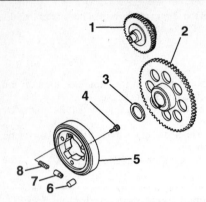

27.3 Starter clutch and gears (220 models)

1	Starter clutch gear	4	Allen bolt
2	Starter idler gear	5	Starter clutch
3	Thrust washer	6	Roller
		7	Cap
		8	Spring

27.4 Remove the screws (arrows) and take off the sprocket retainer

27.5 Slip the sprockets off the starter and crankshaft

27.9 Check the starter clutch rollers (arrow) for wear or damage

27.11 Unscrew the starter clutch Allen bolts (arrows)

27.7 Inspect the starter clutch friction surface (arrow) and the bushing in the sprocket

300 models

Refer to illustrations 27.4 and 27.5

4   Remove the sprocket retainer screws and take off the retainer **(see illustration)**. Use an impact driver if necessary.
5   Slip the sprockets off the starter motor and crankshaft, together with the chain **(see illustration)**.

Inspection

Refer to illustrations 27.7, 27.9 and 27.11

6   If you're working on a 300 model, check the sprockets for worn or broken teeth. Check the bushing inside the driven sprocket for wear. Replace the chain and sprockets as a set if problems are found.
7   Check the one-way clutch friction surface on the starter clutch gear (220) or driven sprocket (300) for scoring or corrosion **(see illustration)**.
8   If you're working on a 300 model, measure the length of the starter chain along any 20 links and compare the measurement to the value listed in this Chapter's Specifications. If it's beyond the specified limit, replace the chain.
9   Check the starter clutch in the back of the alternator rotor for visible wear and damage and replace it as described below if problems are found **(see illustration)**.
10   Place the alternator rotor in the starter clutch. Hold the alternator rotor with one hand so its open side is toward you and the starter clutch gear (220) or driven sprocket (300) is away from you. Hold the gear driven sprocket steady and try to rotate the rotor. The rotor should rotate smoothly counterclockwise, but not at all clockwise.
11   If the rotor rotates both ways or neither way, or if its movement is rough, remove the Allen bolts and separate the starter clutch from the alternator rotor **(see illustration 27.3 or the accompanying illustration)**.

Installation

220 models

12   Install the rollers, springs and spring caps in the starter clutch. Place the starter clutch on the alternator rotor.
13   Apply non-permanent thread locking agent to the threads of the Allen bolts and tighten them to the torque listed in this Chapter's Specifications.

300 models

14   Install the starter clutch on the alternator rotor with its arrow mark facing away from the rotor. Before you tighten the Allen bolts, place the starter driven sprocket in the rotor and try to turn the rotor both ways. It should turn counterclockwise but not clockwise, as described in Step 7. If the rotor turns the wrong way, the starter clutch is installed backwards.
15   Apply non-permanent thread locking agent to the threads of the Allen bolts and tighten them to the torque listed in this Chapter's Specifications.

All models

16   The remainder of installation is the reverse of the removal steps.

28   Wiring diagrams

Wiring diagrams are located at the end of this manual.
Prior to troubleshooting a circuit, check the fuses to make sure they're in good condition. Make sure the battery is fully charged and check the cable connections.
When checking a circuit, make sure all connectors are clean, with no broken or loose terminals or wires. When disconnecting a connector, don't pull on the wires - pull only on the connector housings.

Chapter 4 Part B
Ignition and electrical systems (Prairie models)

Contents

	Section
Alternator stator coils and rotor - check and replacement	18
Battery - charging	4
Battery - inspection and maintenance	3
Brake switch - check and replacement	10
CDI unit - check, removal and installation	23
Charging system - output test	17
Charging system testing - general information and precautions	16
Electrical troubleshooting	2
Fuses - check and replacement	5
Gear position switches – check and replacement	15
General information	1
Handlebar switches - check	13
Handlebar switches - removal and installation	14
Headlight aim - check and adjustment	8
Headlight bulb - replacement	7

	Section
Ignition coil - check, removal and installation	21
Ignition main (key) switch - check and replacement	12
Ignition system – check	20
Ignition timing - general information and check	24
Indicator and speedometer bulbs - replacement	11
Lighting system – check	6
Pick-up coil – check and replacement	22
Regulator/rectifier - check and replacement	19
Spark plug replacement	See Chapter 1
Speedometer and cable - removal and installation	28
Starter circuit - check and component replacement	25
Starter drive – removal, inspection and installation	27
Starter motor - removal and installation	26
Tail light and brake light bulbs - replacement	9
Wiring diagrams	29

4B

Specifications

Fuses

Main fuse	30 amps
Accessory outlet fuse	5 amps

Battery

Type
US models	12V 14 Ah
All except US	12V 19 Ah

Specific gravity
US models	1.270 at 20-degrees C (68-degrees F)
All except US models	1.265 at 20-degrees C (68-degrees F)

Bulbs

Headlights
2WD models	25/25 watts
4WD models	30/30 watts
Tail lights	8 watts
Tail/brake lights	8/27 watts
Indicator lights	Not specified

Charging system

Charging output voltage	Battery voltage to 14 volts
Stator coil resistance	0.33 to 0.49 ohms

Ignition system

Spark plug cap resistance	4750 to 6250 ohms
Ignition coil resistance	
Primary resistance	0.09 to 0.13 ohms
Secondary resistance	3800 to 5800 ohms
Pick-up coil resistance	110 to 140 ohms

Starting system

Starter chain length (20 links)	
Standard	155.8 to 156.1 mm (6.133 to 6.145 inches)
Limit	158.0 mm (6.220 inches)

Torque specifications

Reverse and neutral switches	15 Nm (123 inch-lbs)
Alternator rotor bolt	59 Nm (43 ft-lbs)
Left crankcase cover bolts	8.8 Nm (78 inch-lbs)*
Alternator stator bolts	8.8 Nm (78 inch-lbs)
Pick-up coil mounting screws	2.5 Nm (22 inch-lbs)
Pick-up coil harness retainer screw	4.4 Nm (39 inch-lbs)
Starter stud nut (below cable)	6.9 Nm (61 inch-lbs)
Starter cable nut	4.9 Nm (43 inch-lbs)
Starter mounting bolts	6.9 Nm (61 inch-lbs)
Starter clutch Allen bolts	34 Nm (25 ft-lbs)*

Apply non-permanent thread locking agent to the threads.

1   General information

These vehicles use a 12-volt electrical system with a battery. The components include a crankshaft-mounted permanent-magnet alternator and a solid state voltage regulator/rectifier unit. The alternator consists of a multi-coil stator mounted inside the left engine cover and a permanent magnet rotor mounted on the end of the crankshaft. The regulator maintains the charging system output within the specified range to prevent overcharging. The rectifier converts the AC output of the alternator to direct current (DC) to power the lights and other components and to charge the battery.

All models use an electric starter, mounted behind the engine case. A recoil (pull rope) starter, also standard equipment, is covered in Chapter 2.

Prairie models are equipped with a battery operated, fully transistorized, breakerless ignition system. The system consists of the following components:

   Pick-up coil
   CDI unit
   Battery and fuse
   Ignition coil
   Spark plug
   Engine kill (stop) and main (key) switches
   Primary and secondary (HT) circuit wiring

The transistorized ignition system functions on the same principle as a DC ignition system with the pick-up coil and CDI unit performing the tasks previously associated with the breaker points and mechanical advance system. As a result, adjustment and maintenance of ignition components is eliminated (with the exception of spark plug replacement). **Note:** *Keep in mind that most electrical parts, once purchased, can't be returned. To avoid unnecessary*

Because of their nature, individual electrical components can be checked but not repaired. If ignition system troubles occur, and the faulty component can be isolated, the only cure for the problem is to replace the part with a new one.

expense, make very sure the faulty component has been positively identified before buying a replacement part.

2   Electrical troubleshooting

This procedure is the same as for Bayou models (see Chapter 4A).

3   Battery - inspection and maintenance

1   Most battery damage is caused by heat, vibration, and/or low electrolyte levels, so keep the battery securely mounted, check the electrolyte level frequently and make sure the charging system is functioning properly. **Warning:** *Always disconnect the negative cable first and connect it last to prevent sparks which could the battery to explode.*

2   Refer to Chapter 1 for electrolyte level and specific gravity checking procedures.

3   Check around the base inside of the battery for sediment, which is the result of sulfation caused by low electrolyte levels. These deposits will cause internal short circuits, which can quickly discharge the battery. Look for cracks in the case and replace the battery if either of these conditions is found.

4   Check the battery terminals and cable ends for tightness and corrosion. If corrosion is evident, disconnect the cables from the battery, disconnecting the negative (-) terminal first, and clean the terminals and cable ends with a wire brush or knife and emery paper. Reconnect the cables, connecting the negative cable last, and apply a thin coat of petroleum jelly to the cables to slow further corrosion.

5   The battery case should be kept clean to prevent current leakage, which can discharge the battery over a period of time (especially when it sits unused). Wash the outside of the case with a solution of baking soda and water. Do not get any baking soda solution in the battery cells. Rinse the battery thoroughly, then dry it.

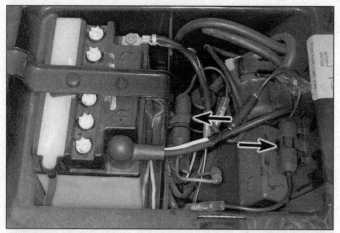

5.1 The main fuse and a spare fuse are located near the battery. . .

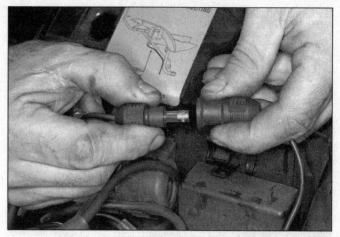

5.2 . . . open the holder for access to the fuse

6   If acid has been spilled on the frame or battery box, neutralize it with a baking soda and water solution, then touch up any damaged paint. Make sure the battery vent tube (if equipped) is directed away from the frame and is not kinked or pinched **(see illustration 12.13 in Chapter 1B)**.

7   If the vehicle sits unused for long periods of time, disconnect the cables from the battery terminals. Refer to Section 4 and charge the battery approximately once every month.

4   Battery - charging

1   If the machine sits idle for extended periods or if the charging system malfunctions, the battery can be charged from an external source.

2   To properly charge the battery, you will need a charger of the correct rating, a hydrometer, a clean rag and a syringe for adding distilled water to the battery cells.

3   The maximum charging rate for any battery is 1/10th of the rated amp-hour capacity. As an example, the maximum charge rate for a 14 amp/hour battery would be 1.4 amps. If the battery is charged at a higher rate, it could overheat, causing the plates inside the battery to buckle.

4   Do not allow the battery to be subjected to a so-called quick charge (high charge rate over a short period of time) unless you are prepared to buy a new battery. The excess heat will warp the plates inside the battery until they touch each other, causing a short that ruins the battery.

5   When charging the battery, always remove it from the machine and be sure to check the electrolyte level before hooking up the charger. Add distilled water to any cells that are low.

6   Loosen the cell caps, hook up the battery charger leads (positive lead to battery positive terminal, negative lead to battery negative terminal), cover the top of the battery with a clean rag, then, and only then, plug in the battery charger. **Warning:** *The hydrogen gas escaping from a charging battery is explosive, so keep open flames and sparks well away from the area. Also, the electrolyte is extremely corrosive and will damage anything it comes in contact with.*

7   Allow the battery to charge until the specific gravity is as specified (refer to Chapter 1 for the specific gravity checking procedure). The charger must be unplugged and disconnected from the battery when making specific gravity checks. If the battery overheats or gases excessively, the charging rate is too high. Either disconnect the charger or lower the charging rate to prevent damage to the battery.

8   If one or more of the cells do not show an increase in specific gravity after a long slow charge, or if the battery as a whole does not seem to want to take a charge, it's time for a new battery.

9   When the battery is fully charged, unplug the charger first, then disconnect the leads from the battery. Install the cell caps and wipe any electrolyte off the outside of the battery case.

10   If the recharged battery discharges rapidly when left disconnected, it's likely that an internal short caused by physical damage or sulfation has occurred. A new battery will be required. A sound battery will tend to lose its charge at about 1-percent per day.

5   Fuses - check and replacement

Refer to illustrations 5.1 and 5.2

1   These models use a 30 amp main fuse and a 5 amp power outlet fuse, located under the seat **(see illustration)**. The fuses are mounted in rubber holders, which are secured in clips. A spare fuse is contained in a plastic holder hung on a wire next to the main fuse.

2   The fuses can be removed and checked visually. Open the rubber cover and pull the fuse out **(see illustration)**. A blown fuse is easily identified by a break in the element.

6   Lighting system – check

This procedure is the same as for Bayou models (see Chapter 4A).

7   Headlight bulb - replacement

This procedure is the same as for Bayou models (see Chapter 4A).

8   Headlight aim - check and adjustment

This procedure is the same as for Bayou models (see Chapter 4A).

9   Tail light and brake light bulbs - replacement

This procedure is the same as for Bayou models (see Chapter 4A).

10   Brake switch - check and replacement

This procedure is the same as for Bayou models (see Chapter 4A).

4B

11.1 Pull the bulb socket out of the speedometer and pull out the bulb

11.2a Remove the screws . . .

11 Indicator and speedometer bulbs - replacement

Refer to illustrations 11.1, 11.2a, 11.2b and 11.2c

1   To remove the speedometer bulb, reach under the handlebar cover and pull the rubber socket out **(see illustration)**.

2   To remove an indicator bulb, remove the screws, washers and collars from the handlebar cover **(see illustrations)**. Lift the cover and pull the bulb sockets out **(see illustration)**.

3   If the socket contacts are dirty or corroded, they should be scraped clean and sprayed with electrical contact cleaner before new bulbs are installed.

4   Push the new bulb into its socket and push the socket back into the speedometer or indicator light housing.

12 Ignition main (key) switch - check and replacement

Check

1   Follow the wiring harness from the ignition switch to the connector and disconnect the connector.

2   Using an ohmmeter, check the continuity of the terminal pairs indicated in the wiring diagrams at the end of the book. Continuity should exist between the terminals connected by a solid line when the switch is in the indicated position.

3   If the switch fails any of the tests, replace it.

Replacement

Refer to illustration 12.6

4   The ignition switch is secured to its bracket by a plastic nut.

5   If you haven't already done so, disconnect the switch electrical connector.

6   Unscrew the nut and lower the switch out of the fender **(see illustration)**.

7   Installation is the reverse of the removal procedure.

13 Handlebar switches - check

1   Generally speaking, the switches are reliable and trouble-free. Most troubles, when they do occur, are caused by dirty or corroded contacts, but wear and breakage of internal parts is a possibility that should not be overlooked. If breakage does occur, the entire switch and related wiring harness will have to be replaced with a new one, since individual parts are not usually available.

2   The switches can be checked for continuity with an ohmmeter or a continuity test light. Always disconnect the battery negative cable, which will prevent the possibility of a short circuit, before making the checks.

3   Follow the wiring harness of the switch in question and disconnect the electrical connectors.

4   Using the ohmmeter or test light, check for continuity between the terminals of the switch harness with the switch in the various posi-

11.2b . . . washers and collars . . .

11.2c . . . then lift the cover, pull out the socket and pull out the bulb

12.6 Unscrew the plastic nut to remove the ignition switch

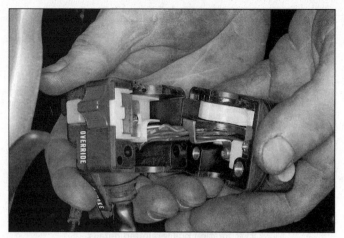

14.1 Separate the housing halves to inspect the individual switches

15.2 The neutral and reverse switches (arrows) are identified by N and R marks cast into the crankcase

tions. Refer to the continuity diagrams contained in the wiring diagrams at the end of the book. Continuity should exist between the terminals connected by a solid line when the switch is in the indicated position.

5   If the continuity check indicates a problem exists, refer to Section 14, disassemble the switch and spray the switch contacts with electrical contact cleaner. If they are accessible, the contacts can be scraped clean with a knife or polished with crocus cloth. If switch components are damaged or broken, it will be obvious when the switch is disassembled.

14   Handlebar switches - removal and installation

Refer to illustration 14.1

1   The handlebar switches are composed of two halves that clamp around the bar. They are easily removed for cleaning or inspection by taking out the clamp screws and pulling the switch halves away from the handlebars **(see illustration)**.

2   To completely remove the switches, the electrical connectors in the wiring harness must be unplugged and the harness separated from the tie wraps and retainers.

3   When installing the switches, make sure the wiring harness is properly routed to avoid pinching or stretching the wires.

15   Gear position switches – check and replacement

Check

Refer to illustration 15.2

1   Remove the oil filter cover from the engine (see Chapter 1).

2   Disconnect the electrical connector from the switch being tested **(see illustration)**.

3   Connect one lead of an ohmmeter to a good ground (bare metal on the engine) and the other lead to the terminal post on the switch being tested.

4   When the Hi/Lo/Reverse shifter is in Neutral, the ohmmeter should read 0 ohms between the neutral switch and ground. In any other range, it should read infinite resistance.

5   When the Hi/Lo/Reverse shifter is in Reverse, the ohmmeter should read 0 ohms between the reverse switch and ground. In any other range, it should read infinite resistance.

6   If a switch is defective, unscrew it from the engine and screw in a new one. Use electrically conductive sealer on the switch threads.

16   Charging system testing - general information and precautions

This procedure is the same as for Bayou models (see Chapter 4A).

17   Charging system - output test

This procedure is the same as for Bayou models (see Chapter 4A).

18   Alternator stator coils and rotor - check and replacement

Stator coil check

Refer to illustration 18.1

1   Follow the stator coil wiring harness from the point where it leaves the left crankcase cover to its connector **(see illustration)**. The connector can be identified by its three yellow wires meeting three black wires.

2   Connect an ohmmeter between each of the terminals in the side of the connector that runs back to the engine (connect the positive

4B

18.1 Remove the left crankcase cover bolts (arrows); the harness leaves the cover just below the decompressor knob

19.4 The regulator/rectifier is at the rear of the vehicle

21.2 Ignition coil mounting details

lead to one of the terminal and the negative lead to each of the two remaining terminals in turn). If the readings are outside the range listed in this Chapter's Specifications, replace the stator as described below.
3   Connect the ohmmeter between a good ground on the vehicle and each of the connector terminals in turn. The meter should indicate infinite resistance (no continuity). If not, replace the stator.

Stator and rotor replacement

4   These procedures are the same as for Bayou models (see Chapter 4A). Refer to Step 1 above for locations of the left crankcase cover screws on Prairie models **(see illustration 18.1)**.

19   Regulator/rectifier - check and replacement

Check

1   The regulator/rectifier should be suspected if the alternator output was significantly too high during the charging system output test or if charging system output never rises and the stator coils are good.
2   Regulator/rectifier testing is a complicated procedure that requires special equipment for complete accuracy. If the regulator/rectifier is suspect, have it tested by a dealer service department or substitute a known good unit.

Replacement

Refer to illustration 19.4
3   Remove the rear fender (see Chapter 7).
4   Disconnect the rectifier/regulator electrical connectors **(see illustration)**. Remove the mounting bolts and lift it off the frame.
5   Installation is the reverse of the removal steps.

20   Ignition system – check

This procedure is the same as for Bayou models (see Chapter 4A).

21   Ignition coil - check, removal and installation

Check

1   This procedure is the same as for Bayou models (see Chapter 4A). Refer to this Chapter's Specifications for coil resistance values.

Removal and installation

Refer to illustration 21.2
2   To remove the coil, refer to Chapter 3 and remove the fuel tank,

then disconnect the spark plug wire from the plug. Unplug the coil primary circuit electrical connectors **(see illustration)**.
3   Support the coil with one hand and remove the mounting bolt, then lift the coil out.
4   Installation is the reverse of removal.

22   Pick-up coil – check and replacement

This procedure is the same as for Bayou models (see Chapter 4A).

23   CDI unit - check, removal and installation

Check

1   The CDI unit is checked by process of elimination (when all other possible causes have been checked and eliminated, the CDI unit is at fault). Because the CDI unit is expensive and can't be returned once purchased, consider having a Kawasaki dealer test the system before you buy a new CDI unit.

Replacement

Refer to illustration 23.3a and 23.3b
2   Refer to Chapter 7 and remove the seat.
3   Disconnect the electrical connector from the CDI unit **(see illustrations)**. Remove its mounting screws and take it off the frame.
4   Installation is the reverse of the removal steps.

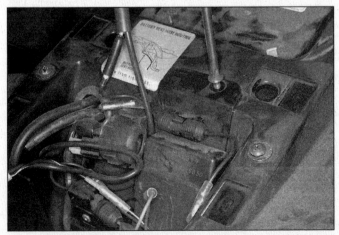

23.3a Remove the screw and lift out the bracket . . .

23.3b ... then disconnect the connector and remove the CDI unit

25.3 The starter relay (bottom) and starter circuit relay (top) are mounted in front of the battery

24 Ignition timing - general information and check

This procedure is the same as for Bayou models (see Chapter 4A).

25 Starter circuit - check and component replacement

1   Remove the seat for access to the starter relay and starter circuit relay (see Chapter 7).
2   Start by taking a good look at all of the wires and connections in the circuit. Disconnect and clean the battery cables and both rends of the heavy cables that run to the starter relay. A common cause of starter problems is corrosion of these terminals. Corrosion that isn't obvious can still be enough to prevent the starter from working. Make sure all wiring is clean, in good condition and tightly connected before you start testing or you won't get accurate results.

Starter relay

Refer to illustration 25.3

Check

Warning: *Make sure the transmission is in Neutral before performing this test.*
3   Locate the starter relay under the seat **(see illustration)**.
4   Disconnect the electrical connector for the two thin wires connected to the relay.
5   Connect a length of wire from the black wire terminal in the connector to the battery positive terminal (the side of the connector that runs to the relay, not the harness side). Connect another length of wire from the battery negative terminal to the yellow/black wire terminal in the connector. The starter should crank the engine. If it doesn't, the problem may be in the starter itself, in the electrical cables between the battery and starter relay, or in the starter relay. If the starter is good and the cables are in good condition and properly connected, the relay is probably at fault.
6   To test the relay further, disconnect its heavy cables. Repeat the test in Step 5 and listen for a clicking sound from the relay when the wires are connected. If there is no sound, the relay is probably bad. To confirm this, connect an ohmmeter between the cable terminals, then repeat Step 5. The ohmmeter should indicate zero ohms when power is applied to the small relay terminals. If not, the relay is bad. Replace it.
7   As a final check on the relay, disconnect all of its cables and connect an ohmmeter between the terminals for the small wires. It should read close to zero ohms. If it reads higher, replace the relay.

Replacement

8   Disconnect the negative cable from the battery.
9   Pull back the rubber covers from the terminal nuts, remove the

nuts and disconnect the starter relay cables **(see illustration 25.3)**. Disconnect the remaining electrical connector from the starter relay.
10   Pull the relay's rubber mount off the metal bracket and pull the relay out of the mount.
11   Installation is the reverse of removal. Reconnect the negative battery cable after all the other electrical connections are made.

Starting circuit relay

Check

12   Locate the relay beneath the seat **(see illustration 25.3)**. Disconnect the connector from the relay.
13   Connect an ohmmeter between relay terminals 3 and 4 **(see illustration 25.13 in Chapter 4A)**. The ohmmeter should indicate no continuity (infinite resistance).
14   Connect a 12-volt battery (the vehicle's battery will work if it's fully charged) between relay terminals 1 and 2. With the battery connected, the ohmmeter should indicate 0 ohms. With the battery disconnected, the ohmmeter should indicate infinite resistance. If the relay doesn't perform as described, replace it.

Replacement

15   If you haven't already done so, disconnect the relay's electrical connector. Pull the relay out of its mounting band and install a new one, then connect the wiring harness.

Starter switch

16   The starter switch is part of the switch assembly on the left handlebar. Refer to Section 14 for checking and replacement procedures.

26 Starter motor - removal and installation

This procedure is the same as for Bayou models (see Chapter 4A).

27 Starter drive – removal, inspection and installation

This procedure is the same as for Bayou models (see Chapter 4A).

28 Speedometer and cable – removal and installation

Cable

Refer to illustrations 28.1, 28.2a and 28.2b

1   Reach beneath the speedometer and unscrew the knurled nut

4B

28.1 Unscrew the knurled nut and pull the cable out of the speedometer

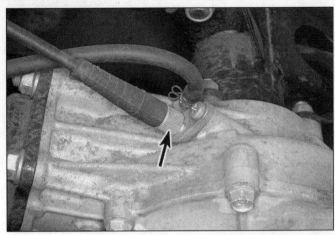

28.2a Unscrew the knurled nut at the rear differential (arrow) . . .

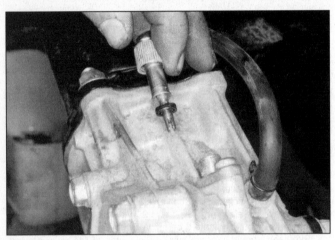

28.2b . . . and pull out the speedometer cable and O-ring

28.4 Pull up the rubber ring from around the speedometer

that secures the cable **(see illustration)**.

2   Follow the cable to the rear differential. Remove the retaining screw, then pull the cable and its O-ring out of the differential **(see illustrations)**.

3   Installation is the reverse of the removal steps. Lubricate both ends of the cable with speedometer cable lubricant.

Speedometer

Refer to illustrations 28.4 and 28.6

4   Pull out the rubber ring that surrounds the speedometer **(see illustration)**.

5   Disconnect the speedometer cable **(see illustration 28.1)**. Pull the bulb socket out of the speedometer.

6   Remove the screws and lift the speedometer mounting insulators out of the brackets **(see illustration)**.

7   Installation is the reverse of the removal steps.

29 Wiring diagrams

Wiring diagrams are at the end of the manual.

Prior to troubleshooting a circuit, check the fuses to make sure they're in good condition. Make sure the battery is fully charged and check the cable connections.

28.6 Remove the screws (arrows) and remove the mounting grommets from the bracket

When checking a circuit, make sure all connectors are clean, with no broken or loose terminals or wires. When disconnecting a connector, don't pull on the wires - pull only on the connector

Chapter 5 Part A
Steering, suspension and final drive (Bayou models)

Contents

	Section
Ball-joint replacement (300 models)	6
Bevel drive unit and output gear (2WD models) removal, inspection and installation	17
Front differential (4WD models) - removal, inspection and installation	16
Front driveaxles (4WD models) - boot replacement and CV joint overhaul	14
Front driveaxles (4WD models) - removal and installation	13
Front driveshaft (4WD models) – removal, inspection and installation	15
Front shock absorbers - removal and installation	8
Front suspension arms - removal, inspection, and installation	9
General information	1
Handlebars - removal, inspection and installation	2
Rear axle - removal, inspection and installation	21

	Section
Rear differential - removal, inspection and installation	22
Rear driveshaft - removal, inspection and installation	20
Rear shock absorbers – removal and installation	10
Rear suspension (complete) – removal and installation	11
Rear suspension links – removal, inspection and installation	12
Steering knuckle bearing replacement (4WD models)	7
Steering knuckles - removal, inspection, and installation	5
Steering shaft - removal, inspection, bearing replacement and installation	3
Sub-transmission and bevel drive gear (4WD models) - removal and installation	19
Sub-transmission shift linkage (4WD models) – removal, inspection and installation	18
Tie-rods - removal, inspection and installation	4

Specifications

Front driveaxles (4WD models)

Inboard joint grease capacity	
Initial amount	25 grams
Final amount	20 grams
Outboard joint grease capacity	40 grams

Torque specifications

Handlebar bracket bolts	
220 models	Not specified
300 models	20 Nm (174 inch-lbs)
Tie-rod nuts	41 Nm (30 ft-lbs)
Tie-rod locknuts	
220 models	27 Nm (20 ft-lbs)
300 models	29 Nm (22 ft-lbs)
Steering shaft nut	29 Nm (22 ft-lbs)
Steering shaft lower bearing bolts	
220 models	Not specified
300 models	20 Nm (174 inch-lbs)
Steering shaft upper bracket bolts	
220 models	26 Nm (19.5 ft-lbs)
300 models	
1986 and 1987	20 Nm (174 inch-lbs)
1988 and later	25 Nm (18 ft-lbs)
Shock absorber bolts (front and rear)	34 Nm (25 ft-lbs)
Front suspension arm pivot bolts	
220 models	88 Nm (65 ft-lbs)
1986 and 1987 300 models	
Upper	34 Nm (25 ft-lbs)
Lower	88 Nm (65 ft-lbs)
1988 and later 300 models (upper and lower)	88 Nm (65 ft-lbs)

Torque specifications (continued)

Ball-joint nuts (300 models)	
1986 and 1987 models	41 Nm (30 ft-lbs)
1988 and later models	
2WD	34 Nm (25 ft-lbs)
4WD (upper stud nut and lower pinch bolt nut)	52 Nm (38 ft-lbs)
Ball-joint to suspension arm (4WD models)	49 Nm (36 ft-lbs)
Knuckle arm pivot shaft nuts (220 models)	35 Nm (25 ft-lbs)
Knuckle arm bolts (4WD models)	49 Nm (36 ft-lbs)
Front suspension link bolts (1986 and 1987)	34 Nm (25 ft-lbs)
Rear suspension trailing link bolts	34 Nm (25 ft-lbs) (1)
Rear suspension lateral link bolts	34 Nm (25 ft-lbs)
Front differential (4WD models)	
Front bracket bolts	25 Nm (18 ft-lbs) (1)
Mounting bolts	37 Nm (27 ft-lbs)
Front driveaxle Allen bolts (4WD models)	8.8 Nm (78 inch-lbs)
Bevel drive unit (2WD models)	
Mounting bolts	25 Nm (18 ft-lbs) (2)
Bearing housing nuts	25 Nm (18 ft-lbs)
Sub-transmission (4WD models)	
8 mm bolts	25 Nm (18 ft-lbs) (3)
6 mm bolts	Not specified
Bevel drive gear nut	
220 models	
1988	78 Nm (58 ft-lbs)
1989 and later	120 Nm (87 ft-lbs)
300 models	
1986 and 1987	
14 mm nut	88 Nm (65 ft-lbs)
16 mm nut	93 Nm (69 ft-lbs)
1988 and later	
2WD	88 Nm (65 ft-lbs)
4WD	120 Nm (87 ft-lbs)
Rear axle housing bolts (2WD)	
220 models	20 Nm (178 inch-lbs)
300 models	
1986 and 1987	20 Nm (178 inch-lbs)
1988 and later	25 Nm (18 ft-lbs)
Rear axle housing nuts (4WD)	34 Nm (25 ft-lbs)
Rear driveshaft housing to differential nuts	
220 models	25 Nm (18 ft-lbs)
300 models	34 Nm (25 ft-lbs)

1   Apply non-permanent thread locking agent to the threads.
2   Apply silicone sealant to the upper front bolt (220 models) and engine oil to all of the others (220 and 300) (see text).
2   Apply non-permanent thread locking agent to the threads of three of the bolts (see text).

1   General information

The steering system consists of knuckles mounted at the outer ends of the front suspension and connected to a steering shaft by tie rods. On 220 models, the knuckles pivot on bolts that pass through the outer end of the control arm. On 300 models, the knuckles pivot between upper and lower ball-joints. The steering shaft on all models is turned by a one-piece handlebar.

The front suspension on 220 models consists of a single control arm on each side of the vehicle. A shock absorber with concentric coil spring is installed between the control arm and frame.

The front suspension on 300 models consists of an upper and lower control arm on each side of the vehicle. A shock absorber with concentric coil spring is installed between the lower control arm and frame on 2WD models and the upper control arm and frame on 4WD models.

The rear suspension on all models consists of trailing links and control arms on each side, supported by a pair of shock absorbers with concentric coil springs.

Final drive consists of a bevel drive unit (2WD) or sub-transmission (4WD) mounted on the left side of the engine. Power from the unit is transmitted through a driveshaft to the rear differential and the rear axle shaft. At the front of 4WD models, a driveshaft transmits power from the sub-transmission to the front driveaxle, which connect to the front wheel hubs. The rear differential on 2WD models can be locked. The front differential on 4WD models is a limited slip type.

2   Handlebars - removal, inspection and installation

1   The handlebars are a one-piece tube. The tube fits into a bracket, which is integral with the steering shaft. If the handlebars must be

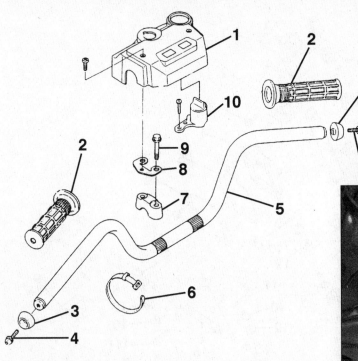

2.3 Handlebar details

1	*Handlebar cover*	7	*Handlebar clamp*
2	*Grip*	8	*Handlebar cover*
3	*Grip end piece*		*bracket*
4	*Bolt*	9	*Bracket bolt*
5	*Handlebar*	10	*Ignition switch (1988*
6	*Wiring harness retainer*		*and later models)*

3.3 Unbolt the bushing halves; on assembly, line up the marks on the sides (arrow)

3.5a Unbolt the lower shaft bearing

removed for access to other components, such as the steering shaft, simply remove the bolts and slip the handlebars off the bracket. It's not necessary to disconnect the cables, wires or brake hose, but it is a good idea to support the assembly with a piece of wire or rope, to avoid unnecessary strain on the cables, wires and the brake hose.

2   If the handlebars are to be removed completely, refer to Chapter 3 for the throttle housing removal procedure, Chapter 6 for the master cylinder removal procedure and Chapter 4 for the switch removal procedure.

Removal

Refer to illustration 2.3

3   If you plan to remove one of the grips, remove its screw while the handlebars are still bolted to the bracket **(see illustration)**.

4   Remove the screws and take off the handlebar cover.

5   Mark the handlebar brackets with a felt pen or punch to they can be reinstalled in the same location (left or right) and facing in the same direction. Remove the handlebar bracket bolts and lift off the brackets. Lift the handlebar out of the bracket.

Inspection

6   Check the handlebar and brackets for cracks and distortion and replace them if any undesirable conditions are found.

Installation

7   Installation is the reverse of the removal steps, with the following additions:

   a) *When installing the handlebar to the brackets, position it so its riser portion is parallel to the steering shaft.*

   b) *Install the handlebar brackets in their original locations and directions, referring to the marks made during removal.*

   c) *First tighten the rear bracket bolts to the torque listed in this Chapter's Specifications, then tighten the front bolts to the specified torque. This will leave a gap between the upper and lower parts of the brackets at the front. Don't try to close this gap by tightening the bolts beyond the specified torque or you may crack the brackets. The gap should be the same at both the left and right brackets, but again, don't try to even it out by tightening beyond the specified torque.*

---

3   Steering shaft - removal, inspection, bearing replacement and installation

Removal

Refer to illustrations 3.3 and 3.5a through 3.5e

1   Remove the handlebars (Section 2).

2   Remove the fuel tank and front fender (see Chapters 3 and 7).

3   Unbolt the steering shaft upper bushing from the frame and remove the oil seals **(see illustration)**.

4   Refer to Section 6 and disconnect the inner ends of the tie-rods.

5   Unbolt the lower bearing from the frame **(see illustrations)**.

6   Remove the steering shaft and lower bearing from the vehicle. Remove the cotter pin and nut from the lower end of the steering shaft.

5A

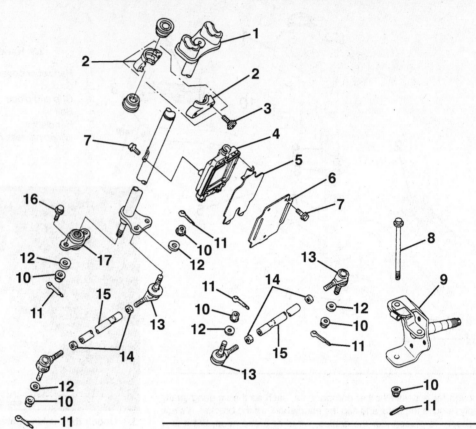

3.5b Steering shaft and linkage (220 models) – exploded view

1   Steering shaft
2   Upper bushing halves
3   Bolt
4   Brake cable equalizer
5   Equalizer seal
6   Equalizer base plate
7   Bolt
8   Steering knuckle pivot shaft
9   Steering knuckle
10 Nut
11 Cotter pin
12 Washer
13 Tie-rod end
14 Tie-rod locknuts
15 Tie-rod
16 Bolt
17 Lower bearing

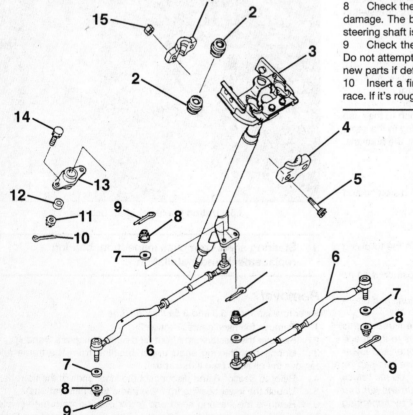

Inspection

7   Clean all the parts with solvent and dry them thoroughly, using compressed air, if available.

8   Check the steering shaft upper bushing for wear, deterioration or damage. The bushing grease seals should be replaced whenever the steering shaft is removed.

9   Check the steering shaft for bending or other signs of damage. Do not attempt to repair any steering components. Replace them with new parts if defects are found.

10 Insert a finger into the steering shaft bearing and turn the inner race. If it's rough, loose or noisy, replace it.

3.5c Steering shaft and linkage (1986 and 1987 300 models) – exploded view

1   Upper bushing forward half
2   Upper bushing grease seals
3   Steering shaft
4   Upper bushing rearward half
5   Upper bushing bolt
6   Right tie-rod
7   Washer
8   Nut
9   Cotter pin
10 Cotter pin
11 Nut
12 Grease seal
13 Lower bearing
14 Bolt
15 Nut

**3.5d Steering shaft and linkage
(1988 and later 300 2WD models) –
exploded view**

1 Steering shaft
2 Grease seals
3 Bolt (1990 on)
4 Bolt (1988 and 1989)
5 Upper bushing rearward half
6 Upper bushing forward half
7 Tie-rod
8 Washer
9 Nut
10 Cotter pin
11 Cotter pin
12 Nut
13 Grease seal
14 Lower bearing
15 Bolt

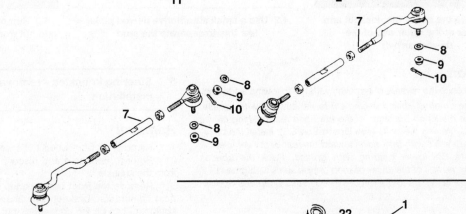

3.5e Steering shaft and linkage (4WD models) – exploded view

1	Steering shaft	13	Tie-rod locknut
2	Steering stop bolt	14	Cotter pin
3	Locknut	15	Nut
4	Washer	16	Grease seal
5	Bolt	17	Shaft lower bearing
6	Upper bushing rearward	18	Bolt
	half	19	Washer
7	Cotter pin	20	Locknut
8	Nut	21	Steering stop bolt
9	Washer	22	Upper bushing grease
10	Tie-rod end		seals
11	Tie-rod locknut	23	Upper bushing forward
12	Tie-rod tube		half

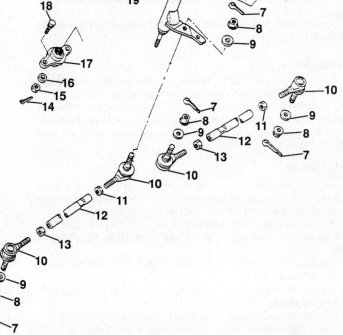

5A

4.1 Remove the cotter pin, locknut and washer at the outer end of the tie-rod (arrow)

4.2 Use a small automotive tie-rod puller like this to separate the stud

4.3 Remove the cotter pin, lockwasher and nut from the inner end of each tie-rod (4WD shown)

Installation

11   Installation is the reverse of removal, with the following additions:

a) *Pack the steering shaft bushing's internal cavities with grease. Align the marks on the sides of the front and rear bushing halves before tightening the bolts* **(see illustration 3.3)**. *Install the bushing grease seals with their splits toward the rear of the vehicle.*

b) *Lubricate the lower bearing with grease. Pack the spaces between the lips of the lower bearing grease seals with grease.*

c) *Tighten all fasteners to the torques listed in this Chapter's Specifications.*

4   Tie-rods - removal, inspection and installation

Removal

Refer to illustrations 4.1, 4.2 and 4.3

1   Remove the cotter pin from the nut at the outer end of the tie-rod **(see illustration)**.

2   Slip an open-end wrench onto the flats of the tie-rod stud and remove the nut. Separate the tie-rod stud from the knuckle **(see illustration)**.

3   Repeat Steps 1 and 2 to disconnect the inner end of the tie rod **(see illustration)**.

Inspection

4   Check the tie-rod shaft for bending or other damage and replace it if any problems are found. Don't try to straighten the shaft.

5   Check the ball-joint boot for cracks or deterioration. Twist and rotate the threaded stud. It should move easily, without roughness or looseness. If the boot or stud show any problems, unscrew the ball-joint from the tie-rod and install a new one.

Installation

6   Measure the distance from each locknut to the end of the threads and make sure it's equal for both tie-rods. If it's incorrect, loosen the locknut and reposition the locknut and ball-joint on the threads.

7   Position the ball-joint at each end of the tie-rod so the studs face in the proper direction (up or down) **(see illustration 3.5b, 3.5c or 3.5d)**.

8   The remainder of installation is the reverse of the removal steps, with the following additions:

a) *Tighten the tie-rod nuts to the torque listed in this Chapter's Specifications.*

b) *Use new cotter pins and bend them to hold the nuts securely.*

c) *Check front wheel toe-in and adjust as necessary (see Chapter 1).*

5   Steering knuckles - removal, inspection, and installation

Removal

1   Remove the front wheel hubs (see Chapter 6).

2   Refer to Section 4 and disconnect the outer end of the tie-rod from the knuckle.

3   Remove the front brake panel (drum brakes) or brake disc and dust shield (disc brakes) (see Chapter 6). The front brake hose (if equipped) can be left connected, but be careful not to twist it and be sure to support the panel or caliper with wire or rope so it doesn't hang by the brake hose.

Bayou 220 models

Refer to illustration 5.4

4   Remove the cotter pin, nut and washer from the bottom end of the steering knuckle pivot shaft **(see illustration)**.

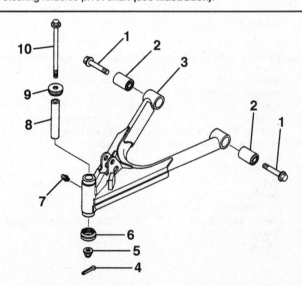

5.4 Front suspension (220 models) – exploded view

1	Suspension arm pivot bolt	6	Seal
2	Bushing	7	Grease fitting
3	Suspension arm	8	Sleeve
4	Cotter pin	9	Seal
5	Pivot shaft nut	10	Steering knuckle pivot shaft

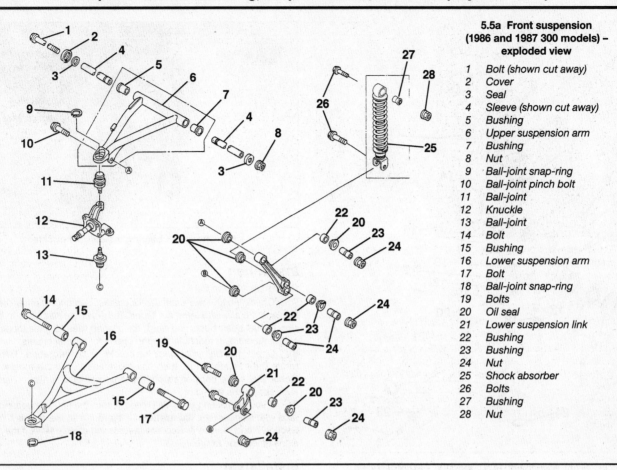

5.5a Front suspension (1986 and 1987 300 models) – exploded view

1 Bolt (shown cut away)
2 Cover
3 Seal
4 Sleeve (shown cut away)
5 Bushing
6 Upper suspension arm
7 Bushing
8 Nut
9 Ball-joint snap-ring
10 Ball-joint pinch bolt
11 Ball-joint
12 Knuckle
13 Ball-joint
14 Bolt
15 Bushing
16 Lower suspension arm
17 Bolt
18 Ball-joint snap-ring
19 Bolts
20 Oil seal
21 Lower suspension link
22 Bushing
23 Bushing
24 Nut
25 Shock absorber
26 Bolts
27 Bushing
28 Nut

Bayou 300 models

Refer to illustrations 5.5a, 5.5b and 5.5c

5 Remove the cotter pin and nut or pinch bolt and nut from the upper and lower ball-joints **(see illustrations)**.
6 Tap the steering knuckle downward to free it from the upper ball-joint stud and upward to free it from the lower ball-joint stud.

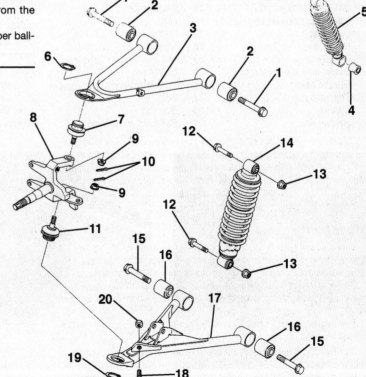

5.5b Front suspension (1988 and later 300 2WD models) – exploded view

1 Bolt	11 Ball-joint
2 Bushing	12 Bolts
3 Suspension arm	13 Nuts
4 Bushing	14 Shock absorber
5 Shock absorber	15 Bolt
6 Ball-joint snap-ring	16 Bushing
7 Ball-joint	17 Suspension arm
8 Knuckle	18 Bolt
9 Ball-joint nut	19 Ball-joint snap-ring
10 Cotter pin	20 Nut

5A

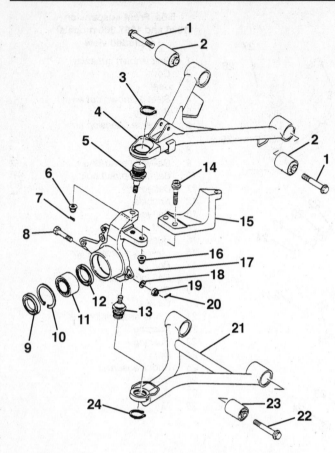

5.9 Check the bearing inside the knuckle

Inspection

Refer to illustration 5.9

7   Check the knuckle carefully for cracks, bending or other damage. Replace it if any problems are found. If the vehicle has been in a collision or has been bottomed hard, it's a good idea to have the knuckle magnafluxed by a machine shop to check for hidden cracks.

8   Check the ball-joint boot for cracks or deterioration. Twist and rotate the threaded stud. It should move easily, without roughness or looseness. If the boot or stud show any problems, refer to Section 6 and replace the ball-joint.

9   If you're working on a 4WD model, turn the knuckle bearing inner race with a finger **(see illustration)**. If it's rough, loose or noisy, refer to Section 7 and replace it. Replace the bearing grease seals if they show signs of leakage or wear.

Installation

10   Installation is the reverse of the removal steps, with the following additions: Use new cotter pins and tighten the ball-joint nut(s) to the torque listed in this Chapter's Specifications.

---

6   Ball-joint replacement (300 models)

Refer to illustrations 6.1, 6.2a and 6.2b

1   Remove the ball-joint snap-ring **(see illustration)**.

2   On 300 2WD models, take the ball-joint out of the suspension arm. On 4WD models, place a large socket on the ball-joint hex and unscrew it from the suspension arm **(see illustrations)**.

5.5c Front suspension (4WD models) – exploded view

1	Bolt	13	Ball-joint
2	Bushing	14	Bolt
3	Ball-joint snap-ring	15	Knuckle arm
4	Upper suspension arm	16	Nut
5	Ball-joint	17	Cotter pin
6	Nut	18	Washer
7	Cotter pin	19	Nut
8	Lower ball-joint pinch bolt	20	Cotter pin
9	Grease seal	21	Suspension arm
10	Snap-ring	22	Bolt
11	Bearing	23	Bushing
12	Grease seal	24	Ball-joint snap-ring

6.1 Remove the snap-ring (upper ball-joint shown)

6.2a Place a large socket over the ball-joint hex . . .

6.2b . . . and unscrew it from the suspension arm

7.1 Pry out the grease seal from each side of the bearing and remove the snap-ring from the outer side

8.3a Remove the upper nut and bolt to detach the shock from the frame . . .

8.3b . . . and the lower nut and bolt to detach the shock from the suspension arm

3   Thread the new ball-joint into the suspension arm and tighten to the torque listed in this Chapter's Specifications.
4   Install the snap-ring and make sure it seats completely in its groove.

7   Steering knuckle bearing replacement (4WD models)

Refer to illustration 7.1
1   Pry out the bearing grease seals **(see illustration)**.
2   Remove the bearing snap-ring from the outer side of the knuckle. Drive the bearing out of the knuckle with a bearing driver or socket that bears against the bearing outer race.
3   Pack a new bearing with grease, then drive it in with the same tool used for removal. The marked side of the bearing faces outward (away from the center of the vehicle). Seat the bearing securely, then install the snap-ring and make sure it fits completely into its groove.
4   Tap in new grease seals with a bearing driver or socket the same diameter as the seals. Make sure the seals seat squarely in their bores, then lubricate the seal lips with grease.

8   Front shock absorbers - removal and installation

Refer to illustrations 8.3a and 8.3b
1   Remove the front fender (see Chapter 7).
2   Securely block both rear wheels so the vehicle won't roll. Refer to Chapter 6 and remove the front wheels.
3   Remove the nuts and bolt at the upper and lower ends of the shock **(see illustrations)**.
4   Installation is the reverse of the removal steps. Tighten the nuts and bolts to the torque listed in this Chapter's Specifications.

9   Front suspension arms - removal, inspection, and installation

Removal

1   Securely block both rear wheels so the vehicle won't roll. Loosen the front wheel nuts with the tires still on the ground, then jack up the front end, support it securely on jackstands and remove the front wheels.
2   Refer to Section 7 and remove the steering knuckle.
3   Detach the shock absorber from the suspension arm (220), lower suspension arm (300 2WD) or upper suspension arm (4WD).
4   If you're working on a 300 model, detach the brake hose clamps from the upper suspension arm.

5   Remove the nuts and bolts at the inner end of the suspension arm **(see illustration 5.4, 5.5a, 5.5b or 5.5c)** and pull the suspension arm out.

Inspection

6   Check the suspension arm for bending, cracks or other damage. Replace damaged parts. Don't attempt to straighten them.
7   Check the rubber bushings at the inner end of the suspension arm for cracks, deterioration or wear of the metal insert. Check the pivot bolts for wear as well. If any bushing problems are visible, have the old bushings pressed out and new ones pressed in by a dealer service department or machine shop.

Installation

8   Installation is the reverse of the removal steps, with the following addition: Tighten the nuts and bolts slightly while the vehicle is jacked up, then tighten them to the torque listed in this Chapter's Specifications while the vehicle's weight is resting on the wheels.

10   Rear shock absorbers – removal and installation

Refer to illustrations 10.3a and 10.3b
1   Remove the rear fender (see Chapter 7).
2   Securely block both front wheels so the vehicle can't roll. Jack up the rear end and support it securely with the rear wheels off the ground.
3   Remove the mounting bolts and nuts at the bottom of the shock, then at the top **(see illustrations)**. Lift the shock out of the vehicle.

5A

10.3a Remove the upper nut and bolt to detach the shock from the frame . . .

10.3b . . . and the lower nut and bolt to detach the shock from the axle

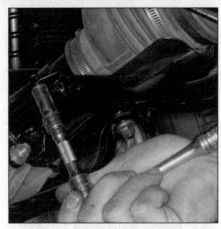

11.4 Unbolt the skid plate from under the rear driveshaft

11.6a Remove the front pivot bolt from the right trailing link . . .

11.6b . . . and from the left trailing link

11.7a Loosen the clamp at the front of the driveshaft boot (arrow) . . .

11.7b . . . and pull the driveshaft out as you remove the rear suspension

4   Installation is the reverse of the removal steps. Tighten the nuts and bolts to the torque listed in this Chapter's Specifications.

11   Rear suspension (complete) – removal and installation

Refer to illustration 11.4, 11.6a, 11.6b, 11.7a, 11.7b and 11.7c

1   The rear suspension and axle can be removed as a complete unit, either for repairs or for access to other components.
2   Support the vehicle under the rear of the floorpan with jackstands or large wooden blocks.
3   Disconnect the rear brake cable(s) and breather hose(s) (see Chapter 6).
4   Remove the skid plate from under the rear differential and driveshaft **(see illustration)**.
5   Remove the upper shock absorber bolts (Section 10).
6   Remove the trailing link front pivot bolts **(see illustrations)**.
7   Disengage the front end of the driveshaft from the sub-transmission or bevel drive unit on the left side of the engine **(see illustrations)**. Roll the suspension back and take it out from under the vehicle **(see illustration)**.
8   Installation is the reverse of the removal steps, with the following additions:
   a) Tighten the nuts and bolts to the torques listed in this Chapter's Specifications.
   b) Adjust the reverse cable (2WD) and brake cable (all models) (see Chapter 1).

11.7c Pull the entire suspension and rear axle to the rear

12   Rear suspension links – removal, inspection and installation

Refer to illustrations 12.1a, 12.1b and 12.5

1   The rear suspension links include two trailing links and two lateral links **(see illustrations)**. The left lateral link consists of an upper and lower piece, which run above the below the forward part of the rear differential.

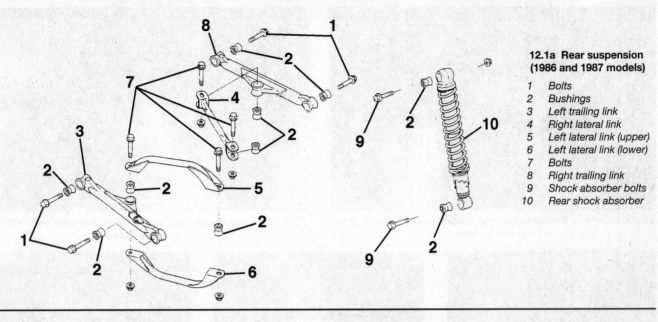

12.1a Rear suspension (1986 and 1987 models)

1   Bolts
2   Bushings
3   Left trailing link
4   Right lateral link
5   Left lateral link (upper)
6   Left lateral link (lower)
7   Bolts
8   Right trailing link
9   Shock absorber bolts
10 Rear shock absorber

2   Support the rear of the vehicle and remove the rear wheels. Support the rear axle with jackstands.
3   Remove the nuts and bolts and remove the link(s) from the vehicle.
4   Inspect the links and replace them if they're cracked or bent. If they're corroded, sand and paint them. Have worn or damaged bushings pressed out and new ones pressed in by a dealer service department or machine shop. Lubricate the new bushings when pressing them in.
5   Installation is the reverse of the removal steps, with the following additions:

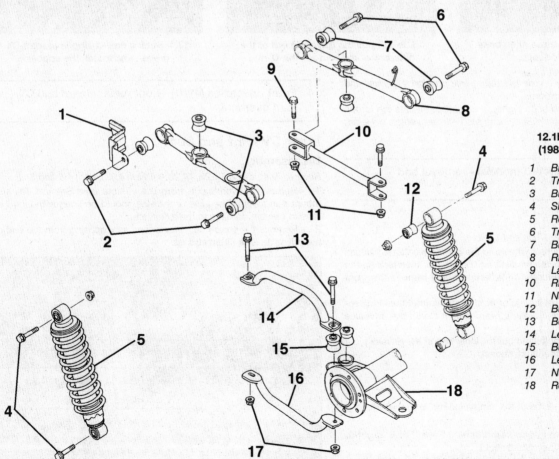

12.1b Rear suspension (1988 and later models)

1   Bracket
2   Trailing link pivot bolts
3   Bushings
4   Shock absorber bolts
5   Rear shock absorber
6   Trailing link pivot bolts
7   Bushings
8   Right trailing link
9   Lateral link bolts
10 Right lateral link
11 Nuts
12 Bushings
13 Bolts
14 Left lateral link (upper)
15 Bushings
16 Left lateral link (lower)
17 Nuts
18 Rear axle housing

5A

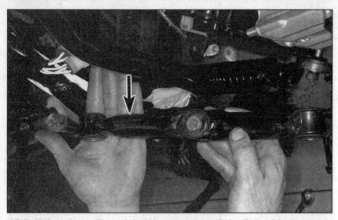

12.5 If there's an F mark in this area, install the link with the mark up and forward

13.2 Pull up the knuckle and separate the outer end of the driveaxle from it

13.3a Remove the three Allen bolts (one bolt hidden) . . .

13.3b . . . pull the driveaxle out of the differential and remove the O-ring

13.4 Stick a new O-ring in place with grease and install the spacer

a) *If there's an F mark on the left trailing link, position it forward and upward* **(see illustration)**.

b) *Tighten the nuts and bolts slightly, then tighten them to the torque listed in this Chapter's Specifications with the vehicle's weight resting on the wheels.*

---

13 Front driveaxles (4WD models) - removal and installation

Removal

Refer to illustrations 13.2, 13.3a and 13.3b

1   Securely block both rear wheels so the vehicle won't roll. Loosen the front wheel nuts with the tires still on the ground, then jack up the front end, support it securely on jackstands and remove the front wheels.

2   Disconnect the lower ball-joint from the steering knuckle (Section 5). Pull the steering knuckle upward until it clears the driveaxle **(see illustration)**.

3   Remove the Allen bolts and pull the inner end of the driveaxle out of the front differential **(see illustrations)**.

Installation

Refer to illustration 13.4

4   Installation is the reverse of the removal steps, with the following additions:

a) *Grease the new O-ring and seat it in its groove. Don't forget to reinstall the spacer* **(see illustration)**.

b) *Tighten the Allen bolts to the torque listed in this Chapter's Specifications.*

14 Front driveaxles (4WD) - boot replacement and CV joint overhaul

Inner CV joint and boot

Disassembly

Refer to illustrations 14.2a, 14.2b, 14.2c, 14.3, 14.4, 14.6 and 14.8

1   Remove the driveaxle from the vehicle (see Section 10) and mount it in a vise. The jaws of the vise should be lined with wood or rags to prevent damage to the axleshaft.

2   Remove the snap-ring, retainer and seal housing from the end of the driveaxle **(see illustrations)**.

14.2a Remove the snap-ring . . .

14.2b . . . and the spacer . . .

14.2c . . . and take the seal housing off the driveaxle

14.3 Pry the boot clamp retaining tabs (arrow) up with a small screwdriver, open the clamps and slide them off the shaft

14.4 Pry the wire ring ball retainer out of the outer race

3   Pry the boot clamp retaining tabs up with a small screwdriver and slide the clamps off the boot **(see illustration)**.
4   Slide the boot back on the axleshaft and pry the wire ring ball retainer from the outer race **(see illustration)**.
5   Pull the outer race off the inner bearing assembly.
6   Remove the snap-ring from the groove in the axleshaft with a pair of snap-ring pliers **(see illustration)**.
7   Slide the inner bearing assembly off the axleshaft.
8   Make match marks on the inner and outer portions of the bearing to identify which side faces out on assembly **(see illustration)**.

Inspection
9   Clean the components with solvent to remove all traces of grease. Inspect the cage, balls and races for pitting, score marks, cracks and other signs of wear and damage. Shiny, polished spots are normal and will not adversely affect CV joint performance.

Reassembly
Refer to illustrations 14.10, 14.16, 14.17a and 14.17b
10   Wrap the axleshaft splines with tape to avoid damaging the boot. Slide the small boot clamp and boot onto the axleshaft, then remove the tape **(see illustration)**.

5A

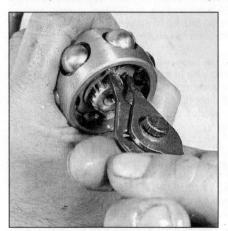

14.6 Remove the snap-ring from the end of the axle

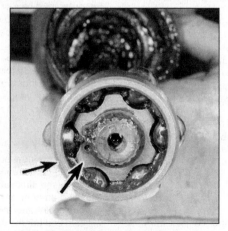

14.8 Apply match marks to the bearing (arrows) to identify which side faces out

14.10 Wrap the splined area of the axle with tape to prevent damage to the boot when installing it

14.16 Equalize the pressure inside the boot by inserting a small, dull screwdriver between the boot and the outer race

14.17a To install the new clamps, bend the tang down and . . .

14.17b . . . fold the tabs over to hold it in place

14.21 Slide the boot away from the joint and off the axleshaft

14.23 With the outer joint clean and dry, rotate it and check for damage; replace the driveaxle if problems are found

11   Install the inner bearing assembly on the axleshaft with the previously made matchmarks facing outward.

12   Install the snap-ring in the groove. Make sure it's completely seated by pushing on the inner bearing assembly.

13   Fill the outer race and boot with the specified type and quantity of CV joint grease (normally included with the new boot kit). Pack the inner bearing assembly with grease, by hand, until grease is worked completely into the assembly.

14   Slide the outer race down onto the inner race and install the wire ring retainer.

15   Wipe any excess grease from the axle boot groove on the outer race. Seat the small diameter of the boot in the recessed area on the axleshaft. Push the other end of the boot onto the outer race.

16   Equalize the pressure in the boot by inserting a dull screwdriver between the boot and the outer race **(see illustration)**. Don't damage the boot with the tool.

17   Install the boot clamps **(see illustrations)**.

18   Install a new circlip on the inner CV joint stub axle.

19   Install the driveaxle as described in Section 10.

Outer CV joint and boot

Disassembly

Refer to illustration 14.21

20   Following Steps 1 through 8, remove the inner CV joint from the axleshaft.

21   Remove the outer CV joint boot clamps, using the technique described in Step 3. Slide the boot off the axleshaft **(see illustration)**.

Inspection

Refer to illustration 14.23

22   Thoroughly wash the inner and outer CV joints in clean solvent and blow them dry with compressed air, if available. **Note:** *Because the outer joint cannot be disassembled, it is difficult to wash away all the old grease and to rid the bearing of solvent once it's clean. But it is imperative that the job be done thoroughly, so take your time and do it right.*

23   Once all the grease has been removed and the solvent blown out, bend the outer CV joint housing at an angle to the driveaxle to expose the bearings, inner race and cage **(see illustration)**. Rotate the joint through its full range of motion and inspect the bearing surfaces for signs of wear. If the bearings are damaged or worn, replace the driveaxle.

Reassembly

24   Slide the new outer boot onto the driveaxle. It's a good idea to wrap vinyl tape around the splines of the shaft to prevent damage to the boot **(see illustration 14.10)**. When the boot is in position, add the specified amount of grease (included in the boot replacement kit) to the outer joint and the boot (pack the joint with as much grease as it will hold and put the rest into the boot). Slide the boot on the rest of the way and install the new clamps **(see illustrations 14.17a and 14.17b)**.

25   Clean and install the inner CV joint and boot by following Steps 10 through 18, then install the driveaxle as outlined in Section 13.

15.2 Loosen the clamp at the front differential . . .

15.3 . . . roll the O-rings back onto the shaft . . .

15.4a . . . open the snap-ring and move it back onto the shaft . . .

15.4b . . . slide the coupling back onto the shaft . . .

15 Front driveshaft (4WD models) – removal, inspection and installation

Removal

Refer to illustrations 15.2, 15.3, 15.4a, 15.4b, 15.5 and 15.6

1   Remove the stamped sheet metal driveshaft cover from the left side of the vehicle.
2   Loosen the clamp that secures the front differential boot to the driveshaft **(see illustration)**.
3   Roll the O-rings out of their grooves on the driveshaft front boot and back onto the shaft **(see illustration)**,
4   Remove the snap-ring that secures the driveshaft's front coupling, then slide the coupling back onto the shaft **(see illustrations)**.
5   Separate the driveshaft from the front differential and remove the spring **(see illustration)**.
6   Pull the driveshaft forward out of the sub-transmission and remove it from the vehicle **(see illustration)**.
7   Clean off all the old grease and check the driveshaft for wear or

5A

15.5 . . . remove the spring . . .

15.6 . . . and slide the universal joint forward away from the sub-transmission

16.3a Remove the upper bolt (arrow) and nut and note how the breather hose fits under the bracket

16.3b Remove the upper bracket bolts (arrows) . . .

16.3c . . . and slide the bracket out

16.4 Remove the rear nuts (arrows) and through-bolts

16.5 Turn the differential and pass it out between the suspension arms

damage. If the splines are damaged, or if the universal joint is worn, replace the driveshaft.

8   Installation is the reverse of the removal steps. Lubricate the splines with grease and use a new snap-ring.

16   Front differential (4WD models) - removal, inspection and installation

Removal

Refer to illustrations 16.3a, 16.3b, 16.3c, 16.4 and 16.5

1   Remove the right front driveaxle and the front driveshaft (Sections 13 and 15). Unbolt the inner end of the left front driveaxle from the differential, but don't pull it out yet.

2   Support the differential with a jack.

3   Remove the upper bracket bolt, then unbolt the bracket and take it out **(see illustrations)**.

4   Remove the two rearward mounting bolts **(see illustration)**.

5   Lift the differential and pull out the left driveaxle. Turn the differential and pass it out between the suspension arms **(see illustration)**. As the breather hose becomes accessible, disconnect it from the differential. If necessary, loosen the pivot bolt at the inner end of the upper suspension arm so the arm can be raised to add removal clearance.

Inspection

Refer to illustration 16.6

6   Loosen the clamp and remove the U-joint boot from the differen-

tial **(see illustration)**. Check the U-joint for wear or damage and replace it if problems are found.

7   Check the oil seal at the driveshaft hole for signs of leakage. Look into the driveaxle holes and check for obvious signs of wear and for damage such as broken gear teeth **(see illustration 16.6)**. Turn the pinion (where the driveshaft enters the differential) by hand (slip the U-joint back on and use it as a handle if necessary).

16.6 Loosen the clamp and remove the U-joint (right arrow); check for damage inside the driveaxle holes (left arrow)

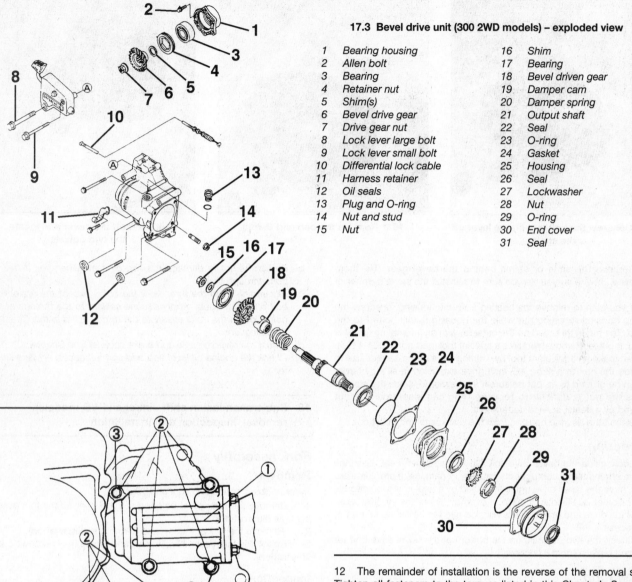

17.3 Bevel drive unit (300 2WD models) – exploded view

1	Bearing housing	16	Shim
2	Allen bolt	17	Bearing
3	Bearing	18	Bevel driven gear
4	Retainer nut	19	Damper cam
5	Shim(s)	20	Damper spring
6	Bevel drive gear	21	Output shaft
7	Drive gear nut	22	Seal
8	Lock lever large bolt	23	O-ring
9	Lock lever small bolt	24	Gasket
10	Differential lock cable	25	Housing
11	Harness retainer	26	Seal
12	Oil seals	27	Lockwasher
13	Plug and O-ring	28	Nut
14	Nut and stud	29	O-ring
15	Nut	30	End cover
		31	Seal

17.4 Bevel drive unit mounting bolts (220 models)

1	Bevel drive unit	3	Apply silicone sealant to
2	Mounting bolts		this bolt

8   Differential overhaul is a complicated procedure that requires several special tools, for which there are no readily available substitutes. If there's visible wear or damage, or if the differential's rotation is rough or noisy, take it to a Kawasaki dealer for disassembly and further inspection.

Installation

9   Lubricate the splines of the U-joint with moly-based multi-purpose grease.
10   Place the differential in the frame.
11   Install the top mounting bracket **(see illustrations 16.3c and 16.3b)**

12   The remainder of installation is the reverse of the removal steps. Tighten all fasteners to the torques listed in this Chapter's Specifications.
13   Fill the differential with the recommended type and amount of oil (see Chapter 1).

5A

17   Bevel drive unit and output gear (2WD models) removal, inspection and installation

Removal

Refer to illustrations 17.3 and 17.4

1   Remove the rear suspension as a unit (Section 11).
2   Remove the shift pedal and reverse lever (Chapter 2A).
3   Remove the nuts that secure the oil seal housing to the rear of the bevel drive unit **(see illustration)**.
4   Remove the bevel drive unit mounting bolts and take the unit off the engine **(see the accompanying illustration, 220 models or illustration 17.3, 300 models)**.
5   Unscrew the bevel drive gear nut from the transmission countershaft **(see illustration 17.3)**. The countershaft will turn as you try to remove the nut. You can spin the nut off with an air wrench if you have one. If not, remove the right crankcase cover and wedge the primary gears (Chapter 2A).

18.1 Unscrew the bolt and lift the lever off the shaft

18.2 Remove the cap and O-ring

18.3 Lift off the cover and locate the two dowels

6   Remove the shim or shims behind the bevel gear. Tie them together with wire so you can be sure to reinstall the same number of shims.

7   If you plan to remove the bearing from the housing, unscrew the bearing housing retaining nut while the housing is still bolted to the engine. The nut is threaded on the outside, with an internal hex, and is staked in place. Removal requires a special tool (part no. 57001-1194). You can make an equivalent tool by welding a nut of the correct size to fit inside the hex to a short 1/2-inch drive extension (a slightly larger nut can be ground to fit, but be sure it's an exact fit, since the staking means the nut is difficult to remove). You can also have the nut removed by a dealer service department.

8   Unbolt the bearing housing from the crankcase and pull it out.

Inspection

9   Look inside the bevel drive unit. Check the driven gear, bearings and the other internal components for wear or damage. If problems are found, have the bevel drive unit overhauled by a dealer service department or other qualified ATV shop. If overhaul is necessary, the backlash of the drive and driven gears will also need to be set up as part of the process.

10   Check the two oil seals on the bottom of the bevel drive unit for wear and replace them if necessary.

Installation

11   Installation is the reverse of the removal steps, with the following additions:

   a) *Use a new gasket.*

b) *Be careful not to damage the two oil seals when you install the bolts through them.*
c) *Ally engine oil to the threads of the bolts, except the upper front bolt on 220 models. Apply silicone sealant to the threads of that bolt. Tighten the bolts evenly to the torque listed in this Chapter's Specifications.*
d) *Adjust the reverse cable and brake cable(s) (see Chapter 1).*
e) *Check the engine oil level and add some if necessary (see Chapter 1).*

---

18   Sub-transmission shift linkage (4WD models) – removal, inspection and installation

---

Fork assembly
Removal
Refer to illustrations 18.1, 18.2 and 18.3

1   Remove the lever pivot bolt and slip the lever off the fork assembly **(see illustration)**.

2   Remove the fork shaft cap and O-ring **(see illustration)**.

3   Unbolt the fork assembly, lift it off and locate the two dowels **(see illustration)**.

Inspection
Refer to illustration 18.4

4   Check the fork for wear or damage, especially at the fingers **(see illustration)**. If it's damaged, remove the shift rod bolt and pry out the

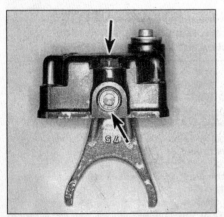

18.4 Remove the bolt and pry out the cap (arrows) to remove the fork shaft; the 75 mark on the fork faces the bolt

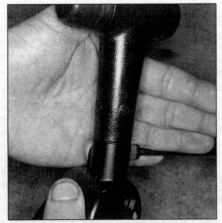

18.7a Remove the screws from the handle . . .

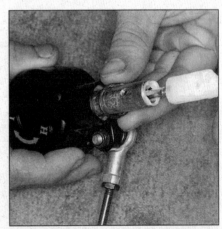

18.7b . . . and slide it off to inspect the internal parts and replace the O-ring

19.8a Sub-transmission mounting bolts

A   *8 mm bolts (without thread locking agent)*
B   *8 mm bolts (with thread locking agent)*
C   *6 mm bolts*

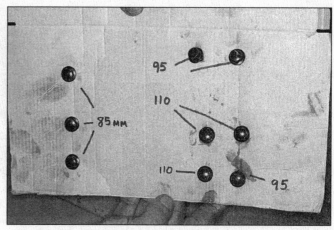

19.8b Place the bolts in a cardboard template to show their lengths and locations

rubber cap at the end of the unit. Push out the shift rod and remove the fork.

Installation

5   Installation is the reverse of the removal steps. Use a new gasket and tighten the bolts to the torque listed in this Chapter's Specifications.

Shift lever and rod

Removal

Refer to illustrations 18.7a and 18.7b

6   Remove the lever mounting bolts and take it off the vehicle.
7   Remove the Phillips screws from the lever shaft and slide the handle off **(see illustrations)**.

Inspection

8   Check the lever cam and shaft for wear or damage. Replace the lever as an assembly if problems are found.
9   Check the ends of the linkage rod for wear or damage. If there are problems, loosen the locknuts, unscrew the ends and screw new ones on.

Installation

10   Installation is the reverse of the removal steps. Install a new O-ring on the lever **(see illustration 18.7b)**.

19 Sub-transmission and bevel drive gear (4WD models) - removal and installation

Removal

Refer to illustrations 19.8a, 19.8b, 19.9, 19.10a, 19.10b and 19.10c

1   Drain the engine oil (see Chapter 1).
2   Remove the rear fender and left footrest (see Chapter 7).
3   Remove the shift pedal and external oil pipe and disconnect the reverse cable from the arm on the left side of the engine (see Chapter 2A).
4   Remove the sub-transmission shift linkage (Section 18).
5   Remove the rear suspension as a unit (Section 11).
6   Remove the front driveshaft (Section 00).
7   Remove the left crankcase cover (see Chapter 4A).
8   Loosen the sub-transmission mounting bolts evenly, then remove the 8 mm bolts, followed by the 6 mm bolts **(see illustration)**. Make a cardboard template and place the 8 mm bolts in it, labeled with their lengths and locations **(see illustration)**.
9   Take the sub-transmission off the engine and locate the dowel **(see illustration)**.
10   The bevel drive gear and its bearing housing must be removed to remove the sub-transmission gasket. Unscrew the nut, using an air wrench if you have one **(see illustration)**. If not, remove the right crankcase cover and wedge the gears on the primary and secondary clutches to prevent the crankshaft from turning while you unscrew the nut (see Chapter 2A). Remove the nut, gear and shim(s), then unbolt the bearing housing and pull it out **(see illustrations)**.

5A

19.9 Pull the sub-transmission off and locate the dowel (arrow)

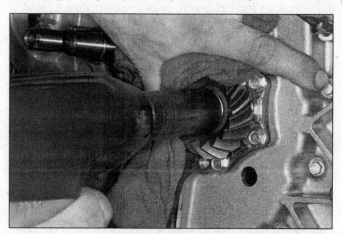

19.10a Unscrew the nut with an air wrench, or if you don't have one, remove the right crankcase cover and wedge the clutch gears

19.10b Remove the nut, bevel drive gear and shim(s)

19.10c Unbolt the bearing housing and pull it off so the gasket can be removed

19.12a Check the seals at the front of the case . . .

19.12b . . . and at the rear

19.14 A special tool is required to unscrew the bearing retainer nut

19.15 Make sure the reverse switch grommet and wiring harness retainer are reinstalled

11   Peel the gasket from the engine and clean the gasket mating surfaces.

Inspection

Refer to illustrations 19.12a, 19.12b and 19.14

12   Check the sub-transmission seals for leakage **(see illustrations)**. If they've been leaking, pry them out and drive in new ones with a socket the same diameter as the seal.

13   Rotate the sub-transmission gears and check them for wear or damage. If problems are found, have the sub-transmission overhauled by a dealer service department or other qualified shop.

14   Rotate the bevel drive gear bearing in its housing. If the bearing is rough, loose or noisy, unscrew the housing's internal nut and replace the bearing **(see illustration)**. This requires a special tool (57001-1194) or equivalent. If you don't have it, have the bearing replaced by a dealer service department or other qualified shop.

Installation

Refer to illustration 19.15

15   Installation is the reverse of the removal steps, with the following additions:

a) Use a new gasket.
b) Seat the reverse switch grommet in its notch **(see illustration)**.
c) Apply non-permanent thread locking agent to the threads of the three forward 8 mm bolts **(see illustration 19.7a)**.
d) Tighten the 8 mm bolts evenly to the torque listed in this Chapter's Specifications, then tighten the 6 mm bolts.
e) Fill the engine with oil (see Chapter 1).

20   Rear driveshaft - removal, inspection and installation

Removal

Refer to illustrations 20.2a, 20.2b and 20.2c

1   Refer to Section 11 and remove the rear suspension.

2   Unbolt the driveshaft housing from the differential, then pull out the driveshaft and remove the spring **(see illustrations)**.

20.2a Remove the nuts that secure the driveshaft housing to the rear differential . . .

20.2b . . . pull the housing off . . .

20.2c . . . and remove the spring

21.6a Remove the left axle housing nuts . . .

21.6b . . . pull out the axle housing and remove the O-ring (and the aluminum gasket on early models) . . .

21.6c . . . and pull the axle shaft out of the housing

Inspection

3   Check the shaft for bending or other visible damage such as step wear of the splines. If the shaft is bent, replace it. If the splines at either end of the shaft are worn, replace the shaft.

4   Hold the driveshaft firmly in one hand and try to twist the universal joint. If there's play in the joint, replace the shaft (but don't confuse play in the joint with its normal motion).

Installation

5   Installation is the reverse of the removal procedure. Tighten the housing nuts to the torque listed in this Chapter's Specifications.

21   Rear axle - removal, inspection and installation

Removal

1   Securely block the front wheels so the vehicle won't roll. Loosen the rear wheel nuts with the vehicle on the ground. Jack up the rear end and support it securely, positioning the jackstands so they won't obstruct removal of the axle. The supports must be secure enough so the vehicle won't be knocked off of them while the axle nuts are loosened. Remove the rear wheels.

2   Remove the rear brake panel(s) and rear wheel hubs (see Chapter 6).

3   Loosen the clamp at the front end of the rear driveshaft's boot (see illustration 11.7a). If you're working on a 2WD model, disconnect the differential locking cable.

4   Support the axle with a jack. Detach the shock absorbers and suspension links from the axle housing (Sections 10 and 12). **Note:** *You can also remove the suspension as a unit (Section 11). This may be easier, depending on the type of axle service you plan to do.*

5   Remove the axle from under the vehicle.

Inspection

Refer to illustrations 21.6a through 21.6f, 21.8a, 21.8b and 21.8c

6   Remove the nuts and detach the axle housing from each side of the differential **(see illustrations)**. Pull the axle shafts out of the housings **(see illustrations)**.

5A

21.6d Remove the right axle housing nuts . . .

21.6e . . . pull out the axle housing and remove the O-ring (and the aluminum gasket on early models) . . .

7   Check the axle shafts for obvious damage, such as step wear of the splines or bending, and replace them as necessary.
8   Rotate the bearing in each axle housing with a finger. Replace the bearings if they're rough, loose or noisy. On the right axle shaft, pry out the grease seal and remove the snap ring, then remove the bearing **(see illustrations)**. On the left axle shaft, remove the bearing, using a blind hole puller if necessary, then remove the grease seal **(see illustration)**. The grease seals should be replaced if they show signs of leakage.

Installation

9   Installation is the reverse of the removal steps, with the following additions:

a) *Use new O-rings and aluminum gaskets (if equipped).*
b) *Lubricate the axle splines with multipurpose grease.*
c) *Tighten all fasteners to the torque listed in this Chapter's Specifications.*
d) *Fill the rear differential with oil (see Chapter 1).*
e) *Check adjustment of the rear brake(s) (see Chapter 1).*

22   Rear differential - removal, inspection and installation

Removal

1   Remove the axle (Section 21) and the rear driveshaft (Section 20). This separates the differential from the other components.

21.6f . . . and pull the axle shaft out of the housing

21.8a Pry the grease seal out of the right axle housing . . .

Inspection

Refer to illustration 22.2
2   Look into the axle holes and check for obvious signs of wear and for damage such as broken gear teeth **(see illustration)**. Also check the seals for signs of leakage. Turn the pinion by hand (slip the driveshaft back on and use it as a handle if necessary).
3   Differential overhaul is a complicated procedure that requires several special tools, for which there are no readily available substitutes. If there's visible wear or damage, or if the differential's rotation is rough or noisy, take it to a Kawasaki dealer for disassembly and further inspection.

Installation

4   Installation is the reverse of the removal steps. Fill the differential with oil (see Chapter 1).

21.8b . . . remove the snap-ring and pull out the bearing

21.8c Remove the bearing and grease seal from the left axle housing

22.2 Look into the axle holes to check for wear and damage

Chapter 5 Part B
Steering, suspension and final drive (Prairie models)

Contents

	Section
Ball-joint replacement	6
Bevel drive unit and output gear - removal, inspection and installation	15
Front differential - removal, inspection and installation	14
Front driveaxle (4WD) - boot replacement and CV joint overhaul	12
Front driveaxles (4WD models) - removal and installation	11
Front driveshaft - removal, inspection and installation	13
Front shock absorbers - removal and installation	8
Front suspension arms - removal, inspection, and installation	9
General information	1
Handlebars - removal, inspection and installation	2

	Section
Rear axle - removal, inspection and installation	16
Rear driveshaft and differential - removal, inspection and installation	20
Rear shock absorber - removal and installation	10
Steering knuckle bearing replacement	7
Steering knuckles - removal, inspection, and installation	5
Steering shaft - removal, inspection, bearing replacement and installation	3
Swingarm - removal and installation	18
Swingarm bearings - check	17
Swingarm bearings - inspection and replacement	19
Tie-rods - removal, inspection and installation	4

Specifications

Torque specifications

Handlebar bracket bolts	27 Nm (20 ft-lbs)
Tie-rod nuts	47 Nm (35 ft-lbs)
Tie-rod locknuts	27 Nm (20 ft-lbs)
Steering shaft nut	29 Nm (22 ft-lbs)
Steering shaft lower bearing bolts	20 Nm (174 inch-lbs)
Steering shaft upper bracket bolts	25 Nm (18 ft-lbs)
Front shock absorber nuts	74 Nm (54 ft-lbs)
Front shock absorber pinch bolt locknuts	52 Nm (38 ft-lbs)
Rear shock absorber bolts	62 Nm (46 ft-lbs)
Front suspension arm pivot bolts	88 Nm (65 ft-lbs)
Ball-joint pinch bolt nuts	42 Nm (31 ft-lbs)
Front differential mounting bolts (4WD models)	42 Nm (31 ft-lbs)
Bevel drive unit mounting bolts	26 Nm (19.5 ft-lbs)*
Bevel drive gear nut	135 Nm (100 ft-lbs)
Rear axle housing to swingarm bolts	52 Nm (38 ft-lbs)*
Rear axle housing to differential nuts	68 Nm (50 ft-lbs)
Swingarm to rear differential nuts	68 Nm (50 ft-lbs)

*Apply non-permanent thread locking agent to the threads.

1 General information

The steering system consists of knuckles mounted at the outer ends of the front suspension and connected to a steering shaft by tie rods. The steering shaft is turned by a one-piece handlebar.

The front suspension consists of a lower suspension arm on each side of the vehicle. A shock absorber with concentric coil spring is installed between the steering knuckle and frame.

The rear suspension consists a single shock absorber with concentric coil spring and a steel swingarm.

Final drive consists of a bevel drive unit mounted on the left side of the engine. Power from the unit is transmitted through a driveshaft to the rear differential and the rear axle shaft. At the front of 4WD models, a driveshaft transmits power from the bevel drive unit to the front driveaxles, which connect to the front wheel hubs. The front differential on 4WD models is a limited slip type.

2.3 Remove the screw at the end of the grip

2.4 Lift the handlebar cover to expose the brackets

2   Handlebars - removal, inspection and installation

1   The handlebars are a one-piece tube. The tube fits into a bracket, which is integral with the steering shaft. If the handlebars must be removed for access to other components, such as the steering shaft, simply remove the bolts and slip the handlebars off the bracket. It's not necessary to disconnect the cables, wires or brake hose, but it is a good idea to support the assembly with a piece of wire or rope, to avoid unnecessary strain on the cables, wires and the brake hose.

2   If the handlebars are to be removed completely, refer to Chapter 3 for the throttle housing removal procedure, Chapter 6 for the master cylinder removal procedure and Chapter 4 for the switch removal procedure.

Removal

Refer to illustrations 2.3, 2.4 and 2.5

3   If you plan to remove one of the grips, remove its screw while the handlebars are still bolted to the bracket **(see illustration)**. The grips are glued to the handlebar ends, so you'll probably have to cut it off.

4   Remove the handlebar cover screws and pull out the rubber ring that surrounds the speedometer. Lift the handlebar cover for access to the bracket bolts **(see illustration)**.

5   Mark the handlebar brackets with a felt pen or punch to they can be reinstalled in the same location (left or right) and facing in the same direction. Remove the handlebar bracket bolts and lift off the brackets. Lift the handlebar out of the bracket **(see illustration)**.

Inspection

6   Check the handlebar and brackets for cracks and distortion and replace them if any undesirable conditions are found.

Installation

7   Installation is the reverse of the removal steps, with the following additions:

a)   When installing the handlebar to the brackets, position it so its riser portion is parallel to the steering shaft.

b)   Install the handlebar brackets in their original locations and directions, referring to the marks made during removal.

c)   First tighten the rear bracket bolts to the torque listed in this Chapter's Specifications, then tighten the front bolts to the specified torque. This will leave a gap between the upper and lower parts of the brackets at the front. Don't try to close this gap by tightening the bolts beyond the specified torque or you may crack the brackets. The gap should be the same at both the left and right brackets, but again, don't try to even it out by tightening beyond the specified torque.

d)   If the handlebar grips were removed, glue new ones to the handlebar.

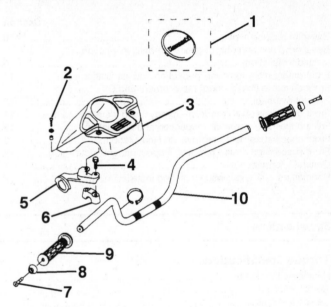

2.5 Handlebar details (Prairie models)

1	Cover (vehicles without speedometer)	5	Handlebar cover bracket
2	Screw, washer and grommet	6	Handlebar bracket
3	Handlebar cover	7	Screw
4	Bracket bolt	8	End cover
		9	Grip
		10	Handlebar

e)   Tighten all fasteners to the torques listed in this Chapter's Specifications.

3   Steering shaft - removal, inspection, bearing replacement and installation

Removal

Refer to illustrations 3.4, 3.6a and 3.6b

1   Remove the handlebars (Section 2).

2   Remove the fuel tank and air cleaner intake duct (see Chapter 3).

3   Remove the front side covers, front fender and front upper cover plate (see Chapter 7).

4   Unbolt the steering shaft upper bushing from the frame and remove the oil seals **(see illustration)**.

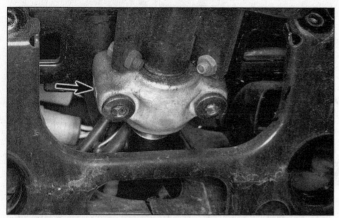

3.4 Remove the Allen bolts; on assembly, make sure the marks on the bracket halves align (arrow)

3.6a Unbolt the lower bearing from the frame

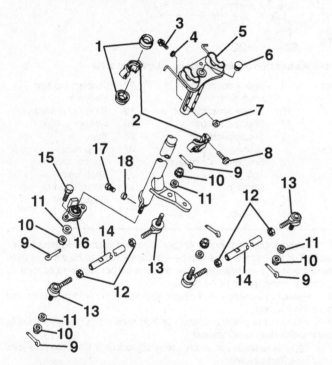

3.6b Steering mechanism (Prairie models) - exploded view

1	Upper bushing grease seals	10	Nut
2	Upper bushing halves	11	Washer
3	Bolt	12	Tie rod locknuts
4	Washer	13	Tie rod end
5	Steering shaft	14	Tie rod tube
6	Cap	15	Bearing bolt
7	Nut	16	Steering shaft bearing
8	Allen bolt	17	Steering stop bolt
9	Cotter pin	18	Stop bolt locknut

5   Refer to Section 4 and disconnect the inner ends of the tie-rods.
6   Unbolt the lower bearing from the frame **(see illustrations)**. Remove the steering shaft and lower bearing from the vehicle.
7   Remove the cotter pin and nut from the lower end of the steering shaft and take the bearing off.

Inspection

8   Clean all the parts with solvent and dry them thoroughly, using compressed air, if available.
9   Check the steering shaft upper bushing for wear, deterioration or

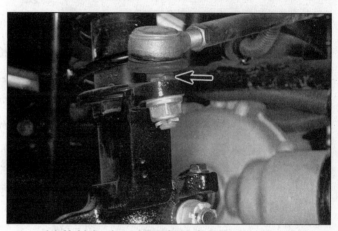

4.1 Hold the tie-rod flats (arrow) with a wrench and unscrew the nut

damage. The bushing grease seals should be replaced whenever the steering shaft is removed.
10   Check the steering shaft for bending or other signs of damage. Do not attempt to repair any steering components. Replace them with new parts if defects are found.
11   Insert a finger into the steering shaft bearing and turn the inner race. If it's rough, loose or noisy, replace it.

Installation

12   Installation is the reverse of removal, with the following additions:
   a) Pack the steering shaft bushing's internal cavities with grease. Align the marks on the sides of the front and rear bushing halves before tightening the bolts **(see illustration 3.4)**. Install the bushing grease seals with their splits toward the rear of the vehicle.
   b) Lubricate the lower bearing with grease. Pack the spaces between the lips of the lower bearing grease seals with grease.
   c) Tighten all fasteners to the torques listed in this Chapter's Specifications.

5B

4   Tie-rods - removal, inspection and installation

Removal

Refer to illustrations 4.1 and 4.3

1   Remove the cotter pin from the nut at the outer end of the tie-rod **(see illustration)**.
2   Slip an open-end wrench over the flats on the tie-rod stud remove the nut **(see illustration 4.1)**. Separate the tie-rod stud from the knuckle **(see illustration 3.6b)**.

4.3 Remove the cotter pins, nuts and washers from the inner tie-rod ends

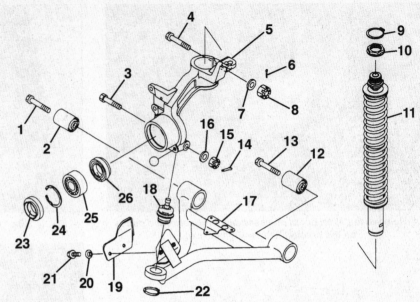

5.4b Front suspension (Prairie models) - exploded view

1	Suspension arm pivot bolt	9	Shock absorber snap-ring	17	Suspension arm
2	Suspension arm bushing	10	Shock absorber nut	18	Ball-joint
3	Ball-joint pinch bolt	11	Shock absorber	19	Ball-joint protector
4	Shock absorber pinch bolt	12	Suspension arm bushing	20	Washer
5	Steering knuckle	13	Suspension arm pivot bolt	21	Bolt
6	Cotter pin			22	Snap-ring
7	Washer	14	Cotter pin	23	Grease seal
8	Nut	15	Nut	24	Snap-ring
		16	Washer	25	Wheel bearing
				26	Grease seal

5.4a Remove the cotter pin, unscrew the nut and remove the bolt completely

3   Repeat Steps 1 and 2 to disconnect the inner end of the tie rod **(see illustration)**. Discard the nuts and use new ones on installation.

Inspection

4   Check the tie-rod shaft for bending or other damage and replace it if any problems are found. Don't try to straighten the shaft.
5   Check the ball-joint boot for cracks or deterioration. Twist and rotate the threaded stud. It should move easily, without roughness or looseness. If the boot or stud show any problems, unscrew the ball-joint from the tie-rod and install a new one.

Installation

6   Measure the distance from each locknut to the end of the threads and make sure it's equal for both tie-rods. If it's incorrect, loosen the locknut and reposition the locknut and ball-joint on the threads.
7   Position the ball-joint at each end of the tie-rod so the studs face in the proper direction (up or down) **(see illustration 3.6b)**.
8   The remainder of installation is the reverse of the removal steps, with the following additions:
   a) Tighten the ball-joint nuts to the torque listed in this Chapter's Specifications.
   b) Use new cotter pins and bend them to hold the nuts securely.
   c) Check front wheel toe-in and adjust as necessary (see Chapter 1).

5   Steering knuckles - removal, inspection, and installation

Removal

Refer to illustrations 5.4a, 5.4b, 5.5, 5.6 and 5.7
1   Remove the front wheel hub (see Chapter 6).

2   Remove the front brake caliper, disc and dust shield (see Chapter 6). The front brake hose can be left connected, but be careful not to twist it and be sure to support the panel or caliper with wire or rope so it doesn't hang by the brake hose.
3   Refer to Section 4 and disconnect the outer end of the tie-rod from the knuckle.
4   Remove the pinch bolt and nut that secure the ball-joint stud to the knuckle **(see illustrations)**.
5   Tap the suspension arm downward to free it from the ball-joint stud **(see illustration)**.
6   If you're working on a 4WD model, pull the knuckle off the outer end of the driveaxle **(see illustration)**.
7   Remove the pinch bolt that secures the lower end of the shock absorber to the knuckle and unbolt the brake hose retainer from the knuckle **(see illustration)**.

5.5 Pull the suspension arm downward to free the ball-joint from the knuckle

5.6 Pull the knuckle off the driveaxle (4WD models)

5.7 Remove the cotter pin and nut (lower arrow) and pinch bolt; unbolt the brake hose retainer (upper arrow)

Inspection

Refer to illustration 5.10

8   Check the knuckle carefully for cracks, bending or other damage. Replace it if any problems are found. If the vehicle has been in a collision or has been bottomed hard, it's a good idea to have the knuckle magnafluxed by a machine shop to check for hidden cracks.
9   Check the ball-joint boot for cracks or deterioration. Twist and rotate the threaded stud. It should move easily, without roughness or looseness. If the boot or stud show any problems, refer to Section 6 and replace the ball-joint.
10   Turn the knuckle bearing inner race with a finger **(see illustration)**. If it's rough, loose or noisy, refer to Section 7 in Chapter 5A and replace it. Replace the bearing grease seals if they show signs of leakage or wear.

Installation

11   Installation is the reverse of the removal steps, with the following additions: Use new cotter pins and tighten the ball-joint nut(s) to the torque listed in this Chapter's Specifications.

6   Ball-joint replacement

1   Separate the knuckle from the suspension arm (Section 5).
2   Remove the ball-joint snap-ring **(see illustration 5.4b)**.
3   Place a large socket on the ball-joint hex and unscrew it from the suspension arm **(see illustrations 6.2a and 6.2b in Chapter 5A)**.
4   Thread the new ball-joint into the suspension arm and tighten to the torque listed in this Chapter's Specifications.
5   Install the snap-ring and make sure it seats completely in its groove.

7   Steering knuckle bearing replacement

     This procedure is the same as for 4WD Bayou models (see Chapter 5A).

8   Front shock absorbers - removal and installation

Refer to illustrations 8.2a and 8.2b
1   Remove the front fender (see Chapter 7).
2   Remove the snap-ring and unscrew the nut from the upper end of the shock absorber **(see illustrations)**.
3   Securely block both rear wheels so the vehicle won't roll. Refer to Chapter 6 and remove the front wheels.
4   Remove the nut and pinch bolt at the lower end of the shock **(see illustration 5.7)**. Tap the knuckle arm down to separate it from the shock absorber.
5   Installation is the reverse of the removal steps. Tighten the nuts and bolts to the torque listed in this Chapter's Specifications.

9   Front suspension arms - removal, inspection, and installation

Removal

Refer to illustration 9.3
1   Securely block both rear wheels so the vehicle won't roll. Loosen the front wheel nuts with the tires still on the ground, then jack up the

5B

5.10 Check the knuckle bearing for rough, loose or noisy rotation

8.2a Remove the shock absorber snap-ring . . .

8.2b . . . and unscrew the nut (a 1-5/8 inch socket will work)

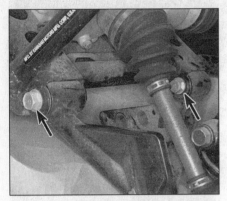

9.3 The heads of the suspension arm bolts (arrows) face the front of the vehicle

10.4a The heads of the shock absorber bolts face the left side of the vehicle (upper bolt shown)

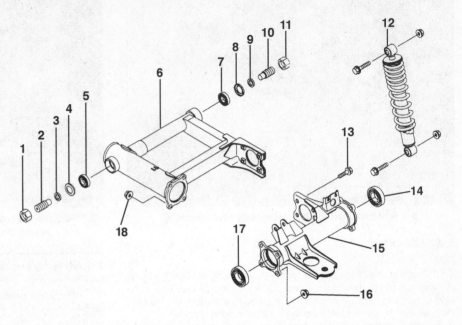

10.4b Rear suspension (Prairie models) - exploded view

1	Swingarm adjusting bolt locknut	10	Swingarm adjusting bolt
2	Swingarm adjusting bolt	11	Swingarm adjusting bolt locknut
3	Collar	12	Rear shock absorber
4	Grease seal	13	Axle housing to swingarm bolt
5	Swingarm bearing	14	Axle shaft bearing
6	Swingarm	15	Axle housing
7	Swingarm bearing	16	Axle housing to differential nut
8	Grease seal	17	Axle shaft bearing
9	Collar	18	Swingarm to differential nut

front end, support it securely on jackstands and remove the front wheels.

2   Detach the steering knuckle from the lower suspension arm (Section 5).

3   Remove the bolts at the inner end of the suspension arm **(see illustration 5.4b and the accompanying illustration)** and pull the suspension arm out.

Inspection

4   This is the same as for Bayou models (see Chapter 5A).

Installation

5   Installation is the reverse of the removal steps, with the following addition: Tighten the bolts slightly while the vehicle is jacked up, then tighten them to the torque listed in this Chapter's Specifications while the vehicle's weight is resting on the wheels.

10   Rear shock absorber - removal and installation

Refer to illustrations 10.4a and 10.4b

1   Remove the rear fender (see Chapter 7).

2   Remove the transmission rear air ducts (see Chapter 2B).

3   Securely block both front wheels so the vehicle can't roll. Jack up the rear end and support it securely with the rear wheels off the ground.

4   Remove the mounting bolts and nuts at the bottom of the shock, then at the top **(see illustrations)**. Lift the shock out of the vehicle.

5   Installation is the reverse of the removal steps. Tighten the nuts and bolts to the torque listed in this Chapter's Specifications.

11   Front driveaxles (4WD models) - removal and installation

Removal

Refer to illustrations 11.3a, 11.3b and 11.4

1   Securely block both rear wheels so the vehicle won't roll. Loosen the front wheel nuts with the tires still on the ground, then jack up the front end, support it securely on jackstands and remove the front wheels.

2   Disconnect the lower ball-joint from the steering knuckle and pull the steering knuckle upward until it clears the driveaxle (Section 5).

11.3a Pry the driveaxle out of the differential . . .

11.3b . . . to free the clip (arrow); be sure to engage the clip with the differential on installation

11.4 Look into the driveaxle holes to check for damage

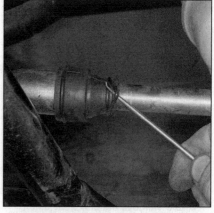

13.2 Roll the O-rings off the boot and onto the narrow part of the driveshaft

3   Pry the inner end of the driveaxle out of the front differential with a taped-over pry bar **(see illustrations)**.
4   Check the driveaxle seal in the differential for leakage **(see illustration)**. If necessary, pry the old seal out and tap a new one in with a seal driver or large socket.

Installation

5   Installation is the reverse of the removal steps, with the following additions:

 a)   *Push the driveaxle into the differential until its clip engages the differential* **(see illustration 11.3b)**. *You should hear a click when this happens.*
 b)   *Check the differential oil level and add some if necessary (see Chapter 1).*

12   Front driveaxle (4WD) - boot replacement and CV joint overhaul

The front driveaxles on Prairie models are supplied as complete assemblies only. If the boots or CV joints are worn or damaged, replace the driveaxle.

13   Front driveshaft - removal, inspection and installation

Removal

Refer to illustrations 13.2, 13.3, 13.4, 15.5a, 13.5b and 13.6
1   Remove the engine cover, left front side cover and left front mud-

13.3 Loosen the boot clamp (left) and move the snap-ring (right) out of its groove onto the narrow part of the driveshaft

guard (see Chapter 7).
2   Roll the O-rings out of their grooves on the driveshaft front boot and back onto the shaft **(see illustration)**.
3   Loosen the clamp on the front boot. Slightly open the snap-ring that secures the driveshaft's front coupling and move it back onto the shaft **(see illustration)**.
4   Slide the coupling back onto the shaft, separate the driveshaft from the front differential and remove the spring **(see illustration)**.
5   Pull the driveshaft forward out of the bevel drive unit and remove it from the vehicle. If it's stuck, place a small hose clamp on the narrow part of the driveshaft, then use a slide hammer with a hook attachment to pull the driveshaft out **(see illustration)**. Remove the O-ring after the

5B

13.4 Separate the driveshaft from the front universal joint and remove the spring

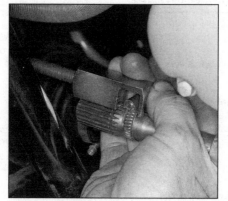

13.5a Use a small hose clamp and a slide hammer with a hook attachment to pull the driveshaft if it's stuck

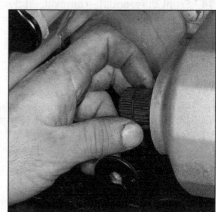

13.5b Remove the O-ring from the bevel drive unit

13.6 Remove the universal joint if necessary; during installation, align the rib (arrow) with the matching rib on the other U-joint boot

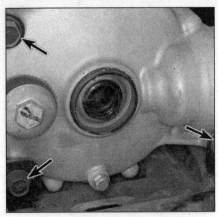

14.3 Front differential mounting bolts (arrows)

14.5 Pry the U-joint off the bevel drive unit; don't loosen the stop screw (arrow)

15.2 Loosen the clamp (arrow) and pull the boot off the bevel drive unit

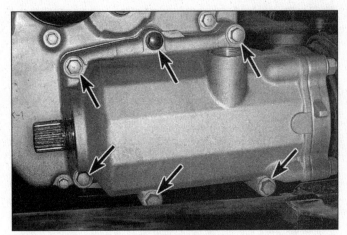

15.3a Bevel drive unit mounting bolts (arrows); note the location of the dark bolt at top center

driveshaft is removed **(see illustration)**.
6   Clean off all the old grease and check the driveshaft for wear or damage. If the splines are damaged, replace the driveshaft. If the universal joint is worn, tap it off the driveshaft and install a new one **(see illustration)**.
7   Installation is the reverse of the removal steps. Lubricate the splines with grease and use a new snap-ring.

14 Front differential - removal, inspection and installation

Removal

Refer to illustration 14.3
1   Remove the front driveaxles and the front driveshaft (Sections 11 and 13).
2   Support the differential with a jack.
3   Remove the mounting bolts **(see illustration)**.
4   Lift the differential and remove it to the right side of the vehicle. As the breather hose becomes accessible, disconnect it from the differential.

Inspection

Refer to illustration 14.5
5   Remove the U-joint from the differential **(see illustration)**. Check the U-joint for wear or damage and replace it if problems are found.
6   Check the oil seal at the pinion shaft hole for signs of leakage. Look into the driveaxle holes and check for obvious signs of wear and

for damage such as broken gear teeth **(see illustration 14.3)**. Turn the pinion (where the driveshaft enters the differential) by hand (slip the U-joint back on and use it as a handle if necessary).
7   Differential overhaul is a complicated procedure that requires several special tools, for which there are no readily available substitutes. If there's visible wear or damage, or if the differential's rotation is rough or noisy, take it to a Kawasaki dealer for disassembly and further inspection.

Installation

8   Lubricate the splines of the U-joint with moly-based multi-purpose grease.
9   Place the differential in the frame.
10   The remainder of installation is the reverse of the removal steps. Tighten all fasteners to the torques listed in this Chapter's Specifications.
11   Fill the differential with the recommended type and amount of oil (see Chapter 1).

15 Bevel drive unit and output gear - removal, inspection and installation

Removal

Refer to illustrations 15.2, 15.3a, 15.3b, 15.4a, 15.4b, 15.5a and 15.5b
1   Remove the front driveshaft and differential (Sections 13 and 14).
2   Loosen the clamp on the universal joint boot and push the boot

15.3b Locate the dowel (arrow); it may have stayed in the engine

15.4a Hold the shaft from turning and unscrew the nut . . .

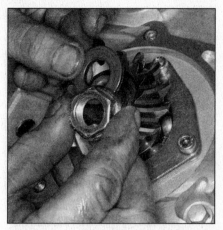

15.4b . . . remove the nut and washer . . .

15.5a . . . the gear and shim(s) behind it . . .

15.5b . . . and the spacer behind the shim(s)

15.7 If necessary, unscrew the Allen bolts and remove the bearing retainer

back off the bevel drive unit **(see illustration)**.

3   Remove the bevel drive unit mounting bolts, take the unit off the engine and locate the dowel **(see illustrations)**.

4   Unscrew the bevel drive gear nut from the transmission countershaft **(see illustration)**. The countershaft will turn as you try to remove the nut. You can spin the nut off with an air wrench if you have one. If not, remove the transmission cover from the right side of the engine. Shift the range selector into a gear (Reverse, High or Low range). Hold the automatic transmission driven pulley with a clutch holding tool and

15.8 The shorter bolt (dark colored) goes in the top center location

unscrew the bevel drive gear nut with a socket. Remove the nut, washer and gear **(see illustration)**.

5   Remove the shim or shims and the spacer behind the bevel gear **(see illustrations)**. Tie them together with wire so you can be sure to reinstall the same number of shims.

Inspection

Refer to illustration 15.7

6   Look inside the bevel drive unit **(see illustration 15.3b)**. Check the driven gear, bearings and the other internal components for wear or damage. If problems are found, have the bevel drive unit overhauled by a dealer service department or other qualified ATV shop. If overhaul is necessary, the backlash of the drive and driven gears will also need to be set up as part of the process.

7   Check the output shaft bearing for rough, loose or noisy rotation (if necessary, remove its retainer) **(see illustration)**. Replace the bearing if problems are found.

Installation

Refer to illustration 15.8

8   Installation is the reverse of the removal steps, with the following additions:

 a) Use a new gasket.
 b) Make sure the bolts are in the correct locations. The dark colored bolt is shorter than the silver ones **(see illustration)**.
 c) Apply non-permanent thread locking agent to the threads of the bolts and tighten them evenly to the torque listed in this Chapter's Specifications.

5B

16.4 The bearing will come out with the axle shaft

16.7a The axle shaft protrudes from the differential like this

16.7b Place the bearing in its bore, then tap it the rest of the way in

16 Rear axle - removal, inspection and installation

Removal

Refer to illustration 16.4

1   Drain the oil from the rear differential (see Chapter 1).
2   Jack up the rear end of the vehicle and support it securely on jackstands. Remove the rear wheels.
3   Remove the rear brake drum and panel (see Chapter 6).
4   Tap the left end of the ale shaft while an assistant supports the right end. The axle shaft will come out of the right end of the axle housing, taking the right axle bearing with it **(see illustration)**.
5   Pull the axle shaft out of the differential and axle housing.

Inspection

6   Check the axle shaft for obvious damage, such as bending or step wear of the splines. Don't try to straighten a bent axle shaft. Replace it if problems are found.

Installation

Refer to illustrations 16.7a and 16.7b

7   Slip the axle shaft into the axle housing and place it in its installed position **(see illustration)**. Place the bearing over it into the axle housing bore **(see illustration)**. Tap the bearing with a socket that bears on the bearing outer race until the bearing seats in the bore.
8   Reinstall the brake panel and drum (see Chapter 6). Reinstall the wheels.
9   Lower the vehicle and fill the rear differential with oil (see Chapter 1).

17 Swingarm bearings - check

Refer to illustration 17.2

1   Refer to Chapter 6 and remove the rear wheels, then refer to Section 10 and remove the rear shock absorber.
2   Grasp the rear of the swingarm with one hand and place your other hand at the junction of the swingarm the frame. Try to move the rear of the swingarm from side-to-side. Any wear (play) in the bearings should be felt as movement between the swingarm and the frame at the front **(see illustration)**. The swingarm will actually be felt to move forward and backward at the front (not from side-to-side). If any play is noted, the bearings should be replaced with new ones (see Section 19).
3   Next, move the swingarm up and down through its full travel. It should move freely, without binding or rough spots. If it doesn't move freely, refer to Sections 18 and 19 for servicing procedures.

18 Swingarm - removal and installation

Removal

Refer to illustrations 18.6, 18.7, 18.8, 18.9a and 18.9b

1   If the swingarm is being removed just for bearing replacement or driveshaft removal, the brake panel and rear axle need not be removed from the swingarm.
2   Raise the rear end of the vehicle off the ground with a jack. Support the rear end of the vehicle securely.

17.2 Check for movement at the gap between the swingarm and frame (arrow)

18.6 Disconnect the breather hose and speedometer cable (if equipped) from the top of the differential

18.7 Loosen the clamp (arrow) that secures the driveshaft boot to the swingarm

18.8 Remove the locknut with a socket, then unscrew the pivot shaft with an Allen wrench

18.9a Pull the drive shaft universal joint . . .

18.9b . . . off the bevel drive unit splines

3   Remove the rear wheels (see Chapter 6).

4   Refer to Section 10 and detach the lower end of the shock absorber from the swingarm.

5   Disconnect the rear brake cables (see Chapter 6).

6   If you're planning to remove the rear axle or brake panel, do it now (see Section 16 or Chapter 6). In any case, disconnect the breather hose and speedometer cable (if equipped) from the differential **(see illustration)**.

7   On the left side of the swingarm, loosen the clamp that secures the driveshaft boot to the swingarm **(see illustration)**.

8   Unscrew the locknut and pivot bolt from each side of the swingarm **(see illustration)**.

9   Pull the swingarm back and away from the vehicle, separating the driveshaft from the bevel drive unit as you do so **(see illustrations)**.

10   If necessary, detach the differential from the swingarm (Section 20). Remove the bolts and separate the axle housing from the swingarm **(see illustration 10.4b)**.

11   Check the pivot bearings in the swingarm for dryness or deterioration. If they're in need of lubrication or replacement, refer to Section 19.

Installation

12   Installation is the reverse of the removal steps, with the following additions:

a) *Tighten the pivot bolts evenly so the gap between the swingarm and frame is 2.6 mm on each side* **(see illustration 17.2)**.

b) *Tighten the swingarm pivot shaft nuts to the torque listed in this*

Chapter's Specifications and make sure the gap on each side didn't change.

c) *Apply non-permanent thread locking agent to the threads of the axle housing bolts if the axle housing was unbolted from the swingarm.*

19   Swingarm bearings - inspection and replacement

Refer to illustrations 19.2a, 19.2b and 19.2c

1   Remove the swingarm (Section 18).

2   Pull the seal collar out of the bearing **(see illustration)**. Pry out the seal and take the bearing out of the swingarm **(see illustrations)**.

3   Clean the bearing thoroughly with solvent and blow it dry. Wipe the old grease from the bearing inner race with a rag.

4   Check the bearing rollers for chips, cracks, pitting or rust. Check the inner race for the same conditions, as well as scoring. If problems are found on either the bearing or the inner race, replace them both as a set. Remove the inner race from the swingarm with a slide hammer.

5   Tap the new inner race into the swingarm with a bearing drive the same diameter as the race.

6   Pack the new bearing with multi-purpose grease and install it in the swingarm. Install the seal, using a socket the same diameter as the seal. Coat the collar with a thin layer of grease and push it into the seal.

7   Repeat Steps 2 through 6 for the other bearing.

8   Installation is the reverse of the removal steps.

5B

19.2a Pull the collar out of the seal

19.2b Pry the seal out of the swingarm

19.2c Pull the bearing out of the swingarm and inspect the inner race

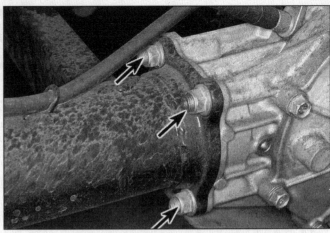

20.2a Remove the axle housing to differential nuts (three nuts shown; one nut hidden)

20.2b Remove the swingarm to differential nuts (three nuts shown; one nut hidden)

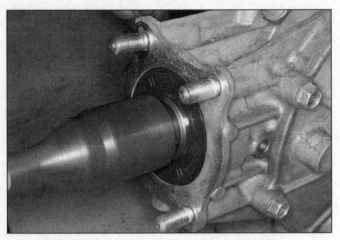

20.3a Pull the driveshaft off the differential pinion . . .

20.3b . . . and remove the spring and O-ring (arrows)

20 Rear driveshaft and differential - removal, inspection and installation

Removal

Refer to illustrations 20.2a, 20.2b, 20.3a and 20.3b

1   Remove the axle (Section 16) and the swingarm (Section 18).

2   Remove the nuts that secure the axle housing and swingarm to the differential **(see illustrations)**. Separate the differential from them, taking the driveshaft with the differential.

3   Pull the driveshaft off the differential pinion and collect the spring **(see illustrations)**.

Inspection

4   Look into the axle holes and check for obvious signs of wear and for damage such as broken gear teeth. Also check the seals for signs of leakage. Turn the pinion by hand (slip the driveshaft back on and use it as a handle if necessary).

5   Differential overhaul is a complicated procedure that requires several special tools, for which there are no readily available substitutes. If there's visible wear or damage, or if the differential's rotation is rough or noisy, take it to a Kawasaki dealer for disassembly and further inspection.

6   Check the shaft for bending or other visible damage such as step wear of the splines. If the shaft is bent, replace it. If the splines at either end of the shaft are worn, replace the shaft.

7   Hold the driveshaft firmly in one hand and try to twist the universal joint. If there's play in the joint, replace the shaft (but don't confuse play in the joint with its normal motion).

Installation

8   Installation is the reverse of the removal steps, with the following additions:

a) *Be sure the driveshaft O-ring and spring are installed on the differential pinion (see illustration 20.3b).*

b) *Fill the differential with oil (see Chapter 1).*

Chapter 6 Part A
Brakes, wheels and tires (Bayou models)

Contents

	Section
Brake fluid level check and fluid change	See Chapter 1
Brake hoses and lines - inspection and replacement	10
Brake lining wear and system check	See Chapter 1
Brake pedal, levers and cables - removal and installation	11
Brake system bleeding	8
Front brake discs - inspection, removal and installation	6
Front brake master cylinder - removal, overhaul and installation	7
Front brakes and wheel bearings (Bayou 220 models) - removal, inspection and installation	2
Front disc brakes - caliper removal, overhaul and installation	5

	Section
Front disc brakes - pad replacement	4
Front drum brakes and wheel bearings (1986 and 1987 300 models) - removal, inspection and installation	3
General information	1
Rear drum brake(s) - removal, inspection and installation	9
Tires - general information	13
Tires and wheels - general check	See Chapter 1
Wheel hubs - removal and installation	14
Wheels - inspection, removal and installation	12

Specifications

General

Brake fluid type	See Chapter 1
Brake shoe lining minimum thickness	See Chapter 1
Brake pad lining minimum thickness	See Chapter 1
Brake pedal height	See Chapter 1

220 models

Brakes

Drum diameter	
Front brakes	
Standard	140.00 to 140.16 mm (5.512 to 5.518 inches)
Limit	140.75 mm (5.541 inches)*
Rear brake	
Standard	160.00 to 160.16 mm (6.299 to 6.305 inches)
Limit	160.65 mm (6.324 inches)*
Brake shoe wear limit	See Chapter 1

Refer to marks cast into the drum (they supersede numbers printed here).

Wheels and tires

Tire pressures	See Chapter 1
Tire tread depth	See Chapter 1

Torque specifications

Front brake drum/hub nuts	34 Nm (25 ft-lbs)
Rear brake drum/hub nuts	147 Nm (108 ft-lbs)
Front brake panel bolts	26 Nm (19.5 ft-lbs)
Rear brake panel reinforcing plate bolts	29 Nm (22 ft-lbs)

6A

300 models

Brakes

Drum diameter	
Front (1986 and 1987 only)	
Standard	160.00 to 160.16 mm (6.299 to 6.305 inches)
Limit	160.65 mm (6.324 inches)*
Rear (2WD models)	
Standard	160.00 to 160.16 mm (6.299 to 6.305 inches)
Limit	160.65 mm (6.324 inches)*
Rear (4WD models)	
Standard	180.00 to 180.14 mm (7.086 to 7.092 inches)
Limit	180.75 mm (7.116 inches)
Front disc thickness	
Standard	3.3 to 3.7 mm (0.130 to 0.145 inch)*
Limit	3.0 mm (0.118 inch)*
Rear disc runout	
Standard	0.2 mm (0.008 inch) or less
Limit	0.3 mm (0.012 inch)
Front pad wear limit	See Chapter 1

Refer to marks cast into the drum or disc (they supersede numbers printed here).

Wheels and tires

Tire pressures	See Chapter 1
Tire tread depth	See Chapter 1

Torque specifications

Front brake drum/hub nuts (1986 and 1987)	34 Nm (25 ft-lbs)
Rear brake drum/hub nuts	145 Nm (110 ft-lbs)
Front brake panel bolts (1986 and 1987)	20 Nm (174 inch-lbs)
Front brake wheel cylinder bolts (1986 and 1987)	7.8 Nm (69 inch-lbs)
Front brake adjuster bolts (1986 and 1987)	7.8 Nm (69 inch-lbs)
Rear brake panel reinforcing plate bolts	
2WD models	29 Nm (22 ft-lbs)
4WD models	34 Nm (25 ft-lbs)
Caliper bleed valve	7.8 Nm (69 inch-lbs)
Caliper mounting bolts	25 Nm (18 ft-lbs)
Caliper pin to bracket (4WD)	18 Nm (156 inch-lbs)
Disc-to-hub bolts	37 Nm (27 ft-lbs)
Pad pins (4WD)	18 Nm (156 inch-lbs)
Rear brake drum drain bolt	29 Nm (22 ft-lbs)
Brake line/hose union bolts	25 Nm (18 ft-lbs)*
Metal line flare nuts (4WD)	20 Nm (174 inch-lbs)
Master cylinder clamp screws	
1986 and 1987	11 Nm (95 inch-lbs)
1988 and later	8.8 Nm (73 inch-lbs)
Brake lever pivot bolt and locknut	5.9 Nm (52 inch-lbs)
Brake pedal nut (2WD only)	29 Nm (22 ft-lbs)

Use new sealing washers each time the union bolts are removed.

1   General information

The vehicles covered in this Part include several different brake designs. Bayou 220 models use front drum brakes, actuated by cables. 1986 and 1987 Bayou 300 models use hydraulically actuated drum brakes at the front. 1988 and later Bayou 300 models use hydraulically actuated disc brakes at the front.

All models use cable-operated rear drum brakes. Bayou 220 and Bayou 300 4WD models have a single rear brake, located at the right end of the rear axle. Bayou 300 2WD models have two rear brakes.

The front brakes on all models are controlled by a lever on the right handlebar. The rear brake has two means of control: a lever on the left handlebar, which can be locked to provide a parking brake, and a pedal on the right side of the vehicle.

All models are equipped with steel wheels, which require very little maintenance and allow tubeless tires to be used. **Caution:** *Brake components rarely require disassembly. Do not disassemble components unless absolutely necessary. If any hydraulic brake line connec-* tion in the system is loosened, the entire system should be disassembled, drained, cleaned and then properly filled and bled upon reassembly. Do not use solvents on internal hydraulic brake components. Solvents will cause seals to swell and distort. Use only clean brake fluid for cleaning. Use care when working with brake fluid as it can injure your eyes and it will damage painted surfaces and plastic parts.

2   Front brakes and wheel bearings (Bayou 220 models) - removal, inspection and installation

Removal

Refer to illustration 2.3

1   Loosen the front wheel nuts. Securely block the rear wheels so the vehicle can't roll. Jack up the front end and support it securely on jackstands.

2   Remove the front wheel.

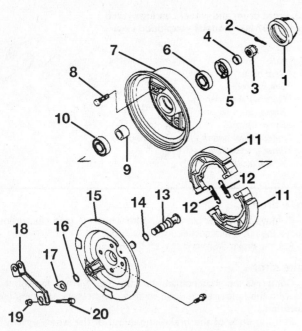

2.3 Front brakes (220 models) - exploded view

1	Trim cap	11	Brake shoes
2	Cotter pin	12	Springs
3	Nut	13	Brake cam
4	Seal collar	14	O-ring
5	Grease seal	15	Brake panel
6	Outer wheel bearing	16	O-ring
7	Brake drum	17	Wear indicator
8	Wheel stud	18	Brake arm
9	Bearing spacer	19	Nut
10	Inner wheel bearing	20	Pinch bolt

Brake drum

3   Pull off the front hub cover and remove the cotter pin from the front hub nut **(see illustration)**. Remove the nut with a socket and breaker bar.
4   Pull the brake drum off together with the front wheel bearings and seals.

Brake shoes

5   Pull the brake shoes apart and fold them toward each other to release the spring tension. Remove the shoes and springs from the brake panel.

Brake panel

6   Unscrew the brake cable adjuster wing nut all the way. Slip the cable out of the adjuster pin, then pull the pin out of the brake adjuster lever.
7   Remove the snap-ring and detach the cable from the bracket on the brake panel.
8   Remove the four brake panel bolts and take it off the steering knuckle.

Inspection

9   Check the linings for wear, damage and signs of contamination from road dirt or water. If the linings are visibly defective, replace them.
10   Measure the thickness of the lining material (just the lining material, not the metal backing) and compare with the value listed in the Chapter 1 Specifications. Replace the shoes if the material is worn to the minimum or less.
11   Check the ends of the shoes where they contact the brake cam and anchor pin. Replace the shoes if there's visible wear.

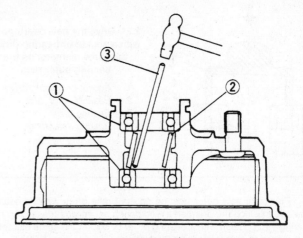

2.19 Push the spacer aside with the drift and drive out the old bearings

1	Bearings	2	Spacer	3	Drift

12   Check the anchor pin for wear or damage. It's an integral part of the brake panel, so the panel will have to be replaced if the anchor pin isn't serviceable.
13   If the brake cam is loose in its bore or if the O-rings show any signs of leakage, remove the brake cam from the panel. Make alignment marks on the brake cam and adjuster lever with a felt pen so they can be reassembled in their relative positions. Remove the lever pinch bolt, slide the lever and wear indicator off the brake cam and pull the cam out of the brake panel. Inspect the cam and its bore for wear and replace worn parts, then reverse the disassembly sequence to reinstall the brake cam and adjuster lever.
14   Check the brake drum for wear or damage. Measure the diameter at several points with a drum micrometer (or have this done by a dealer service department). Very small scratches can be polished away with fine emery cloth (polish the whole drum surface evenly). If the measurements are uneven (indicating that the drum is out-of-round) or if there are scratches deep enough to snag a fingernail, the drum can be resurfaced by a dealer service department or other qualified shop, as long as it isn't ground larger than the service limit listed in this Chapter's Specifications. The drum must be replaced if the diameter is greater than the maximum listed in this Chapter's Specifications.
15   Check the waterproof seal on the edge of the brake panel for wear (caused by rubbing against the brake drum). Also check for damage such as cuts and tears. If the seal is worn or damaged, replace it.
16   Remove the collar from the grease seal in the center of the brake drum. Check the seal for wear or damage. If its condition is in doubt, pry it out and drive in a new seal with a socket the same diameter as the seal. Turn the bearings in the brake drum with a finger. If their movement is rough, noisy or loose, replace them.

Wheel bearing replacement

Refer to illustrations 2.19 and 2.21
17   The front wheel bearings are mounted in the brake drums.
18   Remove the seal collar from the outer seal. Pry out the inner and outer seals out of the drum.
19   Insert a soft metal drift into the hub from the outside **(see illustration)**. Push the spacer out of the way with the drift and place the end of the drift against the inner bearing. Tap gently against the inner bearing, on opposite sides of the bearing, to drive it from the drum. Insert the drift from the other side and drive the outer bearing out in the same way.
20   Pack the new bearings with multi-purpose grease. Work the grease into the spaces between the bearing balls. Hold the outer race and rotate the bearing inner race as you pack it to distribute the grease.

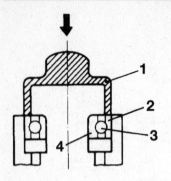

2.21 Drive the new bearings in with a socket or bearing driver the same diameter as the bearing outer race

1   Socket or bearing driver
2   Bearing outer race
3   Bearing balls
4   Bearing inner race

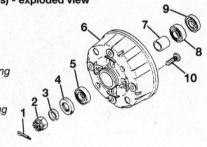

3.3 Front drum and wheel bearings (1986 and 1987 300 models) - exploded view

1   Cotter pin
2   Nut
3   Seal collar
4   Grease seal
5   Outer wheel bearing
6   Brake drum
7   Brake drum
8   Inner wheel bearing
9   Inner grease seal
10 Wheel stud

21   Place the new outer bearing on the brake drum with its sealed side out. Position the drum on a workbench or similar surface. Tap the bearing into position with a bearing driver or socket the same diameter as the bearing outer race **(see illustration)**.
22   Turn the drum over and install the inner bearing in the same manner.

Installation

23   Installation is the reverse of the removal steps, with the following additions:

a) Tighten the brake panel bolts to the torque listed in this Chapter's Specifications.
b) If you removed the brake cam, lubricate it with high temperature brake grease where it fits into the brake panel.
c) Apply a thin film of high-temperature brake grease to the shoe contact areas of the brake cam and anchor pin, as well as to the shoe contact areas on the brake panel. Be sure not to get any grease on the brake drum or linings.
d) Place the shoes on the brake panel with their flat ends against the brake cam and their dished ends over the anchor pin.
e) Lubricate the drum seal with high temperature brake grease. Be sure not to get any grease on the inside of the drum; if you do, clean it off with a non-residue solvent such as brake cleaner or lacquer thinner.
f) Be sure to insert the collar in the dust seal.
g) Tighten the hub nut to the torque listed in this Chapter's Specifications and install a new cotter pin. If necessary, tighten the nut to align the hole in the spindle with the slots in the nut. Don't loosen the nut.
h) Once the nut is tightened properly, bend the cotter pin to secure it.
i) Refer to Chapter 1 and adjust the brakes.

3   Front drum brakes and wheel bearings (1986 and 1987 300 models) - removal, inspection and installation

Warning: *If a front wheel cylinder indicates the need for an overhaul (usually due to leaking fluid or sticky operation), BOTH front wheel cylinders should be overhauled and all old brake fluid flushed from the system. Also, the dust created by the brake system may contain asbestos, which is harmful to your health. Never blow it out with compressed air and don't inhale any of it. An approved filtering mask should be worn when working on the brakes. Do not, under any circumstances, use petroleum-based solvents to clean brake parts. Use clean brake fluid or brake system cleaner only!*

Removal

Refer to illustrations 3.3 and 3.5

1   Loosen the front wheel nuts. Securely block the rear wheels so the vehicle can't roll. Jack up the front end and support it securely on jackstands.
2   Remove the wheel cap and front wheel.

Brake drum

3   Remove the cotter pin from the front hub nut **(see illustration)**. Remove the nut with a socket and breaker bar.
4   Pull the brake drum and hub off the spindle.

Brake shoes

5   Compress the shoe holders, turn the pins 1/4 turn to align their ends with the holder slots, then remove the holders and pins **(see illustration)**.
6   Pull the ends of the brake shoes out of the wheel cylinders. Remove the shoes and springs from the brake panel.

Brake panel

7   If you're planning to remove the wheel cylinders, remove the brake hose union bolt and sealing washers from the brake panel. Place the end of the hose in a container so the brake fluid can drain or else wrap a plastic bag over the end of the hose with a rubber band to prevent loss of brake fluid. If you're removing the brake panel for access to another component such as the spindle, the brake hose can be left connected.
8   Remove the four brake panel bolts and lift it off the knuckle together with the wheel cylinders.

Wheel cylinders

9   Unscrew the bleed valve (this will be easier to do while the wheel cylinder is bolted to the brake panel).
10   Remove the wheel cylinder mounting bolts and take the cylinders off the panel.

Inspection

11   Check the linings for wear, damage and signs of contamination from road dirt or water. If the linings are visibly defective, replace them.
12   Measure the thickness of the lining material (just the lining material, not the metal backing) and compare with the value listed in the Chapter 1 Specifications. Replace the shoes if the material is worn to the minimum or less.
13   Check the ends of the shoes where they contact the wheel cylinders and adjusters and replace them if they're worn or damaged.
14   Pull back the rubber cups on the wheel cylinders. Slight moisture inside the cups is normal, but if fluid runs out, overhaul the wheel cylinders as described below.
15   Check the brake drum for wear or damage. Measure the diameter at several points with a drum micrometer (or have this done by a dealer service department). Very small scratches can be polished away with fine emery cloth (polish the whole drum surface evenly). If the measurements are uneven (indicating that the drum is out-of-round) or if there are scratches deep enough to snag a fingernail, the drum can be resurfaced by a dealer service department or other qualified shop, as long as it isn't ground larger than the service limit listed in this Chapter's Specifications. The drum must be replaced if the diameter is greater than the maximum listed in this Chapter's Specifications.

Wheel cylinders and adjusters

16   Remove the boot(s) from the cylinder(s) **(see illustration 3.5)**. Pull

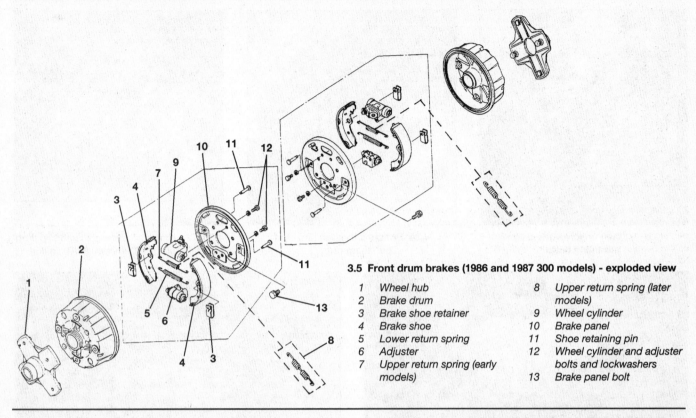

3.5 Front drum brakes (1986 and 1987 300 models) - exploded view

1	Wheel hub	8	Upper return spring (later
2	Brake drum		models)
3	Brake shoe retainer	9	Wheel cylinder
4	Brake shoe	10	Brake panel
5	Lower return spring	11	Shoe retaining pin
6	Adjuster	12	Wheel cylinder and adjuster
7	Upper return spring (early		bolts and lockwashers
	models)	13	Brake panel bolt

the pistons and cups out of the cylinder.

17 Check the piston and cylinder bore for wear, scratches and corrosion. If there's any doubt about their condition, replace the cylinder as an assembly. Even barely visible flaws can reduce braking performance.

18 The piston cups and boots are not available separately. If they show wear, damage, swelling or other problems, replace both front wheel cylinders.

19 Check the adjuster components for wear or damage and replace as necessary.

20 Assembly is the reverse of the disassembly steps, with the following additions:

a) *Coat the cylinder bore with clean brake fluid. Install the pistons with the wide sides of the piston cups entering the bore first. Be sure not to turn back the lips of the cups.*

b) *Lubricate the adjuster wheels with high temperature brake grease.*

Wheel bearing replacement

21 This is the same as for 220 models (see Section 2).

Installation

22 Apply high temperature grease to the ends of the springs and to the ends of the shoes where they contact the adjusters and wheel cylinder pistons. Apply a thin smear of grease to each of the brake shoe contact points on the brake panel.

23 Hook the springs to the shoes **(see illustration 3.5)**.

24 Pull the shoes apart and position their ends in the wheel cylinders and adjusters.

25 Install the pin holders and pins. Compress the holders and turn the pins 90-degrees so the pins secure the holders.

26 The remainder of installation is the reverse of the removal steps, with the following additions:

a) *Tighten all fasteners to the torques listed in this Chapter's Specifications.*

b) *Use new sealing washers on the brake hose union bolt.*

c) *Tighten the hub nut to the torque listed in this Chapter's Specifications and install a new cotter pin. If necessary, tighten the nut to*

align the hole in the spindle with the slots in the nut. Don't loosen the nut. Once the nut is tightened properly, bend the cotter pin to secure it.

d) *Refer to Chapter 1 and adjust the brakes.*

4 Front disc brakes - pad replacement

Refer to illustrations 4.2a, 4.2b, 4.3a, 4.3b, 4.3c and 4.3d

Warning: *The dust created by the brake system may contain asbestos, which is harmful to your health. Never blow it out with compressed air and don't inhale any of it. An approved filtering mask should be worn when working on the brakes.*

1 Support the front of the vehicle securely on jackstands and remove the front wheels.

2 Loosen the pad pins while the caliper is still bolted to the steering knuckle **(see illustration)**. Remove the caliper mounting bolts and lift

4.2a Loosen the pad pins while the caliper is still attached . . .

6A

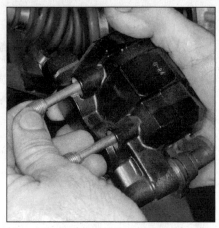

4.2b . . . then unscrew the caliper mounting bolts

4.3a Unscrew the pad pins and pull them out . . .

4.3b . . . rotate the outer pad and slip it off the slider pin (4WD shown; 2WD similar). . .

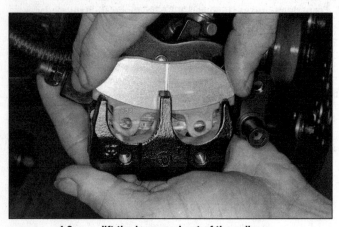

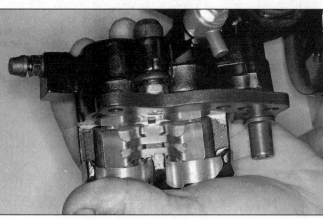

4.3c . . . lift the inner pad out of the caliper . . .

4.3d . . . and remove the pad spring

the caliper off **(see illustration)**.

3   Unscrew the pad pins and pull out the pads **(see illustrations)**. Remove the pad spring from the caliper **(see illustration)**.

4   Inspect the pad spring and replace it if it's rusted or damaged.

5   Refer to Chapter 1 and inspect the pads.

6   Check the condition of the brake disc (see Section 6). If it's in need of machining or replacement, follow the procedure in that Section to remove it. If it's okay, deglaze it with sandpaper or emery cloth, using a swirling motion.

7   Remove the cover from the master cylinder reservoir and siphon out some fluid. Push the piston into the caliper as far as possible, while

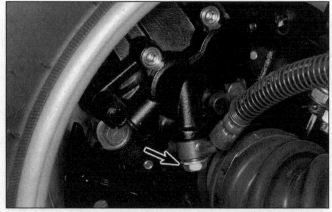

5.1 If you remove the union bolt (arrow), be sure to use a new sealing washer on each side of the bolt during assembly

checking the master cylinder reservoir to make sure it doesn't overflow. If you can't depress the pistons with thumb pressure, try using a C-clamp. If either piston sticks, remove the caliper and overhaul it as described in Section 10.

8   Install the spring and new pads. Install the retaining pins and tighten them slightly.

9   Install the caliper on the steering knuckle, sliding the brake disc between the pads. Install the caliper mounting bolts and tighten them to the torque listed in this Chapter's Specifications, then tighten the pad pins to the torque listed in this Chapter's Specifications.

10   Install the wheels and lower the vehicle. Operate the right brake lever several times to seat the pads. Check the operation of the brakes carefully before riding the vehicle.

5   Front disc brakes - caliper removal, overhaul and installation

Warning: *If a caliper indicates the need of an overhaul (usually due to leaking fluid or sticky operation), all old brake fluid must be flushed from the system. Also, the dust created by the brake system may contain asbestos, which is harmful to your health. Never blow it out with compressed air and don't inhale any of it. An approved filtering mask should be worn when working on the brakes. Do not, under any circumstances, use petroleum-based solvents to clean brake parts. Use brake cleaner or denatured alcohol only!*

Removal

Refer to illustration 5.1

Note: *If you're planning to disassemble the caliper, read through the*

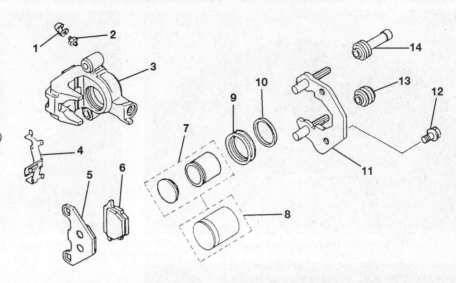

5.4a Brake caliper (300 2WD models) - exploded view

1   Bleed valve cap
2   Bleed valve
3   Caliper body
4   Pad spring
5   Outer pad
6   Inner pad
7   Piston (1988 through 1990 models)
8   Piston (1991 and later models)
9   Dust seal
10   Piston seal
11   Caliper bracket
12   Mounting bolt
13   Boot
14   Boot

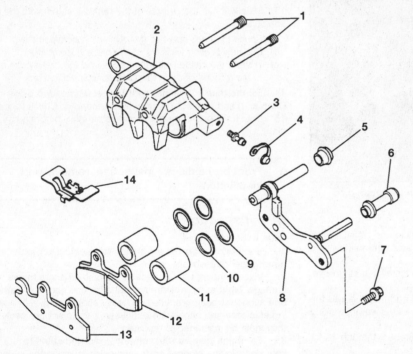

5.4b Brake caliper (300 4WD models) - exploded view

1   Pad pins
2   Caliper body
3   Bleed valve
4   Bleed valve cap
5   Boot
6   Boot
7   Mounting bolt
8   Caliper bracket
9   Piston seals
10   Dust seals
11   Pistons
12   Inner pad
13   Outer pad
14   Pad spring

overhaul procedure, paying particular attention to the steps involved in removing the piston with compressed air. If you don't have access to an air compressor, you can use the vehicle's hydraulic system to force the pistons out instead. To do this, remove the pads and pump the brake lever. The hydraulic pressure will push the pistons out of the bores.

1   Securely support the front end of the vehicle on jackstands and remove the front wheels. Remove the brake hose fitting bolt and disconnect the brake hose from the caliper **(see illustration)**. Wrap the end of the hose in a plastic bag, tightly secured with a rubber band, to prevent excess fluid loss and contamination.

2   Unscrew the caliper mounting bolts and lift it off the steering knuckle **(see illustration 4.2b)**.

Overhaul

Refer to illustrations 5.4a and 5.4b

3   Remove the brake pads and anti-rattle spring from the caliper (see Section 4, if necessary). Clean the exterior of the caliper with

denatured alcohol or brake system cleaner.

4   Slide the caliper body off the bracket and remove the rubber bushings **(see illustrations)**.

5   Pack a shop rag into the space that holds the brake pads. Use compressed air, directed into the caliper fluid inlet, to remove the piston(s). Use only enough air pressure to ease the piston out of the bore. If a piston is blown out forcefully, even with the rag in place, it may be damaged. **Warning:** *Never place your fingers in front of a piston in an attempt to catch or protect it when applying compressed air, as serious injury could occur.*

6   Using a wood or plastic tool, remove the piston seals. Metal tools may cause bore damage.

7   Clean the pistons and bores with denatured alcohol, clean brake fluid or brake system cleaner and blow them dry with filtered, unlubricated compressed air.

8   Inspect the surface of the piston for nicks and burrs and loss of plating. Check the caliper bore, too. If surface defects are present, the caliper must be replaced. If the caliper is in bad shape, the master

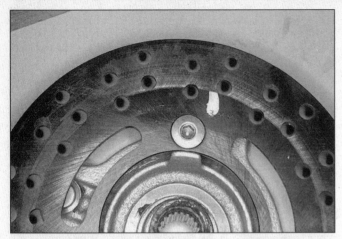

6.4 The minimum thickness is stamped in the disc

6.6a Remove the cotter pin, nut and washer . . .

6.6b . . .and pull the hub off together with the brake disc

cylinder should also be checked.

9   Lubricate the piston seal with clean brake fluid and install it in its groove in the caliper bore. Make sure the seal seats completely and isn't twisted.

10   Lubricate the dust seal with brake fluid and install it in its groove, making sure it seats correctly.

11   Lubricate the piston with clean brake fluid and install it into the caliper bore. Using your thumbs, push the piston all the way in, making sure it doesn't get cocked in the bore.

12   If you're working on a 4WD model, repeat Steps 9 through 11 for the other piston.

6.6c Remove the bolts (arrows) to detach the disc shield

Installation

13   Installation is the reverse of the removal steps, with the following additions:

   a) *Space the pads apart so the disc will fit between them.*

   b) *Use new sealing washers on the brake hose fitting.*

   c) *Tighten the caliper mounting bolts and the brake hose union bolt to the torques listed in this Chapter's Specifications.*

14   Fill the master cylinder with the recommended brake fluid (see Chapter 1) and bleed the system (see Section 5). Check for leaks.

15   Check the operation of the brakes carefully before riding the vehicle.

---

6   Front brake discs - inspection, removal and installation

Disc inspection

Refer to illustration 6.4

1   Securely support the front of the vehicle on jackstands and remove the front wheels.

2   Visually inspect the surface of the disc for score marks and other damage. Light scratches are normal after use and won't affect brake operation, but deep grooves and heavy score marks will reduce braking efficiency and accelerate pad wear. If the discs are badly grooved they must be machined or replaced.

3   To check disc runout, mount a dial indicator to the steering knuckle, with the plunger on the indicator touching the surface of the disc about 1/2-inch from the outer edge. Slowly turn the wheel and watch the indicator needle, comparing your reading with the limit listed in this Chapter's Specifications. If the runout is greater than allowed, check the hub bearings for play (see Chapter 1). If the bearings are worn, replace them and repeat this check. If the disc runout is still excessive, the disc will have to be replaced.

4   The disc must not be machined or allowed to wear down to a thickness less than the allowable minimum listed in this Chapter's Specifications. The thickness of the disc can be checked with a micrometer. If the thickness of the disc is less than the minimum allowable, it must be replaced. The minimum thickness is normally stamped into the disc **(see illustration)**.

Removal

Refer to illustrations 6.6a, 6.6b, 6.6c and 6.7

5   Remove the brake caliper (see Section 5).

6   Remove the cotter pin and unscrew the nut that secures the hub to the spindle (2WD) or driveaxle outer end (4WD) **(see illustration)**. Pull the hub and brake disc off the spindle or driveaxle **(see illustra-**

6.7 Remove the disc-to-hub bolts with an Allen wrench

7.4 Unscrew the union bolt (arrow); use new sealing washers when you reinstall it

7.5 Remove the clamp bolts (arrows) and take the master cylinder off

tion). If necessary, unbolt the disc shield and remove it from the knuckle (see illustration).

7   Mark the relationship of the disc to the wheel, so it can be reinstalled in the same position. Remove the bolts that retain the disc to the wheel (see illustration). Loosen the bolts a little at a time, in a criss-cross pattern, to avoid distorting the disc.

8   Once the disc is removed from the hub, inspect the wheel bearings, located inside the hub. Replace them if they're worn or damaged, using the same procedure as for front drum brakes (see Section 2).

Installation

9   Position the disc on the hub, aligning the previously applied matchmarks (if you're reinstalling the original disc). In all cases, the marked side of the disc faces away from the hub.

10   Install the bolts, tightening them a little at a time in a criss-cross pattern, to the torque listed in this Chapter's Specifications. Clean off all grease from the brake disc using acetone or brake system cleaner.

11   Install the brake disc shield if it was removed. Install the hub and brake disc on the spindle. Install the nut, tighten it to the torque listed in this Chapter's Specifications, then secure it with a new cotter pin.

12   Install the brake caliper (Section 5) and wheel.

13   Operate the brake lever several times to bring the pads into contact with the disc. Check the operation of the brakes carefully before riding the vehicle.

7   Front brake master cylinder - removal, overhaul and installation

1   If the master cylinder is leaking fluid, or if the lever doesn't produce a firm feel when the brake is applied and bleeding the brakes does not help, master cylinder overhaul is recommended.

2   Before disassembling the master cylinder, read through the entire procedure and make sure that you have the correct rebuild kit. Also, you will need some new, clean brake fluid of the recommended type, some clean rags and internal snap-ring pliers.

Caution 1: To prevent damage to the finish from spilled brake fluid, always cover the fuel tank and front fender when working on the master cylinder.

Caution 2: Disassembly, overhaul and reassembly of the brake master cylinder must be done in a spotlessly clean work area to avoid contamination and possible failure of the brake hydraulic system components.

Removal

Refer to illustrations 7.4 and 7.5

3   Loosen, but do not remove, the screws holding the reservoir cover in place.

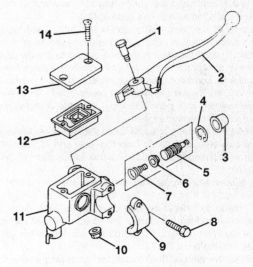

7.7 Master cylinder - exploded view

1	Lever pivot bolt	8	Clamp bolt
2	Lever	9	Clamp
3	Cap	10	Pivot bolt locknut
4	Snap-ring	11	Cylinder body
5	Piston	12	Diaphragm
6	Cup	13	Reservoir cover
7	Spring	14	Cover screw

4   Place rags beneath the master cylinder to protect the finish in case of brake fluid spills. Remove the union bolt (see illustration) and separate the brake hose from the master cylinder. Wrap the end of the hose in a clean rag and suspend the hose in an upright position or bend it down carefully and place the open end in a clean container. The objective is to prevent excess loss of brake fluid, fluid spills and system contamination.

5   Remove the master cylinder mounting bolts (see illustration) and separate the master cylinder from the handlebar.

Overhaul

Refer to illustration 7.7

6   Remove the locknut from the underside of the lever pivot screw, then remove the screw and detach the lever from the master cylinder.

7   Carefully remove the rubber dust boot from the end of the piston (see illustration).

6A

8.5 Pull back the cap (arrow) to expose the bleed valve

8   Using snap-ring pliers, remove the snap-ring and slide out the piston, the cup seals and the spring. Lay the parts out in the proper order to prevent confusion during reassembly.

9   Clean all of the parts with clean brake fluid. **Caution:** *Do not, under any circumstances, use a petroleum-based solvent to clean brake parts. If compressed air is available, use it to dry the parts thoroughly (make sure it's filtered and unlubricated). Check the master cylinder bore for corrosion, scratches, nicks and score marks. If damage is evident, the master cylinder must be replaced with a new one. If the master cylinder is in poor condition, then the wheel cylinders or calipers should be checked as well.*

10   Remove the old cup seals and install the new ones. Make sure the lips of the cup seals face away from the lever end of the piston. If a new piston is included in the rebuild kit, use it regardless of the condition of the old one.

11   Before reassembling the master cylinder, soak the piston and the rubber cup seals in clean brake fluid for ten or fifteen minutes. Lubricate the master cylinder bore with clean brake fluid, then carefully insert the piston and related parts in the reverse order of disassembly. Make sure the lips on the cup seals do not turn inside out when they are slipped into the bore.

12   Depress the piston, then install the snap-ring (make sure the snap-ring is properly seated in the groove with the sharp edge facing out). Install the rubber dust boot (make sure the lip is seated properly in the piston groove).

13   Install the brake lever and tighten the pivot bolt locknut.

Installation

14   Attach the master cylinder to the handlebar.

15   Make sure the word UP on the master cylinder clamp is upright, then tighten the bolts to the torque listed in this Chapter's Specifications **(see illustration 7.5)**. Tighten the top bolt fully, then tighten the lower bolt. **Caution:** *Don't try to close the gap at the lower bolt mating surface or the clamp may break.*

16   Connect the brake hose to the master cylinder, using new sealing washers. Tighten the union bolt to the torque listed in this Chapter's Specifications.

17   Refer to Section 8 and bleed the air from the system.

8   Brake system bleeding

Refer to illustration 8.5

1   Bleeding the hydraulic brakes on models so equipped is simply the process of removing all the air bubbles from the brake fluid reservoir, the lines and the wheel cylinders or calipers. Bleeding is necessary whenever a brake system hydraulic connection is loosened, when a component or hose is replaced, or when the master cylinder, wheel cylinders or calipers are overhauled. Leaks in the system may also

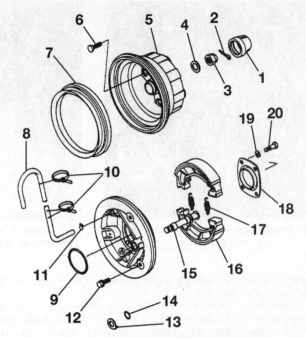

9.3a Rear drum brake - exploded view

1	Trim cap	11	Breather hose clamp
2	Cotter pin	12	Drain bolt
3	Nut	13	Wear indicator
4	Washer	14	O-ring
5	Brake drum	15	Brake cam
6	Wheel stud	16	Brake shoes
7	Drum seal	17	Return springs
8	Breather hose	18	Reinforcing plate
9	Brake panel O-ring	19	Lockwasher
10	Breather hose retainers	20	Bolt

allow air to enter, but leaking brake fluid will reveal their presence and warn you of the need for repair.

2   To bleed the brake, you will need some new, clean brake fluid of the recommended type (see Chapter 1), a length of clear vinyl or plastic tubing, a small container partially filled with clean brake fluid, some rags and a wrench to fit the brake bleed valve.

3   Cover the fuel tank and other painted components to prevent damage in the event that brake fluid is spilled.

4   Remove the reservoir cap and slowly pump the brake lever a few times, until no air bubbles can be seen floating up from the holes at the bottom of the reservoir. Doing this bleeds the air from the master cylinder end of the line. Reinstall the reservoir cap.

5   Attach one end of the clear vinyl or plastic tubing to the wheel cylinder or caliper bleed valve **(see illustration 3.5 or the accompanying illustration)** and submerge the other end in the brake fluid in the container.

6   Check the fluid level in the reservoir. Do not allow the fluid level to drop below the lower mark during the bleeding process.

7   Carefully pump the brake lever three or four times and hold it while opening the bleed valve. When the valve is opened, brake fluid will flow out of the wheel cylinder or caliper into the clear tubing and the lever will move toward the handlebar.

8   Retighten the bleed valve, then release the brake lever gradually. Repeat the process until no air bubbles are visible in the brake fluid leaving the wheel cylinder or caliper, and the lever is firm when applied. Remember to add fluid to the reservoir as the level drops. Use only new, clean brake fluid of the recommended type. Never reuse the fluid lost during bleeding.

9   Repeat this procedure at the other wheel. Be sure to check the fluid level in the master cylinder reservoir frequently.

9.3b Remove the cotter pin and unscrew the nut, then remove the washer

9.3c This type of drum puller has hollow bolts that thread into the studs . . .

9.3d . . . a threaded shaft pushes against the axle shaft, pulling the holder and brake drum outward

9.3e Pull off the brake drum and seal; don't get grease on the shoes

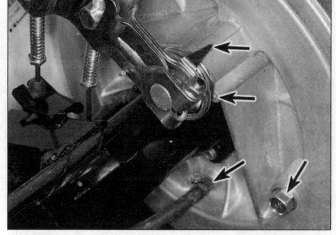

9.4 Remove the drain bolt and disconnect the breather hose (lower arrows); note how the wear indicator and spring are installed (upper arrows)

10 Replace the reservoir cap, wipe up any spilled brake fluid and check the entire system for leaks. **Note:** *If bleeding is difficult, it may be necessary to let the brake fluid in the system stabilize for a few hours (it may be aerated). Repeat the bleeding procedure when the tiny bubbles in the system have floated out.*

9 Rear drum brake(s) - removal, inspection and installation

Removal

Refer to illustrations 9.3a through 9.3e, 9.4, 9.6a, 9.6b, 9.6c, 9.7, 9.8a, 9.8b and 9.8c

1 Securely support the rear end of the vehicle on jackstands and remove the rear wheel from the side being worked on.
2 Disconnect the brake cable(s) from the brake arm(s) (Section 11).
3 Remove the cotter pin, hub nut and washer, then pull the brake drum off the axle **(see illustrations)**. If the drum is difficult to remove, use a puller **(see illustrations)**.
4 Disconnect the breather hose and unscrew the drain bolt from the brake panel **(see illustration)**.
5 If you're working on a 2WD model, fold the brake shoes into a V and remove them from the brake panel. Disengage the springs from the shoes.
6 If you're working on a 4WD model, pull the springs free with a

9.6a Pull off the return springs with a hook . . .

hook **(see illustration)**. Remove the snap-rings and plate from the pivot ends of the shoes, then separate the shoes and slide them off the pivots **(see illustrations)**.

6A

9.6b . . . remove the snap-ring and retaining plate . . .

9.6c . . . then spread the shoes off the brake cam and slip them off the pivot posts

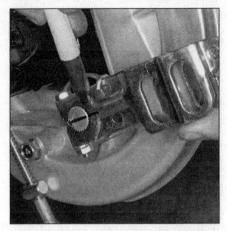

9.7 Mark the position of the arm on the brake cam, then remove the nut and pinch bolt

9.8a Unbolt the reinforcing plate . . .

9.8b . . . and pull it off the brake panel; note how the raised center of the plate faces the brake panel

9.8c Take the brake panel off the axle and remove the gasket

7   Mark the position of the adjusting lever on the brake cam, then remove the pinch bolt and take the lever off **(see illustration)**.

8   Remove the reinforcing plate and O-ring from the brake panel, then take the brake panel off the axle housing **(see illustrations)**.

Inspection

Refer to illustration 9.9

9   Inspection is the same as for front drum brakes, described in Sec-tion 2. Refer to the maximum diameter stamped in the drum **(see illus-tration)**.

Installation

Refer to illustration 9.10

10   Installation is the reverse of the removal steps, with the following additions:

9.9 The maximum diameter is cast in the drum

9.10 Lubricate the brake cam shaft with high temperature brake grease

10.2 Check the hoses for cracks, especially where they meet the metal fittings (arrow)

a) If you removed the brake cam, apply a thin coat of multipurpose grease to the shaft **(see illustration)**.
b) Apply a thin film of high-temperature brake grease to the brake cam and the pivot areas of the anchor pin(s), as well as to the shoe contact areas on the brake panel. Be sure not to get any grease on the brake drum or linings.
c) Place the shoes on the brake panel with their flat ends against the brake cam and their rounded ends over the anchor pin(s).
d) Lubricate the drum seal with high temperature brake grease. Be sure not to get any grease on the inside of the drum; if you do, clean it off with a non-residue solvent such as brake cleaner or lacquer thinner.
e) Tighten the hub nut to the torque listed in this Chapter's Specifications and install a new cotter pin. If necessary, tighten the nut further to align the cotter pin hole in the axle with the slots in the nut. Don't loosen the nut.
f) Once the nut is tightened properly, bend the cotter pin to secure it.
g) Refer to Chapter 1 and adjust the brakes.

10   Brake hoses and lines - inspection and replacement

Inspection

Refer to illustration 10.2

1   Once a week, or if the vehicle is used less frequently, before every use, check the condition of the brake hoses.
2   Twist and flex the rubber hoses while looking for cracks, bulges and seeping fluid. Check extra carefully around the areas where the hoses connect with metal fittings, as these are common areas for hose failure **(see illustration)**.

Replacement

Refer to illustrations 10.3a, 10.3b, 10.3c and 10.5

Flexible hoses

3   Cover the surrounding area with plenty of rags and unscrew the union bolt or flare nut. Pull out the clip or detach the hose from any retainers that may be present and remove the hose **(see illustrations)**.

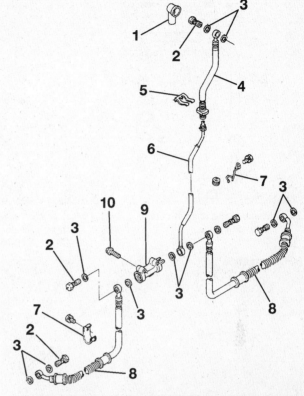

10.3a Front brake line details (1986 and 1987 300 models)

1	Rubber cap	6	Metal line
2	Union bolt	7	Retainer, grommet and bolt
3	Sealing washers	8	Lower hoses
4	Master cylinder hose	9	Hose fitting
5	Hose clip	10	Bolt

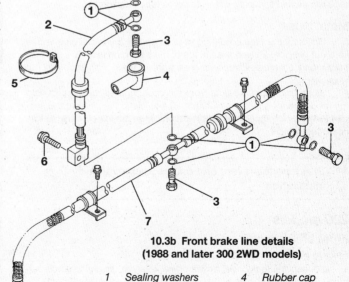

**10.3b Front brake line details
(1988 and later 300 2WD models)**

1	Sealing washers	4	Rubber cap
2	Master cylinder hose	5	Retainer
3	Union bolt	6	Bolt
		7	Lower line

6A

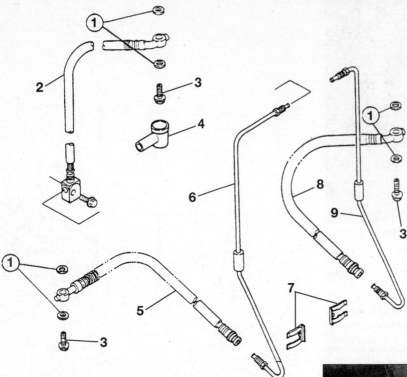

10.3c Front brake line details (1988 and later 300 2WD models)

1   *Sealing washers*
2   *Master cylinder hose*
3   *Union bolt*
4   *Rubber cap*
5   *Lower left hose*
6   *Metal line*
7   *Hose clips*
8   *Lower right hose*
9   *Metal line*

4   Position the new hose, making sure it isn't twisted or otherwise strained, between the two components. Make sure the metal tube portion of the banjo fitting at the brake panel or caliper is located between the stoppers.

5   Install the union bolts, using new sealing washers on both sides of the fittings, and tighten them to the torque listed in this Chapter's Specifications. If the hose is connected by a flare nut, hold it with one wrench and tighten the flare nut with another wrench. Make sure the clips are seated securely in their grooves **(see illustration)**.

Metal pipes

6   Unscrew the flare nut fitting at each end of the metal pipe with a flare nut wrench. Thread the fittings of the new pipe in with fingers so they won't be cross-threaded, then tighten them with the flare nut wrench.

7   Flush the old brake fluid from the system, refill the system with the recommended fluid (see Chapter 1) and bleed the air from the system (see Section 8). Check the operation of the brakes carefully before riding the vehicle.

11   Brake pedal, levers and cables - removal and installation

220 models

Front brake cables

Refer to illustration 11.1

1   Loosen the lockwheel at the brake lever on the right handlebar, then loosen the adjuster all the way. Line up the adjuster slot with the slots in the lever and bracket, then rotate the upper cable out of the slots and lower the cable end out of the lever **(see illustration)**.

2   Unscrew the cable adjuster wingnut off the end of one of the lower front cables at the brake panel. Remove the snap-ring that secures the lower cable, then pull the cable out of the end plug. Slip the end plug sideways out of the brake arm, pull the cable out of the

10.5 Be sure the hose clips are secure in their grooves

brake arm and slide the washer off the cable. Once the cable is disconnected from the brake arm, slip the washer and end plug back on and screw the wingnut on so the parts won't be lost.

3   Repeat Step 2 for the other lower cable.

4   Detach the cables from the equalizer, separate them from any retainers and remove them from the vehicle.

5   Installation is the reverse of the removal steps, with the following additions:

a) *Lubricate the cable ends with multi-purpose grease.*
b) *Make sure the cables are secure in their slots and retainers.*
c) *Adjust brake lever play as described in Chapter 1.*

Parking brake cable

Refer to illustration 11.6

6   Loosen the lockwheel at the brake lever on the right handlebar, then loosen the adjuster all the way. Line up the adjuster slot with the slots in the lever and bracket, then rotate the upper cable out of the slots and lower the cable end out of the lever **(see illustration)**.

7   Disconnect the lower end of the cable from the intermediate lever at the brake pedal. Free the cable from any retainers and take it out.

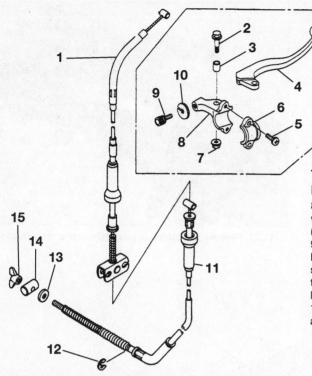

11.1 Front brake cable and lever details (220 models)

1	Upper cable	9	Cable adjuster
2	Brake lever pivot bolt	10	Adjuster locknut
3	Bushing	11	Lower cable
4	Brake lever	12	Snap-ring
5	Clamp screw	13	Washer
6	Clamp	14	Cable end plug
7	Pivot bolt locknut	15	Adjusting wingnut
8	Lever bracket		

Rear brake cable

8   At the brake pedal intermediate lever, remove the cotter pin and washer, then remove the clevis pin and detach the cable from the lever (**see illustration 11.6**).

9   Unscrew the cable adjuster wingnut off the end of the cable at the brake panel. Pull the cable out of the end plug and slip the end plug sideways out of the brake arm. Pull the cable out of the brake arm, slip the end plug back on and screw the wingnut on so the parts won't be lost.

10   Installation is the reverse of the removal steps, with the following additions:

a) Lubricate the clevis pin and the rear end of the cable with multi-purpose grease.

b) Adjust brake pedal height and freeplay as described in Chapter 1.

11.6 Parking brake and rear brake cable details (220 models)

1	Parking brake cable
2	Clevis pin
3	Rear brake cable
4	Adjusting wingnut
5	Pinch bolt
6	Brake arm
7	Pinch bolt nut
8	Cable end plug
9	Washer
10	Cotter pin
11	Spring
12	Intermediate lever
13	Washer
14	Lever to pedal link
15	Washer
16	Cotter pin
17	Spring
18	Locknut
19	Adjusting bolt
20	Pedal

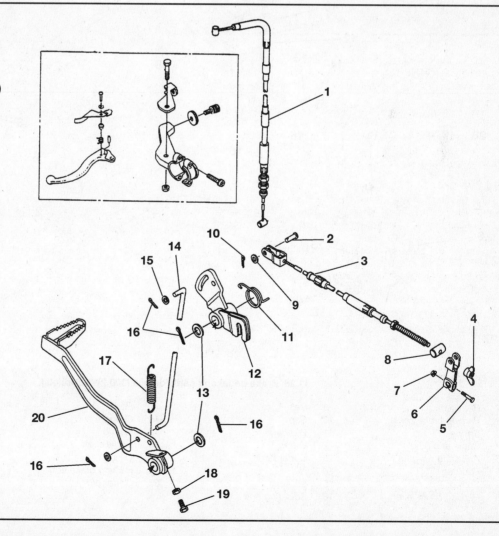

6A

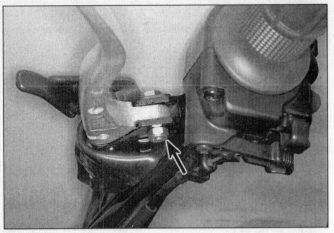

11.22 Remove the locknut (arrow), then unscrew the pivot bolt

11.23 Remove the clamp screws (arrows) to detach the lever

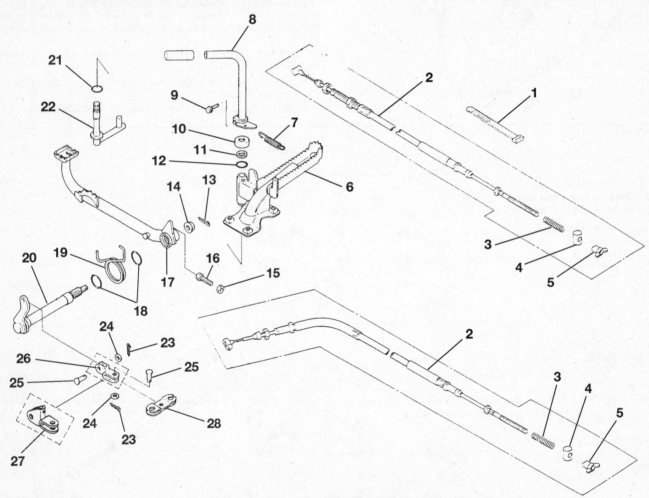

11.25 Brake pedal and cable details (300 2WD models)

1	Retainer	9	Bolt	17	Pedal	24	Washer
2	Parking brake cable	10	Cap	18	O-ring	25	Clevis pin
3	Spring	11	Washer	19	Spring	26	Equalizer link (1988
4	Cable end plug	12	O-ring	20	Pedal shaft		through 1990 models)
5	Adjusting wingnut	13	Cotter pin	21	O-ring	27	Equalizer link (1991 and
6	Footpeg	14	Nut	22	Parking brake arm		later models)
7	Spring	15	Locknut	23	Cotter pin	28	Equalizer
8	Parking brake lever	16	Adjusting bolt				

11.36 Rotate the cable (upper arrow) around to the removal slot (lower arrow) and lower it out of the lever

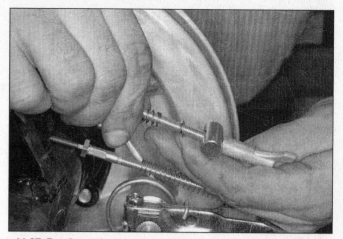

11.37 Put the spring, washer, end plug and locknut back on the cable so they won't be lost

Brake pedal and intermediate lever

11   Disconnect the cables from the intermediate lever as described above.

12   Unhook the pedal return spring. Remove the cotter pin and washer and slide the pedal off the pivot shaft **(see illustration 11.6)**.

13   Unhook the return spring from the intermediate lever. Remove the cotter pin and washer, slide the intermediate lever off the pivot shaft and remove the return spring.

14   Installation is the reverse of the removal steps, with the following additions:

a) *Lubricate the intermediate lever and pedal shafts with multi-purpose grease.*

b) *Use new cotter pins.*

c) *Refer to Chapter 1 and adjust brake pedal height and freeplay.*

Brake lever

15   Disconnect the cable from the brake lever as described in Step 2 above.

16   If the machine has a brake light switch, refer to Chapter 4 and remove it.

17   Remove the lever mounting screws and take it off the handlebar **(see illustration 11.1)**.

18   Installation is the reverse of the removal steps.

19   Refer to Chapter 1 and adjust brake lever freeplay.

Parking brake lever

Refer to illustrations 11.22 and 11.23

20   Disconnect the cable from the parking brake lever as described in Step 2 above.

21   To remove the lock lever, note how the spring fits, then remove the screw and take the lever off **(see illustration 11.6)**.

22   To remove the parking brake lever, remove its locknut and bolt **(see illustration)**. Take the lever off.

23   To remove the lever bracket, remove its mounting screws **(see illustration)**.

24   Installation is the reverse of the removal steps, with the following additions:

a) *Tighten the bracket screws securely, but don't overtighten them and break the bracket.*

b) *Lubricate the lever pivot bolt with multi-purpose grease.*

c) *Adjust the lever as described in Chapter 1.*

300 2WD models

Refer to illustration 11.25

Rear brake cables

25   Unscrew the cable adjuster wingnut off the end of the cable at the brake panel **(see illustration)**. Pull the cable out of the end plug and

slip the end plug sideways out of the brake arm. Pull the cable out of the brake arm, slip the end plug back on and screw the wingnut on so the parts won't be lost.

26   At the equalizer, turn the cable to align with the slot, then lower the cable end plug out of the equalizer.

27   Installation is the reverse of the removal steps, with the following additions:

a) *Lubricate the clevis pin and the rear end of the cable with multi-purpose grease.*

b) *Adjust brake pedal height and freeplay as described in Chapter 1.*

Brake pedal

28   Remove the cotter pin, washer and clevis pin and disconnect the equalizer pivot from the brake pedal shaft **(see illustration 11.25)**.

29   Remove the cotter pin and nut from the brake pedal shaft. Remove the pedal, O-rings and return spring.

30   Installation is the reverse of the removal steps, with the following additions:

a) *Lubricate the pedal shaft with multi-purpose grease.*

b) *Use new cotter pins.*

c) *Refer to Chapter 1 and adjust brake pedal height and freeplay.*

Parking brake lever

31   The parking brake lever is on the right side of the vehicle and locks the brake pedal.

32   Unhook the return spring from the parking brake lever **(see illustration 11.25)**.

33   Remove the lever pivot bolt and lift it off the post. Remove the seal, washer, O-ring and post.

34   Installation is the reverse of the removal steps. Grease the O-rings and lever pivot.

Brake lever

35   The brake lever is part of the master cylinder on these models (see Section 7).

300 4WD models

Rear brake cables

Refer to illustrations 11.36, 11.37, 11.39 and 11.40

36   Loosen the lockwheel at the brake lever on the left handlebar, then loosen the adjuster all the way. Line up the adjuster slot with the slots in the lever and bracket, then rotate the upper cable out of the slots and lower the cable end out of the lever **(see illustration)**.

37   Unscrew the cable adjuster wingnut off the end of the parking brake cable at the brake panel **(see illustration)**. Pull the cable out of the end plug and slip the end plug sideways out of the brake arm. Pull the cable out of the brake arm, slip the end plug back on and screw the wingnut on so the parts won't be lost.

6A

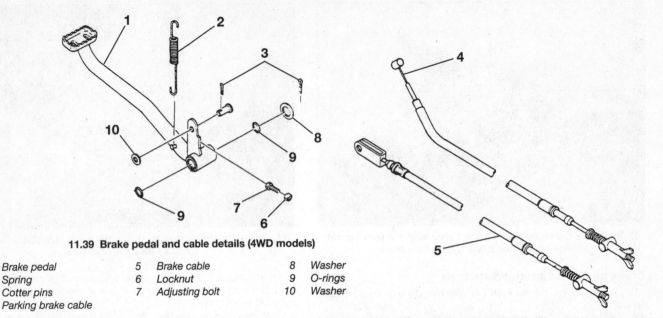

11.39 Brake pedal and cable details (4WD models)

1	Brake pedal	5	Brake cable	8	Washer
2	Spring	6	Locknut	9	O-rings
3	Cotter pins	7	Adjusting bolt	10	Washer
4	Parking brake cable				

38   Remove the cotter pin, washer and clevis pin to disengage the brake cable from the pedal.

39   Repeat Step 37 to disengage the brake pedal cable from the lever on the brake panel **(see illustration)**.

40   Push the rubber pieces forward on the cables with a screwdriver **(see illustration)**. Pull the cable housings out of the brackets, then slip the cables out of the bracket slots.

41   Free the cables from their retainers and remove them from the vehicle.

42   Installation is the reverse of the removal steps, with the following additions:

   a) *Lubricate the cable end plugs with multi-purpose grease.*
   b) *Adjust the brake pedal and parking brake lever as described in Chapter 1.*

Brake pedal

43   Disconnect the brake cable from the pedal as described above.

44   Remove the cotter pin, washer and clevis pin, then slide the pedal off the shaft and remove the O-rings **(see illustration 11.37)**.

45   Installation is the reverse of the removal steps, with the following additions:

   a) *Lubricate the pedal shaft and O-rings with multi-purpose grease.*
   b) *Use new cotter pins.*
   c) *Refer to Chapter 1 and adjust brake pedal height and freeplay.*

Parking brake lever

46   This procedure is the same as for 220 models, described above.

Brake lever

47   The brake lever is part of the master cylinder on these models (see Section 7).

12   Wheels - inspection, removal and installation

Inspection

1   Clean the wheels thoroughly to remove mud and dirt that may interfere with the inspection procedure or mask defects. Make a general check of the wheels and tires as described in Chapter 1.

2   The wheels should be visually inspected for cracks, flat spots on the rim and other damage. Since tubeless tires are involved, look very

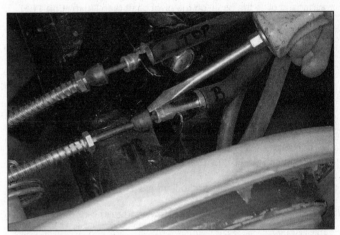

11.40 Push the rubber piece forward on the cable, then pull the cable housing rearward and slip the cable through the bracket slot

closely for dents in the area where the tire bead contacts the rim. Dents in this area may prevent complete sealing of the tire against the rim, which leads to deflation of the tire over a period of time.

3   If damage is evident, the wheel will have to be replaced with a new one. Never attempt to repair a damaged wheel.

Removal

4   Securely block the wheels at the opposite end of the vehicle from the wheel being removed, so it can't roll.

5   Loosen the lug nuts on the wheel being removed. Jack up one end of the vehicle and support it securely on jackstands.

6   Remove the lug nuts and pull the wheel off.

Installation

7   Position the wheel on the studs. Make sure the directional arrow on the tire points in the forward rotating direction of the wheel.

8   Install the wheel nuts with their tapered sides toward the wheel. This is necessary to locate the wheel accurately on the hub.

9   Snug the wheel nuts evenly in a criss-cross pattern.

10   Remove the jackstands, lower the vehicle and tighten the wheel nuts, again in a criss-cross pattern.

Deflate the tire and remove the valve core. Release the bead on the side opposite the tire valve with an ATV bead breaker, following the manufacturer's instructions. Make sure you have the correct blades for the tire size (using the wrong size blade may damage the wheel, the tire or the blade). Lubricate the bead with water before removal (don't use soap or any type of lubricant).

TIRE CHANGING SEQUENCE

Turn the tire over and release the other bead.

If one side of the wheel has a smaller flange, remove and install the tire from that side. Use two tire levers to work the bead over the edge of the rim.

Before installing, ensure the tire is suitable for the wheel. Take note of any sidewall markings such as direction of rotation arrows, then work the first bead over the rim flange.

Use tire levers to start the second bead over the rim flange.

Hold the bead while you work the last section of it over the rim flange. Install the valve core and inflate the tire, making sure not to overinflate it.

6A

14.4 Pull or pry the trim cap from the hub . . .

14.5 . . . remove the cotter pin, unscrew the nut and remove the washer . . .

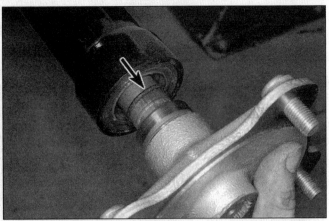

14.7 . . . slide the hub off the splines and remove the O-ring (arrow); pry the seal out of the axle if it has been leaking

bead of the tire is substantial, much more than required for motorcycle tires, and is beyond the capabilities of an individual working with normal tire irons or even a normal bead breaker. A special bead breaker is required for ATV tires; it produces a great deal of force and concentrates it in a relatively small area.

3   Also, repair of the punctured tire and replacement on the wheel rim requires special tools, skills and experience that the average do-it-do-it-yourselfer lacks.

4   For these reasons, if a puncture or flat occurs with an ATV tire, the wheel should be removed from the vehicle and taken to a dealer service department or a repair shop for repair or replacement of the tire. The accompanying illustrations can be used as a guide to tire replacement in an emergency, provided the necessary bead breaker is available.

13   Tires - general information

1   Tubeless tires are used as standard equipment on this vehicle. Unlike motorcycle tires, they run at very low air pressures and are completely unsuited for use on pavement. Inflating ATV tires to excessive pressures will rupture them, ruining the tire.

2   The force required to break the seal between the rim and the

14   Wheel hubs - removal and installation

Removal

Refer to illustrations 14.4, 14.5 and 14.7

1   The hubs on wheels with drum brakes are integral with the drums. See Section 2 or 3 for removal and installation procedures. The hubs on wheels with disc brakes are removed together with the brake discs (see Section 6).

2   This section applies to the left rear wheel hubs on Bayou 220 and Bayou 300 4WD models (no brake is used at this hub).

3   Refer to Section 12 and remove the wheel(s).

4   Remove the trim cap from the hub **(see illustration)**.

5   Bend back the cotter pin and pull it out of the hub nut **(see illustration)**.

6   Unscrew the hub nut and remove the washer.

7   Pull the hub off the axle shaft. Remove the O-ring **(see illustration)**.

8   If the seal at the end of the axle housing has been leaking, pry it out. Press in a new seal with a piece of pipe or similar tool that will fit over the axle shaft.

Installation

Refer to illustration 14.9

9   Installation is the reverse of the removal steps, with the following additions:

a) *Use a new O-ring and place it in the hub groove* **(see illustration)**.

b) *Lubricate the axle shaft and hub splines with multi-purpose grease.*

c) *Tighten the hub nut to the torque listed in this Chapter's Specifications. If necessary, tighten it an additional amount to align the cotter pin slots. Don't loosen the nut to align the slots.*

d) *Install a new cotter pin and bend it to secure the nut.*

14.9 The O-ring fits in the hub like this

Chapter 6 Part B
Brakes, wheels and tires (Prairie models)

Contents

	Section
Brake fluid level check and fluid change	See Chapter 1
Brake hoses and lines - inspection and replacement	8
Brake lining wear and system check	See Chapter 1
Brake pedal, levers and cables - removal and installation	9
Brake system bleeding	6
Front brake calipers - removal, overhaul and installation	3
Front brake discs - inspection, removal and installation	4
Front brake master cylinder - removal, overhaul and installation	5

	Section
Front brakes - pad replacement	2
General information	1
Rear drum brake - removal, inspection and installation	7
Tires - general information	11
Tires and wheels - general check	See Chapter 1
Wheel hubs - removal and installation	12
Wheels - inspection, removal and installation	10

Specifications

Brakes

Brake fluid type	See Chapter 1
Brake shoe lining minimum thickness	See Chapter 1
Brake pad lining minimum thickness	See Chapter 1
Brake pedal height	See Chapter 1
Drum diameter	
Standard	180.00 to 180.14 mm (7.086 to 7.092 inches)
Limit	180.75 mm (7.116 inches) (1)
Front disc thickness	
Standard	3.3 to 3.7 mm (0.130 to 0.145 inch)
Limit	3.0 mm (0.118 inch) (1)
Front disc runout	
Standard	0.2 mm (0.008 inch) or less
Limit	0.3 mm (0.012 inch)
Front pad wear limit	See Chapter 1

Wheels and tires

Tire pressures	See Chapter 1
Tire tread depth	See Chapter 1

Torque specifications

Rear axle nuts	185 Nm (135 ft-lbs)
Rear brake panel bolts	29 Nm (22 ft-lbs)
Rear brake drum drain bolt	29 Nm (22 ft-lbs)
Caliper bleed valve	5.4 Nm (48 inch-lbs)
Caliper mounting bolts	25 Nm (18 ft-lbs)
Slider pin-to-bracket	Not specified
Allen head slider pin	18 Nm (156 inch-lbs)
Disc-to-hub bolts	37 Nm (27 ft-lbs)
Pad bolts	18 Nm (156 inch-lbs)
Brake line/hose union bolts	25 Nm (18 ft-lbs) (2)
Master cylinder clamp screws	8.8 Nm (73 inch-lbs)
Brake lever pivot bolt and locknut	5.9 Nm (52 inch-lbs)

1   *Refer to marks cast into the drum or disc (they supersede numbers printed here).*
2   *Use new sealing washers each time the union bolts are removed.*

6B

2.2a Bend back the lockwasher tabs and loosen the pad bolts
while the caliper is still attached . . .

2.2b . . . then unscrew the caliper mounting bolts

1 General information

The vehicles covered in this Part use a single-piston hydraulic disc brake at each front wheel and a single cable-operated rear drum brake, located at the right end of the rear axle.

The front brakes are controlled by a lever on the right handlebar. The rear brake has two means of control: a lever on the left handlebar, which can be locked to provide a parking brake, and a pedal on the right side of the vehicle. Prairie models are equipped with steel wheels, which require very little maintenance and allow tubeless tires to be used. **Caution:** *Brake components rarely require disassembly. Do not disassemble components unless absolutely necessary. If any hydraulic brake line connection in the system is loosened, the entire system should be disassembled, drained, cleaned and then properly filled and bled upon reassembly. Do not use solvents on internal hydraulic brake components. Solvents will cause seals to swell and distort. Use only clean brake fluid for cleaning. Use care when working with brake fluid as it can injure your eyes and it will damage painted surfaces and plastic parts.*

2 Front brakes - pad replacement

Refer to illustrations 2.2a, 2.2b, 2.3a, 2.3b and 2.3c
Warning: *The dust created by the brake system may contain asbestos, which is harmful to your health. Never blow it out with compressed air*

and don't inhale any of it. An approved filtering mask should be worn when working on the brakes.

1   Support the front of the vehicle securely on jackstands and remove the front wheels.

2   Bend back the lockwasher tabs and loosen the pad bolts while the caliper is still bolted to the steering knuckle **(see illustration)**. Remove the caliper mounting bolts and lift the caliper off **(see illustration)**.

3   Unscrew the pad bolts and pull out the pads **(see illustrations)**. Remove the pad spring from the caliper **(see illustration)**.

4   Inspect the pad spring and replace it if it's rusted or damaged.

5   Refer to Chapter 1 and inspect the pads.

6   Check the condition of the brake disc (see Section 4). If it's in need of machining or replacement, follow the procedure in that Section to remove it. If it's okay, deglaze it with sandpaper or emery cloth, using a swirling motion.

7   Remove the cover from the master cylinder reservoir and siphon out some fluid. Push the piston into the caliper as far as possible, while checking the master cylinder reservoir to make sure it doesn't overflow. If you can't depress the piston with thumb pressure, try using a C-clamp. If the piston sticks, remove the caliper and overhaul it as described in Section 8.

8   Install the spring and new pads, making sure to install the pad shim on the correct side and facing the correct direction. Install the pad bolts and tighten them slightly.

9   Install the caliper on the steering knuckle, sliding the brake disc between the pads. Install the caliper mounting bolts and tighten them to the torque listed in this Chapter's Specifications, then tighten the

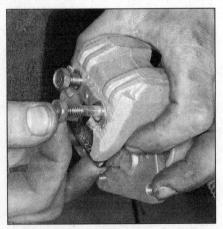

2.3a Unscrew the pad bolts and
pull them out . . .

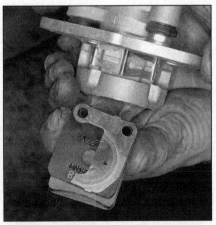

2.3b . . . and remove the pads; note the
direction of the arrowhead mark on the
inner pad's shim

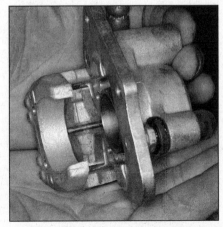

2.3c Remove the pad spring

3.2 Remove the union bolt (arrow) and replace both sealing washers; loosen the Allen head slider pin . . .

3.3 . . . and loosen the lower slider pin with an open-end wrench

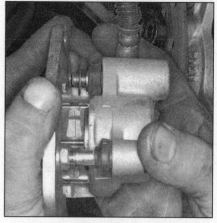

3.6a Slide the caliper off the bracket; don't lose the lockwasher on the Allen head slider pin

pad bolts to the torque listed in this Chapter's Specifications.

10   Install the wheels and lower the vehicle. Operate the right brake lever several times to seat the pads. Check the operation of the brakes carefully before riding the vehicle.

3 Front brake calipers - removal, overhaul and installation

Warning: *If a caliper indicates the need of an overhaul (usually due to leaking fluid or sticky operation), all old brake fluid must be flushed from the system. Also, the dust created by the brake system may contain asbestos, which is harmful to your health. Never blow it out with compressed air and don't inhale any of it. An approved filtering mask should be worn when working on the brakes. Do not, under any circumstances, use petroleum-based solvents to clean brake parts. Use brake cleaner or denatured alcohol only!*

Removal

Refer to illustrations 3.2 and 3.3

1   Securely support the front end of the vehicle on jackstands and remove the front wheels. **Note:** *If you're planning to disassemble the caliper, read through the overhaul procedure, paying particular attention to the steps involved in removing the piston with compressed air. If you don't have access to an air compressor, you can use the vehicle's hydraulic system to force the pistons out instead. To do this, remove the pads and pump the brake lever. The hydraulic pressure will push the pistons out of the bores.*

2   Remove the brake hose fitting bolt and disconnect the brake hose from the caliper **(see illustration)**. Wrap the end of the hose in a plastic bag, tightly secured with a rubber band, to prevent excess fluid loss and contamination.

3   If you're planning to overhaul the caliper, remove the rubber cap and loosen the Allen head slider pin while the caliper bracket is still bolted to the knuckle **(see illustration 3.2)**. If you're planning to remove the slider pin from the bracket, loosen it now also **(see illustration)**.

4   Unscrew the caliper mounting bolts and lift it off the steering knuckle **(see illustration 2.2b)**.

Overhaul

Refer to illustrations 3.6a, 3.6b and 3.14

5   Remove the brake pads and anti-rattle spring from the caliper (see Section 2, if necessary). Clean the exterior of the caliper with denatured alcohol or brake system cleaner.

6   Slide the caliper body off the bracket and remove the rubber bushings **(see illustrations)**.

7   Pack a shop rag into the space that holds the brake pads. Use

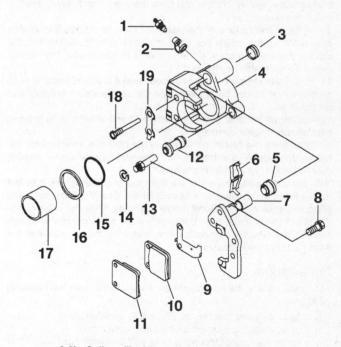

3.6b Caliper (Prairie models) - exploded view

1	Bleed valve	11	Outer pad
2	Bleed valve cap	12	Pin boot
3	Allen head slider pin cap	13	Allen head slider pin
4	Caliper body	14	Lockwasher
5	Pad spring	15	Piston seal
6	Pin boot	16	Dust seal
7	Caliper bracket	17	Piston
8	Bolt	18	Pad bolt
9	Pad shim	19	Lockwasher
10	Inner pad		

compressed air, directed into the caliper fluid inlet, to remove the piston. Use only enough air pressure to ease the piston out of the bore. If a piston is blown out forcefully, even with the rag in place, it may be damaged. **Warning:** *Never place your fingers in front of a piston in an attempt to catch or protect it when applying compressed air, as serious injury could occur.*

8   Using a wood or plastic tool, remove the piston seals. Metal tools may cause bore damage.

6B

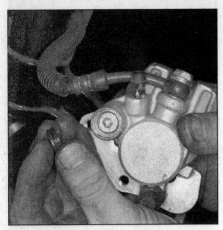

3.14 Install the rubber cap over the Allen head slider pin after it's tightened

4.3a Remove the cotter pin, locknut and washer

4.3b You may need a puller like this one to get the hub off the splines

9   Clean the pistons and bores with denatured alcohol, clean brake fluid or brake system cleaner and blow them dry with filtered, unlubricated compressed air.

10   Inspect the surface of the piston for nicks and burrs and loss of plating. Check the caliper bore, too. If surface defects are present, the caliper must be replaced. If the caliper is in bad shape, the master cylinder should also be checked.

11   Lubricate the piston seal with clean brake fluid and install it in its groove in the caliper bore. Make sure the seal seats completely and isn't twisted.

12   Lubricate the dust seal with brake fluid and install it in its groove, making sure it seats correctly.

13   Lubricate the piston with clean brake fluid and install it into the caliper bore. Using your thumbs, push the piston all the way in, making sure it doesn't get cocked in the bore.

14   If you removed the slider pin from the bracket, tighten it to the torque listed in this Chapter's Specifications. Coat the slider pins with silicone grease and install the rubber bushings. Slide the caliper onto the pin in the bracket, then tighten the Allen head pin to the torque listed in this Chapter's Specifications. Install the rubber cap over the Allen head bolt (see illustration).

Installation

15   Installation is the reverse of the removal steps, with the following additions:

   a) Space the pads apart so the disc will fit between them.
   b) Use new sealing washers on the brake hose fitting.
   c) Tighten the caliper mounting bolts and the brake hose union bolt to the torques listed in this Chapter's Specifications.

16   Fill the master cylinder with the recommended brake fluid (see Chapter 1) and bleed the system (see Section 5). Check for leaks.

17   Check the operation of the brakes carefully before riding the vehicle.

4   Front brake discs - inspection, removal and installation

Disc inspection

1   This procedure is the same as for Bayou models (see Chapter 6A).

Removal

Refer to illustrations 4.3a and 4.3b

2   Remove the wheel and the brake caliper (see Section 3).

3   Remove the cotter pin and unscrew the nut that secures the hub to the spindle (2WD) or driveaxle outer end (4WD) (see illustration).

Pull the hub and brake disc off the spindle or driveaxle, using a puller if necessary (see illustration). If necessary, unbolt the disc shield and remove it from the knuckle.

4   Mark the relationship of the disc to the wheel, so it can be reinstalled in the same position. Remove the bolts that retain the disc to the wheel (see illustration 6.6c in Chapter 6A). Loosen the bolts a little at a time, in a criss-cross pattern, to avoid distorting the disc.

Installation

5   Position the disc on the hub, aligning the previously applied matchmarks (if you're reinstalling the original disc). In all cases, the marked side of the disc faces away from the hub.

6   Install the bolts, tightening them a little at a time in a criss-cross pattern, to the torque listed in this Chapter's Specifications. Clean off all grease from the brake disc using acetone or brake system cleaner.

7   Install the brake disc shield if it was removed. Install the hub and brake disc on the spindle or driveaxle. Install the nut, tighten it to the torque listed in this Chapter's Specifications, then secure it with a new cotter pin.

8   Install the brake caliper (Section 5) and wheel.

9   Operate the brake lever several times to bring the pads into contact with the disc. Check the operation of the brakes carefully before riding the vehicle.

5   Front brake master cylinder - removal, overhaul and installation

This procedure is the same as for Bayou models (see Chapter 6A).

6   Brake system bleeding

Refer to illustration 6.1

This procedure is the same as for Bayou models (see Chapter 6A). A bleed valve is located under a rubber cap on each caliper (see illustration).

7   Rear drum brake - removal, inspection and installation

Removal

Refer to illustrations 7.1, 7.4a, 7.4b, 7.5a, 7.5b, 7.6a, 7.6b, 7.7a, 7.7b, 7.9a and 7.9b

1   Disconnect the breather hose from the brake panel (see illustra-

6.1 There's a bleed valve (arrow) under the rubber cap
on each caliper

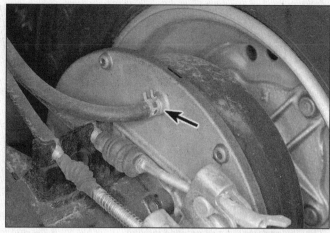

7.1 Disconnect the breather hose from the brake panel

7.4a Remove the skid plate bolt from the
bottom (arrow) . . .

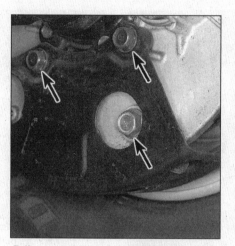

7.4b . . . and from the top (upper arrows),
then remove the drain bolt (lower arrow)

7.5a Unscrew the locknut and axle nut,
then pry out the plate . . .

tion). Securely support the rear end of the vehicle on jackstands and
remove the right rear wheel.
2   Disconnect the brake cables from the brake arm (Section 9).
3   Remove the rear hub (Section 12).
4   Remove the drum skid plate and unscrew the drain bolt **(see**

illustrations).
5   Unscrew the locknut and axle nut, pry off the drum plate and pry
off the drum cover seal **(see illustrations)**.
6   Remove the drum cover screws and pry the cover off the drum
(see illustrations).

7.5b . . . and the drum cover seal

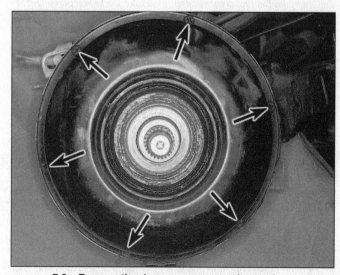

7.6a Remove the drum cover screws (arrows) . . .

6B

7.6b . . . and use the pry notches (arrow) to separate the cover from the brake panel

7.7a Pull the drum off . . .

7.7b . . . and pull the O-ring out of its groove

7.9a Unscrew the brake panel bolts . . .

7.9b . . . pull the panel off and remove the O-ring

7   Pull the brake drum off and remove the O-ring **(see illustrations)**.
8   Refer to Section 9 in Chapter 6A to remove the brake shoes, brake arm and cam.
9   Remove the brake panel bolts, then take the brake panel and O-ring off the axle housing **(see illustrations)**.

Inspection

10   Inspection is the same as for front drum brakes, described in Section 2 of Chapter 6A.

Installation

11   Installation is the same as for Bayou models (see Chapter 6A). In addition, tighten the axle nut and locknut to the torque listed in this Chapter's Specifications.

8   Brake hoses and lines - inspection and replacement

Inspection

1   This is the same as for Bayou models (see Chapter 6A).

Replacement

2   Prairie brake lines and hoses are the same as for 1988 and later Bayou 300 2WD models (see Chapter 6A).

9   Brake pedal, levers and cables - removal and installation

Rear brake cables

1   The brake pedal cable and parking brake cable on Prairie models are the same as for 1988 and later Bayou 300 2WD models (see Chapter 6A).

9.3 Remove the brake cable clevis pin (left) and the trim cap (right)

9.4a Remove the cotter pin from the brake pedal shaft . . .

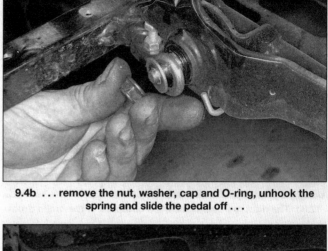

9.4b . . . remove the nut, washer, cap and O-ring, unhook the spring and slide the pedal off . . .

9.6a . . . unhook the spring from the bracket . . .

9.6b . . . then remove the spring and remaining O-ring

Brake pedal

Refer to illustrations 9.3, 9.4a, 9.4b, 9.6a and 9.6b

2   Remove the right floorboard (see Chapter 7).
3   Remove the cotter pin, washer and clevis pin and disconnect the brake cable from the pedal **(see illustration)**. Remove the trim cap from the pedal shaft.
4   Remove the cotter pin from the pedal pivot shaft **(see illustration)**. Unscrew the nut and remove the washer, cap and O-ring **(see illustration)**.
5   Unhook the spring from the brake pedal and slip the pedal off the shaft.
6   Unhook the spring from the bracket, take it off and remove the O-ring **(see illustrations)**.
7   Installation is the reverse of the removal steps, with the following additions:

 a) Lubricate the pedal shaft with multi-purpose grease.
 b) Use a new cotter pin.
 c) Refer to Chapter 1 and adjust brake pedal height and freeplay.

Parking brake lever

8   This procedure is the same as for Bayou 220 models (see Chapter 6A).

Brake lever

9   The brake lever is part of the master cylinder on these models (see Chapter 6A).

10   Wheels - inspection, removal and installation

Inspection

1   Clean the wheels thoroughly to remove mud and dirt that may interfere with the inspection procedure or mask defects. Make a general check of the wheels and tires as described in Chapter 1.
2   The wheels should be visually inspected for cracks, flat spots on the rim and other damage. Since tubeless tires are involved, look very closely for dents in the area where the tire bead contacts the rim. Dents in this area may prevent complete sealing of the tire against the rim, which leads to deflation of the tire over a period of time.
3   If damage is evident, the wheel will have to be replaced with a new one. Never attempt to repair a damaged wheel.

Removal

4   Securely block the wheels at the opposite end of the vehicle from the wheel being removed, so it can't roll.
5   Loosen the lug nuts on the wheel being removed. Jack up one end of the vehicle and support it securely on jackstands.
6   Remove the lug nuts and pull the wheel off.

Installation

7   Position the wheel on the studs. Make sure the directional arrow on the tire points in the forward rotating direction of the wheel.
8   Install the wheel nuts with their tapered sides toward the wheel. This is necessary to locate the wheel accurately on the hub.

6B

12.3a The right rear hub is installed outboard of the brake drum

12.3b The left rear hub is installed on the end of the axle

9   Snug the wheel nuts evenly in a criss-cross pattern.
10   Remove the jackstands, lower the vehicle and tighten the wheel nuts, again in a criss-cross pattern.

11   Tires - general information

1   Tubeless tires are used as standard equipment on this vehicle. Unlike motorcycle tires, they run at very low air pressures and are completely unsuited for use on pavement. Inflating ATV tires to excessive pressures will rupture them, ruining the tire.
2   The force required to break the seal between the rim and the bead of the tire is substantial, much more than required for motorcycle tires, and is beyond the capabilities of an individual working with normal tire irons or even a normal bead breaker. A special bead breaker is required for ATV tires; it produces a great deal of force and concentrates it in a relatively small area.
3   Also, repair of the punctured tire and replacement on the wheel rim requires special tools, skills and experience that the average do-it-yourselfer lacks.
4   For these reasons, if a puncture or flat occurs with an ATV tire, the wheel should be removed from the vehicle and taken to a dealer service department or a repair shop for repair or replacement of the tire. The illustrations in Chapter 6A can be used as a guide to tire replacement in an emergency, provided the necessary bead breaker is available (see page 6A-19).

12   Wheel hubs - removal and installation

Removal

Refer to illustrations 12.3a and 12.3b
1   The hubs on wheels with disc brakes are removed together with the brake discs (see Section 4). This section applies to the rear wheel hubs.
2   Refer to Section 10 and remove the wheel(s).
3   Bend back the cotter pin and pull it out of the hub nut **(see illustrations)**.
4   Unscrew the hub nut, remove the washer and pull the hub off the axle shaft.

Installation

5   Installation is the reverse of the removal steps, with the following additions:

   a) *Lubricate the axle shaft and hub splines with multi-purpose grease.*
   b) *Tighten the hub nut to the torque listed in this Chapter's Specifications. If necessary, tighten it an additional amount to align the cotter pin slots. Don't loosen the nut to align the slots.*
   c) *Install a new cotter pin and bend it to secure the nut.*

Chapter 7 Part A
Bodywork and frame (Bayou models)

Contents

	Section
Cargo racks - removal and installation	3
Frame - general information, inspection and repair	8
Front fender and side covers - removal and installation	5
Fuel tank covers - removal and installation	4

	Section
General information	1
Rear fender - removal and installation	6
Seat - removal and installation	2
Skidplates and footpegs - removal and installation	7

1 General information

This Chapter covers the procedures necessary to remove and install the fenders and other body parts. Since many service and repair operations on these vehicles require removal of the fenders and/or other body parts, the procedures are grouped here and referred to from other Chapters.

In the case of damage to the fenders or other body parts, it is usually necessary to remove the broken component and replace it with a new (or used) one. The material that the fenders and other plastic body parts is composed of doesn't lend itself to conventional repair techniques. There are, however, some shops that specialize in "plastic welding", so it would be advantageous to check around first before throwing the damaged part away.

Note: *When attempting to remove any body panel, first study the panel closely, noting any fasteners and associated fittings, to be sure of returning everything to its correct place on installation. In most cases, the aid of an assistant will be required when removing panels, to help avoid damaging the surface. Once the visible fasteners have been removed, try to lift off the panel as described but DO NOT FORCE the panel - if it will not release, check that all fasteners have been removed and try again. Where a panel engages another by means of lugs and grommets, be careful not to break the lugs or to damage the bodywork. Remember that a few moments of patience at this stage will save you a lot of money in replacing broken panels!*

2 Seat - removal and installation

Refer to illustrations 2.1, 2.2 and 2.3

1   Lift the seat latch **(see illustration)** and lift the back end of the seat.

2   Disengage the front end of the seat from the bracket **(see illustration)** and lift the seat off the vehicle.

3   Installation is the reverse of removal. Position the seat stopper posts in their holes **(see illustration)**.

2.1 Release the seat latch . . .

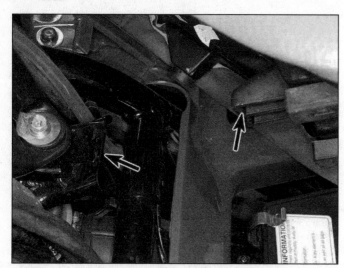

2.2 . . . lift the back end of the seat and disengage the hook at the front from the bracket (arrows)

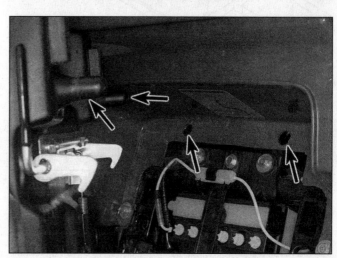

2.3 Fit the stopper posts into their holes

7A

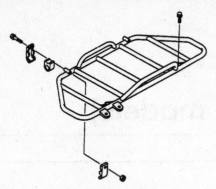

3.1a Front cargo rack - all Bayou 220, 1986 and 1987 Bayou 300 2WD models

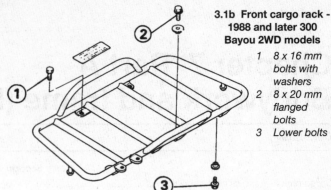

3.1b Front cargo rack - 1988 and later 300 Bayou 2WD models

1   8 x 16 mm bolts with washers
2   8 x 20 mm flanged bolts
3   Lower bolts

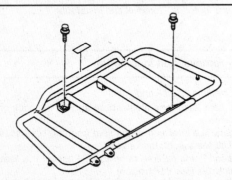

3.1c Front cargo rack - 300 Bayou 4WD models

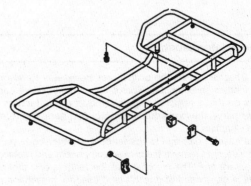

3.1d Rear cargo rack - all Bayou 220, 1986-1987 Bayou 300 2WD models

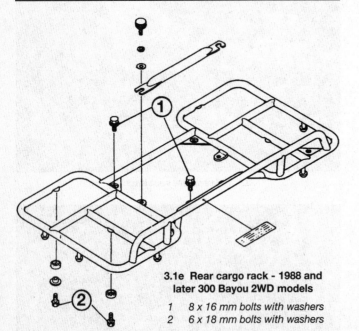

3.1e Rear cargo rack - 1988 and later 300 Bayou 2WD models

1   8 x 16 mm bolts with washers
2   6 x 18 mm bolts with washers

3   Cargo racks - removal and installation

Refer to illustrations 3.1a through 3.1f

1   The front and rear cargo racks are secured by bolts **(see illustrations)**.
2   To remove a cargo rack, unscrew the bolts. Note the bolt lengths and the locations of any collars.

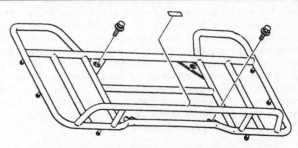

3.1f Rear cargo rack - Bayou 300 4WD models

3   Lift off the rack and place the bolts back in their holes in the rack. Tie them into position with rubber bands or wire so they can be reinstalled in their original locations.
4   Installation is the reverse of the removal steps.

4   Fuel tank covers - removal and installation

Refer to illustrations 4.2a through 4.2g, 4.3a and 4.3b

1   All models have front and rear fuel tank covers, secured by screws. Bayou 300 2WD models also have a top cover.
2   Remove the front cover screws (and collars if equipped) **(see illustrations)**. On 300 4WD models, unhook the plastic tabs **(see illustrations)**. Take the cover off.
3   To remove the rear cover, remove the seat (Section 2). Remove the screws and disengage the tabs **(see illustrations 4.2a through 4.2d and the accompanying illustrations)**.
4   Installation is the reverse of the removal steps.

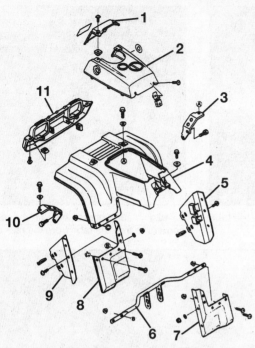

4.2a Front bodywork - Bayou 220 models

1	Fuel tank front cover	7	Fender flap
2	Fuel tank rear cover	8	Fender flap
3	Fender bracket	9	Side cover
4	Front fender	10	Fender bracket
5	Side cover	11	Headlight trim
6	Fender bracket		

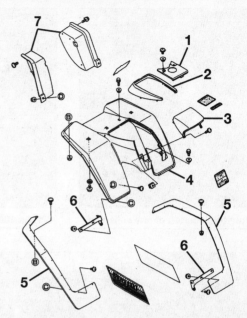

4.2b Front bodywork - 1986 and 1987 Bayou 300 models

1	Fuel tank top cover	5	Fender flap
2	Fuel tank front cover	6	Fender bracket
3	Fuel tank rear cover	7	Side covers
4	Front fender		

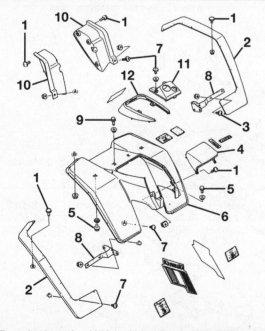

4.2c Front bodywork - 1988 and later Bayou 300 2WD models

1	6 x14 mm screws	7	6 x 18 mm black screws
2	Fender flaps	8	Fender bracket
3	6 x 18 mm black screw	9	8 x 20 mm flanged bolt
4	Fuel tank rear cover	10	Side cover
5	6 x 16 mm flanged bolts	11	Fuel tank top cover
6	Front fender	12	Fuel tank front cover

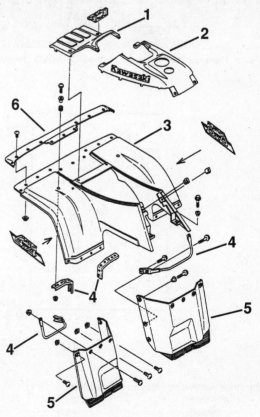

4.2d Front bodywork - Bayou 300 4WD models

1	Fuel tank front cover	4	Fender brackets
2	Fuel tank rear cover	5	Fender flap
3	Front fender	6	Fender trim

7A

4.2e Note the location of any collars in bolt holes

4.2f On 300 4WD models, unhook the tabs from the slots . . .

4.2g . . . and press down on the rear corners to free the tabs from the rear cover

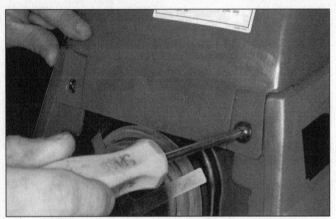

4.3a Remove the top cover screws (300 4WD shown) . . .

4.3b . . . and the retaining clips

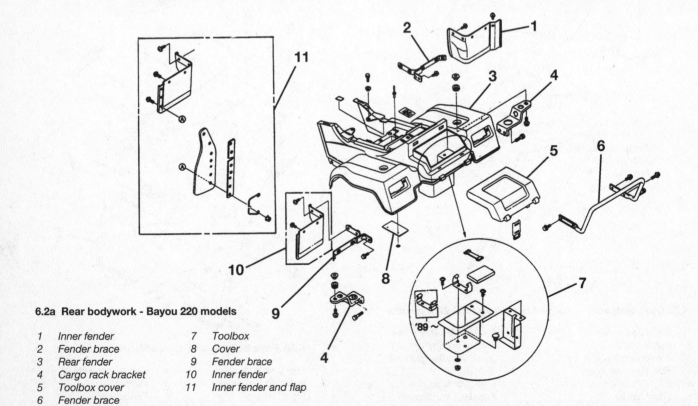

6.2a Rear bodywork - Bayou 220 models

1	Inner fender	7	Toolbox
2	Fender brace	8	Cover
3	Rear fender	9	Fender brace
4	Cargo rack bracket	10	Inner fender
5	Toolbox cover	11	Inner fender and flap
6	Fender brace		

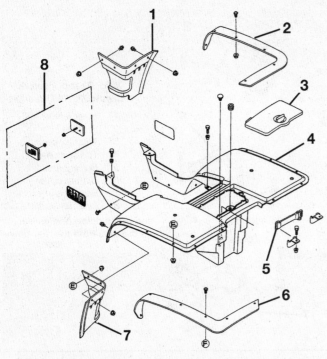

6.2b Rear bodywork - 1986 and 1987 Bayou 300 models

1	Inner fender	5	Battery strap
2	Fender flap	6	Fender flap
3	Toolbox cover	7	Inner fender
4	Rear fender	8	Reflectors (Canadian models)

5 Front fender and side covers - removal and installation

1   The front fender is a one-piece unit that spans the front of the vehicle and covers both front tires. A separate flap is attached to each side of the center unit.

2   Remove the cargo rack mounting bolts and lift the cargo rack off, taking care not to scratch the plastic fender (Section 3).

3   Disconnect the headlight electrical connectors, located beneath the fender.

4   Remove the seat and fuel tank covers (Sections 2 and 4).

5   Remove the side cover screws and nuts and take the side covers out from under the fender.

6   Remove the fender mounting bolts and screws and lift the fender off the vehicle **(see illustrations 4.2a through 4.2d)**. Have an assistant support one side if necessary, so the fender can be lifted off without scratching it. Tilt the fender forward and lift it off.

7   Installation is the reverse of removal.

6 Rear fender - removal and installation

Refer to illustrations 6.2a, 6.2b, 6.2c and 6.2d

1   Remove the seat and rear cargo rack (Sections 2 and 3).

2   Remove the fender bolts, nuts and screws **(see illustrations)**.

3   If necessary, remove the fender flaps.

4   Installation is the reverse of removal.

6.2c Rear bodywork - 1988 and later Bayou 300 2WD models

1   Inner fender (1990 and later models)
2   Inner fender (1988 and 1989 models)
3   6 x 18 mm black screws
4   6 x 14 mm screws
5   Reflector (Canadian models)
6   Fender brace
7   Fender flap
8   Battery retainer
9   Battery cover
10   6 x 20 mm bolts with washers
11   Battery carrier
12   Toolbox cover
13   6 x 18 mm bolts with washers
14   Inner fender (1990 and later models)
15   Inner fender (1988 and 1989 models)
16   Rear fender

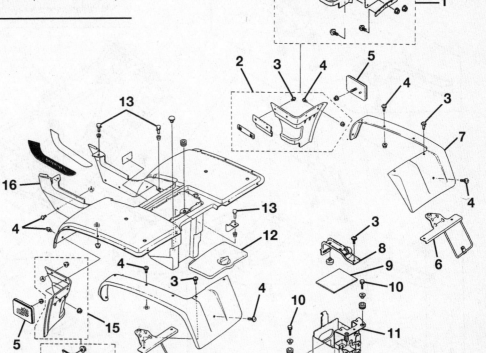

7A

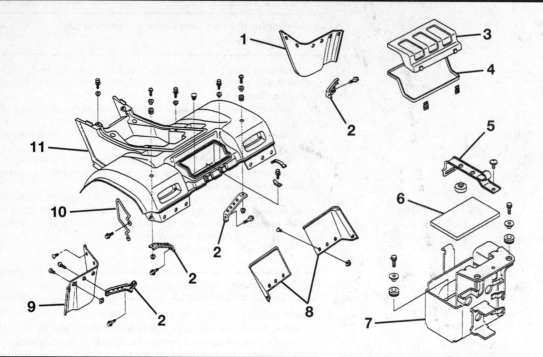

**6.2d Rear bodywork -
Bayou 300 4WD models**

1 Inner fender
2 Bracket
3 Toolbox cover
4 Toolbox seal
5 Battery retainer
6 Battery cover
7 Battery carrier
8 Inner fenders
9 Inner fender
10 Brace
11 Rear fender

7   Skidplates and footpegs - removal and installation

Refer to illustrations 7.1a, 7.1b, 7.1c and 7.1d
1   Skid plates and footpegs are secured to the frame by bolts. To remove a skid plate or footpeg, unscrew its bolts and take it out **(see illustrations)**.
2   Installation is the reverse of the removal steps.

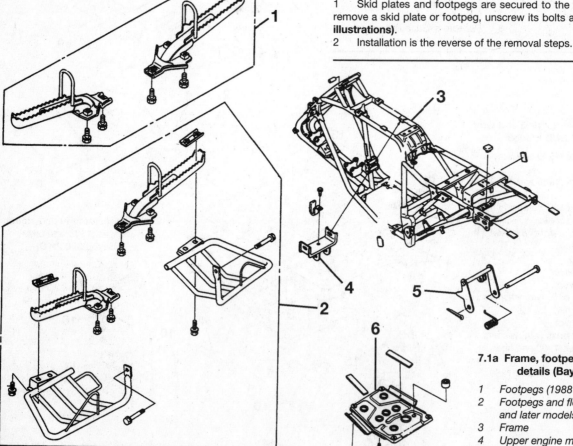

**7.1a Frame, footpeg and skidplate
details (Bayou 220)**

1 Footpegs (1988 and 1989 models)
*2 Footpegs and floorboards (1990
and later models)*
3 Frame
4 Upper engine mounting bracket
5 Seat latch
6 Skidplate

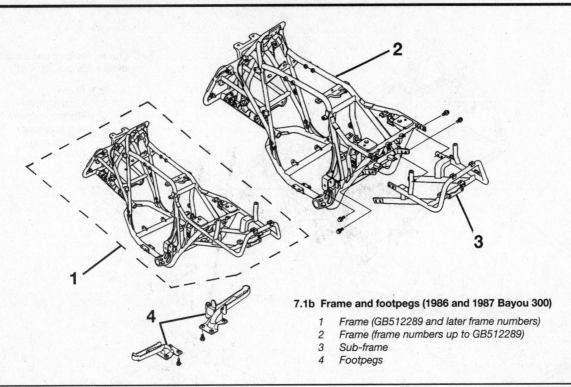

7.1b Frame and footpegs (1986 and 1987 Bayou 300)

1   *Frame (GB512289 and later frame numbers)*
2   *Frame (frame numbers up to GB512289)*
3   *Sub-frame*
4   *Footpegs*

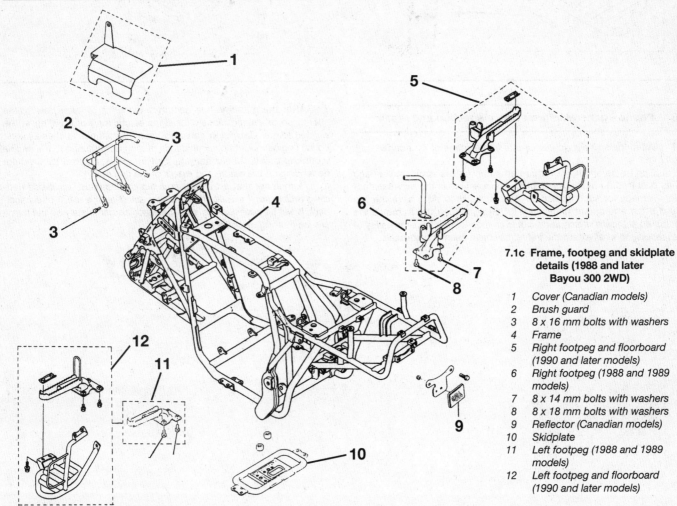

7.1c Frame, footpeg and skidplate details (1988 and later Bayou 300 2WD)

1   *Cover (Canadian models)*
2   *Brush guard*
3   *8 x 16 mm bolts with washers*
4   *Frame*
5   *Right footpeg and floorboard (1990 and later models)*
6   *Right footpeg (1988 and 1989 models)*
7   *8 x 14 mm bolts with washers*
8   *8 x 18 mm bolts with washers*
9   *Reflector (Canadian models)*
10 *Skidplate*
11 *Left footpeg (1988 and 1989 models)*
12 *Left footpeg and floorboard (1990 and later models)*

7A

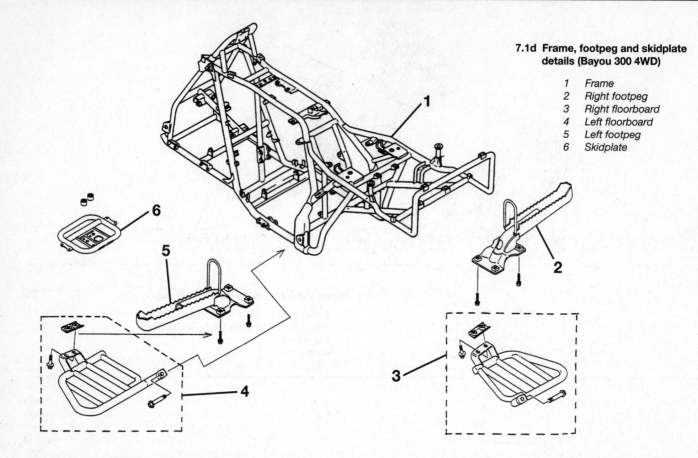

7.1d Frame, footpeg and skidplate details (Bayou 300 4WD)

1   *Frame*
2   *Right footpeg*
3   *Right floorboard*
4   *Left floorboard*
5   *Left footpeg*
6   *Skidplate*

8   Frame - general information, inspection and repair

1   All models use a double-cradle frame made of cylindrical steel tubing.
2   The frame shouldn't require attention unless accident damage has occurred. In most cases, frame replacement is the only satisfactory remedy for such damage. A few frame specialists have the jigs and other equipment necessary for straightening the frame to the required standard of accuracy, but even then there is no simple way of assessing to what extent the frame may have been overstressed.

3   After the machine has accumulated a lot of miles, the frame should be examined closely for signs of cracking or splitting at the welded joints. Corrosion can also cause weakness at these joints. Loose engine mount bolts can cause ovaling or fracturing to the engine mounting points. Minor damage can often be repaired by welding, depending on the nature and extent of the damage.
4   Remember that a frame that is out of alignment will cause handling problems. If misalignment is suspected as the result of an accident, it will be necessary to strip the machine completely so the frame can be thoroughly checked.

Chapter 7 Part B
Bodywork and frame (Prairie models)

Contents

	Section
Cargo racks and brush guards - removal and installation	3
Frame - general information, inspection and repair	8
Front fender and side covers - removal and installation	5
Fuel tank cover - removal and installation	4

	Section
General information	1
Rear fender - removal and installation	6
Seat - removal and installation	2
Skidplates and floorboards - removal and installation	7

1 General information

This Chapter covers the procedures necessary to remove and install the fenders and other body parts. Since many service and repair operations on these vehicles require removal of the fenders and/or other body parts, the procedures are grouped here and referred to from other Chapters.

In the case of damage to the fenders or other body parts, it is usually necessary to remove the broken component and replace it with a new (or used) one. The material that the fenders and other plastic body parts is composed of doesn't lend itself to conventional repair techniques. There are, however, some shops that specialize in "plastic welding", so it would be advantageous to check around first before throwing the damaged part away.

Note: *When attempting to remove any body panel, first study the panel closely, noting any fasteners and associated fittings, to be sure of returning everything to its correct place on installation. In most cases, the aid of an assistant will be required when removing panels, to help avoid damaging the surface. Once the visible fasteners have been removed, try to lift off the panel as described but DO NOT FORCE the panel - if it will not release, check that all fasteners have been removed and try again. Where a panel engages another by means of lugs and grommets, be careful not to break the lugs or to damage the bodywork. Remember that a few moments of patience at this stage will save you a lot of money in replacing broken panels!*

2 Seat - removal and installation

Refer to illustrations 2.1a and 2.1b

1 Pull the cable handle to unhook the seat latches **(see illustrations)**.

2 Disengage the front end of the seat from the bracket and lift the seat off the vehicle.

3 Installation is the reverse of removal. Position the tab on the front end of the seat under the catch at the rear of the fuel tank.

2.1a Pull the cable handle . . .

2.1b . . . to disengage the seat latches

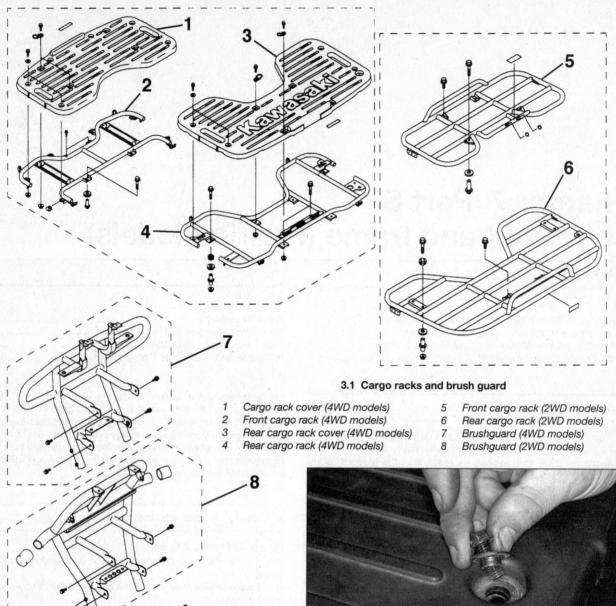

3.1 Cargo racks and brush guard

1	Cargo rack cover (4WD models)	5	Front cargo rack (2WD models)
2	Front cargo rack (4WD models)	6	Rear cargo rack (2WD models)
3	Rear cargo rack cover (4WD models)	7	Brushguard (4WD models)
4	Rear cargo rack (4WD models)	8	Brushguard (2WD models)

3.2a Don't forget to reinstall the bolt collars

3.2b Some of the cargo rack nuts are this removable clip design

3   Cargo racks and brush guards - removal and installation

Refer to illustrations 3.1, 3.2a and 3.2b

1   The brush guard and the front and rear cargo racks are secured by bolts **(see illustration)**.

2   To remove a brush guard or cargo rack, unscrew the bolts. Note the bolt lengths and the locations of any collars and nuts **(see illustrations)**.

3   Lift off the rack and place the bolts back in their holes in the rack. Tie them into position with rubber bands or wire so they can be reinstalled in their original locations.

4   Installation is the reverse of the removal steps.

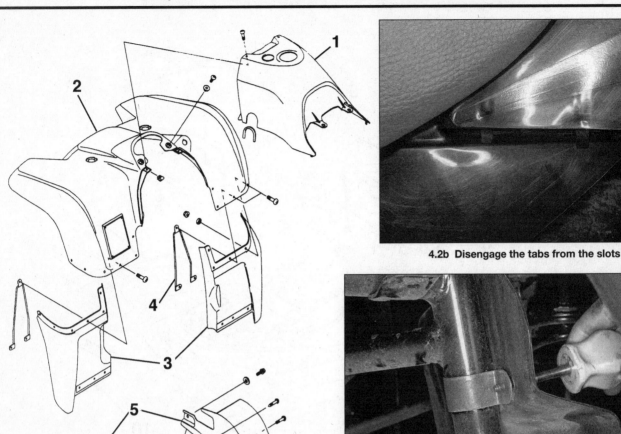

4.2b Disengage the tabs from the slots

5.5a Semi-circular clamps secure the side covers to the frame

4.2a Front bodywork (Prairie models)

1	Fuel tank cover	2	Front fender	4	Fender brace
		3	Fender flaps	5	Side covers

4   Fuel tank cover - removal and installation

Refer to illustrations 4.2a and 4.2b

1   Unscrew the cap from the fuel tank.
2   Remove the cover screws (and collars if equipped) **(see illustration)**. Unhook the plastic tabs **(see illustration)**. Take the cover off.
3   Put the cap back on the fuel tank right away. Don't leave it uncapped.
4   Installation is the reverse of the removal steps.

5   Front fender and side covers - removal and installation

Refer to illustrations 5.5a and 5.5b

1   The front fender is a one-piece unit that spans the front of the vehicle and covers both front tires. A separate flap is attached to each

5.5b Lift the side cover over the tire and remove it to the rear

side of the center unit.
2   Remove the cargo rack mounting bolts and lift the cargo rack off, taking care not to scratch the plastic fender (Section 3).
3   Disconnect the headlight electrical connectors, located beneath the fender.
4   Remove the seat and fuel tank cover (Sections 2 and 4).
5   Remove the side cover screws, nuts and clamps and take the side covers out from under the fender **(see illustration 4.2a and the accompanying illustrations)**.

7B

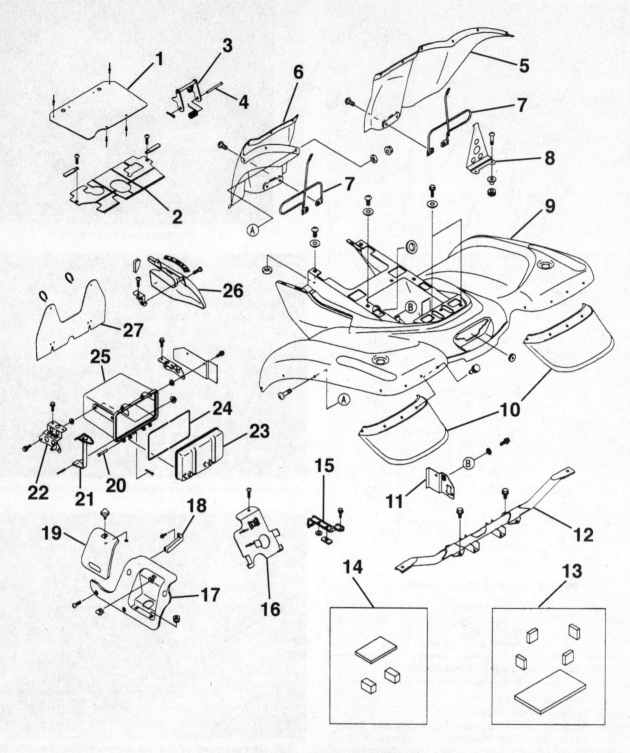

6.2a Rear bodywork (Prairie models)

1	Engine front cover	9	Rear fender	14	Battery dampers (except
2	Engine cover	10	Fender flap		US models)
3	Seat latch	11	Electrical component	15	Battery retainer
4	Pin		bracket	16	Engine cover
5	Fender flap	12	Rear fender stay	17	Engine cover
6	Fender flap	13	Battery dampers (US	18	Engine cover bracket
7	Brace		models)	19	Engine cover
8	Brace			20	Pin

21	Toolbox band
22	Toolbox bracket
23	Toolbox cover
24	Toolbox gasket
25	Toolbox
26	Shift lever cover
27	Cover

6.2b Remove the brace from the battery holder . . .

6.2c and remove the collars from the grommets

6   Remove the fender mounting bolts and screws and lift the fender off the vehicle (see illustration 4.2a). Have an assistant support one side if necessary, so the fender can be lifted off without scratching it. Tilt the fender forward and lift it off.
7   Installation is the reverse of removal.

6   Rear fender - removal and installation

Refer to illustrations 6.2a, 6.2b and 6.2c
1   Remove the seat and rear cargo rack (Sections 2 and 3). Remove the battery (see Chapter 1).
2   Remove the fender bolts, nuts and screws (see illustrations).
3   If necessary, remove the fender flaps (see illustration 6.2a).
4   Installation is the reverse of removal.

7   Skidplates and floorboards - removal and installation

Refer to illustration 7.1
1   Skid plates and floorboards are secured to the frame by bolts. To remove a skid plate or floorboard, unscrew its bolts and take it out

(see illustration).
2   Installation is the reverse of the removal steps.

8   Frame - general information, inspection and repair

1   All models use a double-cradle frame made of cylindrical steel tubing (see illustration 7.1).
2   The frame shouldn't require attention unless accident damage has occurred. In most cases, frame replacement is the only satisfactory remedy for such damage. A few frame specialists have the jigs and other equipment necessary for straightening the frame to the required standard of accuracy, but even then there is no simple way of assessing to what extent the frame may have been overstressed.
3   After the machine has accumulated a lot of miles, the frame should be examined closely for signs of cracking or splitting at the welded joints. Corrosion can also cause weakness at these joints. Loose engine mount bolts can cause ovaling or fracturing to the engine mounting points. Minor damage can often be repaired by welding, depending on the nature and extent of the damage.
4   Remember that a frame that is out of alignment will cause handling problems. If misalignment is suspected as the result of an accident, it will be necessary to strip the machine completely so the frame can be thoroughly checked.

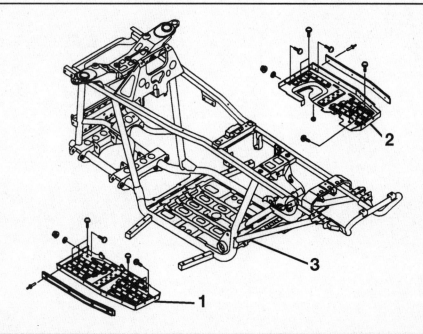

7.1 Floorboards and frame (Prairie models)

1   Left floorboard
2   Right floorboard
3   Frame

7B

Notes

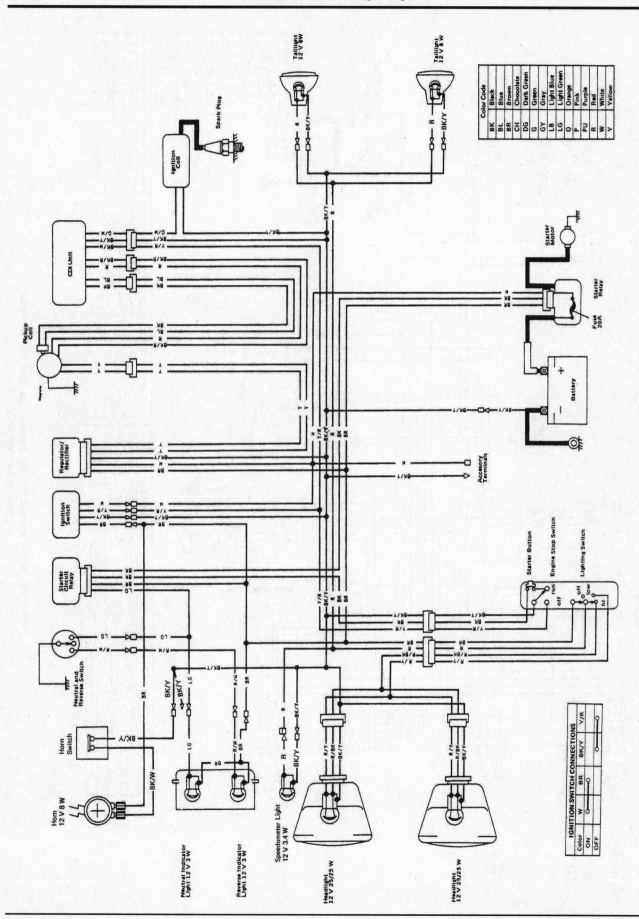

Wiring diagram – Bayou 220 (1988 through 1995 US, Canadian and UK models, 1988 through early 1995 (A8) European models)
(Horn: Australia only - Speedometer: Europe only)

Color Code	
BK	Black
BL	Blue
BR	Brown
CH	Chocolate
DG	Dark Green
G	Green
GY	Gray
LB	Light Blue
LG	Light Green
O	Orange
P	Pink
PU	Purple
R	Red
W	White
Y	Yellow

IGNITION SWITCH CONNECTIONS

Color	W	BR	BK/Y	Y/R
ON				
OFF				

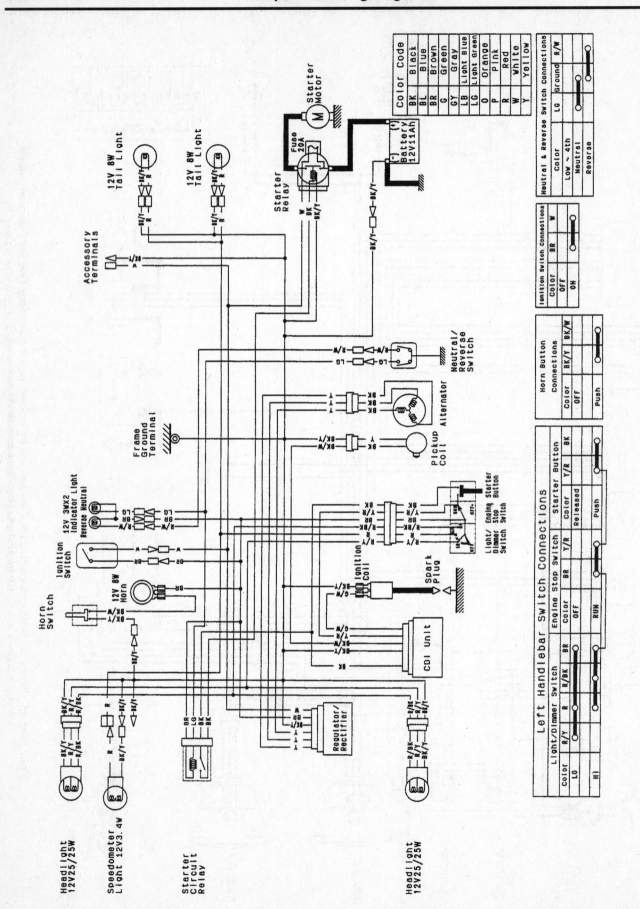

Wiring diagram – Bayou 220 (1996 and later US, Canada, Australia)
(Horn – Australia only)

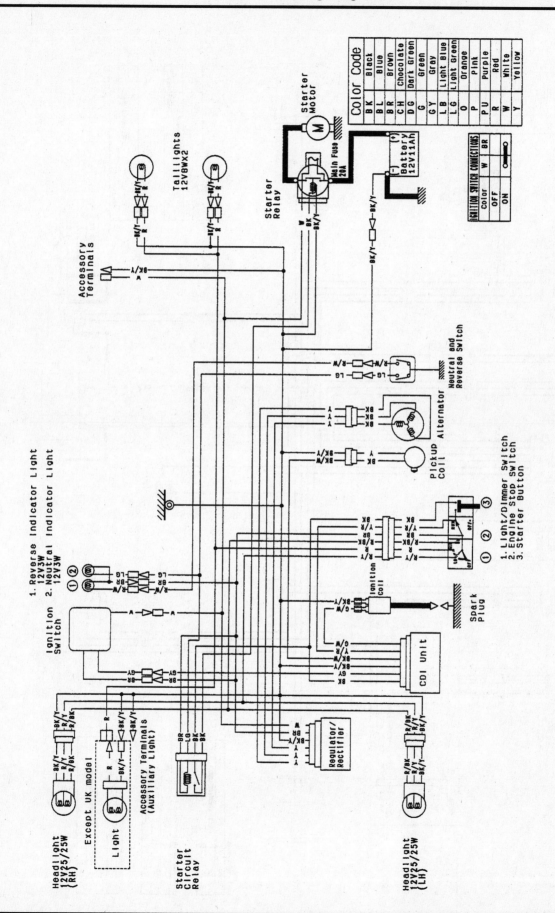

Wiring diagram – Bayou 220 (1996 and later UK models, late 1995 (A8A) and later European models)

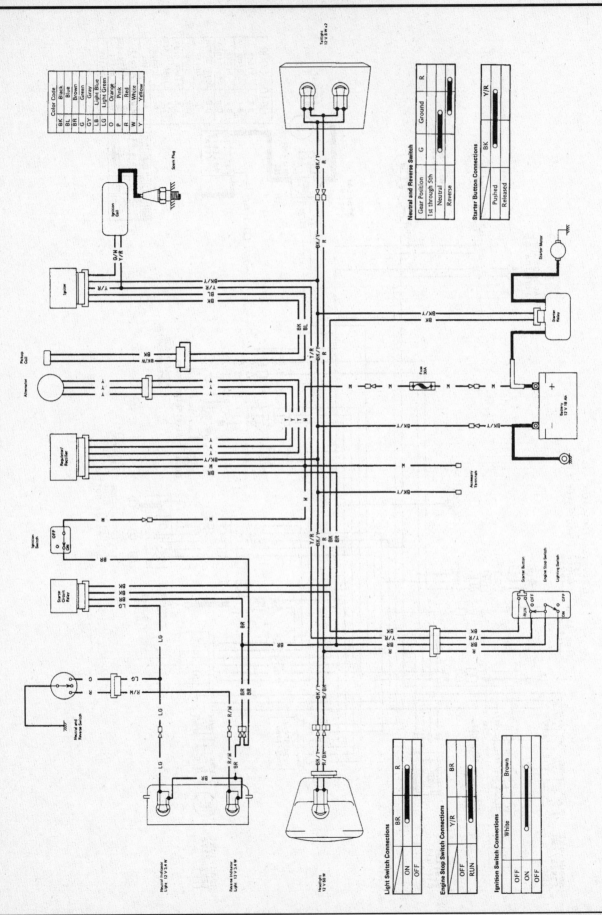

Wiring diagram – Bayou 300 (1986 and 1987 models)

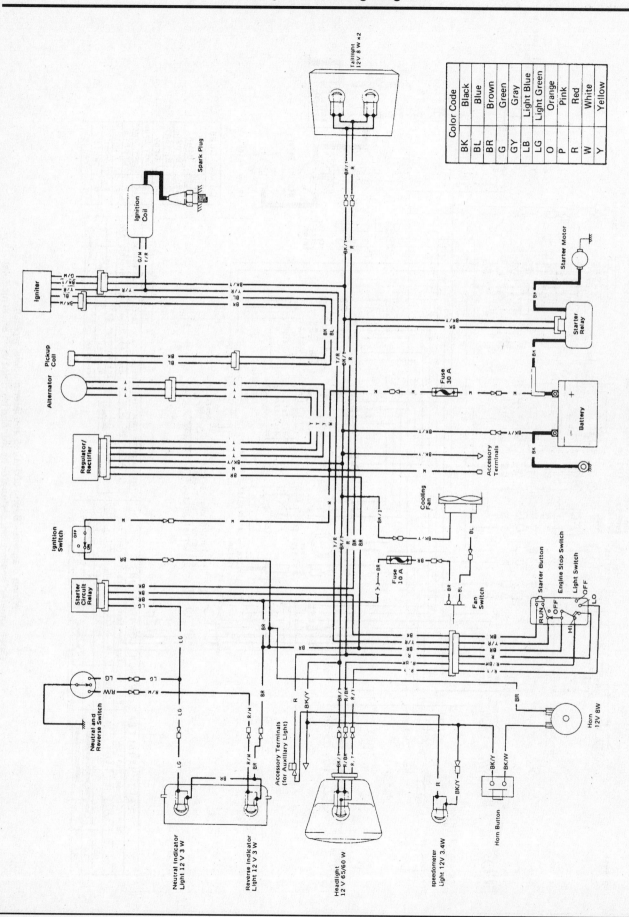

Wiring diagram - Bayou 300 (1988 through 1994 models)
(Speedometer, cooling fan, lights and horn not used on all models)

Color Code		
BK	Black	
BL	Blue	
BR	Brown	
G	Green	
GY	Gray	
LB	Light Blue	
LG	Light Green	
O	Orange	
P	Pink	
R	Red	
W	White	
Y	Yellow	

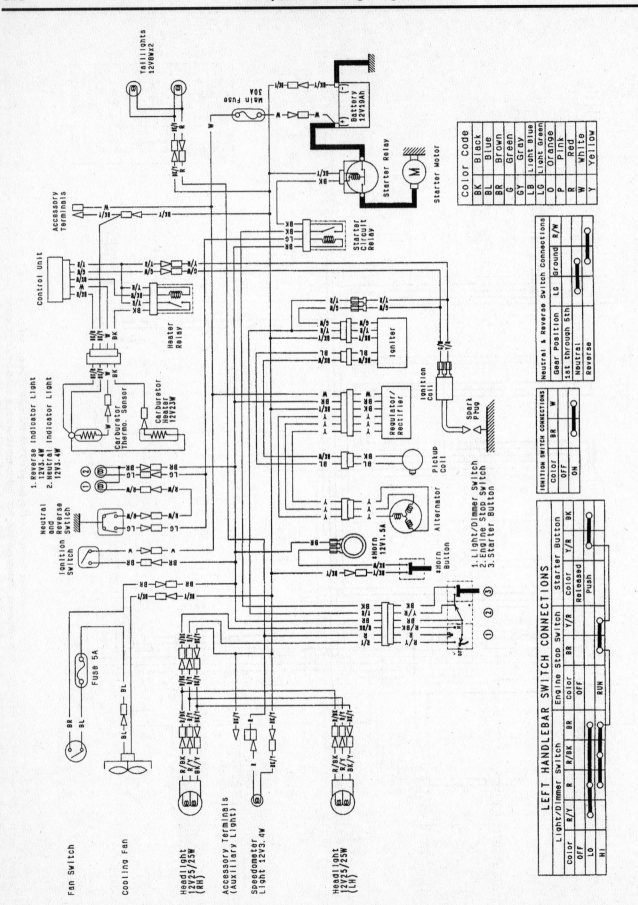

Wiring diagram – Bayou 300 (1995 and later models, typical)
(Speedometer, cooling fan, carburetor heater and horn not used on all models)

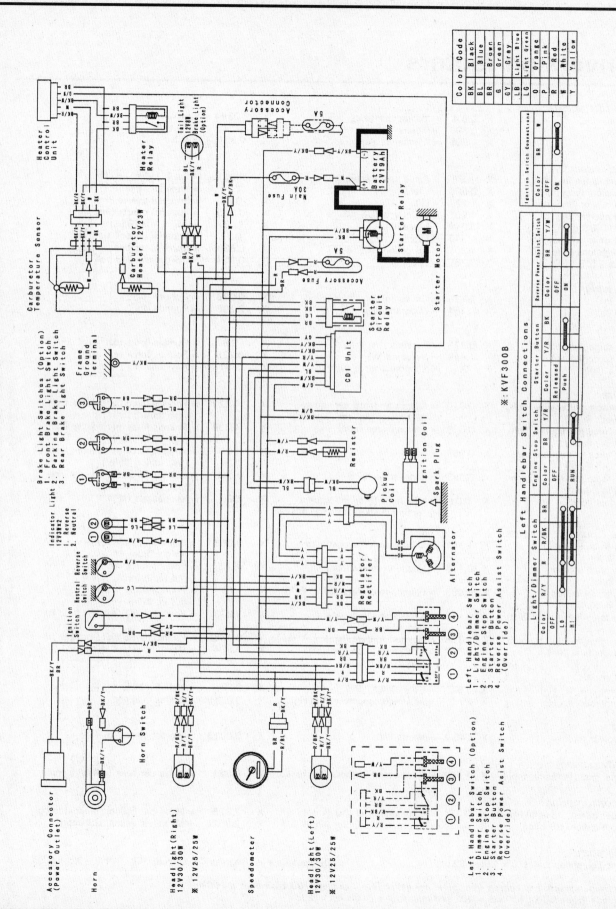

Wiring diagram – Prairie models
(Speedometer and horn not used on all models)

Conversion factors

Length (distance)

Inches (in)	X 25.4 = Millimeters (mm)	X 0.0394 = Inches (in)
Feet (ft)	X 0.305 = Meters (m)	X 3.281 = Feet (ft)
Miles	X 1.609 = Kilometers (km)	X 0.621 = Miles

Volume (capacity)

Cubic inches (cu in; in^3)	X 16.387 = Cubic centimeters (cc; cm^3)	X 0.061 = Cubic inches (cu in; in^3)
Imperial pints (Imp pt)	X 0.568 = Liters (l)	X 1.76 = Imperial pints (Imp pt)
Imperial quarts (Imp qt)	X 1.137 = Liters (l)	X 0.88 = Imperial quarts (Imp qt)
Imperial quarts (Imp qt)	X 1.201 = US quarts (US qt)	X 0.833 = Imperial quarts (Imp qt)
US quarts (US qt)	X 0.946 = Liters (l)	X 1.057 = US quarts (US qt)
Imperial gallons (Imp gal)	X 4.546 = Liters (l)	X 0.22 = Imperial gallons (Imp gal)
Imperial gallons (Imp gal)	X 1.201 = US gallons (US gal)	X 0.833 = Imperial gallons (Imp gal)
US gallons (US gal)	X 3.785 = Liters (l)	X 0.264 = US gallons (US gal)

Mass (weight)

Ounces (oz)	X 28.35 = Grams (g)	X 0.035 = Ounces (oz)
Pounds (lb)	X 0.454 = Kilograms (kg)	X 2.205 = Pounds (lb)

Force

Ounces-force (ozf; oz)	X 0.278 = Newtons (N)	X 3.6 = Ounces-force (ozf; oz)
Pounds-force (lbf; lb)	X 4.448 = Newtons (N)	X 0.225 = Pounds-force (lbf; lb)
Newtons (N)	X 0.1 = Kilograms-force (kgf; kg)	X 9.81 = Newtons (N)

Pressure

Pounds-force per square inch (psi; lbf/in^2; lb/in^2)	X 0.070 = Kilograms-force per square centimeter (kgf/cm^2; kg/cm^2)	X 14.223 = Pounds-force per square inch (psi; lbf/in^2; lb/in^2)
Pounds-force per square inch (psi; lbf/in^2; lb/in^2)	X 0.068 = Atmospheres (atm)	X 14.696 = Pounds-force per square inch (psi; lbf/in^2; lb/in^2)
Pounds-force per square inch (psi; lbf/in^2; lb/in^2)	X 0.069 = Bars	X 14.5 = Pounds-force per square inch (psi; lbf/in^2; lb/in^2)
Pounds-force per square inch (psi; lbf/in^2; lb/in^2)	X 6.895 = Kilopascals (kPa)	X 0.145 = Pounds-force per square inch (psi; lbf/in^2; lb/in^2)
Kilopascals (kPa)	X 0.01 = Kilograms-force per square centimeter (kgf/cm^2; kg/cm^2)	X 98.1 = Kilopascals (kPa)

Torque (moment of force)

Pounds-force inches (lbf in; lb in)	X 1.152 = Kilograms-force centimeter (kgf cm; kg cm)	X 0.868 = Pounds-force inches (lbf in; lb in)
Pounds-force inches (lbf in; lb in)	X 0.113 = Newton meters (Nm)	X 8.85 = Pounds-force inches (lbf in; lb in)
Pounds-force inches (lbf in; lb in)	X 0.083 = Pounds-force feet (lbf ft; lb ft)	X 12 = Pounds-force inches (lbf in; lb in)
Pounds-force feet (lbf ft; lb ft)	X 0.138 = Kilograms-force meters (kgf m; kg m)	X 7.233 = Pounds-force feet (lbf ft; lb ft)
Pounds-force feet (lbf ft; lb ft)	X 1.356 = Newton meters (Nm)	X 0.738 = Pounds-force feet (lbf ft; lb ft)
Newton meters (Nm)	X 0.102 = Kilograms-force meters (kgf m; kg m)	X 9.804 = Newton meters (Nm)

Vacuum

Inches mercury (in. Hg)	X 3.377 = Kilopascals (kPa)	X 0.2961 = Inches mercury
Inches mercury (in. Hg)	X 25.4 = Millimeters mercury (mm Hg)	X 0.0394 = Inches mercury

Power

Horsepower (hp)	X 745.7 = Watts (W)	X 0.0013 = Horsepower (hp)

Velocity (speed)

Miles per hour (miles/hr; mph)	X 1.609 = Kilometers per hour (km/hr; kph)	X 0.621 = Miles per hour (miles/hr; mph)

Fuel consumption*

Miles per gallon, Imperial (mpg)	X 0.354 = Kilometers per liter (km/l)	X 2.825 = Miles per gallon, Imperial (mpg)
Miles per gallon, US (mpg)	X 0.425 = Kilometers per liter (km/l)	X 2.352 = Miles per gallon, US (mpg)

Temperature

Degrees Fahrenheit = (°C x 1.8) + 32

Degrees Celsius (Degrees Centigrade; °C) = (°F - 32) x 0.56

*It is common practice to convert from miles per gallon (mpg) to liters/100 kilometers (l/100km), where mpg (Imperial) x l/100 km = 282 and mpg (US) x l/100 km = 235

DECIMALS to MILLIMETERS

Decimal	mm	Decimal	mm
0.001	0.0254	0.500	12.7000
0.002	0.0508	0.510	12.9540
0.003	0.0762	0.520	13.2080
0.004	0.1016	0.530	13.4620
0.005	0.1270	0.540	13.7160
0.006	0.1524	0.550	13.9700
0.007	0.1778	0.560	14.2240
0.008	0.2032	0.570	14.4780
0.009	0.2286	0.580	14.7320
		0.590	14.9860
0.010	0.2540		
0.020	0.5080		
0.030	0.7620		
0.040	1.0160	0.600	15.2400
0.050	1.2700	0.610	15.4940
0.060	1.5240	0.620	15.7480
0.070	1.7780	0.630	16.0020
0.080	2.0320	0.640	16.2560
0.090	2.2860	0.650	16.5100
		0.660	16.7640
0.100	2.5400	0.670	17.0180
0.110	2.7940	0.680	17.2720
0.120	3.0480	0.690	17.5260
0.130	3.3020		
0.140	3.5560		
0.150	3.8100		
0.160	4.0640	0.700	17.7800
0.170	4.3180	0.710	18.0340
0.180	4.5720	0.720	18.2880
0.190	4.8260	0.730	18.5420
		0.740	18.7960
0.200	5.0800	0.750	19.0500
0.210	5.3340	0.760	19.3040
0.220	5.5880	0.770	19.5580
0.230	5.8420	0.780	19.8120
0.240	6.0960	0.790	20.0660
0.250	6.3500		
0.260	6.6040		
0.270	6.8580	0.800	20.3200
0.280	7.1120	0.810	20.5740
0.290	7.3660	0.820	21.8280
		0.830	21.0820
0.300	7.6200	0.840	21.3360
0.310	7.8740	0.850	21.5900
0.320	8.1280	0.860	21.8440
0.330	8.3820	0.870	22.0980
0.340	8.6360	0.880	22.3520
0.350	8.8900	0.890	22.6060
0.360	9.1440		
0.370	9.3980		
0.380	9.6520		
0.390	9.9060		
		0.900	22.8600
0.400	10.1600	0.910	23.1140
0.410	10.4140	0.920	23.3680
0.420	10.6680	0.930	23.6220
0.430	10.9220	0.940	23.8760
0.440	11.1760	0.950	24.1300
0.450	11.4300	0.960	24.3840
0.460	11.6840	0.970	24.6380
0.470	11.9380	0.980	24.8920
0.480	12.1920	0.990	25.1460
0.490	12.4460	1.000	25.4000

FRACTIONS to DECIMALS to MILLIMETERS

Fraction	Decimal	mm	Fraction	Decimal	mm
1/64	0.0156	0.3969	33/64	0.5156	13.0969
1/32	0.0312	0.7938	17/32	0.5312	13.4938
3/64	0.0469	1.1906	35/64	0.5469	13.8906
1/16	0.0625	1.5875	9/16	0.5625	14.2875
5/64	0.0781	1.9844	37/64	0.5781	14.6844
3/32	0.0938	2.3812	19/32	0.5938	15.0812
7/64	0.1094	2.7781	39/64	0.6094	15.4781
1/8	0.1250	3.1750	5/8	0.6250	15.8750
9/64	0.1406	3.5719	41/64	0.6406	16.2719
5/32	0.1562	3.9688	21/32	0.6562	16.6688
11/64	0.1719	4.3656	43/64	0.6719	17.0656
3/16	0.1875	4.7625	11/16	0.6875	17.4625
13/64	0.2031	5.1594	45/64	0.7031	17.8594
7/32	0.2188	5.5562	23/32	0.7188	18.2562
15/64	0.2344	5.9531	47/64	0.7344	18.6531
1/4	0.2500	6.3500	3/4	0.7500	19.0500
17/64	0.2656	6.7469	49/64	0.7656	19.4469
9/32	0.2812	7.1438	25/32	0.7812	19.8438
19/64	0.2969	7.5406	51/64	0.7969	20.2406
5/16	0.3125	7.9375	13/16	0.8125	20.6375
21/64	0.3281	8.3344	53/64	0.8281	21.0344
11/32	0.3438	8.7312	27/32	0.8438	21.4312
23/64	0.3594	9.1281	55/64	0.8594	21.8281
3/8	0.3750	9.5250	7/8	0.8750	22.2250
25/64	0.3906	9.9219	57/64	0.8906	22.6219
13/32	0.4062	10.3188	29/32	0.9062	23.0188
27/64	0.4219	10.7156	59/64	0.9219	23.4156
7/16	0.4375	11.1125	15/16	0.9375	23.8125
29/64	0.4531	11.5094	61/64	0.9531	24.2094
15/32	0.4688	11.9062	31/32	0.9688	24.6062
31/64	0.4844	12.3031	63/64	0.9844	25.0031
1/2	0.5000	12.7000	1	1.0000	25.4000

8

Index

A

Air cleaner housing, removal and installation
Bayou models, 3A-8
Prairie models, 3B-6
Alternator stator coils and rotor, check and replacement
Bayou models, 4A-8
Prairie models, 4B-5

B

Balancer, crankshaft (Prairie models), 2B-25
Ball-joint replacement
Bayou 300 models, 5A-8
Prairie models, 5B-5
Battery
charging
Bayou models, 4A-3
Prairie models, 4B-3
inspection and maintenance
Bayou models, 4A-3
Prairie models, 4B-2
Bevel drive unit and output gear, removal, inspection and installation
Bayou (2WD) models, 5A-17
Prairie models, 5B-8
Bodywork and frame, Bayou models, 7A-1 through 7A-8
cargo racks, removal and installation, 7A-2
frame, general information, inspection and repair, 7A-8
front fender and side covers, removal and installation, 7A-5
fuel tank covers, removal and installation, 7A-2
rear fender, removal and installation, 7A-5
seat, removal and installation, 7A-1
skidplates and footpegs, removal and installation, 7A-6
Bodywork and frame, Prairie models, 7B-1 through 7B-6
cargo racks and brush guards, removal and installation, 7B-2
frame, general information, inspection and repair, 7B-5
front fender and side covers, removal and installation, 7B-3
fuel tank cover, removal and installation, 7B-3
rear fender, removal and installation, 7B-5
seat, removal and installation, 7B-1
skidplates and floorboards, removal and installation, 7B-5
Brake switch, check and replacement
Bayou models, 4A-6
Prairie models, 4B-3
Brakes, wheels and tires, Bayou models, 6A-1 through 6A-20
front brake calipers, removal, overhaul and installation, 6A-6
front brake discs, inspection, removal and installation, 6A-8
front brake master cylinder, removal, overhaul and installation, 6A-9
front brake pad replacement, 6A-5
front brakes and wheel bearings, removal, inspection and installation
220 models, 6A-2
1986 and 1987 300 models, 6A-4
general information, 6A-2

hoses and lines, inspection and replacement, 6A-13
pedal, levers and cables, removal and installation, 6A-14
rear drum brake(s), removal, inspection and installation, 6A-11
system bleeding, 6A-10
tires, general information, 6A-20
wheel hubs, removal and installation, 6A-20
wheels, inspection, removal and installation, 6A-18
Brakes, wheels and tires, Prairie models, 6B-1 through 6B-8
front brake calipers, removal, overhaul and installation, 6B-3
front brake discs, inspection, removal and installation, 6B-4
front brake master cylinder, removal, overhaul and installation, 6B-4
front brake pad replacement, 6B-2
general information, 6B-2
hoses and lines, inspection and replacement, 6B-6
pedal, levers and cables, removal and installation, 6B-6
rear drum brake, removal, inspection and installation, 6B-4
system bleeding, 6B-4
tires, general information, 6B-8
wheel hubs, removal and installation, 6B-8
wheels, inspection, removal and installation, 6B-7
Brush guards (Prairie models), removal and installation

C

Cam chain tensioner, removal and installation
Bayou models, 2A-10
Prairie models, 2B-6
Carburetor
disassembly, cleaning and inspection
Bayou models, 3A-5
Prairie models, 3B-4
overhaul, general information
Bayou models, 3A-3
Prairie models, 3B-3
reassembly and float height check
Bayou models, 3A-7
Prairie models, 3B-4
removal and installation
Bayou models, 3A-4
Prairie models, 3B-3
Carburetor heater (Prairie models), removal, inspection and installation, 3B-4
Cargo racks, removal and installation
Bayou models, 7A-2
Prairie models, 7B-2
CDI unit, check, removal and installation
Bayou models, 4A-12
Prairie models, 4B-6
Charging system
output test
Bayou models, 4A-8
Prairie models, 4B-5
testing, general information and precautions
Bayou models, 4A-7
Prairie models, 4B-5

Cooling fan (Bayou 300 [UK] models), check, removal and
installation, 4A-7
Crankcase components, inspection and servicing
    Bayou models, 2A-39
    Prairie models, 2B-21
Crankcase, disassembly and reassembly
    Bayou models, 2A-38
    Prairie models, 2B-19
Crankshaft and connecting rod, removal, inspection and
installation
    Bayou models, 2A-43
    Prairie models, 2B-25
Cylinder head and valves, disassembly, inspection and
reassembly
    Bayou models, 2A-17
    Prairie models, 2B-7
Cylinder head, decompression lever, camshaft and rocker arms,
removal, inspection and installation
    Bayou models, 2A-11
    Prairie models, 2B-6
Cylinder, removal, inspection and installation
    Bayou models, 2A-20
    Prairie models, 2B-7

E

Electrical troubleshooting
    Bayou models, 4A-3
    Prairie models, 4B-2
Engine, clutch and transmission, Bayou models,
2A-1 through 2A-44
    cam chain tensioner, removal and installation, 2A-10
    crankcase components, inspection and servicing, 2A-39
    crankcase, disassembly and reassembly, 2A-38
    crankshaft and connecting rod, removal, inspection and
        installation, 2A-43
    cylinder head and valves, disassembly, inspection and
        reassembly, 2A-17
    cylinder head, decompression lever, camshaft and rocker arms,
        removal, inspection and installation, 2A-11
    cylinder, removal, inspection and installation, 2A-20
    engine disassembly and reassembly, general information, 2A-10
    engine, removal and installation, 2A-9
    external shift mechanism, removal, inspection and
        installation, 2A-32
    oil screen and pump, removal, inspection and installation, 2A-33
    piston rings, installation, 2A-23
    piston, removal, inspection and installation, 2A-21
    primary clutch, removal, inspection and installation, 2A-26
    recoil starter, removal, inspection and installation, 2A-36
    recommended break-in procedure, 2A-44
    reverse shift mechanism and reverse-neutral switch, removal,
        inspection and installation, 2A-31
    secondary clutch and release mechanism, removal, inspection and
        installation, 2A-27
    transmission shafts, balancer shaft and shift drum, removal,
        inspection and installation, 2A-41
    valves/valve seats/valve guides, servicing, 2A-17
Engine, clutch and transmission, Prairie models,
2B-1 through 2B-26
    automatic transmission
        air ducts, removal and installation, 2B-8
        drive belt
            removal, inspection and installation, 2B-10
            width and play check, 2B-11
        general information, 2B-8
        outer cover and seal, removal, inspection and installation, 2B-9
        pulleys, disassembly, inspection and reassembly, 2B-13
        pulleys, inner cover and seal, removal and installation, 2B-11

    cam chain tensioner, removal and installation, 2B-6
    crankcase components, inspection and servicing, 2B-21
    crankcase, disassembly and reassembly, 2B-19
    crankshaft, connecting rod and balancer, removal, inspection and
        installation, 2B-25
    cylinder head and valves, disassembly, inspection and
        reassembly, 2B-7
    cylinder head, decompression lever, camshaft and rocker arms,
        removal, inspection and installation, 2B-6
    cylinder, piston and rings, removal, inspection and
        installation, 2B-7
    engine disassembly and reassembly, general information, 2B-6
    engine, removal and installation, 2B-4
    external oil pipe and oil cooler, removal and installation, 2B-7
    high-low and reverse gears, shafts and shift mechanism, removal,
        inspection and installation, 2B-22
    high-low and reverse shift mechanism, removal, inspection and
        installation, 2B-17
    oil pump, removal, inspection and installation, 2B-18
    recoil starter, removal, inspection and installation, 2B-19
    recommended break-in procedure, 2B-26
    shift lever, adjustment, 2B-17
    valves/valve seats/valve guides, servicing, 2B-6
Exhaust system, removal and installation
    Bayou models, 3A-10
    Prairie models, 3B-8
External shift mechanism (Bayou models), removal, inspection
and installation, 2A-32

F

Frame, general information, inspection and repair
    Bayou models, 7A-8
    Prairie models, 7B-5
Front brake calipers, removal, overhaul and installation
    Bayou models, 6A-6
    Prairie models, 6B-3
Front brake discs, inspection, removal and installation
    Bayou 220 models, 6A-8
    Prairie models, 6B-4
Front brake master cylinder, removal, overhaul and installation
    Bayou 220 models, 6A-9
    Prairie models, 6B-4
Front brakes and wheel bearings, removal, inspection and
installation, 6A-2
    Bayou 220 models, 6A-2
    Bayou 300 models (1986 and 1987), 6A-4
Front brakes, pad replacement
    Bayou models, 6A-5
    Prairie models, 6B-2
Front differential, removal, inspection and installation
    Bayou models, 5A-16
    Prairie models, 5B-8
Front driveaxle (4WD), boot replacement and CV joint overhaul
    Bayou models, 5A-12
    Prairie models, 5B-7
Front driveaxles (4WD models), removal and installation
    Bayou models, 5A-12
    Prairie models, 5B-6
Front driveshaft, removal, inspection and installation
    Bayou models, 5A-15
    Prairie models, 5B-7
Front drum brakes and wheel bearings, removal, inspection and
installation
    Bayou 220 models, 6A-2
    Bayou 300 models, 6A-4
Front fender and side covers, removal and installation
    Bayou models, 7A-5
    Prairie models, 7B-3

Front shock absorbers, removal and installation
Bayou models, 5A-9
Prairie models, 5B-5
Front suspension arms, removal, inspection, and installation
Bayou models, 5A-9
Prairie models, 5B-5
Fuel and exhaust systems, Bayou models, 3A-1 through 3A-10
air cleaner housing, removal and installation, 3A-8
carburetor
disassembly, cleaning and inspection, 3A-5
overhaul, general information, 3A-3
reassembly and float height check, 3A-7
removal and installation, 3A-4
fuel level gauge (1988 and later), removal, inspection and
installation, 3A-3
fuel level, check and adjustment, 3A-8
fuel tank
and gauge, removal and installation, 3A-2
cleaning and repair, 3A-3
idle fuel/air mixture adjustment, 3A-3
throttle and choke cables, removal, installation and
adjustment, 3A-9
Fuel and exhaust systems, Prairie models, 3B-1 through 3B-8
air cleaner duct and housing, removal and installation, 3B-6
carburetor
disassembly, cleaning and inspection, 3B-4
overhaul, general information, 3B-3
reassembly and float height check, 3B-4
removal and installation, 3B-3
carburetor heater, removal, inspection and installation, 3B-4
fuel level gauge, removal, inspection and installation, 3B-2
fuel level, check and adjustment, 3B-4
fuel tank
and gauge, removal and installation, 3B-2
cleaning and repair, 3B-2
idle fuel/air mixture adjustment, 3B-2
throttle and choke cables, removal, installation and
adjustment, 3B-6
Fuel tank cover, removal and installation
Bayou models, 7A-2
Prairie models, 7B-3
Fuses, check and replacement
Bayou models, 4A-4
Prairie models, 4B-3

G

**Gear position switches, check and replacement
(Prairie models), 4B-5**
General specifications, 0-8

H

Handlebar switches
check
Bayou models, 4A-7
Prairie models, 4B-4
removal and installation
Bayou models, 4A-7
Prairie models, 4B-5
Handlebars, removal, inspection and installation
Bayou models, 5A-2
Prairie models, 5B-2
Headlight aim, check and adjustment
Bayou models, 4A-5
Prairie models, 4B-3
Headlight bulb, replacement
Bayou models, 4A-5
Prairie models, 4B-3

**High-low and reverse gears, shafts and shift mechanism, removal,
inspection and installation, Prairie models, 2B-22**
**High-low and reverse shift mechanism, removal, inspection and
installation, Prairie models, 2B-17**

I

Identification numbers, 0-6
Idle fuel/air mixture adjustment
Bayou models, 3A-3
Prairie models, 3B-2
**Ignition and electrical systems, Bayou models,
4A-1 through 4A-14**
alternator stator coils and rotor, check and replacement, 4A-8
battery
charging, 4A-3
inspection and maintenance, 4A-3
brake switch, check and replacement, 4A-6
CDI unit, check, removal and installation, 4A-12
charging system
output test, 4A-8
testing, general information and precautions, 4A-7
cooling fan (UK 300 models), check, removal and installation, 4A-7
electrical troubleshooting, 4A-3
fuse, check and replacement, 4A-3
handlebar switches
check, 4A-7
removal and installation, 4A-7
headlight aim, check and adjustment, 4A-5
headlight bulb, replacement, 4A-5
ignition coil, check, removal and installation, 4A-11
ignition main (key) switch, check and replacement, 4A-7
ignition system, check, 4A-10
ignition timing, general information and check, 4A-12
indicator bulbs, replacement, 4A-6
lighting system, check, 4A-4
pick-up and exciter coils, check and replacement, 4A-11
regulator/rectifier, check and replacement, 4A-10
starter circuit, check and component replacement, 4A-12
starter drive, removal, inspection and installation, 4A-13
starter motor, removal and installation, 4A-13
tail light and brake light bulbs, replacement, 4A-6
Ignition and electrical systems, Prairie models, 4B-1 through 4B-8
alternator stator coils and rotor, check and replacement, 4B-5
battery
charging, 4B-3
inspection and maintenance, 4B-2
brake switch, check and replacement, 4B-3
CDI unit, check, removal and installation, 4B-6
charging system
output test, 4B-5
testing, general information and precautions, 4B-5
electrical troubleshooting, 4B-2
fuses, check and replacement, 4B-3
gear position switches, check and replacement, 4B-5
handlebar switches
check, 4B-4
removal and installation, 4B-5
headlight aim, check and adjustment, 4B-3
headlight bulb, replacement, 4B-3
ignition coil, check, removal and installation, 4B-6
ignition main (key) switch, check and replacement, 4B-4
ignition system, check, 4B-6
ignition timing, general information and check, 4B-7
indicator and speedometer bulbs, replacement, 4B-4
lighting system, check, 4B-3
pick-up coil, check and replacement, 4B-6
regulator/rectifier, check and replacement, 4B-6
speedometer and cable, removal and installation, 4B-7

starter circuit, check and component replacement, 4B-7
starter drive, removal, inspection and installation, 4B-7
starter motor, removal and installation, 4B-7
tail light and brake light bulbs, replacement, 4B-3
Ignition coil, check, removal and installation
Bayou models, 4A-11
Prairie models, 4B-6
Ignition main (key) switch, check and replacement
Bayou models, 4A-7
Prairie models, 4B-4
Ignition system, check
Bayou models, 4A-10
Prairie models, 4B-6
Ignition timing, general information and check
Bayou models, 4A-12
Prairie models, 4B-7
Indicator bulbs, replacement
Bayou models, 4A-5
Prairie models, 4B-4

L

Lighting system, check
Bayou models, 4A-4
Prairie models, 4B-3

O

Oil cooler, removal and installation (Prairie models), 2B-7
Oil pump, removal, inspection and installation
Bayou models, 2A-33
Prairie models, 2B-18
Oil screen and pump, removal, inspection and installation

P

**Pick-up and exciter coils, check and replacement,
Bayou models, 4A-11**
Pick-up coil, check and replacement, Prairie models, 4B-6
**Primary clutch, removal, inspection and installation, Bayou
models, 2A-26**

R

Rear axle, removal, inspection and installation, 5A-20
Bayou models, 5A-21
Prairie models, 5B-10
Rear differential, removal, inspection and installation
Bayou models, 5A-21
Prairie models, 5B-12
Rear driveshaft, removal, inspection and installation
Bayou models, 5A-20
Prairie models, 5B-11
Rear drum brake(s), removal, inspection and installation
Bayou 220 models, 6A-11
Prairie models, 6B-4
Rear fender, removal and installation
Prairie models, 7B-5
bodywork and frame Bayou models, 7A-5
Rear shock absorber, removal and installation
Bayou models, 5A-9
Prairie models, 5B-6
Recoil starter, removal, inspection and installation
Bayou models, 2A-36
Prairie models, 2B-19
Regulator/rectifier, check and replacement
Bayou models, 4A-10
Prairie models, 4B-6

S

Safety first!, 0-14
Seat, removal and installation
Bayou models, 7A-1
Prairie models, 7B-1
**Secondary clutch and release mechanism, removal, inspection
and installation (Bayou models), 2A-27**
Shift lever, adjustment (Prairie models), 2B-17
Skidplates, removal and installation
Bayou models, 7A-6
Prairie models, 7B-5
**Speedometer and cable, removal and installation,
Prairie models, 4B-7**
Starter circuit, check and component replacement
Bayou models, 4A-12
Prairie models, 4B-7
Starter drive, removal, inspection and installation
Bayou models, 4A-13
Prairie models, 4B-7
Starter motor, removal and installation
Bayou models, 4A-13
Prairie models, 4B-7
Steering knuckle bearing replacement
Bayou (4WD) models, 5A-9
Prairie models, 5B-5
Steering knuckles, removal, inspection, and installation
Bayou models, 5A-6
Prairie models, 5B-4
**Steering shaft, removal, inspection, bearing replacement and
installation**
Bayou models, 5A-3
Prairie models, 5B-2
**Steering, suspension and final drive, Bayou models,
5A-1 through 5A-22**
ball-joint replacement (300 models), 5A-8
bevel drive unit and output gear (2WD models) removal, inspection
and installation, 5A-17
front differential (4WD models), removal, inspection and
installation, 5A-16
front driveaxles (4WD models)
boot replacement and CV joint overhaul, 5A-12
removal and installation, 5A-12
front driveshaft (4WD models), removal, inspection and
installation, 5A-15
front shock absorbers, removal and installation, 5A-9
front suspension arms, removal, inspection,
and installation, 5A-9
handlebars, removal, inspection and installation, 5A-2
rear axle, removal, inspection and installation, 5A-20
rear differential, removal, inspection and installation, 5A-21
rear driveshaft, removal, inspection and installation, 5A-20
rear shock absorbers, removal and installation, 5A-9
rear suspension (complete), removal and installation, 5A-10
rear suspension links, removal, inspection and installation, 5A-10
steering knuckle bearing replacement (4WD models), 5A-9
steering knuckles, removal, inspection, and installation, 5A-6
steering shaft, removal, inspection, bearing replacement and
installation, 5A-3
sub-transmission and bevel drive gear (4WD models), removal and
installation, 5A-19
sub-transmission shift linkage (4WD models), removal, inspection
and installation, 5A-18
tie-rods, removal, inspection and installation, 5A-6
**Steering, suspension and final drive, Prairie models,
5B-1 through 5B-12**
ball-joint replacement, 5B-5
bevel drive unit and output gear, removal, inspection and
installation, 5B-8
front differential, removal, inspection and installation, 5B-8

front driveaxle (4WD)
    boot replacement and CV joint overhaul, 5B-7
    removal and installation, 5B-6
front driveshaft, removal, inspection and installation, 5B-7
front shock absorbers, removal and installation, 5B-5
front suspension arms, removal, inspection, and installation, 5B-5
handlebars, removal, inspection and installation, 5B-2
rear axle, removal, inspection and installation, 5B-10
rear driveshaft and differential, removal, inspection and
    installation, 5B-11
rear shock absorber, removal and installation, 5B-6
steering knuckle bearing replacement, 5B-5
steering knuckles, removal, inspection, and installation, 5B-4
steering shaft, removal, inspection, bearing replacement and
    installation, 5B-2
swingarm
    bearings
        check, 5B-10
        inspection and replacement, 5B-11
    removal and installation, 5B-10
tie-rods, removal, inspection and installation, 5B-3
**Sub-transmission and bevel drive gear (4WD Bayou models),
    removal and installation, 5A-19**
**Sub-transmission shift linkage (4WD Bayou models), removal,
    inspection and installation, 5A-18**

T

Tail light and brake light bulbs, replacement
    Bayou models, 4A-6
    Prairie models, 4B-3
Throttle and choke cables, removal, installation and adjustment
    Bayou models, 3A-9
    Prairie models, 3B-6
Tie-rods, removal, inspection and installation
    Bayou models, 5A-6
    Prairie models, 5B-3
Tires, general information
    Bayou models, 6A-20
    Prairie models, 6B-8
**Transmission shafts, balancer shaft and shift drum, removal,
    inspection and installation, Bayou models, 2A-41**
Transmission, automatic, Prairie models
    air ducts, removal and installation, 2B-8
    drive belt, removal, inspection and installation, 2B-10
    drive belt, width and play check, 2B-11
    general information, 2B-8
    outer cover and seal, removal, inspection and installation, 2B-9
    pulleys
        disassembly, inspection and reassembly, 2B-13
        inner cover and seal, removal and installation, 2B-11
Troubleshooting, 0-16
**Tune-up and routine maintenance, Bayou models,
    1A-1 through 1A-18**
    air cleaner, filter element and drain tube cleaning, 1A-9
    battery electrolyte level/specific gravity, check, 1A-12
    brake lever and pedal freeplay, check and adjustment, 1A-7
    brake system, general check, 1A-6
    choke, operation check, 1A-11
    clutch, check and freeplay adjustment, 1A-10
    cylinder compression, check, 1A-16
    differential oil, change, 1A-18
    driveaxle and driveshaft boots, inspection, 1A-11
    engine oil and filter, change, 1A-14

    exhaust system, inspection, 1A-13
    fasteners, check, 1A-11
    fluid levels, check
        brake fluid (hydraulic brakes), 1A-5
        differential oil, 1A-6
        engine oil, 1A-5
    fuel system, check and filter cleaning, 1A-14
    idle speed, check and adjustment, 1A-13
    lubrication, general, 1A-11
    reverse cable, check and adjustment, 1A-11
    routine maintenance intervals, 1A-4
    spark arrester, cleaning, 1A-18
    spark plug, replacement, 1A-15
    steering system, inspection and toe-in adjustment, 1A-17
    suspension, check, 1A-13
    throttle freeplay and speed limiter, check and adjustment, 1A-10
    tires/wheels, general check, 1A-8
    valve clearances, check and adjustment, 1A-16
**Tune-up and routine maintenance, Prairie models,
    1B-1 through 1B-14**
    air cleaner, filter element and drain tube cleaning, 1B-7
    battery electrolyte level/specific gravity, check, 1B-9
    brake lever and pedal freeplay, check and adjustment, 1B-6
    brake system, general check, 1B-5
    choke, operation check, 1B-8
    cylinder compression, check, 1B-13
    differential oil, change, 1B-14
    driveaxle and driveshaft boots, inspection, 1B-8
    engine oil and filter, change, 1B-11
    exhaust system, inspection, 1B-10
    fasteners, check, 1B-8
    fluid levels, check, 1B-4
        brake fluid (hydraulic brakes), 1B-4
        differential oil, 1B-5
        engine oil, 1B-4
    fuel system, check and filter cleaning, 1B-12
    idle speed, check and adjustment, 1B-10
    lubrication, general, 1B-10
    routine maintenance intervals, 1B-3
    spark arrester, cleaning, 1B-14
    spark plug, replacement, 1B-12
    steering system, inspection and toe-in adjustment, 1B-14
    suspension, check, 1B-10
    throttle freeplay and speed limiter, check and adjustment, 1B-8
    tires/wheels, general check, 1B-6
    valve clearances, check and adjustment, 1B-13

V

Valves/valve seats/valve guides, servicing
    Bayou models, 2A-17
    Prairie models, 2B-6

W

Wheel hubs, removal and installation
    Bayou models, 6A-20
    Prairie models, 6B-8
Wheels, inspection, removal and installation
    Bayou models, 6A-18
    Prairie models, 6B-7